Movies and Midrash

Movies and Midrash

Popular Film and Jewish Religious Conversation

Wendy I. Zierler

Foreword by
Eugene B. Borowitz

Published by State University of New York Press, Albany

© 2017 State University of New York

All rights reserved

Printed in the United States of America

No part of this book may be used or reproduced in any manner whatsoever without written permission. No part of this book may be stored in a retrieval system or transmitted in any form or by any means including electronic, electrostatic, magnetic tape, mechanical, photocopying, recording, or otherwise without the prior permission in writing of the publisher.

For information, contact State University of New York Press, Albany, NY
www.sunypress.edu

Production, Eileen Nizer
Marketing, Anne M. Valentine

Library of Congress Cataloging-in-Publication Data

Names: Zierler, Wendy I., author.
Title: Movies and midrash : popular film and Jewish religious conversation / Wendy I. Zierler ; foreword by Eugene B. Borowitz.
Description: Albany : State University of New York Press, [2017] | Includes bibliographical references and index.
Identifiers: LCCN 2016040642 (print) | LCCN 2016042266 (ebook) | ISBN 9781438466156 (hardcover : alk. paper) | ISBN 9781438466149 (pbk. : alk. paper) | ISBN 9781438466163 (ebook)
Subjects: LCSH: Motion pictures—Religious aspects—Judaism. | Motion pictures—Moral and ethical aspects.
Classification: LCC PN1995.5 .Z54 2017 (print) | LCC PN1995.5 (ebook) | DDC 791.43/682961—dc23
LC record available at https://lccn.loc.gov/2016040642

10 9 8 7 6 5 4 3 2 1

To the memory of my mentor and friend,
Rabbi Dr. Eugene B. Borowitz
(1924–2016)

Contents

List of Illustrations		ix
Foreword by Rabbi Eugene B. Borowitz		xi
Acknowledgments		xv
Introduction		1
Chapter 1	*The Truman Show*: Truth	25
Chapter 2	*Magnolia*: Confession and Redemption	41
Chapter 3	*The Descendants*: Birthright: Consent versus Descent	59
Chapter 4	On *Memento*: Remaking Memory from the Outside In	77
Chapter 5	Crimes, Misdemeanors, and Sin	95
Chapter 6	*Forrest Gump*: Cleverness and Simplicity	117
Chapter 7	*The King's Speech*: Speaking God's Word	133
Chapter 8	*Stranger than Fiction*: God as Author	151
Chapter 9	*A Serious Man*: Parables of Jewishness	169
Chapter 10	*Exam*: Tests, Trials, and Attachments	189

Chapter 11	*The Hunger Games*: In God's Image	209
Conclusion	*Moonrise Kingdom*: And the Youth Shall See Visions	233
Appendix I	On the Design of "Reel Theology," from e-mail archives	237
Appendix II	More Movies and Midrash: Additional Film Resources	243
Notes		249
Bibliography		285
Index		297

Illustrations

Figure 1.1	*The Truman* Show, Truman Sees the Light	26
Figure 2.1	*Magnolia*, Wise Up	50
Figure 3.1	*The Descendants*, Looking at the Land in Kauai	64
Figure 3.2	*The Descendants*, Archipelago	67
Figure 4.1	*Memento*, Remember Sammy Jankis	81
Figure 5.1	*Crimes and Misdemeanors*, Comedy is Tragedy Plus Time	98
Figure 5.2	*Crimes and Misdemeanors*, Judah Talks Morality with the Rabbi Ben	102
Figure 5.3	*Crimes and Misdemeanors*, Judah's Confession	108
Figure 6.1	*Forrest Gump*, Forrest Traps the Feather in his Copy of *Curious George*	121
Figure 7.1	*The King's Speech*, The Duke's Speech at Wembley Stadium	134
Figure 7.2	*The King's Speech*, Watching Hitler	140
Figure 8.1	*Stranger Than Fiction*, Flours	162
Figure 9.1	*A Serious Man*, Sussman's Teeth	177
Figure 9.2	*A Serious Man*, Marshak	185
Figure 10.1	*Exam*, Blonde Looks Through Deaf's Glasses	193

Figure 11.1a	Dorothea Lange, Migrant Mother	213
Figure 11.1b	*Hunger Games,* Dorothea Lange-Like Portrait	213
Figure 11.2	*Hunger Games,* Laying Rue to Rest in a Bed of Flowers	216
Figure 11.3	*Hunger Games,* Registering the Children at the Reaping	219
Figure 12.1	*Moonrise Kingdom,* The Bishop Kids Listen to Benjamin Britten	234

Foreword

By Rabbi Eugene B. Borowitz*

The very first day I met Wendy Zierler, when she interviewed for her position in Feminist Studies at HUC-JIR, I knew that I wanted to teach a course with her. Years ago, I had started something related, a course dealing with novels by those three or four Jews [Roth, Malamud, Bellow, Singer] who had burst onto the literary scene. I had hoped to expand to other fields, such as film. I dared to try to teach Jewish novels to alumni, but realized after the first few years of doing this that I wasn't competent to be teaching this material. I could see the horizons beckoning me. I had never studied literature, though. I tried to write English about related ideas and thoughts. I could discuss the material reasonably and add to it what Jews thought about religion, belief, and the like, but I was disappointed by the limits of what I could do from my vantage point as a theologian. I knew it was important. I knew that it was something I had an affinity for, but no real knowledge or ability for this particular kind of literary analysis. I knew that even we philosophical types needed to pay attention to what the imaginative types were doing.

---

*Rabbi Dr. Eugene B. Borowitz (February 24, 1924–January 22, 2016) was the leading theologian of Reform Judaism. The founding editor of *Sh'ma: A Journal of Jewish Responsibility* and the author of seventeen books, including the landmark *Renewing the Covenant: A Theology for the Postmodern Jew*, he served as rabbi of the Community Synagogue in Port Washington, New York; Director of Education for the Union of American Hebrew Congregations (now the Union for Reform Judaism); and on the faculty of Hebrew Union College–Jewish Institute of Religion from 1962 to 2015.

For years already, Christians had been conducting these sorts of religious discussions around film, but not Jews. The reason that Jews did not do this was they considered it *goyish*, both the theological and the analytical part; they would rather avoid talking about what you needed to believe and feel, wanted rather to talk about other less uncomfortable things. Talking about belief disturbed a lot of people. People didn't want to be on display that way.

My hope for the course was that people would see what was positive in the films, and once they acquired that sense they would see what was "kosher" in this material. The idea was to create an environment where people could identify the believing material if expressed in a humanized and personal way and find a way to take it seriously.

Novels and films, like the Jewish enterprise of Aggadah, are something very serious.

In our Reel Theology course, there were movies that I resisted at first, such as *American Beauty*. I was skeptical about what people had done with aesthetics: aesthetics in worship, thinking only about the right kind of lights on the *bima*, about music, trappings, superficiality. This aesthetic approach was not very thoughtful, not one in which people were willing to ask hard questions. I wanted intellectual seriousness that was also deeply believing; this was not of a piece with an overly aestheticized form of Reform Judaism. We had the same problem with Jewish music: how might one find a way for cantors to communicate depth and not just something pretty?

My colleagues Arnold Wolf and Steven Schwarzchild and I were eager to think both more personalistically and yet not let that collapse into mushy feeling. It didn't seem sensible to most people, the thinking ones, that you could combine hard thinking and deep believing, or the same thing in reverse. Lots of people thought that if you could get people to talk about how something moved them, that would be something, but if you started taking it seriously or you started making demands on them as a consequence, then you'd run into problems.

Back then, there were very few people to talk to. There were very few people who took ideas seriously. They couldn't believe that the "Higher Aesthetic" could command; what did it all require them to do? That troubled them. Reform Jewish leaders had certain areas that they took seriously, but Believing and God did not come easily to them.

In teaching together, did Wendy Zierler and I help people believe? I believe so. By 2001, when Wendy arrived at the College, I was very serious about teaching about Jewish belief. I had developed a career by working with high school kids from all over the country at Reform summer camp, where you could do things with kids that you couldn't do in other places; where we could let the students do it themselves, a kind of religious democratization but led by people who could help them take the endeavor seriously. The idea there was to involve the kids and have them take responsibility for what they had been hearing and learning. You don't like the services, the music: do it yourselves, but take it seriously! That worked out very well. That helped develop the Reform summer camp movement. I wanted to see something like that with our students at the College.

Looking back on the Reel Theology course, I remember how wonderful it was when the students began to delve in and take it seriously, when they got involved in the discussion, and meant it, when I saw commitment. So many students came to get a job and to learn how to do the job well. But there were also some students who believed in what we were doing. They cared about it.

For me, that was the point of the course: not that students should know something specific, but that, in the process of back and forth, they should see that they cared about something and become invested.

They knew that we cared. We taught this course because we believed in something and it meant something to us.

And they knew that we considered what we were doing real Torah study. We began every class with the *bracha* (blessing) of "*La'asok bedivrei Torah*"—to occupy yourself in the study of Torah.

With regard to making this blessing at the beginning of every Reel Theology class, the feeling was that when approached in the proper way, there is *bracha* (blessing) in this material. The experience validated the *bracha*. I learned that one day, when in a hurry, having been running around and having put my stuff down in class, I started the lesson straightaway. A student suddenly stopped me and said, Dr. Borowitz, what, no *bracha*?

Concerning the gendered dynamic of teaching with a younger, female colleague, it is true that students approached me, the elder colleague, with a certain fear and awe, but this dynamic shifted over time. I only tried to do what was true. Yes, I wanted the students to take the stuff we were working with very seriously. I didn't want them doing some rote thing that they didn't particularly care about or that I was somehow compelling them to do. The believing was what I wanted to see.

—Stamford, CT, August 2014

Acknowledgments

Any book that takes fifteen years to write incurs many debts of gratitude. First and foremost, I need to acknowledge Rabbi Dr. Eugene Borowitz, z"l, without whom this project never would have come to be. The relationship we formed and the lessons that I learned by teaching with him are an ongoing gift. He is sorely missed. Thanks also to his daughters, Lisa, Nan, and Drucy, for permission to include the foreword along with excerpts from my e-mail correspondence with their father, which appear in the appendices.

Thanks to former Dean, now President, Aaron Panken of Hebrew Union College–Jewish Institute of Religion (henceforth HUC-JIR) for hiring me in 2001 and for supporting the Reel Theology course from its inception, including providing initial funding for the purchase of VHS tapes of films—one marker of how quickly things change in the media world. Thanks as well to former HUC-JIR President David Ellenson for his collegiality and enthusiasm for the Reel Theology concept, to Provost Michael Marmur for providing a much-appreciated HUC-JIR subvention grant to support the publication of this volume, and to all my colleagues at the New York School for their warm collegiality.

Since spring 2002 I have been blessed to share the ideas that have made their way into these pages with wonderful groups of students and colleagues at HUC-JIR and elsewhere. Audiences at the Central Conference of American Rabbis, the Union for Reform Judaism Biennial, the North American Scholars Circle of the Shalom Hartman Institute, the Posen Foundation, the Wexner Foundation, and congregations throughout the United States listened to the ideas in this book and helped shape my thinking. Thanks to Oklahoma City University, which invited me to deliver the Neustadt lectures in 2016, and to the Valley Beit Midrash, where I gave film-related lectures on two separate occasions in 2012 and 2017.

Since the bulk of the writing of this book occurred from 2014 to 2016, I am particularly grateful to my Reel Theology classes at Park Avenue Synagogue in 2014 to 2016; Yeshivat Chovevei Torah, fall 2014; and Temple Gates of Prayer, 2016, for serving as crucial interlocutors. Special thanks also go to the dedicated 2015 Reel Theology students at HUC-JIR (Nicole Auerbach, Andy Feldman, Alexandra Klein, Vladimir Lapin, Adam Lutz, Sarah Marion, Elle Muhlbaum, Alona Nir, Rachel Silverstein, Samantha Shabman, Tova Schaller, and Natan Trief), whose insights and observations have greatly enriched these chapters. Special thanks to Rabbis Joshua Strom and Kevin Kleinman for introducing me to the film *Stranger than Fiction*, to Andy Dubin to initiating me to Wes Anderson's *Moonrise Kingdom*, and to Sam Pearlson and Ben Shefter for introducing me to *Exam*.

Early research assistance was provided by my former student and fellow film enthusiast Debra Griboff. More recent and invaluable assistance has come from HUC-JIR librarians extraordinaire Tina Weiss and Yoram Bitton, who accommodated my seemingly endless requests for interlibrary loan books on religion and film and helped me attain Blu-ray copies of films to produce the illustrations in this book. Crucial technical support at various junctures was provided by Gregg Alpert, Andrew Greene, and T. J. Williams.

Longtime colleague, collaborator, and treasured friend Carole Balin provided helpful feedback on several chapters. Additional helpful input came from Staci Ford, Lawrence Hoffman, Thomas Leitch, Adriane Leveen, Michael Meyer, Vanessa Ochs, David G. Myers, and Gordon Slethaug. Many thanks as well to the two readers for State University of New York Press, who read the manuscript with special care and offered excellent suggestions for revision. The editorial staff at SUNY Press, most notably Rafael Chaiken, was responsive and helpful at every possible point along the way.

Andrew Silberstein and Leah Krakinowski suffered through *Magnolia* with me the very first time and are now wary of my ever choosing the film for shared family movie nights. But they still keep inviting us back for weekends and holidays. Many, many thanks.

Endless love and thanks go to my husband, Daniel Feit, and our children, Shara, Yona, and Amichai Zierler Feit, for sitting through many subpar movies with me as well as many visionary, transcendent films. Every day you help me see what is worth looking at again and what really matters. Thanks as well to my parents, in-laws, and siblings for rooting for me and supporting all that I continue to do.

Earlier versions of material in this book appeared in a variety of publications:

- "In Search of a Feminist Interpretation of the Akedah," *Nashim: A Journal of Jewish Women's Studies & Gender Issues* 9 (Spring 2005).

- "Holy Fools on the Road," in *Hit the Road Jack: Essays on the Culture of the American Road*, ed. Staci Ford and Gordon Slethaug (Montreal: McGill/Queens University Press, 2012).

- "God in the Age of Twitter," *Tikkun* (March/April, 2010).

- "Trying to Say Something, Something: *Magnolia* and Confession," in *We Have Sinned: Sin and Confession in Judaism*, ed. Lawrence Hoffman (Woodstock, VT: Jewish Lights, 2012).

- "On *Memento*: Remaking Memory from the Outside In," in *Between Tradition and Modernity: Rethinking an Old Opposition*, ed. Michael Meyer and David G. Myers (Detroit: Wayne State University Press, 2014).

- "Midrashic Adaptation: The Ever-Growing Torah of Moses," in Thomas Leitch ed., *The Oxford Handbook of Adaptation Studies* (Oxford: Oxford University Press, 2016), https://global.oup.com/academic/?cc=us&lang=en&.

Introduction

Eugene Borowitz, *z"l*, and the Beginnings of "Reel Theology"

I was a teenager in Toronto when I first encountered the writing and editorial vision of Rabbi Dr. Eugene Borowitz, a man who would go on to become my colleague and mentor at Hebrew Union College–Jewish Institute of Religion (HUC-JIR) and my partner in the project that has become this book. My older brother, an aspiring rabbi, subscribed to *Sh'ma*, and it was on the pages of that slim journal that I read my first articles about pluralism, halakhic change, women's ordination, and Jewish feminism, among many other things. As founding editor of *Sh'ma*, Gene Borowitz helped open my eyes to other ways of thinking than those of my immediate Orthodox community and modeled the kind of interdenominational postmodern conversation that enabled me to become a committed feminist and pluralist, capable of straddling and inhabiting various worlds at the same time.

I did not know this when I applied and interviewed, but it was Dr. Borowitz who insisted that HUC-JIR create the position in Feminist Studies that I would come to occupy in July 2001 after a six-year expat stint at the University of Hong Kong. He was on the search committee that hired me for this position, and I remember being awed and excited to meet him in the flesh. It wasn't for another year and a half, however, when we shared several hours together on the most tragic day in the history of New York City, that our intellectual and collegial relationship really began.

On Tuesday morning, September 11, 2001, I boarded the Bx10 bus that stopped in front of our house and dropped me off at the 231st Street 1/9 subway station. I was busy working on my teaching notes and fretting about the faulty plumbing in the old house we had recently moved into in Riverdale when I heard the first hazy, unintelligible bits of news about a plane and the World Trade Center. Why I didn't get off the bus and make my way home right there and then remains unclear to me. At the time, new to my job, I could think only of the class I was supposed to teach at 12:20 PM. It was only when we were all told to get off the subway at 34th Street, and I walked outside to a 7th Avenue where not a single car or bus was running, and people were walking uptown in the middle of the road, and cars and vans were pulled up alongside the curbs with their doors wide open so that people passing by could listen to the radio, and I heard the news of the first tower falling, and my cell phone wasn't working, and none of the payphones were working either, that I realized that I would not be teaching that 12:20 class after all, and I became truly frightened. Was Daniel, my husband, okay? We had moved back to New York from Hong Kong only a few weeks earlier, and I had no real concept of where his office was in Lower Manhattan. I knew it wasn't in the World Trade Center, but was it nearby? I knew he took the subway to work and that he passed through the Chambers Street/World Trade Center station on his way to work. Had he gotten there safely? While every other New Yorker seemed to be walking uptown away from what was later to be called Ground Zero, I began running downtown in the direction of HUC-JIR for the very purpose of getting to a phone to find out whether Daniel was safe. Of course, I had no luck with that either. After walking southeast across town to 1 West 4th Street, I sat in my office for more than three excruciating hours later before I got word, through an aunt, that Daniel had made his way safely out of lower Manhattan on a ferry to New Jersey.

    Dr. Borowitz was also at the college that fateful Tuesday, as he had a similar teaching schedule to mine. (It is for this reason, in fact, that for the first few years that we taught Reel Theology, we offered the course on Tuesday afternoons and dubbed it "Tuesdays with Gene and Wendy" after Mitch Albom's best-seller, *Tuesdays with Morrie*, the first text and film of the course.) Bewildered and shocked, we ran into each other in the college library, both of us looking for something to do as we awaited news about the roads and trains. For several hours, we sat down and tried—rather unsuccessfully—to make preliminary sense of what we had just seen and heard. Later that day, when the West Side Highway reopened, we shared a cab ride uptown and looked out the window at a New York that would never again be the same.

Shortly after the High Holiday recess that followed soon after 9/11, I ran into Dr. Borowitz again on the Common Level of the HUC-JIR building. Having shared that afternoon together, we exchanged solicitous, post-9/11, post–New Year greetings, and then he made me an unexpected proposition. Would I be open to the idea of teaching a course with him next semester that brought together discussion of Jewish theology with popular novels and film? Of course, I would, I said; I was flattered by the invitation. Later I began to panic—something that was becoming rather regular for me in this new New York City life of mine. After all, Dr. Borowitz—it took me a while to feel comfortable calling him Gene—had been rather vague about his ideas for this course. Years ago, in the Bellow-Malamud-Roth heyday, he had taught a course on Jewish American literature and its relevance to Jewish religious life, and he had always wanted to return to some version of that effort. But now there were other reigning influences in American culture, with film and other forms of popular culture dominating the attention of Jews and non-Jews alike. It struck him that all of this needed some attention in the College. Did I think I could come up with something? He had two films that he knew he wanted to teach, but otherwise, he would leave the rest up to me. "Great," I said. "Oh no," I thought. What exactly should such a course be about? Jewish films and TV shows and books? Or secular TV shows and films and books that somehow raised religious theological issues? Socio-anthropological patterns of religious ritual and behavior in popular culture? Meaning on the cultural "streets" of America after 9/11? All of the above?

Not long after that, my husband made me another proposition. Our time in New York City, to say the least, had not gotten off to a good start. With our new location, new jobs, new community, and new house, the renovations of which could not have been going worse, and most of all, with the tragic events of 9/11, we had hardly breathed in weeks. What would I say to the idea of both of us taking off a few hours off from work to take a walking tour around the city? I agreed to the idea on the condition that as we walked, he'd help me figure out what I should teach for this course with Eugene Borowitz. "Fine," he said. We'd walk and talk about God and the Movies.

And that was what we did. Daniel picked up a copy of *New York for the Independent Traveler*[1] and chose a walking route in the Village, not far from my office. I picked a notebook that I could use to jot down ideas as we walked. On a late Tuesday afternoon, but a few short weeks after that fateful Tuesday morning, we hit the streets, pretending to be tourists, in the hope of getting to know another side of this city that had become our new home.

This particular book-guided walk through the East and West Villages was attentive to quirky detail and required us to look closely at things, to search our surroundings to identify traces of meaning and history. These are the kinds of things we saw: strange, unexpected places, such as 75½ Bedford Street, the narrowest house in the Village, only nine and a half feet wide. (Apparently poet Edna St. Vincent Millay lived in that house for one year, in 1923.) And "Twin Peaks" at 102 Bedford Street, a Hansel-and-Gretel–looking house described in our guidebook as "one of the strangest houses in this village of strange buildings." We saw places that once upon a time used to accommodate something or someone else, such as the remnant of the second cemetery of the Spanish and Portuguese Synagogue (1805), most of which was destroyed as a result of the construction of 11th Street. And Washington Mews, not far from the Washington Square Park Arch, that used to house stables and now is simply a "charming alley." And 82 Washington Place West, which used to be home to the great novelist Willa Cather. We visited Chumley's, a literary speakeasy tucked between Barrow and Bedford Streets, frequented in the early parts of the twentieth century by the literary likes of F. Scott Fitzgerald, John Dos Passos, and Theodore Dreiser, which closed in 2007 as a result of a chimney and wall collapse but is finally due to reopen.

It is in the nature of walking and looking around to make associations. And so, as we walked along, taking in bits of civic and literary history, some of them Jewish, we thought and talked about what popped into our heads. At 18 11th Street, formerly a house that was accidentally destroyed by a bomb detonated by the 1960s radical group the Weathermen, I was reminded of Philip Roth's pre-9/11 Pulitzer Prize–winning novel *American Pastoral*, which features a young Jewish girl from the 1960s who blows up her local New Jersey post office. "That might be a good book to read in this course," I said out loud. And that's how it unfolded, associatively. As we walked and ticked off the list of recommended Village sites, we also began compiling a parallel list of popular and significant books, movies, and TV shows: *Tuesdays with Morrie*, *Harry Potter*, *The Sopranos*, *The Truman Show*, and *American Beauty*. In the barroom at Chumley's, under black-and-white photos of Hemingway, Dreiser, and other literary legends, we ventured a list of classic themes that ought to be covered in a course that engages issues of religious and theological importance: Good and Evil, Truth and Sin, Free Will, Memory, Cleverness versus Simplicity in matters of faith, images and representations of God, patterns of Confession and Repentance, and the religious function of Beauty.

I have chosen to tell this story of the meandering genesis of the first syllabus for the course Reel Theology because it serves as a parable for some of the enduring motivations and goals of the course and now this book. Daniel and I took that walk for a few reasons. First, we needed some time to be together. Second, New York is one of the greatest cities in the world, but as fate would have it, we had moved there on the eve of the worst calamities ever to befall the city (and the country of which it serves as the cultural capital). In short, we needed an opportunity to look more closely at our city and see what still makes it such an important, enchanting, and stimulating place to live—to rescue our sense of its value at a time when tragic events were making it hard for us to lay claim to enduring values. Third, like most people in our stage of family and professional life, we were always rushing somewhere, always in a hurry. When we walked in the city, making our way from the subway to our offices or to some store or another, we viewed our surroundings in a state of half-consciousness, passing by people and things on our way to other people and things. For one afternoon, we needed to walk more slowly, to pay more attention to detail, to leave ourselves open to the possibility of the Unexpected.

Both the Reel Theology course and *Movies and Midrash* have proceeded from similar needs and yearnings. People need time to be together, to have joint experiences around shared stories and myths, to share a quest for meaning. As a society, we have become more interconnected through wireless and digital technologies and at the same time more disconnected, insofar as we are now able to shop, entertain ourselves, and carry on myriad conversations without having to leave our homes or interact physically with another body. Television, film, and other media have become the streets that we roam and the source of our myths and stories, but in the same way that most of us race unconsciously through the physical streets of the cities we inhabit, we shuttle across the byways of popular culture in a state of partial awareness. We keep multiple screens up before our eyes but look at none of them carefully. Our attention forever slips, glides, and lurches. We consume video and media culture the way we consume fast food, but how much cultural and spiritual nourishment do we actually take in? What value attaches to that which we do assimilate? What does it mean when so many people are calling in to vote on the next *American Idol* or winner of *The Voice* or binge watching *Orange Is the New Black*, *House of Cards*, and *Transparent*? Is there any larger, spiritual, or even theological message to be culled from these flickering images and fads, these seemingly evanescent pop culture obsessions? If prodded to look more closely, might we become closer, more astute and appreciative readers of both our cities and our celluloid/cyber/video neighborhoods? And could this kind of closer reading of culture at large be brought into conversation with the work that we do in Jewish schools, college classrooms, synagogues, and youth groups?

My husband and I had a ready-made guidebook that instructed us on what to look for to make our walk around the city interesting and meaningful. There is currently no such guide, however, that looks in depth at influential or significant movies or other screen phenomena and makes them interesting, meaningful, and textually relevant to a religiously interested Jewish audience.[2] Insofar as Jews have been major filmmakers, writers, comedians, and entertainers, there are scores of books about Jews in the movie industry, in broadcasting, comedy, and the like.[3] But there is no extant book that presents a Jewish "Reel Theology," that is, a method of "reading" film and popular culture in a way that is textually and religiously edifying for a Jewish reader.[4] This book attempts to be such a guide, offering examples of how it can be done.

Christian Precedents

While there have been no scholarly works to date on Jewish faith and film, there is a veritable library of books on film and religion, mostly from a decidedly Christian perspective, which has helped shape and define the agenda for this project. While I do not intend to provide a comprehensive overview of all of this literature, as there are several books, articles, and bibliographies that do just that,[5] I would like to point out some of the central ideas and trends that arise from the already vast literature so as to situate this book in the existing conversation and make clear how my method both coheres with and departs from previous work on the subject.

The earliest articles and books on film and religion arose from a twin awareness of the waning influence of the church and organized religion on American life and the concomitant, rising influence of film and media culture. One of the first Christian theologian-scholars to embrace the possibilities of secular film was Harvard Divinity School Professor Harvey G. Cox, who as early as 1962 wrote an article that criticized film and media as the "consciousness industry" that "drones a perpetual liturgy celebrating the symbols on which the societal power rests" but also praised those "prophetic films" that "probe the soft spots of a culture's claim to ultimacy."[6] Cox's sense that sacred messages might be discerned in such media as secular film was echoed and amplified in his classic 1965 book *The Secular City*, which urged fellow Christians to embrace the secularization of religious concepts in urban American life: "Far from being something Christians should be against," Cox argued, "secularization represents an authentic consequence of Biblical faith. Rather than oppose it, the task of Christians should be to support and nourish it."[7]

Paul Tillich (1886–1965) makes similar arguments in his earlier book *Theology of Culture* (1959):

> If religion is the state of being grasped by an ultimate concern, this state cannot be restricted to a special realm. The unconditional character of this concern implies that it refers to every moment of our life, to every space and every realm. The universe is God's sanctuary. Every workday is a day of the Lord, every supper, a Lord's supper, every work the fulfillment of a divine task, every joy a joy in God. In all preliminary concerns ultimate concern is present, consecrating them. Essentially the religious and the secular are not separate realms. Rather, they are within each other.[8]

Building on these ideas, the first scholars of film and religion began looking to avant-garde as well as popular film as new sources of religious symbolism. "It has become a commonplace for theologian and non-theologian alike," writes Carle Skrade, in the introduction to *Celluloid and Symbols* (1970), one of the earliest essay anthologies on theology and film,

> to state and probe the awesome gap which has developed between the church and our society as a whole. As matters stand, increasing numbers of our society see the church not a good or a bad, but simply as irrelevant . . . For the first time

since Gutenberg, we are turned from word-consciousness to consciousness of the visual image. It is to the films that we can, perhaps must, look for the self-interpretation of our period; here were can find out age's "religious" questions, our age's askings about the meaning of existence.[9]

Since these early books, Protestant and Catholic scholars and writers such as John May and Michael Bird, Robert K. Johnston, Craig Detweiler, Barry Taylor, and Anthony Clarke[10] have mounted similar arguments, pursuing the connections and analogies between (Christian) religious teachings and secular popular culture. By and large, these books have served the function of "interfaith dialogue"[11] between the worlds of the church and of Hollywood, working to bridge the chasm between religious commitment and popular culture—in Bryan Stone's words, to dispel the notion that all cinema is "sinema." As Stone writes in *Faith and Film*,

> [t]he cinema is regularly and quite amazingly a source of revelation about ourselves and our world—about the "signs of the times." The cinema reveals what we value as human beings, our hopes and our fears. It asks our deepest questions, expresses our mightiest rage, and reflects our most basic dreams . . . There remains in human beings a deep hunger for images, sound, pictures, music and myth. Film offers us a creative language—an imaginative language of movement and sound—that can bridge the gap between the rational and the aesthetic, the sacred and the secular, the church and the world, and thereby throw open fresh new windows on a very old gospel.[12]

Stone's turn-of-the-twenty-first-century book is part of an ever-mounting group of popular as well as scholarly works on the subject written by committed Christians—in some cases, ordained ministers and theologians—who feel the need to engage in critical dialogue with culture at large as a means of strengthening the church and creating a theological approach to this ever-increasing set of influences and cultural practices.[13]

Other works, written from a more eclectic and less church-bound position, have chronicled the ways in which younger Americans have channeled religious energies away from the church and toward other forms of popular culture. In *Virtual Faith: The Irreverent Spiritual Quest of Generation X*, for example, Tom Beaudoin, a former student of Harvey Cox, describes the way that his generation of X'ers remained ambivalent or hostile toward "religion" while at the same time claiming a sense of "spirituality" that often consisted of a hodgepodge of theological symbols and traditions. Beaudoin "began to notice how the popular culture was suffused with religious references. Our popular songs, music videos, and movies were about sin, salvation, and redemption, among other themes. Contrary to common perception, we appeared to have a very theological culture."[14] In Beaudoin's particular case, the eclectic quest for the meaning of popular culture ultimately led him to reembrace his Catholic upbringing. Even this seemingly subversive study ultimately reaffirmed Christian commitments.

Another class of studies emerged from religion and/or film departments and, as such, pursued a more ecumenical, comparative agenda, looking at film and religion in the broadest possible, sociological/anthropological terms.[15] John C. Lyden demonstrates this approach in his book *Film as Religion*, where he draws on the teachings of Paul Tillich, Rudolph Otto, and anthropologist Clifford Geertz to examine the quest for the numinous or the world "as it ought to be" in popular American films.[16] Similarly, in *Screening the Sacred: Religion, Myth and Ideology in Popular American Film*, religious studies professors Joel W. Martin and Conrad E. Ostwalt use what they term theological, mythological, and ideological criticism to analyze the interplay between popular film and religion writ large.[17] Other religion scholars, such as Melanie Wright, Gregory Watkins, and William Blizek,[18] have investigated the interrelationships, meanings, ideologies, and effects of film, using religion and biblical texts reciprocally to interpret movies and movies, to critique religion. Unlike the church-bound writers, these scholars analyze and problematize religion rather than promote a particular doctrine or religious perspective. With the proliferation of writings from both theologically oriented and religion department scholars, one has also begun to see a greater interest in the theory and distinctive visuality of film, such as in the work of Melanie Wright, Roy Anker, Steve Nolan, Jonathan Brant, and S. Brent Plate.[19] Often with the development of a field comes disagreement, and some scholars, such as Plate, Wright, and especially Nolan, have leveled trenchant criticisms against the ideological predispositions of their predecessors and their focus on narrative rather than film technique and theory. As Jonathan Brant argues, however, "these critics with their rallying cry of 'film qua film' produce more heat than light because they are just as situated, just as guilty of ideology and more freighted rhetoric, as the authors they denounce."[20]

I will say outright that as a literature professor who is interested in bringing film into conversation with Jewish faith as it expresses itself in the Jewish textual tradition, I too tend to emphasize the narrative and literary aspects of film, though not to the exclusion of salient visual elements. I do not believe, however, that in order to do justice to film one needs to restrict one's view to a consideration of the visual. I note as well that while I appreciate the sophistication of film theory and semiotics, the arcane jargon thereof often obscures rather than clarifies and undermines the very notion of trying, through popular, accessible film, to reach people where they are. In film analysis, I believe, one ought to avail oneself of theory where relevant, and certainly to become acquainted with the terminology and craft of filmmaking. But one ought not be compelled, as if dogmatically, to respond through one particularly critical/theoretical lens. Throughout these chapters I attempt, where germane, to call attention to issues of editing, camera angle, framing, lighting, color, and sound,[21] as well as to allusions to other films. But I highlight these elements in conjunction with issues of narrative construction, character, dialogue, theme, and other relevant literary elements.

Given my academic background in literary and feminist criticism and my teaching audience, I also find myself torn between the ecumenical and critical approaches of the religion departments and the staunch, religious investment of the avowedly Christian writers. It is not enough for me, as a literature professor at a rabbinical seminary and a teacher of classes in Jewish adult education contexts throughout the country, to show my students how to regard film, TV, popular music, or spectator sports as sociological or anthropological forms of general religious expression, however interesting and compelling these arguments may be. I am drawn by studies of religion and film that reflect an engaged or invested theological perspective. At the same time, I do not feel satisfied reading or assigning books that equate theology with Christian doctrine. I read one book on religious film, the product of a conference in Rome "that attracted over fifty participants, representing six continents and sixteen different countries, including several third-world nations . . . by far the most diverse groups of critics, scholars and filmmakers and students of film that had ever, in the knowledge of the participants, ever been brought to together in one place,"[22] only to realize that not a single Jewish voice is represented in the volume, despite the claim to great diversity. I read other books, such as Christopher Deacy's *Faith and Film* and Clive Marsh and Gaye Ortiz's *Explorations in the Theology of Film*, where faith and theology are seen as synonymous with Christianity, or where Christianity is the preferred if not default interpretive lens.[23] William Telford's tripartite definition of "theology," culled from an otherwise excellent anthology of essays on film and theology titled *Cinema Divinité*, is about as good as it gets on this score:

> What do I mean by "theology?" The word "theology" can be used in three major ways, depending on how widely or narrowly one defines it. At its narrowest, it is used to refer to systematic reflection on nature and work of God. A slightly wider definition would see it as a systematic reflection on Christian doctrine, embracing in addition the traditional categories of Christology (the person of Christ), soteriology (the work of Christ), pneumatology (the Spirit), cosmology (the nature of the world), ecclesiology (the Church), and ethics. At its widest, it would embrace other religions and be understood as reflection upon what various religious traditions might regard as the ultimate reality (the sacred, the holy, the external).[24]

Telford's "slightly wider definition" refers to a set of theological terms, attitudes, and commitments that are thoroughly Christian and incompatible with a Jewish reading practice. And though Telford goes on in his essay to declare a preference for the third, widest definition of theology, he admits nevertheless to a "particular emphasis on Christianity" that is typical of so much of this literature. As a Jew, one begins to feel like an eavesdropper listening belatedly and surreptitiously to a long-standing Christian conversation.

Following but also departing from the lead of many of my Christian colleagues, I have set out to construct a distinctively religious, Jewish dialogue with film. Given the vast influence of media culture on all of our lives, I am interested in finding out what Jewish tradition, text, and theology might have to say about the lessons and themes that arise from influential and compelling works of film and popular culture. I do so not to exclude Christian readers from the learning I wish to undertake, but to expand the film-religion audience to include the Jewish community and to do so in an unapologetically Jewish text-oriented way. I am eager to find not only "Saint Paul at the Movies" (to borrow from the title of not just one but two Christian theological books on film[25]), but also Abraham, Moses, Sarah, David, the rabbis, medieval and modern Jewish thinkers, and modern Hebrew poets. In presenting this argument for the need for a book of this sort, however, I am reminded of early feminist observations on the need to provide a woman's perspective on literature, history, and religion. As in the case of the feminist call for the reconfiguration of knowledge, history, and society, it is not enough, however, to take the extant conversations on religion and film, add in a Jewish voice, and stir.

Toward a Jewish Reel Theology

And so, while the first Reel Theology course may have originated associatively and meanderingly, over the course of the years our teaching, reading, and thinking about this subject coalesced into a distinctive vision and method, combining close analysis of film narrative and visuality with a study of an array of classical and modern Jewish texts. As in the case of Harvey Cox and his disciples, Gene Borowitz and I were intent on finding ways to identify sacredness in the secular world outside the walls of the seminary and the synagogue. In marked contrast to Cox, however, who celebrated secularization as a desired end, a process in which the biblical stories of Creation, Exodus, and the prohibition against idolatry were universalized and ramified in general, universal society[26]—we have engaged the secular not as an end in and of itself but as a means of deep textual engagement and Jewish religious return.

As far back as 1973 with the publication of his National Jewish Book Award–winning book, *The Mask Jews Wear*, which charged American Jews with being "modern Marranos"—assimilationists whose Americanized lifestyle represses an inner Jewish core—Eugene Borowitz was searching for a way back from a classically Reform, German Jewish philosophical orientation that outlined Jewish belief in the most universalized, generalized way possible. His theological work became a quest both for a systematic framing of his Liberal Jewish belief in God, Torah, and Israel and for a way to bring Jewish particularity, covenantal duty, and thick Jewishness back to Liberal Judaism without sacrificing the modern values of autonomy and self-determination. In this pursuit, he was joined later in life by a group of younger postmodern philosophers and theologians called the Textual Reasoners, who were disillusioned with modernism and Orthodoxy as well as with generalized Jewish philosophy with its pretenses of capital-T Truth—scholars who, in Peter Ochs's formulation, were interested in giving "rabbinic and ecclesial tradition both the benefit of the doubt and the benefit of doubt."[27] Gene's contribution to the first book by this group, published in the same year that he and I began teaching together, offers a compelling explanation of his motivations in joining pedagogical/theological ranks with me, a modern Orthodox feminist and a close reader of literary texts rather than a theologian. Here are a few statements from that essay:

> Jewish philosophy today suffers from what generalization has done to Jewishness. When Jewish thinkers can transcend the secularity of the general philosophical guild, they identify Jewish belief with having a proper understanding of God and seek to supply that in terms of a philosophically responsible statement. But that accomplishment, for all its value, only brings us to the faith of the Noachides, that is, people in general, human beings. Without also positing the election of Israel and the truth of Torah, that is, without the particularity which philosophic generalization eschews, we do not stand in the covenant of Sinai and have a recognizable Jewish character. A similar reductionism occurs when mitzvah is redefined as ethics . . . Valorizing the ethical commandments may produce exemplary Benei Noach, but it will not produce Benei Yisrael . . . This line of thought has led some thinkers among us to suggest that we could link philosophy and particularity by a close reading of Jewish texts. This procedure might well produce the therapy we seek . . . Engagement with our texts, then, commends itself as therapy for the generalizing ills of Jewish philosophy and may also help us create a new way of thinking about Judaism.[28]

Gene was chagrined that most American Liberal Jews had come to define themselves more by their universalistic, Noachide dispositions and their exposure to the world at large than by Judaism in its particularity. In this, his thinking matched that of Franz Rosenzweig, another theologian marked by his turning away from the generalizing tendencies of German Jewish philosophy toward an embrace of Jewish particularism.

Inverted Midrash: On Method

In his draft address, "Upon the Opening of the Jüdisches Lehrhaus," Franz Rosenzweig sees the modern Jewish turn to "the realms of alien knowledge of the 'outside book' " as occasioning the birth of a new kind of Jewish learning:

> It is learning in reverse order. A learning that no longer starts from the Torah and leads into life, but the other way around: from life, from a world that knows nothing of the Law or pretends to know nothing, back to the Torah. That is the sign of the time.[29]

Rosenzweig refers to post-Emancipation, modern Jewish alienation from the Torah and traditional Jewish learning and memory as a form of illness that begets its own cure, allowing one to draw on the resources of one's outside learning to return to and strengthen one's Jewish core.

What Rosenzweig called "learning in reverse order," Eugene Borowitz and I termed "inverted midrash." Rabbinic midrash often elucidates or underscores the meaning of a classical text by introducing a parable. The rabbis commonly quote a verse and point to a exegetical difficulty with the text and then introduce a story or parable with the words "*mashal lemah hadavar domeh*" (a parable: to what can the saying be likened?). Today many Jews in synagogues are inadequately acquainted with biblical sources; exposure to classical Jewish texts is as likely to puzzle as to inspire. And so in our Reel Theology course, and by extension in this book, we become practitioners of inverted midrash. We begin our learning with the profound matters that are raised by thoughtful, artistically rendered novels and movies and seek to show how they are analogous to or intersect with one or another aspects of Jewish thought, text study, practice, memory, and knowledge. The assumption is that readers of this book, like the students in our courses over the years, will first see the "assigned" films and after doing so will follow along with the "midrashic" engagements, analysis, and interpretation.

Following this notion of "inverted midrash," each chapter in this book looks at a significant secular film that visually and thematically highlights a central theme in Jewish thought, text, or practice: Truth, Memory, Sin, Confession, Legacy, the idea of God as Author and of Moses as speaking God's word, Simplicity versus Cleverness in Faith, the spiritual value of tests, and the Jewish notion of being created in the image of God. Building on the idea of inverted midrash and the idea of the mashal, an additional chapter looks at the function and theology of the parable form. The first part of each chapter is devoted to a close reading of the film and its major narrative and visual elements, noting how form enriches meaning and so forth. The second part elaborates on the related Jewish theme in relation to the Jewish textual tradition. In some cases, the textual section focuses on an analogous biblical episode or book; in others, it targets materials from rabbinic literature, classical and modern Jewish thought, or Jewish literature. This eclectic approach reflects my own wide-ranging interests in Jewish studies, as well as a sense that Jewish culture is necessarily multifarious and multivalent and that it unfolds in different genres over time. Over the years of developing our course, film and theme choices were made around the significance and artistic merit of the material "out there" and the centrality of certain central themes to Jewish theology or religious practice.[30] Films lent themselves to discussion if they were rich enough to admit multiple interpretations; indeed, the importance of study and ongoing interpretation as a religious activity with no simple answers and no easy, tidy structure emerges in several of the chapters of this book. In addition to artistry, theme, susceptibility to interpretation, and/or cultural impact, *Magnolia*, *The Descendants*, *Stranger Than Fiction*, *The Hunger Games*, and *Exam* were chosen because they afforded the opportunity for feminist analysis.

A note on comprehensiveness: while I do believe that each of films and themes treated in the book is significant with rich artistic and thematic content, I make no claim here to being thoroughly representative or completely up-to-date. The assumption of this method is that the work is never "reely" done; there are so many issues that are central and important to Jewish religious and national life, and so many works of film, video, television, and literature are coming out all the time. Contemporary concerns and fads change from day to day. The hope, in offering this partial, idiosyncratic, and eclectic approach to bridging Judaism and film, is to show other interested students of Judaism and religion how rich this material can be and how they themselves can carry on the conversation.

Note that the term "inverted midrash" and the title *Movies and Midrash* are meant not just to be clever or alliterative but also to illustrate an interpretive disposition that follows from midrashic tradition. Like early Hellenistic biblical exegesis, which registered the contact between Judaism and Hellenism, or later rabbinic midrash, a genre that developed as a response to the crisis of the destruction of the temple and the need to bridge the gap between biblical faith and contemporary reality,[31] so too, our practice of inverted midrash is meant to address and bridge the gap between the estranged reality of many contemporary Jews and the Jewish religious past. As scholar Lesleigh Cushing Stahlberg notes,

> The crises to which midrash responds are distinctly Jewish; it attempts to bridge time and tradition at moments of historical and religious uncertainty. The function of midrash becomes teaching about tradition at the very moments that the tradition seems most in danger of losing its footing or its relevance. . . . Midrash always recontextualizes the Bible, making it relevant (and present) in the interpreter's context.[32]

The goal of both classical midrash and by analogy, of this book, is to renew and reanimate the textual tradition. As the rabbis teach in Pesikta de-Rav Kahana 12:12,

> לא תהא תורה עליך כפרוס דוגמא ישנה, אלא כפרוס דוגמא חדשה שיש לה שנים
> או שלשה ימים, הלא כתבתי לך שלישים (שם /משלי כ"ב/), שלשם כת'. בן עזיי
> או' לא כפרוס דוגמא שיש לה שנים או שלשה ימים, אלא כפרוס דוגמא בן יומה.

> Let the Torah never be for you an antiquated decree, but rather like a decree freshly issued, no more than two of three days old . . . [Indeed,] Ben Azzai said: not even as old as a decree issued two or three days ago, but as a decree issued this very day.[33]

The desire to renew and reanimate the biblical text is classically reflected in the way in which rabbinic midrash often responds and refers closely to the Hebrew original of the biblical text; likewise, the analyses in these chapters is grounded in similar kinds of close, Hebrew-based reading of texts. With regard to the proposed analogy between movies and midrash, in the same way in which the visual stories in movies often employ conventional, popular character types and plots to engage audiences, and in the best cases convey big ideas, *meshalim* use exceedingly popular and common figures (a king or a father) to interpret a verse but more importantly to probe the reality of God. As Brad Young explains,

> [t]he reality of God is revealed through the word-pictures of a parable. They [the rabbis] challenged the mind on the highest intellectual level by using simple stories that made common sense out of the complexities of religious faith and human experience. On the one hand, in finite terms God is beyond human comprehension, but on the other, his infinite majesty may be captured in vivid stories of daily life.[34]

To be sure, the idea of inverted midrash is not meant to advance some simplistic, one-to-one correspondence between the rabbinic culture of antiquity and our present-day reality or to suggest in any way that the Jewish textual lessons that unfold in this book are somehow anticipated or explicitly coded in any of the films themselves. Here too the specific use and form of the midrashic mashal prove instructive. As David Stern explains, in the classical king mashal, the text has several parts: the quoting of a verse, followed by the story about a king and the like, and then the narrative's application, the nimshal, which typically ends with the citing of a verse, the mashal's proof-text:

> Yet while the message is inscribed—enacted as it were—in both the narrative and the accompanying exegesis, it is never stated explicitly; indeed, the mashal's effectiveness in persuading its audience of the truth of its message lies in its refusing to state that message explicitly, thereby making the audience deduce for themselves the two enactments. . . . The duplication serves both as a hermeneutical safeguard—since the audience can "check" their interpretation of the narrative against their understanding of the exegesis, and vice versa—and as an opening for additional subtleties of meaning, since by inserting discrepancies in the space between the mashal-proper and the nimshal, by introducing differences into the larger

pattern of resemblance, the mashal's author can deliberately complicate his audience's act of interpretation as well as the mashal's own message.[35]

Insofar as, in this exploration, Jewish text study and theological discussion are the "nimshal" of the movie "mashal," a similar set of discrepancies, gaps, or incomplete analogies opens up between the given film and the chosen Jewish textual application. This is to be expected and in fact desired. The goal or expectation of this experience is not that films decode or speak directly for our Jewish tradition or experience, but that they provoke discussion and engagement; the gaps between the worldview of the film and Jewish tradition matter here as much as the correspondences. At bottom, the method of inverted midrash strives for an illustration and reframing of old ideas through the introduction of new images and stories.

To some extent, the method outlined here in this book is already common practice in congregations and classrooms all across America. Since beginning to teach Reel Theology, I have been contacted many times by rabbis and educators who have shared with me their movie-inspired High Holiday sermons and their blockbuster-billed lesson plans. These sermonic and classroom contexts themselves follow from midrashic tradition. According to Stern, "the most frequent occasions for the recitation of meshalim . . . were the delivery of the sermon in the synagogue and the study of Torah in the academy . . . From deathbed to pulpit, then, the mashal was an exceedingly popular, widely used literary form."[36] Even so, in antiquity and in our own day, there has been a common tendency to dismiss such popular forms, as suggested in a midrash of Song of Songs Rabbah 1:1:8, in which the mashal genre itself is subjected to a series of parables, likening it to a variety of mundane tools, including, finally, a penny candle:

ורבנן אמרין אל יהי המשל הזה קל בעיניך שע"י המשל הזה אדם יכול לעמוד
בד"ת, משל למלך שאבד זהב מביתו או מרגליות טובה לא ע"י פתילה כאיסר הוא
מוצא אותה כך המשל הזה לא יהיה קל בעיניך שע"י המשל אדם עומד על ד"ת.

Our rabbis say: Let not the mashal [parable] be made light of in your eyes, for by means of the parable one can understand Torah. A parable [to what can it be likened?]: To a king for whom gold or a precious pearls have gone missing from his house. Does he not find it by means of a wick worth a small Roman coin? In the same way the parable should not be made light of in your eyes, for by means of the parable one can understand Torah.³⁷

Echoing the rabbis, this book makes an argument for the seriousness of serious film study as a way of taking hold not just of film meanings but also of Torah. Here I take up the lead of film and religion scholar S. Brent Plate, who writes about the recreational nature of film watching in relation to what he terms the "re-creational" experience of serious film analysis. According to Plate, "Recreation is a way to re-create the world, which often means taking a step back from the world to see how it is put together, if only to figure out how it can be rearranged."³⁸ Brent explains what he means by this by referring to the Jewish observance of the Sabbath:

> Judaism has a strong tradition of understanding the Sabbath as the *completion* of creation, that on the seventh day God did not refrain from creating as much as God created the Sabbath. The Sabbath according to this view, is the "real world," the rest of the week a necessary other world. . . . If the Sabbath is the day we turn "to the mystery of creation" and "from the world of creation to the creation of the world," then film mimics this very process. Film makes us wonder about the world again, makes us say 'wow!" and offers images that allow us to see things in a new way . . . To be active consumers and participants in front of the film screen, altar or Sabbath table—in order to maintain the hyphen in re-creation—it is necessary to at times to dissect and analyze, to take things apart and then recombine them.³⁹

For Plate, the form of film, which gives off the impression of seamless reality, but in actuality is composed of 800 to 1,200 edited shots in a ninety-minute film, specifically calls for this kind of taking apart. Midrashic tradition adopts a similar tack by, on the one hand, asserting the divine unity of the Bible, and then, as a matter of course, dismembering the unity, analyzing it word by word, verse by verse, creating breaks between the divine utterances and then stitching them back together through ongoing, engaged running commentary.

Re-creative Alienation: Images, Idols, and Interpretive Imagination

What follows in the act of midrashic/filmic interpretation is a dialectical process of retreat and return, of drawing back and drawing close, one that Eugene Borowitz argues in *The Mask Jews Wear* is a necessary part of the Jewish position in contemporary culture:

> Today mankind desperately needs people who are creatively alienated. To be satisfied in our situation is either to have bad values or to understand grossly what man can do. Simply to be opposed to "the system" leads to quixotic protests that work to entrench the established wrong and promote despair and passivity. Creative alienation implies sufficient withdrawal from our society to judge it critically, but also the will and flexibility to keep finding and trying ways to correct it. I think Jewishness offers a unique means of gaining and maintaining such creative alienation.[40]

Borrowing both from Borowitz and Plate, I would like to suggest that a practice of Jewish Reel Theology entails a stance of "re-creative alienation," at once acknowledging and appreciating the power and artistry of popular film but also standing at a Jewish cultural and interpretive remove. It is this stance of "re-creative alienation" that allows one to immerse oneself in the screen image of our culture without succumbing to a form of contemporary idolatry.[41]

I mention idolatry here, as there is no way to write a book about Jewish faith and film without in some way addressing the position of Jewish tradition with respect to visual representation. We are all familiar with the injunction in the Decalogue against making images (Exodus 20:4–5):

לֹא-תַעֲשֶׂה לְךָ פֶסֶל, וְכָל-תְּמוּנָה, אֲשֶׁר בַּשָּׁמַיִם מִמַּעַל, וַאֲשֶׁר בָּאָרֶץ מִתָּחַת--וַאֲשֶׁר בַּמַּיִם, מִתַּחַת לָאָרֶץ. לֹא-תִשְׁתַּחֲוֶה לָהֶם, וְלֹא תָעָבְדֵם:

> **4.** You shall not make for yourself a sculptured image, or any likeness of what is in the heavens above, or on the earth below, or in the waters under the earth **5.** You should not bow down unto them, nor serve them . . .[42]

Based on the verses above, the notion has emerged that Jewish tradition rejects not just the fashioning of images of gods or God, but, according to some, all forms of representational visual art, as species of idolatry.[43]

And yet, even as the Bible prohibits the creation of idolatrous graven objects, the tablets of the law are themselves "idolic," graven with the words of the Ten Commandments.[44] Even the Shema prayer (Deut. 6:4–9), our primary monotheistic, liturgical statement, entails the deployment of salient visual markers—the *mezuzot* placed on doorposts, the *totafot* (phylacteries) placed on one's arms and between one's eyes. Art historian Vivien Mann notes that the prohibition against sculptured images actually supports rather than rejects the "role and inherent power of images." They would not be prohibited if they did not work their cultural magic. The presence in the Tabernacle of such images as Ark of the Covenant and the cherubim points to the use of images even among the biblical faithful. Mann notes the telling additional example of Ezekiel 4, in which the prophet is enjoined to draw an image of Jerusalem, as a means of depicting its future siege.[45]

How, then, does one assume or arrive at a Jewish stance toward images? To be sure, the biblical prophets commonly rail against the spiritual backsliding of the Israelites who betray their relationship with God by fashioning and worshipping man-made images. In the Talmud, idolatry is condemned as one of the three major sins for which one must suffer martyrdom rather than transgress. An entire Talmudic tractate, Avodah Zarah, is devoted to the laws on how to deal with idol worshippers and their culture. At the same time, rabbinic literature offers evidence of the need to operate and circulate within a world where statuary and images are ubiquitous. As Yaron Eliav notes, "[p]ublic sculptures were the "mass media" of the Roman world. They populated urban centers throughout the empire, serving as what art historians call a "plastic language" that communicated political, religious, and social messages."[46] One might expect, based on the prohibition against idolatry, that all this statuary would produce a constant clash of cultures. As Eliav notes, however, "[i]n the sphere of culture and religion, conflict and amity both coexist and intertwine."[47] So while some rabbis perceived all statues as idols and therefore anathema to the Jew, others "classified statues into different categories, distinguishing between those that transgress Jewish norms and those that did not constitute a problem."[48] For example, the Mishnah in Tractate Avodah Zarah (3:4) records a conversation between Proclos, son of Plosphos, and

Rabban Gamliel that takes place in the bathhouse of Aphrodite in Acco. Proclos challenges Rabban Gamliel over his willingness to bathe in the presence of an idol, and Rabban Gamliel answers as follows:

> I came not within her limits, she came within my limits. [People] do not say "Let us build a bath as an adornment for [the statue of] Aphrodite," but "Let us make a [statue of] Aphrodite as an adornment for the bath." . . . It is said, "Their gods [Deuteronomy 12:3]: what is treated as a god is prohibited, what is not treated as a god is permitted.[49]

Rabban Gamliel's willingness to frequent a place that was adorned by idols stemmed from a conviction that the idols were incidental to the bathhouse rather than central to the space, and that not all statues were meant to be worshipped. This sort of position, Eliav argues, allowed Jews to "live a 'normal' Jewish life in the presence of Roman sculpture.[50]

Let us follow up on Eliav's premise that "[p]ublic sculptures were the "mass media" of the Roman world. Can the Mishnah quoted above serve, then, as a guide for a contemporary Jewish appreciation and study of mass media culture? Perhaps. And yet there is an obvious difference between finding a way to get by in an alien culture that contradicts one's basic values and delving into, even celebrating, that culture. In this sense, Rabban Gamliel's flexibility is only partly useful to those of us looking for a Jewish way into popular culture and film. It might permit me to walk through Times Square for the purpose of finding my way to the subway, the billboards and images flashing in my peripheral vision. It would not permit me, however, to enter a theater, switch on a TV, or surf from one YouTube video to another. Unlike Rabban Gamliel's argument about the incidental nature of the Aphrodite statues in the bathhouse, the images on the movie or television screen are not mere adornment; they are the main attraction.

Other Talmudic precedents, such as rabbinic discussions of whether one is allowed to go to a *te'atron* (theater), present similar impediments. According to the position of Rabbi Meir, one is forbidden from going to the theater because of the injunction against idolatry; statues typically adorned the theaters. According to the sages, however, this constitutes the prohibition only when idol worship actually took place at the theater. Otherwise, the prohibition derives from theater's status as a *"moshav leitzim*," a place of frivolous activity.⁵¹ Either way, of course, attendance at the theater is forbidden. This rejectionist position forms the basis of the contemporary ultra-Orthodox practice of refraining from going to the movies or even owning a television.⁵²

For those of us who are committed to engaging the broader cultural world, the aforementioned rabbinic/halakhic sources likely will not prevent us from entering a movie theater or watching a TV show. These sources might, however, serve as a model for how to view and engage these cultural products from a Jewish point of view. Prior, ancient discussions might prompt us to consider what constitutes idolatry or frivolity in the present-day context and to use our media engagement as an occasion to develop a religiously minded, "re-creational" stance. There is no question that we live in an image-saturated culture that often lauds, even worships, physical beauty, youth, money, success, sexual pleasure, and material possessions. Hollywood blockbusters that trade in violence and explicit sexuality have dulled our critical sensibilities, while twenty-four-hour cable news has blunted our emotions. Text and instant messaging, Twitter and Facebook, and the "two-screen experience" offered by so many hit TV shows all feed us micro bits of culture and human interaction and condition us to be less rather than more attentive, to focus vaguely on many things at once, and to engage life only in an instantaneous, superficial way.

A Jewish approach to film and popular culture stands against that kind of thinking. It presupposes that as human beings, uniquely created in the image of a Creator God who is depicted in Genesis 1 as speaking, seeing, distinguishing among things, and pronouncing Creation good, we have an ethical/theological critical ability to sort out the valuable and edifying from the morally vapid, mind-deadening, and theologically noxious. Often people watch movies to escape reality, to have images wash over them unthinkingly. More than any other artistic medium, the unexamined realism of film—along with the convention of watching on a big screen, in the dark, effectively blocking out reality⁵³—enables this kind of escapism. As scholar John Lyden notes, "[w]e desire alternate worlds because we find our own imperfect; but such desires to flee also entail a desire to return, renewed and refreshed, to the everyday."⁵⁴ The ability of film to reproduce our world completely as well as to imagine other worlds provides an opportunity for considering our world in all of its exquisite, perplexing, and exasperating detail as well as for envisioning alternatives. As Neil P. Hurley writes, "[t]he first step in any liberation process is the adoption of a critical stance."[55] Assuming an active, critically alert, open-minded set of watching and reading practices is the necessary first step to a Jewish Reel Theology. The next step is to bring the central themes of any given cultural work into conversation with Jewish text and Jewish thought, for as Emmanuel Levinas teaches, Torah study constitutes a "reading or study of a text that protects itself from the eventual idolatry of this very text, by renewing, through continual exegesis—the immutable letters and hearing breath of the living God in them."[56]

1

The Truman Show

Truth

If one of the preconditions of a Reel Theology is the development of a critical stance with respect to our ubiquitous screen culture, there are movies that dramatize that very issue. Peter Weir's 1998 film *The Truman Show* opens with a close shot of Christof, the "creator" of the show within the film, who lauds the singular authenticity of its lead actor (Truman). Christof defends his "reality TV" creation by insisting that, as a culture, we have become "tired of actors giving up phony emotions," tired of pyrotechnics and special effects. Truman, he argues, is an antidote to all of this cultural fakery. "While the world he inhabits is, in some respects, counterfeit," Christof claims, "there is nothing fake about Truman himself"[1]—a statement that is ostensibly true yet skirts the border of truth insofar as everything around Truman, all his assumptions about himself and his life, are, in fact, scripted and false. Learning how to watch *The Truman Show* entails a decoding of all this media fakery, even as one accepts that there is no true way to flee the superstructure of words and images that it represents.

Frequently, throughout this opening monologue close-up, especially when referring to the idea of phoniness, Christof looks up and to the left, an artistic affectation and obvious sign of duplicity. The entire opening montage show, featuring "testimony" about the truthfulness of the show from its principal actors, smacks of dishonesty and suggests the ways in which truth and reality are deliberately obscured within the tightly crafted and controlled world of images known as Seahaven.

Truman himself, however, knows nothing about these lies or the thousands of cameras, cast members, and people watching him the world over. Seen at first through a concealed camera in the bathroom medicine cabinet, boyishly playacting as a mountain climber who fears that he will never reach the summit, Truman seems at best a lovable dupe. The women's cosmetic products strategically placed in the medicine cabinet that frames the screen attest to the truth he does not yet know: that his whole life is a vehicle for Christof's studio to sell things: clothes, cosmetics, furniture, kitchen implements, and Truman kitsch. The medicine cabinet screen suggests enclosure and limited possibilities. Yet Truman's adventure monologue, with its intimations of intrepid travel to faraway destinations—there are no mountains to scale in Seehaven!—also foreshadows the emotional, intellectual, and physical journey toward truth that Truman will eventually undertake over the course of the film. "Tell me something I don't already know," Truman says to himself as he playacts. To gain this new knowledge and make this journey, Truman must first wake up from his enforced innocence to experience a spark of consciousness and new knowledge. He must stop letting his wife, Meryl, mother him, as she does in this scene, calling up to Truman that he's going to be late. He must separate and individuate and begin to sense all on his own that something is not right in Seahaven.

Shortly thereafter, when Truman goes out to his car to leave for work, the next-door neighbor's dog jumps on him, a scene that is filmed from a low angle shot that makes Truman suddenly seem very tall and important; capable, perhaps, of great insight. Immediately following this, Truman sees a stage light plunge from the sky to the ground before him, a mock let-there-be-light moment that shows the limits of Christof's purported authority as creator and turns on a lamp of critical awareness within Truman.[2]

Figure 1.1. Truman Sees the Light.

Truman had formerly been given to clichéd speech ("That's the whole kit and caboodle!" "That's the whole ball of wax!") and limited by the phobias and obstacles set before him by Christof's script writers (who stage the drowning of his father to make him forever frightened of sea travel and spirit away his love interest, Lauren/Sylvia, before he can develop a real relationship with her). After the stage light falls, however, Truman gradually begins to discern the ersatz, production-set nature of his life in Seahaven. Before being dragged off of the set of Truman's life, Sylvia had attempted to inform Truman that everyone was watching him and that his whole life was a show. Her unique, sad eyes, symbolic of the possibility of individual vision, experience, and critical insight, haunt him as he continues to detect cracks in the veneer of his simulated, regulated, too-perfect life in Seahaven. Increasingly unhappy and suspicious, Truman makes various unsuccessful attempts to escape the island by plane, bus, car, and foot. His failed forays are filmed by the many cameras planted everywhere, accentuating the closely monitored and limited nature of his world. In one particularly desperate scene, Truman, having run into the forest by the nuclear power plant, is wrestled to the ground by several men in hazmat suits, a camera recording his subjection from a bird's-eye angle, as if from heaven above.

For a time, Truman's desperate quest for the truth is held at bay by Christof's decision to reunite Truman with his supposedly dead father. This plot turn is executed with the help of Truman's best friend, Marlon, who lies outright to Truman, with the words fed to him through an earpiece by Christof. If there were some grand plot, Marlon says, he would have to be in on it, which of course, he is! During a subsequent call-in-show interlude, ironically called "Tru-talk," Sylvia calls in and denounces Christof as a liar and manipulator. Christof defends his actions on the grounds that Truman is better off anyway living in Seahaven than in the sick outside world. Seahaven is how the world truly ought to be. In fact, Christof claims, Truman's failure until this point to uncover the reality of his life proves that he actually "prefers his cell."

In the end, Chistof's bogus claim is roundly refuted as Truman finally defies his longstanding sea phobia and takes a ship to the edge of the film set, having endured the final dramatic storm unleashed against him by Christof to deter him from his journey. Crashing into a wall of fake sky, Truman then climbs a set of stairs (as if to heaven) and exits the phony Seahaven world through a dark door leading to who knows where. Truman's journey of discovery reveals the sham nature of his media-generated reality and its would-be god, Christof.

Notably, throughout the film, Christof demonstrates much of what Judeo-Christian tradition has long taught about God: he is a creator; with his ubiquitous, providential camera-eyes, he is seemingly omniscient, omnipresent, and omnipotent. In accordance with the God portraits of Genesis 1–3, he cues the sun and brings forth the rain and attempts to control his creature's access to knowledge.[3] Like God in the book of Jonah, he summons a storm on the sea to force his way on his recalcitrant messenger. At times he is a punitive ruler; at others, he is paternal, even loving, stroking the image of Truman on the screen as a father would a son, cooing over memories of Truman as a young boy. The ever-formulaic nature of Truman's life and times in Seahaven as designed by its director-creator (reminiscent of the creation story in Genesis 1, which repeats the formula "and there was evening and there was morning" after each day of Creation) is perhaps best encapsulated by the cheery morning greeting Truman repeatedly offers his neighbors and audience: "If I don't see you, good afternoon, good evening and good night." Who, we wonder, fed Truman that hokey 1950s TV host line? And what does he himself live for? Does he have any chance of writing his own script or establishing core values of his own? Is he doomed forever to bend to the will of false God Christof and the idolatrous media world into which he was born?

In the last scene of the film, Truman stands by the dark doorway of the Seahaven set and listens as Christof reveals (by loudspeaker) his identity as the "creator of a television show" starring Truman himself. This moment by the door, in which Christof speaks to Truman, attempting to dissuade him from walking through that door, calls to mind Franz Kafka's famous parable "Before the Law,"[4] in which a gatekeeper stands before the door and bars the man from the country from entering the Law—a multivalent symbol of power, freedom, truth, righteousness, and the great scheme of things; of God as lawgiver and the Ground of all Meaning. How does one gain access to any of these? How does one even attempt to comprehend these master narratives and construct a narrative of one's own?

Kafka's parable is somber and pessimistic. While the man from the country grows old and dwindles in darkness, light radiates from the door of the Law, to which the man will never gain entry. Ultimately Kafka's man from the country must bow and submit to this dark destiny, forever at a remove from the light.

In contrast, Truman stands before an open door. There is no radiance emanating from the other side, yet he embraces that dark unknown. The final bow that Truman takes right before he exits stands not for obeisance but for rebellion against the cheery, blinding norms of Christof's determined, protected world. If sort-of-God Christof insists that because he has been providentially watching Truman his whole life—and besides, Truman is too afraid to act on his own—Truman ought not leave Seahaven, Truman implicitly says, I'd rather not see you or be seen by you any more, thank you very much. We, like the filmed audience within the film, cannot help cheering him on as he bravely walks right through that door and Sylvia rushes to greet him.

A modernist, Freudian reading of Truman's exit at the film's end might suggest that Truman has been cured of his religious neurosis and is now ready to live a healthy life, free of the pseudo-God. An existentialist reading might similarly suggest that he has learned to reject the religiously scripted or media-staged meanings previously made for him and is now ready to make meaning of his own.[5]

But is there really any way to find ultimate meaning outside words, signs, symbols, and images—that is, outside the realm of human language and image media? As a film, comprised of several shows within a show, about the need to be wary of the film and television, *The Truman Show* indicates, in frank terms, the extent to which we cannot, and perhaps should not, attempt to flee the superstructure of words, images, cameras, and screens that governs our sense of selfhood and freedom. We remain, in some sense, enclosed in the system, dependent on it to frame and communicate our values.

A postsecular, religious, "reely theological" reading of the film thus entails both a smashing of Christof-like idols and an affirmation of what God really is. From my text-centered, covenant-centered, Jewish vantage point, I maintain a belief that central to the uncovering of God in our lives is a recognition of the sacredness of words and our godly indwelling within language, for it is our ability to freely communicate, create, and relate in words, signs, and thought images, both to each other and to God, that identifies us as created *betzelem Elohim* (in the image of God).[6] It is for this reason that the Torah imagines the creation of the world through a speech act; that Moses, the giver of the Torah, is repeatedly presented in the Bible as speaking *devarim* [words]; and that in Hebrew, the Ten Commandments are called *dibrot* and are engraved on two tablets, another form of graven image. As suggested by Truman's incipient relation with Sylvia, truth and God inhere in real, freely chosen relationships; in love as expressed in symbols, words, and pictures, cut and pasted together and acknowledged with open eyes.

Nowadays, we are no longer as surprised by the idea of reality TV. What was mere fiction in that 1998 is very much our reality. For that reason, more than ever, we need to have a sense of where religion and God arise from our media-soaked existence. Where is our godly reality in this world of constant texts, Twitter, YouTube, and Web downloads? What structures in our lives allow us to identify eternal moments of significance in language, learning, human action, conversation, and relationships? And how can we fill our time not with noisy verbiage, but with the language of transcendence and truth? *The Truman Show*, in featuring a protagonist who is searching for personal truth in his media-fabricated world, helps facilitate this discussion. "We do not believe," says Jesuit minister Richard Leonard in *Movies That Matter*, "that God created us as playthings, brought into being for God's amusement . . . It is not accident that the name of Truman's escape boat is the Santa Maria—the ship that Columbus captained in 1492. We believe that God's greatest enjoyment is to be our companion as we explore the many horizons of the world, becoming the men and women God created us to be."[7]

Truth, God, and Humankind: *The Truman Show* and the Book of Jonah

In the process of outlining the ways in which the *Truman Show*'s Christof pretends to be God, I briefly referred above to the God of the biblical book of Jonah, a prophet who dared to escape the directive of God. I'd like to return now to the story of Jonah, this time drawing a more explicit analogy between the protagonists of both of these works, beginning with their names.

In marked contrast to the Hollywood-star names of his purported wife, mother, father, and best friend (Meryl, Angela, Kirk, and Marlon, respectively), Truman's name quite literally sets him apart as the lone True Man in his specious world. It is this name, assigned to him at birth by Christof, that defines Truman and eventually helps him to escape the control of his supposed Burbank family, that is, of Christof's studio. The biblical Jonah is similarly marked and defined by his name. We know nothing at all about the background of this oddball prophet other than his name, *Yonah ben Amittai*. Scholars have assigned various meanings to his first name. Penina Galpaz-Feller links the name *Yonah* with the Hebrew root ינה, which is associated elsewhere in the Bible (in Isaiah and Nahum) with mourning and lament, a reading that is supported by Jonah's recurrent death wish as well as his eventual doomsday prophecy to Nineveh.[8] Bruce Vawter connects the name ironically to Nineveh, "sacred to the goddess Ishtar, whose fertility symbols were often a dove or a fish," linking Jonah, his escape attempts, and his ultimate fate to the very city he tries to avoid confronting.[9] According to Aviva Zornberg, "Yonah, a dove, communicates something essential about him: elusive, always in flight."[10] The name Yonah also links the book of Jonah with the Noah story, another biblical narrative that features a singular man, a sea voyage, a big storm, and the predicted annihilation of a whole civilization. In the biblical story of Noah, a *yonah* (dove) is sent out to ascertain whether the floodwaters have subsided, serving as a messenger or mediator between the sealed-off ark and the outside world.[11] Seahaven, in a sense, is Truman's ark; both Yonah ben Amitai and Truman, sharing aspects of the dove, are chosen to play roles and deliver messages beyond their sealed worlds that do not accord with their nature or their inchoate, inner sense of truth. Unbeknownst to him, Truman's whole life involves acting a part for an audience, and so his quest for truth involves exposing the lies of this role and finding a way out. "Was any of it real?" he asks Christof in their culminating conversation. "You were," contends Christof, "which is what made you so interesting to watch." But Christof is not granted the last word. Sylvia, watching this sequence, stares at the screen and says, "Please, God," appealing to a different sort of God, one who supports rather than thwarts the exercise of free will. Truman's final intoning of "If I don't see you, good afternoon, good evening, and good night," constitutes a final rejection of Christof's revelation of "reality" and the answer to Sylvia's prayer.

The biblical book of Jonah, of course, is a theological work that upholds rather than renounces God's truth, even as it allows God's messenger to express and work through a series of personal objections to it. In contrast to *The Truman Show*, where Truman's natural desire to explore and break out is systematically thwarted, and thus his escape marks the culmination of his maturation and emancipation, the escape attempt staged in the book of Jonah marks only the beginning of Jonah's journey toward understanding. Truman's story climaxes with his ascent up the soundstage steps and his exit through the door. Jonah's journey begins with a similar vocabulary of ascent, with the communication of the word of the Lord (*devar-Adonai*) to Jonah that he "arise and go to Nineveh, that great city, for their wickedness has come up before Me."[12] But Jonah insists on burrowing inward rather than venturing outward, on going down instead of up. Underscoring this choice, the Hebrew verb *vayeired* (and he went down) recurs several times in the first chapter of the book, as Jonah first goes down to Joppa to escape God's bidding, descends into the ship bound for Tarshish (1:3), and descends even further into the innermost part of the ship as the God-sent tempest threatens to break the ship apart. Jonah then falls asleep (*vayeiradem*—a verb that plays on *vayeired* and suggests an even further decline). Truman also "goes down and sleeps" insofar as his escape to see begins with a retreat to his basement, to his trunk childhood memorabilia and mementos of Sylvia. But this proves to be a feigned sleep, a ruse, using a plastic snowman and a tape-recorded snore, to facilitate his getaway at sea. And though Truman's journey also includes a descent into the sea as Christof unleashes the storm on him, his quest ultimately entails an awakening, a heightening of critical consciousness. Whereas Truman's quest entails an awakening and a heightening of critical consciousness, Jonah deadens his consciousness and goes under, so as to deny God's bidding. In contrast to Truman, who wants to break out from the childishly perfect world of Seahaven, Jonah rejects his prophetic errand to the broader world and seeks a haven of somnolence at sea.

Throughout the book of Jonah, reflecting Jonah's resistance to God's will and God's counterresistance, certain words or roots appear and then reappear in opposing contexts or meanings. If God pursues Jonah and casts (*heitil*) a mighty wind onto the sea (*el hayam*, 1:4), Jonah counters by advising the God-fearing sailors to "cast me forth into the sea" (1:12; *hatiluni el hayam*). Jonah initially sets out to flee (1:3; *livro'aḥ*) by ship to Tarshish. In being thrown overboard, he hopes to abscond into the deepest depths of death, as if to flee responsibility by returning to the watery bars (*briḥehah*) of the earth (2:7).

Compare this moment to Truman's heroic call to whoever is controlling the storm over his boat: "You are going to have to kill me first!" Christof, determined to maintain ratings and control Truman at all costs, agrees to halt the storm over Truman's boat only when it seems that Truman is dead. In the book of Jonah, however, God wants Jonah neither to escape nor to regress nor to die. As such, he appoints a fish to swallow Jonah up and prevent his ultimate descent, allowing him some time back in the womb so that he can be reborn, this time with a willingness to do God's will.

As for Jonah in the belly of the fish, he couldn't be happier. He now has exactly what he wants: an enclosed world, cut off from all human responsibility, but without death, at least as long as he is not done in by the digestive juices in the guts of the big fish.

Canadian poet A. M. Klein captures this mood of escapist jubilation in the following rhyming, poetic depiction of Jonah's happy lair in the belly of the whale:

> Within the whale's belly
> Good Jonah at home
> Ate fish made of jelly
> And drank frothy foam.[13]

Klein's poem takes its singsong, rhyming, celebratory cues from Jonah's Thanksgiving song from the belly of the fish, a paean to the God who answered his prayers that repeatedly refers to God's "holy temple" (2:5, 2:8), suggesting that for Jonah, the fish's belly is its own kind of long-sought, sacred sanctuary. To be sure, Klein's rendition of Jonah's life in the whale is more sensual and secular than Jonah's prayer. In the fish's belly, Klein's Jonah has all of his aesthetic, romantic, and gustatory needs fulfilled, and he "roisters" with his mermaid until God summarily dishes him out onto the seashore. Still, if we chuckle at the idea of Jonah roistering and carousing in the whale's belly, there is something equally funny about the biblical Jonah's designation of the intestinal tract of the fish as a holy temple. Here is Jonah, the erstwhile fugitive, now trapped with no way out, nevertheless pledging to bring thanksgiving sacrifices. Just a little while ago, he yearned for nothing more than to go down and die, and now he praises God for raising him up. Only in being cocooned in the fish for three days with no hope of escape does Jonah find a way to thank and praise (if not apologize to) God and imagine living on, prompting God, of course, to direct the fish to spit Jonah up onto dry land.

"If Jonah wishes that much to die," asks Elie Wiesel, "why does he cling to life? Why [later in the book] does he seek the coolness of the shade [of the gourd vine], when he should do nothing to avoid suffering? His is a peculiar combination of life-force and death wish. Which is more real?"[14] Wiesel's attempt here to grapple with the inconsistency of Jonah's personality, to untangle the contradictions and discern what is "real," indirectly points to one of the central teachings of the book of Jonah, that is, the enduring truth of changeability and, by extension, the malleability of truth within the divine–human relationship. Things change in this book, Jonah's moods and aspirations among them. Words take on meanings and countermeanings, indicating that interpretation, intention, and decision are not fixed. Rather they change in response to the circumstances, something that Jonah does not entirely appreciate. In BT. Sanhedrin 89b, the rabbis call attention to the double meaning of the word *nehepakhet* and, as a consequence, the indeterminate meaning of the message that Jonah is told to deliver to the people of Nineveh: "Jonah was originally told that Nineveh would be turned [*nehepakhet*] but did not know whether for good or for evil."[15] As Yvonne Sherwood observes, "the word that Jonah is given is a hinged word, a curse-blessing, a word that declines to fill its obvious referential responsibilities."[16] Is it possible that the very contingency of God's message itself disturbed Jonah, that is, the impossibility of knowing, in advance, whether the people would be overthrown and destroyed or turned around, and therefore saved?

As readers, we share in this sense of indeterminacy, insofar as we are not initially apprised of the reasons behind Jonah's refusal to bring God's message to Nineveh. Left without an explicit motive, we might deduce on our own that Jonah escapes to Tarshish because of either compassion for Nineveh or a simple, selfish desire not to leave his comfort zone and get involved in the affairs of strangers.[17] In chapter 4, however, we find out that Jonah's wish to escape the divine errand, and by extension to die, derives from his objection to God's willingness to forgive Nineveh should they repent. When the people of Nineveh enact their dramatic, universal turn toward God, and God stays the decree against them, Jonah complains bitterly to God:

> Please, O LORD, was this not my word when I was still in my own land? This is why I hastened to flee to Tarshish; for I knew that You are a compassionate and gracious God, slow to anger, abounding in kindness, and abundant in mercy, repenting of evil. Now LORD, please take my life, for I would rather die than live. (4:2–3)[18]

The above list of God's attributes recalls a similar litany from Exodus 34:6—"The LORD, the LORD God, compassionate and gracious, slow to anger, abounding in kindness and truth (*emet*)"[19]—a list of divine attributes proclaimed in the wake of God's instruction to Moses to prepare a second set of tablets of the Law. By the logic of strict justice, which is how Jonah seems to define the world *emet*, God should have annihilated the Israelites in the desert as punishment for the sin of the Golden Calf, but God gives them a second chance as well as a second set of tablets to replace the ones Moses smashed. Yonah ben Amittai's reprise of Exodus 34:6 replaces *emet* with God's readiness to repent of evil, suggesting that truth and the acceptance of repentance are mutually exclusive. Himself notoriously inconsistent, given to contradictions, mood swings, and changes of heart, Jonah wants God to be completely Other and unchanging, to issue decrees that are immovable and immutable, even if facts change on the ground and the initial assessment no longer proves to be true. To him, Divine Truth needs to be a thing eternal and apart, forever unaffected by the ephemera and chimera of human behavior. Feeling like a false prophet or the servant of a mercurial God, Jonah calls for *moti* (my death), another canny wordplay. For Jonah, in the absence of what he considers divine *emet*, the only other available, inalterable truth is death.

But Jewish tradition represents *emet* in diverse ways, reflecting its many meanings and contexts. As Peter Ochs writes, "[i]n Hebrew Scripture, in rabbinic literature, and for most Jewish thinkers, truth is a characteristic of human relationships. Truth is fidelity to one's word, keeping promises, saying with the lips what one says in one's heart, bearing witness to what one has seen."[20] A word that includes the first, last, and middle letters of the Hebrew alphabet,[21] *emet*, as an attribute of God, stands for an all-encompassing mode that accommodates the full range of experience and divine-human relationships. If human beings are willing to change and are created in the image of God, then it follows, in truth, that God would be willing to change and respond accordingly.

Note that God's earlier order to the fish to spit Jonah up onto dry land comes shortly after Jonah's reference, in his prayer from the belly of the fish, to those who maintain "empty folly," thereby forsaking "*ḥasdam*" (the compassion bestowed upon them). Often in the Bible, the words *ḥesed* and *emet* appear as a pair.[22] Here Jonah not only rejects that pairing, but also connects *ḥesed* with *ya'azovu* (they shall forsake or give up), foreshadowing his own desire as elaborated in 4:2 to renounce *ḥesed* as contradictory to his own identity as *Ben Amitai*, "son of my truths." In setting Jonah back on dry land after a mere mention of the notion of *ḥesed* (even if in a negative context), God shows great forbearance, allowing Jonah a second chance to bring the message to Nineveh and thereby internalize a lesson about the relationship between lovingkindness and truth. Jonah's outsized anger and repeated call for his own death, first in response to the dramatic repentance of the people of Nineveh and then to the shriveling up of the gourd plant, all suggest that for Jonah, this lesson does not go down easily.

In fact, at the end of the book of Jonah, we never really find out whether Jonah changes his own mind about the idea of God's *ḥesed ve'emet*. The book ends with a rhetorical question from God:

> "You cared about the plant, which you did not work for and which you did not grow, which appeared overnight and perished overnight. And should I not care about Nineveh, that great city, in which there are more than twelve myriad persons who do not yet know their right hand from their left, and many beasts as well?" (4:10–11)[23]

Does God really get the final word here? Does the absence here of a response from Jonah prove that he has finally acquiesced to God's view? Or does it represent a form of ongoing, silent protest? The open-endedness of the ending of the book of Jonah seems to suggest that even in this case, where God goes to great lengths and exerts considerable pressure to compel a prophet to convey a message, the prophet, indeed, the human being, is left with his own Free Will to decide whether or not to agree. Ultimately, human beings are free to choose God's way or the highway. The true God allows people to make such choices.

Clearly, there were those who found the ambiguous ending of the book of Jonah unsettling and wanted therefore to enclose the message of the book in a more predictable frame. The three extra verses from the end of the book of Micah that were added by the rabbis to the *haftarah* reading of Jonah on Yom Kippur afternoon clearly aim to resolve the uncertainty. *Titen emet leya'akov veḥesed le'avraham*—"You will show truth to Jacob and lovingkindness to Abraham,"[24]—reads the final verse of Micah (Micah 7:20), which closes the Yom Kippur *haftarah*. If Jonah ultimately refused to accept the coupling of *ḥesed* and *emet*, well, here it is for the congregation. That truth is associated here with the biblical Jacob, hardly the most straightforward man in his early life, shows that truth is not a monolith, but rather a multivalent, ever-burgeoning thing. People grow, learn, and change, and that is what God wants, even if Jonah—birdbrained, stubborn, and free—refuses to admit it.

There is a beautiful commentary in Midrash Yonah (sixteenth century) that imagines (despite the textual evidence to the contrary) that Jonah actually experienced a complete change of heart and confessed this to God. According to this midrash, which goes to great length to elaborate on the size of Nineveh, with its many markets, alleyways, courtyards, and houses and its many innocent children, the people of Ninveh repented so fully and radically that they went above and beyond to right all wrongs and return all formerly lost and stolen goods. In one case, a man who buys a ruined house from another man and finds a stash of gold hidden in the ruin tries to hand the gold over to the former owner of the ruin, but the former owner refuses to accept it, saying that the buyer is entitled to this treasure. The seller and the buyer take the matter to a judge, each of them renouncing the gold lest they accept something stolen to which they are not entitled and bring the wrath of God upon the world. In response, the judge decides to look back several generations into the history of this property and finds the proper inheritor. "It was about this very moment," Midrash Yonah says, "that David proclaimed, *Truth springs out of the earth*" [Psalms 85:12]. According to the midrash, God receives the repentant Ninvenites' prayers right away and says, "I forgive." At the same time, Jonah falls on his face before the Holy One of Blessing and says, "Master of the Universe, forgive my sins and absolve my iniquity that I fled from You to the sea. For I did not know Your ways, and now I know the strength of your ways and your power, as it is written, *for I know that You are a gracious God, compassionate.*"[25] According to this midrash, the miraculous, newly found piety, magnanimity, and justice of the people of Nineveh ultimately provoke stubborn Jonah to change his mind about the relationship between repentance and truth, realizing that from repentance come even greater acts of compassion and justice. More than that, Jonah learns from the Ninvehnites that he too must confess and reckon with his own mistakes. From their example, Jonah realizes that he can change his mind and still remain true to himself. He can admit before God that he was wrong and receive forgiveness. Jonah's former truths are deflated, and a new set of convictions forms in their stead.

It's So True That It's Funny/It's So Funny That It's True: Jonah as Comedy

To be sure, the actual biblical text does not go nearly as far as the midrash in its description of the contrition of Ninveh. And it remains completely mum about the possibility of Jonah changing his attitude. In fact, according to the text, Jonah is so sullen and serious about his principles and so immovably convinced that he is right that it's funny. Indeed, many scholars read the book of Jonah as a profoundly humorous book,[26] another feature that aligns it with *The Truman Show*. The comedy in *The Truman Show* derives in part from the distinctive screen personality of Jim Carrey, an actor whose performances are typically over-the-top but who nevertheless underplays these qualities in this film so as to allow Truman's sense of his phony surroundings—what Freud refers to in *Jokes and Their Relation to the Unconscious* as the relationship between "bewilderment and enlightenment"[27]—to slowly emerge. The rest of the comedy in *The Truman Show* comes from the exaggerated efforts and ridiculous gaffes made by those who work in Christof's studio as they try to maintain the show and the illusion of Truman's life and by the larger audience's unacknowledged, slavish loyalty to the show.

The comedy in the book of Jonah derives similarly from the interplay between understatement and exaggeration. At the beginning of the book, Jonah, like a comic, antiheroic straight man, doesn't say much. When God sends him to Nineveh, he simply runs in the other direction. When the ship begins to toss, he flees to the lower deck. Jonah's sullen understatement contrasts markedly with the extravagant action of everyone and everything around him: the remarkable fear of God demonstrated by the sailors, the hugeness of the fish that swallows Jonah up and of the city of Nineveh; the flamboyant show of repentance staged by the king of Nineveh, who commands everyone in the town, man and beast alike, to fast, don sack cloth, and "call mightily to God" (3:8).

As the book progresses, Jonah speaks up more and more, but in ways that only serve only to highlight his own, buffoonish recalcitrance and narrow-mindedness. He thanks God from the belly of the whale but does not apologize. He calls out to the people of Nineveh to prophesy their doom, only to mourn their salvation when it comes. He complains unto death about the death of a plant he has neither created nor tended. Will he ever learn? Jonah is a schlemiel prophet, one who does not want to fulfill his duty but cannot seem to escape. When he tries to fall asleep, someone wakes him up. When he tries to sink low into death, a fish scoops him up and then gives birth to him anew by spitting him back onto dry land. He is a cartoon prophet, flattened by God, but somehow, against his will, he always pops back to life. According to Rachel Adler,

"Jonah is a parody, burlesquing other Biblical stories and punning outrageously. It is also the most carnivalesque of biblical books, rich in monstrosities, curiosities, spectacles and monkeyshines."[28] In Adler's view, the liturgical reading of this comic book on Yom Kippur afternoon, just as our spirits and blood sugar are waning, is meant to provoke us "to see in comic perspective the bodies we are so righteously afflicting and the spirits we are so assiduously burnishing."[29] We cannot help laughing at Jonah's foibles, and as we erupt into laughter, some of the truths of our own Jonah-like evasiveness and our own antiheroic tendencies also burst out into the open.

All this brings to mind scholar John Morreall's observations about humor as a virtue. "In the comic frame of mind," Morreaull argues, "we get out of our mental ruts to think flexibly . . . The comic mind is always ready to consider another possible perspective. In this way, comic thinking fosters objectivity and rationality. We break free of thinking in the here and now and the real and the practical. Instead of seeing things from our own personal perspective, we can see them in the big picture."[30]

And so the book of Jonah, like *The Truman Show*, teaches that the truth can be funny. Moreover, even God—if not Christof, who rarely smiles!—can have a sense of humor. According to Meir Shalev,

> God smiles in the face of Jonah's anger. The smile isn't described in words, but can be read between the lines. "Are you really angry?" He asks the furious prophet, and the reader can read these words out loud to prove that they cannot be said without a faint mocking smile. If I am right, that is, if God smiled when he said these words, it is God's first smile, the first, last, and only smile in the Bible.[31]

If all this is so, perhaps the best way to classify the book of Jonah is as religious comedy. One of the aims of comedy, and indeed of religious life, is to reveal hidden truths. Comedy opens a window to the limitations of human knowledge, as does religion. Both comedy and religion expose cracks in our smug veneer and assault our sense of superiority. They both also allow for surprising moments of reprieve, for salvation in the face of assumed doom. Late in the day on Yom Kippur, lightheaded and tired, we read the book of Jonah and discover these giddy truths. We imagine a God who smiles and forgives Jonah, a prophet who laments God's *ḥesed* even as he enjoys it amply himself.³² We laugh at Jonah and at ourselves, at our own intolerance and hypocrisy, trusting God to untangle the truth of it all. Like Truman at the end of *The Truman Show*, we stand at the top of those heavenly steps and smile at God's open door.

2

Magnolia

Confession and Redemption

In *Visible Fictions*, John Ellis outlines the difference between the images projected by television as opposed to cinema: "It is a characteristic of broadcast TV," writes Ellis, "that the viewer is larger than the image: the opposite of cinema. It seems to be a convention also that the TV image is looked down on, rather than up to as in cinema . . . There is no surrounding darkness, no anonymity of the fellow viewers, no large image, no lack of movement amongst the spectators, no rapt attention."[1] In *The Truman Show*, specific attention is given to the spectatorship of Truman's fans, who at times watch in rapt attention and at other times fall asleep in front of the screen. As a TV image, Truman's life in Seahaven is elevated and idealized but also treated casually, as merely another channel to watch. Truman is looked up at by the patrons in a bar, who view his brightly colored life from a TV suspended from the ceiling, but not in the sense of being a model for behavior. He is the subject of prurient but also passing interest, a life to be eavesdropped on until the show finally comes to an end and channels are changed for the sake of finding some other way to pass the time.

In Paul Thomas Anderson's *Magnolia* (1999),[2] another film that also unfolds in Burbank, California, the lesser, devalued, casual TV images that flit across the screen help convey the sense of diminished humanity and morality, not just on-screen but off-screen as well. Whereas *The Truman Show* (the show within the movie) conjures up an "idyllic" Seahaven, *Magnolia*, released only one year after *The Truman Show*, focuses on all that is sordid about life in Burbank. Everyone and everything around

Truman is impossibly clean, tidy, wholesome, but fake. By contrast, *Magnolia* offers a relentlessly realistic, brilliantly acted, ensemble view of TV producers, game-show hosts, and contestants, a world shot through and interpenetrated with promiscuity, profanity, and other forms of betrayal.

Two of the characters in the film are drug addicts. Another, a game-show host, is an unconfessed child molester. Yet another, the producer of this same game show, serially betrays the wife of his youth and then abandons her when she is dying of cancer to the care of their fourteen-year-old son. This producer's son, clearly damaged by the betrayals of his father, carries on this tradition of abuse and becomes a "celebrity" in his own right, developing a video self-help program called *Seduce and Destroy* to teach men how to dominate and humiliate women. The image-saturated world of *Magnolia* is literally and figuratively cancerous, with two characters dying of cancer[3] and others suffering the effects of malignant parental abuse. Given all of this, the very idea of reading *Magnolia* within a theological context might seem questionable. And yet it is precisely its sin-riven "community" and its unflinching, fleeting portraits that make *Magnolia* such a rich resource for a discussion of religious concepts such as confession and repentance.

Recall the significance of Truman's name (and the eponymous name of the reality TV show based on his life) to our reading of that film. Names matter in *Magnolia* too, helping to clarify the film's approach to its subject matter and milieu. Indeed, *Magnolia*'s frank approach to its characters is indicated early on by the name of the first of the LA-based characters to appear in the film, Frank T. J. Mackie. Ironically, this name is itself a lie, part of an invented, misogynist Hollywood persona assumed by the Tom Cruise character, to help him hide and deflect the painful experience of his mother's death and his father's abandonment. Over the course of the film, a forthright African American female journalist endeavors to get Frank to confess this lie, but without success. It is only when contacted about his father's impending death that Frank finally faces his past, frankly.

If *The Truman Show* dramatizes the need to debunk a sham TV-generated idyll/idol, *Magnolia* portrays a series of characters with glitzy screen images who in reality are steeped in and damaged by sin and abuse. These are people who desperately need to face and confess their pain and their misdeeds to turn in a better direction. The film shows how iniquity ramifies, leading to broad consequences not just for the sinners but also for their children, a kind of visitation of the sins of fathers on their innocent children (see Ex. 34:7). Things that happened in the past continue to visit and beleaguer the characters in the present. And while the film concedes that there is an element of randomness in life that might mitigate one's control over the entirety of one's fate, how one treats the members of one's family or those under one's tutelage is shown to be a matter of choice, not chance. The responsibility to do right by one's children cannot be evaded. And failure to do right has its inevitable consequences.

To demonstrate this point, *Magnolia* begins with a prologue, narrated by sleight-of-hand artist Ricky Jay, which tells and visually depicts three different stories about freak occurrences. In the first story, a pharmacist is murdered in Greenberry Hill, London, by three men, coincidentally named Green, Berry, and Hill. In the second, a pilot in Reno, Nevada, having been dealt a bad hand the day before by a blackjack dealer, flies too close to the lake and accidentally kills that same blackjack dealer, who happens at that very moment to be scuba diving in the lake. In the third, a teenage boy named Sydney Barringer jumps off the roof of his Los Angeles building and would have been saved by a net that had been spread out below had he not been first shot and killed by his mother. Unbeknownst to Mrs. Barringer, Sydney had loaded the family shotgun in the hope that his parents, who frequently threatened each other with it, would kill each other once and for all. The gun goes off accidentally just as Sydney is whizzing by his parents' open window, killing Sydney instead.

These three stories are thematically linked insofar as each includes coincidental death. With each successive story, however, the measure of coincidence is diminished by a countervailing element of malice or intent. Thus, with regard to the final story, the narrator insists, in his "humble opinion," "that this is not just 'Something That Happened.' This cannot be 'One of those things . . .' This, please, cannot be that. And for what I would like to say, I can't. This Was Not Just a Matter of Chance."[4]

That these lines are narrated by artist Ricky Jay (who often tells such historical stories in his routines and appears in person later in the film) presents the viewer/listener with an interpretive conundrum. As a master of illusion and deception, Ricky Jay would seem to be a suspect narrator. At the same time, his expertise in the design and intent of the card trick suggests that he is someone not easily duped, who knows the difference between happenstance and intent and therefore ought to be trusted. Indeed, as Ricky Jay insists, the harm brought to Sydney in the last story cannot be understood simply as the result of random chance.

The parents in this story should never have saturated their child's life with so much anger and contention such that he would want to kill himself to escape it. They should never have threatened each other repeatedly with a shotgun. They should have loved and lived better.

The idea of randomness or chance as presented in the first two stories of the prologue thus becomes a kind of thematic diversion that a theologically interested viewer of the film must look past to get the main point.[5] It is true that many of the characters in this film are drawn together by happenstance, but one cannot relegate the key elements of one's life to coincidence. If one views the world and human behavior solely through the prism of randomness, there are no meanings to actions or events and no grounds for morality, accountability, and repentance. *Magnolia* does not actually espouse the view that the world is random and therefore meaningless, even as it introduces in rapid succession a seemingly unrelated series of LA-based characters and stories.[6] The real interpretive key to the film lies not in the notion of chance but in the familial structure presented in the last vignette of the prologue. This familial triangle, featuring an abusive father, a mother, and an unhappy only child, is reiterated and recycled in various forms in just about all of the interlocking stories that unfold over the 24-hour period depicted in the film. It is this cycle of familial abuse that the film exposes and forces toward repair.[7] "One is the loneliest number," goes the Harry Nilsson song (sung here by Aimee Mann) that accompanies the rapid-fire opening sequence of the main body of the film. Songs are important in this film, this one underscoring not just the loneliness of the only children introduced here but also the aloneness of all the other characters as well. The fact, however, that all of the stories and characters are introduced in one rapid-fire montage, set to a song about the number one, links these lonely characters and their fates to one overall thematic structure. Throughout the film, which features music both diegetically (as part of the story and action of the film itself) and nondiegetically (in soundtrack form), the Aimee Mann songs in particular play an important function, creating a sense of cultural community for the characters.

The following is a list and description of the characters in the order in which they appear in this initial sequence that highlights both their abject loneliness and interconnectedness:

1. Frank T. J. Mackie (pseudonym), founder and host of *Seduce and Destroy*, only son of Lily and Earl Partridge,

whose mother is now dead and who is completely estranged from his father.

2. Claudia Wilson, a cocaine addict, given to picking up men at the Smiling Peanut Bar for sex and drugs and to watching TV and listening to music at the same time at very high volumes. Her father is TV game show host Jimmy Gator, from whom she is completely estranged, and her mother is Rose.

3. Jimmy Gator, host of a quiz show called *What Kids Know*, now in its thirty-third year. In this opening sequence, Jimmy is diagnosed with terminal cancer in the presence of his wife, Rose (whom he frequently cheats on). Soon after this sequence, Jimmy goes to see his daughter Claudia, but she will not see him and tells him she hopes he "burns in hell."

4. Rose Gator, devoted wife of Jimmy Gator, who is distraught over Jimmy's diagnosis and later by her suspicions that Jimmy abused Claudia, explaining why Claudia will not speak with him.

5. Stanley Spector, only child of Rick Spector. A socially marginal child genius and champion contestant on *What Kids Know* who is being pushed to keep on winning on the show so that the father, a failed actor, can take the money.

6. Quiz kid Donnie Smith, a former quiz show champion and only child whose parents stole all his winnings when he was young and who was later struck by lightning, impairing his cognitive ability. He is now a hapless, lonely adult who moons for a young bartender with braces on his teeth who works at the Smiling Peanut Bar (the same bar frequented by Claudia Wilson). As the opening of the film he is preparing himself to get braces, thinking that it will attract the bartender.

7. Earl Partridge, producer of television shows (including *What Kids Know*). A man given to profanity and infidelity, he is dying of cancer and has a deathbed wish to see his estranged son.

8. Phil Parma, Earl's nurse, who later learns that Earl's son is none other than Frank T. J. Mackie, and who sets about to contact him to bring about a reunion.

9. Linda Partridge, Earl's young, drug-addicted, and unfaithful wife, who like Earl is given to extreme verbal profanity, exacerbated by the anxiety surrounding Earl's impending death.
10. Jim Kurring, a well-meaning Christian police officer, who, according to the personal ad played in this sequence, is "really interested in meeting someone who likes quiet things." Jim's earnest goodness, his desire, as he says out loud to himself, "to do well in this life and in this world correct a wrong or right a situation," is at odds with the tough-guy image of the LAPD that renders him something of an outcast. He means well but cannot seem to garner the respect of his peers, nor can he see the darker side of the behavior of the people around him.

On the most basic level, these characters are connected to one another by their common loneliness; by their watching (or participating in) the same television programs, such as Jimmy Gator's quiz show, which often plays in the background of the separate stories; as well as by their location in Los Angeles on or near Magnolia Boulevard (hence the title of the film). More significantly, as symbolized by the overlapping petals of the Magnolia flower that serves as the "cover" of the film, their lives are drawn together in a network of doublings, repetitions, and intersections. There are two quiz-kid contestants in the film (Donnie and Stanley), two drug addicts (Claudia and Linda), two cancer patients (Earl and Jimmy), two complaints of a disturbance answered by Officer Kurring (the scene at the apartment of a black woman named Marcie, resulting in the discovery of a murder, and the noise complaint against Claudia Wilson), two break-ins (Donnie's into his former place of employment and Stanley's, into his school), and three suicide attempts (Sydney Barringer in the prologue, Linda Partridge, and Jimmy Gator).

Names function in the film in a similarly doubled or reiterative way. There are two mothers named after flowers (Lily and Rose), symbolizing shared, vulnerable beauty; neither of these mothers manages to protect her children from abuse or abandonment, though Rose (a flower with thorns) will turn, however belatedly, against Jimmy Gator's abuse. Earl Partridge and Jimmy Gator both have phony, stage-sounding, animal-related last names that bring to mind television shows (*The Partridge*

Family) and suggest an identity entirely subsumed by their work and its predatory, abusive aspects. As previously mentioned, Frank T. J. Mackie's assumed name and misogynist identity is a ploy to avoid frankness about his own past experience caring for and losing his mother to cancer. By contrast, the two upright men in the film, the police officer and the nurse, have names that reflect habits of kindness and service: Kurring (caring) and Phil (love). Phil's last name, Parma, together with the role he plays in administering the morphine to Earl, thereby ushering him into unconsciousness, also calls to mind the Greek word *Pharmakos*, meaning "sacrament, remedy, or poison." Phil presides over this event as a secular priest offering a final sacrament. He cannot heal the cancer but he can ease the pain, and he willingly sits by Earl's bedside until the moment he dies, something his own wife, Linda, cannot muster the courage to do.

Almost all of the characters in this film use massive amounts of profane language, a measure of their spiritual malaise and its effects on others. Marcie, the black woman, at whose home Jim Kurring investigates a disturbance, swears profusely, as does the little boy, Dixon, who seems to know the truth about the murder committed at Marcie's home.[8] Earl Partridge calls everyone vulgar names, even his son when he was a boy; Linda curses excessively, as does Jimmy Gator, whose daughter, the childhood victim of his sexual advances, swears vituperatively back at him. In this film, the "f" word is emblematic of the abuse of both language and sex, with people more often "fucking" than making love. In the opening sequence of the film, we see Jimmy Gator screwing an anonymous woman and Claudia being fucked for cocaine. Frank has learned well from the example of his father and elevates the profane to an art form, teaching men how to "respect the cock and tame the cunt." In the infomercial that opens the main body of the film, he declares the "bottom line" to be one of language: "the magical key to unlocking the female analytical mindset." As such, Frank devotes his considerable verbal acumen to the purpose of humbling and objectifying women. Once again, the two exceptions to this rule are Phil and Jim, innocents of a sort who voice objections to the use of profane language. Early the film, Phil asks Earl, "How come every word you use is either 'cocksucker,' 'shitballs' or 'fuck?' " Similarly, Jim tells young Dixon to watch his language and balks at Claudia's ready use of profanity. As such, both of them represent an alternative approach not just to language but also to love, a naïve approach that remains disturbingly alien to the reigning ethos of Magnolia Boulevard.[9]

Magnolia: Confession and Repentance

With its interlocking structure and themes, *Magnolia* can also be seen as mirroring, albeit in secular, non–synagogue-based terms, the Jewish experience of the Yom Kippur *vidui* (confession), bringing together in a kind of congregation several characters with stories that unfold over the course of twenty-four hours. All of this conveys the notion that even in our atomized, alienated world, where people sit alone watching their televisions (or their computers), there are still shared narratives and experiences that link people together and can catalyze change. As on Yom Kippur eve, where we declare our readiness to pray and repent together with the sinners, *Magnolia* assumes that our human experiences of virtue and sin are interconnected. In terms of the process of confession, the film supports the notion that for a confession to work, one needs to speak it aloud so that it can be heard. Jewish liturgical tradition teaches that confession is often best uttered in the presence of a group, as *Ashamnu* (We have sinned), in first-person plural.

This point may seem counterintuitive. For many, the group nature of the *vidui* makes it seem inauthentic and formulaic. Who bares his or her soul and confesses his or her sins publicly in front of so many people? Who confesses in the first-person plural? Does it not make more sense for me to confess in private the sins I have actually committed than to recite a confession in the encyclopedic A-to-Z acrostic form of the *Ashamnu* and *'Al ḥet* prayers?

To be sure, there is a need and a purpose to private confession. And *Magnolia* dramatizes several such moments. Linda Partridge confesses her marital infidelities to her lawyer in the hope of being disowned from Earl's will. Haunted by the specter of imminent death, Jimmy Gator confesses his infidelities to Rose (though falling short of admitting his abuse of Claudia). Later in the film, after his botched attempt to rob his former employers to get money for his orthodontia, Donnie confesses his mistakes to Officer Jim Kurring and receives forgiveness.

At the same time, Magnolia also situates confession within a communal context. The climactic moment in the film occurs when Earl Partridge, the terminally ill cancer patient who cheated on his wife, abandoned her when she was sick, and left his child (Jack, now known as Frank) to deal with the physical and emotional repercussions, awakens long enough from his drug-induced haze to make a frank deathbed confession of past sins.[10] It is filmed as an extremely long take and intercut toward its conclusion with scenes featuring all of the other characters in the film so as to widen its scope. The source lighting in this confession scene, coming from two side bed lamps, is also notable for its marked naturalness and honesty, especially when contrasted with the dramatic, hyped-up lighting used to illuminate Frank in the Seduce-and-Destroy seminar scene that immediately precedes this long take.

"I'm trying to say something, something," Earl says, a language doubling that can be explained by the effects of his medication, but that also echoes the doubling that is common to the film and to its general message about plural or interconnected experience:

> Mistakes like this . . . you don't make. Sometimes . . . you make some and okay. Not okay, sometimes, you make other ones. Know that you should do better . . . The goddamn regret. The goddamn regret! And I'll die. Now I'll die, and I'll tell you what . . . the biggest regret of my life. I let my love go. What did I do? I'm 65 years old. And I'm ashamed. Million years ago. The fucking regret and guilt, these things . . . don't ever let anyone ever say to you . . . you shouldn't regret anything. Don't do that! Don't. You regret what you fucking want. Use that. Use that. Use that regret for anything, anyway you want. You can use it, okay? Oh God. This is a long way to go with no punch. A little moral . . . story, I say. Love. Love. Love. This fucking life . . . oh oh . . . it's so fucking hard. So long. Life ain't short. It's long. It's long goddammit. God damn. What did I do? What did I do? What did I do? What did I do? Phil, Phil, help me. Please. What did I do?[11]

Earl's confession then leads into a sequence of secular liturgical worship/*vidui* as nine of ten characters in the film join in a serial singing of Aimee Mann's "Wise Up" as it plays on the radio, with each character taking up a part of the song that pertains most to his or her own vices or sins, the camera zooming in for a close-up of each individual singer, symbolic of the act of prayerful introspection. We have already seen in the opening montage how Anderson uses another Aimee Mann song, "One,"

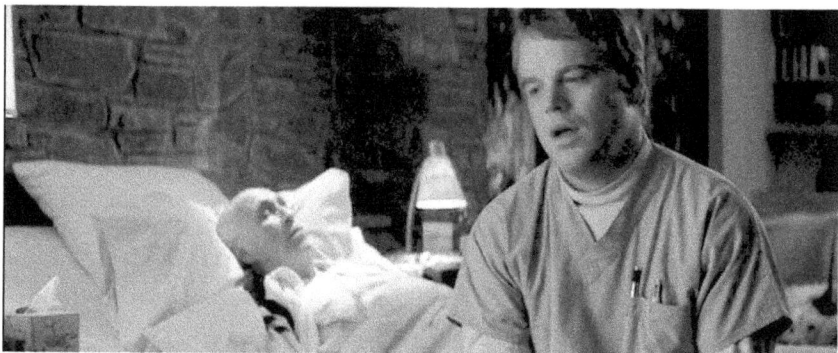

Figure 2.1. *Magnolia*, Wise Up.

to create unity among the diverse characters. Here, too, the Aimee Mann song plays a specific function, supporting the narrative and augmenting its central themes.

In this particular climactic scene, all the characters sing the same song but find a way to identify their own experience within this collective chant. The sequence calls to mind the wondrous potential of *vidui* (confession) and *teshuvah* (repentance) to change one's nature and overturn the past. Two of the characters manage to sing while in a state of unconsciousness, suggesting that even a rote liturgical recitation with little or no consciousness of what the confession says may result in a seemingly miraculous coming to terms with one's actual sins—as one "wisens up."[12]

Weather forecasts, set against images of clouds, punctuate the film, culminating with this scene, which takes place against a backdrop of heavy rain. A mixed universal symbol, rain connotes heavenly punishment as well as blessing, an eruption of emotion or sympathy—the heavens weeping along with the various pained characters—and a cleansing or purification from sin.

Shortly thereafter, a freak incident occurs, reminiscent of the prologue, which turns this rainstorm into something altogether bizarre and maybe miraculous and opens up the film even further to theological interpretation. While Jim Kurring is driving down the street, a frog falls down from the sky onto his windshield, initiating a rain of frogs that recalls the biblical plague of frogs (Exodus 8:2).[13] In contrast to the book of Exodus, however, where a plague of frogs that emerges from below-ground is unleashed against Pharaoh as a punishment, serving only to further harden Pharaoh's heart, the frogs that rain down from the sky in *Magnolia* signal a breakthrough that changes the lives of several of the characters for the good—that is, with one notable exception.

Jimmy Gator, who has never confessed to Claudia, meets his end during this frog rain. A frog falls down through a skylight above him and sets off the gun that he has been holding to his guilty head, an instance of poetic justice that contrasts sharply with the tragic, accidental death of Sydney Barringer in the prologue.

For others, however, the frog rain marks a major turnaround. Jim Kurring spots Donnie trying to break into his employer's building, but in an act of grace, instead of arresting him for robbery, Kurring encourages Donnie to return the money and take real stock of his life. Shortly thereafter, the gun that Kurring had lost during a rain-soaked police operation falls down from the sky and lands right in front of him—a reward, it seems, for his kindness.

In other story lines, the frog rain marks a long-deferred reunion of parent and child. As Adele Reinhartz summarizes,

> Rose is on her way to see Claudia when the frog rain hits; she has an accident but nevertheless makes it to her daughter's apartment, where they wait out the rain and renew their relationship. Frank spends the night of the frog rain at his dying father's side; in the morning after Earl's death, Frank visits Linda [who had overdosed] in the hospital and for the first time acknowledges her role in his father's life and her presence in his own. Stanley enjoys the frog rain, which seems to give him the courage later in the night to wake his father up and to inform him calmly but firmly that he must be nicer to him from now on. After helping Donnie, Jim returns to Claudia's apartment where she has huddled with her mother against the amphibian terrors of the night. He talks to her slowly and seriously, and so quietly that we viewers can barely catch a word. But we see the result: a slow, tentative, but radiant smile from Claudia, her first smile and the final, cautiously optimistic image in the movie as a whole.[14]

Together with the miraculous singing to "Wise Up," the frog rain scene becomes a moment that calls attention to the capacity of film not just to amaze visually but also to depict wondrous transformation. As *Rolling Stone* critic Peter Travers writes in his adulatory review of the film,

> Anderson has made a movie of constant astonishments, including a cast sing-along to a ballad by Aimee Mann and a rain of frogs (check your Bible, Exodus 8:8)[15] that serves as a millennial wake-up call. Even if all his bold strokes don't pay off, Anderson takes risks that make you hopeful about the future of movies. His *Magnolia* is a near miracle.[16]

Judaism as Confession

My analysis of the film has already referred to the biblical source of the wondrous frog rain as well as the notion of collective liturgical confession. I would like now to delve into a deeper discussion of confession as a central aspect of Judaism and its broader, redemptive message.

The originator of biblical *vidui* or confession of guilt is, in fact, Jacob's son Judah, whose name, which means both thanks (see Gen. 29:35) and admission, derives from the same root, *y.d.h.*, as the word *vidui* (confession). As Elie Kaunfer has suggested, "[t]he word Judaism comes from our ancestor Judah, so presumably, being Jewish means being like Judah," that is, "admitting when you're wrong."[17]

It is Judah who comes up with idea of selling his brother Joseph into slavery instead of killing him (Gen. 37:26–27), and thus it is he who bears primary responsibility for the long, painful separation between Joseph, his brothers, and his father. Already in chapter 38, however, in the seemingly non sequitur story of Judah and Tamar, Judah begins to demonstrate the capacity to admit sin and assume responsibility.

We saw in the case of Jonah the way in which the repetition of the verb *y.r.d* signals a disconsolate disposition and marks a trajectory of escape. At the beginning of chapter 38, Judah is similarly described as "going down from his brethren" (Gen. 38:1), indicating an inability, after the selling of Joseph into slavery, to face his brothers and his sense of guilt. This description also echoes Jacob's disconsolate declaration at the end of the previous chapter ("No, in mourning shall I go down to my son to Sheol" (Gen. 37: 35) and suggests that Judah has become haunted by his father's grief, something he will eventually have to confront. Judah marries a woman named Bat-Shua and has three sons with her, the eldest of whom marries a woman named Tamar but then dies without having had a child. In accordance with Levirate practice, Tamar is given in marriage to Judah's second son, Onan, but when he too dies, Judah balks at giving Tamar to his last remaining son, Shelah. Trapped in a condition of living widowhood, Tamar disguises herself as a prostitute and has relations with none other than Judah himself, who promises her a goat kid as payment. Judah gives Tamar his staff, his signet, and his cord as a guarantee of this future payment. When Tamar is later found to be pregnant (with Judah's child) and Judah condemns her to death by burning for her harlotry, Tamar sends him these articles to Judah as visual mnemonic cues, saying "*haker na*" (Gen. 38:25; Acknowledge whose signet seal, cords, and staff these are). Judah recognizes his possessions and immediately admits that Tamar is in the right: "Judah recognized [them], and said: 'She is more in the right than I; for certainly, I did not give her to my son Shelah'" (Gen. 38:26).

Judah's confession stands out as first time in the Bible where anyone admits wrongdoing and accepts responsibility. Adam and Eve do not admit to God when they eat the forbidden fruit. Cain does not confess to the murder of his brother Abel. Jacob neither acknowledges nor apologizes to Isaac for deceiving him over the birthright. Judah's singular admission of guilt in the case of his treatment of Tamar sets an bold example for his brothers, who some time later will admit their culpability for selling Joseph into slavery, albeit only to one another ("*aval asheimim anaḥnu al aḥeinu*" [Genesis 42:21; Oh, we are being punished on account of our brother]).[18] Judah's admission of culpability concerning the Tamar affair also presages his own public declaration of responsibility (in the case of the goblet incident) before Joseph himself: "*Vayomer Yehudah, mah nomar l'adoni, ma nedabber umah nitztadak*" (Gen. 44:16; And Judah said: "What can we say to my lord? How speak and how justify ourselves? God has found out the iniquity of your servants; here we are, my lord's slaves—both we and the one who was caught with the goblet in his possession!"). Judah doesn't yet know that the viceroy is his brother; he has no way of knowing how this admission reverberates with echoes of his prior mistreatment of his brother. Still, his language communicates a deep, authentic sense of contrition, such that it eventually becomes part of our High Holiday repentance liturgy.

Judah's role as inventor of *vidui* as "Judah-ism" comes to the fore very clearly in the following midrash, where his admission of guilt furnishes the reason why the tribe of Judah is granted the kingship and why Jews are called "Yehudim" rather than "Re'uveinim" or "Shimonim."

> JUDAH, YOUR BROTHERS SHALL PRAISE YOU (Gen. 49:8; *yodukha*). You admitted your part in the incident of Tamar; you brethren will acknowledge you as King over them. Rabbi Shimon Bar Yohai said: Let all your brothers be called by your name. No one says "I am a Reuveni," "I am a Shimoni," rather "I am a Yehudi" (a Jew). R. Yehuda Bar Simon said, "It is like the king who had twelve sons and one of their names was his most favorite. Part of it was given to that one son and the rest was shared among his brothers."[19]

It is worth calling attention to the mashal about a king who has a favorite name that closes this midrash. The inclusion of a king mashal in this context certainly coheres with the kingship theme of the midrash. But what additional insight does it provide? What does it mean to say that the king (who stands for God) has a favorite name that he gives to one child in particular but also gives in smaller measure to the rest of the sons too? Suggested here is that given its meaning, the name Judah has a value or power that both the chosen son and the rest of the sons ought to possess. God, the king in the mashal, wants the flesh-and-blood kings of Judah to model the ability to bear responsibility and admit wrongdoing, and he wants the rest of his people to learn from their confessional habits.

Notably, a goat or goat kid figures at several major junctures in the Joseph/Judah cycle in relation to the theme of confession. Recall that the brothers slaughter a goat to dip Joseph's coat in blood and fake his death (Gen 37:31), that Judah promises Tamar a goat kid as payment for her "services," and that both these events occasion a confession. In Leviticus, the connection between *vidui* and goats becomes even more salient, as confession is carried out within a sacrificial temple context. In the Yom Kippur ritual of the scapegoat, as elaborated in Leviticus 16:21, Aaron the priest is commanded to "lay both his hands upon the head of the live goat and confess (*hitvadah*) over him all the iniquities of the children of Israel and all their transgressions, even all their sins; and he shall put them upon the head of the goat, and shall send him away by the hand of an appointed man into the wilderness."[20]

With the destruction of the Temple, the practice of *vidui* changes once again, shifting away from the arena of sacrifice to that of communal prayer, with the act of verbal *vidui* serving as the necessary first step in the process of repentance.[21] In the book of Daniel, for example, the exilic prophet documents his own confession and prayer on behalf of his exiled community:

> And I prayed unto the LORD my God, *and made confession*, and said: "O Lord, the great and awful God, who keeps covenant and mercy with them that love You and keep Your commandments, we have sinned, and have dealt iniquitously, and have done wickedly, and have rebelled, and have turned aside from Your commandments and from Your ordinances." (Daniel 9:4–5; emphasis added)[22]

Daniel's confession of the sins of the community culminates with a prophecy from the angel Gabriel promising the return of the exiled Jews to Jerusalem. Confession here, as in the books of Ezra and Nehemiah, thus becomes associated with *teshuvah* in the broadest possible sense, referring not just to repentance but also to a national return to the land of Israel.

Teshuva as a Return of Fathers to Sons and Sons to Fathers

Israeli scholar Tzvi Luz writes the following about the redemptive and/or messianic aspects of *teshuvah*:

> There is a dialectic tension evident here, since *teshuvah* is at once restorative and utopian in its character; it is an effort to return to an ancient model, an ideal state that is imagined to have existed in the past (before man sinned in the Garden of Eden), but also simultaneously, an endeavor to reach a perfect future, radically different from any reality that now exists or has existed in the past (the messianic era). Every movement for religious renewal that has appeared within Judaism, from the very beginning of its history, may thus be defined as a movement of *teshuvah*.[23]

I'd like to link these observations about the utopian aspects of *teshuvah* with the metaphor of reconciliation between fathers and sons that figures so prominently both at the end of the Joseph/Judah cycle and at the end of *Magnolia*.

The scene of Joseph reuniting with his elderly father, Jacob, is one of the only such scenes of father-son togetherness in the Bible. Again and again, our tradition depicts fathers who parent badly or in a way that is calculated to alienate their sons and sons who simply refuse the good bestowed upon them by their fathers, preferring instead to rebel and turn away. The book of Genesis alone offers us several instances of unresolved tensions between fathers and sons. Abraham tries to sacrifice Isaac, and thereafter they are never seen together again. Isaac prefers Esau over Jacob, and Jacob (with the encouragement of his mother) tricks him in return. Jacob prefers Joseph over his other sons, who trick them both, such that Jacob spends decades assuming that his beloved son is dead, only to find out that Joseph is actually alive and ruling in Egypt. (All that time, Joseph makes no effort to contact his father and inform him of his whereabouts, another chilling fact.) By the time they finally reunite, Jacob is already a broken man, one who describes the days of his life to Pharaoh as bitter and short. Jacob and Joseph's reunion is thus at best bittersweet, a short interlude that serves as a preamble to the eventual enslavement of the children of Israel in Egypt. The father–son relationship cycle seems unendingly bleak.

Despite or perhaps because all of this father–son strife, the last verse of the last prophetic book of the Bible (Malachi 3:23–24)[24] imagines that on the day of redemption, Elijah the prophet, harbinger of the messiah, "shall turn the heart of the fathers to the children, and the heart of the children to their fathers," indicating just how hard such reconciliations are to bring about. This kind of familial reconciliation and repair is the very stuff of messianic redemption.

This has enduring theological implications. If Jewish tradition often likens God to a heavenly Father and the faithful to His sons, then the state of father–son relationships in the Bible does not bode well for this relationship. If fathers and sons, standing in for the divine Father and the children of Israel, cannot get along in the Bible, then what can we expect from our modern, emancipated, post-Holocaust community?

By the same token, the *Magnolia* depicts a contemporary LA community where fathering has become so corrupt, caustic, and misogynist an institution that it no longer seems capable of serving as an apt metaphor for God or anything at all redemptive. One might even discern a patricidal/deicidal strain in the film, insofar as two of the abusive fathers are killed off by the end of the film.

I am reminded, however, of the scene toward the end of *Magnolia* where Frank, having been sought out by Phil at Earl's behest and summoned to Earl's deathbed, yells and hurls invective at Earl but then begs him not to die. Frank's outpouring at Earl's bedside suggests that while the corrosive, imperious, and misogynist model of fathering and of God the Father ought to meet its demise, the theological metaphor of God as a beneficent and caring parent has not lost its power and relevance. And while Rose's recognition of the truth concerning her husband's abuse of Claudia comes woefully late, her swift decision to leave the dying Jimmy to be with Claudia (against the backdrop of the miraculous frog rain) represents an alternative, redemptive, maternal model of care and compassion. Perhaps, for real *teshuvah* to take place, that is, a real turning of children back to parents and parents back to children, we must not only confess our sins before God, but also demand a change from our God concept as well. Put differently, insofar as our figuration of God as embodiment of Ultimate Concern influences our behavior, we must strive to reconceptualize what we mean when we think of God as divine parent.[25] We must imagine, pray, and confess to a God-parent who conforms not to some retrograde patriarchal model, but to our highest, frankest, noblest ideals.

In the Bible, the verb "confess" is *lehitvadot*, a hitpa'el verb root.[26] The hitpa'el form typically connotes reflexive or reciprocal action. The verb *lehitpalel*, to pray, takes the same form. If we read *lehitpalel* and *lehitvadot* as reflexive verbs, we might conclude that, like Officer Jim Kurring, who frequently talks to himself in his car about what he hopes to accomplish as a police officer, pronouncing a series of self-motivational prayers, we perform our prayers and confessions to ourselves. Read as reciprocal verbs, however, *lehitpalel* and *lehitvadot* imply that others too participate with us in our prayers and confessions. According to our tradition, those who pray or confess together have a catalyzing effect on one another. They shore up one another's resolve to change and improve. But our tradition also assumes that our confessions and prayers have a catalyzing effect on God. We confess, turn away from the past, and pray that in the future this changes not only us but also our experience of and relationship with God as father, mother, lawgiver, caregiver, and forgiving, loving friend.

3

The Descendants

Birthright: Consent versus Descent

We move now from a discussion of familial relations as a model for theological encounter to a discussion of familial inheritance as a model for Jewish national belonging. This is a tricky discussion in America. We live in a culture that generally prizes consent over descent and individual achievement over birthright. We laud those who are able to transcend the limitations of their background and birthplace and achieve economic, educational, and geographic (where needed) mobility. Though we appreciate familial duty, we assign even greater value to romance, to the notion of freely choosing a mate and a destiny. We do not like the idea of being limited by the biological claims of heredity, blood, or the tenets of previous generations.

As Werner Sollors explains,

> [d]escent relations are those defined by anthropologists as relations of "substance" (by blood or nature); consent relations describe those of "law" or "marriage." Descent language emphasizes our positions as heirs, our hereditary qualities, liabilities and entitlements; consent language stresses our abilities as mature free agents and "architects of our fates" to choose our spouses, our destinies, and our political systems . . . [A]n attack on the system of hereditary privilege has American overtones; and modern democratic political and family relations are described in terms of the consent of the governed, the age of consent or consenting adults.[1]

The Descendants, directed by Alexander Payne (2011)[2] and based on a novel by the same title by Kaui Hart Hemmings,[3] directly challenges this opposition of consent and descent, telling the story of Matt King, the descendant of a Hawaiian princess and a white banker, who consents to re-embrace his birthright and acknowledge the larger, transcendent claims of descent and homeland. *The Descendants* also investigates the problematic implications of traditional, patriarchal figurations of family, birthright, and inheritance, and gestures toward a more complicated and nuanced feminist conception.

The film opens with Matt confronting several crises simultaneously. At the center is Matt's wife, Elizabeth, an inveterate thrill seeker drawn to dangerous water sports, who is now lying in Queen's Hospital in a coma as a result of a boating accident. Usually the "back-up parent, the under-study,"[4] Matt has been forced in the wake of Elizabeth's accident to assume primary responsibility for their two daughters, Alex (seventeen) and Scottie (ten), both of whom have been acting out in ways that challenge the limits of Matt's parenting experience.

At the same time, Matt is confronting a major decision regarding the King family trust, a bequest to his extended family that goes back to the 1860s and his great-great-great-grandmother Princess Margaret Ke'alohilani, purportedly one of the last descendants of King Kamehameha I, who united the Hawaiian islands and established the kingdom of Hawaii in 1810. In his capacity as the sole trustee of the trust, Matt King is responsible for the disposition of the last 25,000 pristine acres of "pure virgin land" still being held by the family. (The gendered, sexualized nature of this description of the land is not incidental to the main concerns of the film.) A land sale is currently being negotiated seven years in advance of the dissolution of the trust as a result of the "rule against perpetuities"—a law whose very name challenges the notion of enduring birthright or perpetual familial claim to land. The King family has agreed to meet soon about the sale, with Matt saddled with the task of making the final decision. Under the shadow of his wife's impending death, Matt is thus being called upon to assume sole responsibility not just for his immediate biological descendants (his children) but also for his familial inheritance as a descendant of Hawaiian royalty and of an elite banking family.[5]

The film opens with a black screen and the sound of a whirring motor that fades into a scene of Elizabeth waterskiing and smiling. The screen then fades again to black, a visual pattern that jarringly signals a falling away from prior happiness and expectations. Following this are the opening credits, which are superimposed over floating batik images of hibiscus flowers—the Hawaiian state flower—and accompanied by a Hawaiian song by slack guitarist-songwriter Gabby Pahinui about the winds of Hawaii, a "lei that I adore above all others, and a home that is so delightful to visitors."[6]

Elizabeth's smile, the hibiscus flowers, the soulful native music about Hawaiian winds, and the leis all set up an expectation of an Edenic story, one that is quickly shattered by the opening voice-over of Matt King as he laments the simplistic notions of people on the mainland about what it means to live in Hawaii:

> My friends on the mainland think just because I live in Hawaii, I live in paradise. Like a permanent vacation. We're all just out here sipping Mai Tais, shaking our hips, and catching waves. Are they insane? Do they think we're immune to life? How could they possibly think that our families are less screwed up, our cancers less fatal, our heartbreaks less painful. Hell, I haven't been on a surfboard for fifteen years . . . For the last twenty-three days I've been living in a paradise of IVs and urine bags and tracheal tubes. Paradise? Paradise can go fuck itself.[7]

Accompanying this voice-over is a montage of Oahu life decidedly east of Eden: scenes of hyperdevelopment, heavy traffic, homeless people, a woman in a wheelchair, an old Asian woman walking unsteadily and clasping one side of her face, another woman living in a shack on the beach, and finally the view from the window of Elizabeth's hospital room. The camera then slowly zooms in on Elizabeth herself, her inert, ailing body emerging as a synecdoche for the despoliation of the island and for larger familial and social ills.

At this early stage of the film, Matt is still laboring under the ironic misconception that Elizabeth's accident and comatose state are merely a wake-up call; eventually she will revive, he will nurse her back to health, and together they will reconstitute their marriage and family. Matt soon learns from her doctor, however, that Elizabeth is not going to wake up, and therefore he goes to collect his oldest daughter, Alex, from her boarding school so as to begin the process of informing other family members and friends about Elizabeth's impending death. (He finds Alex at the boarding school late at night not in her room but drunk and carousing on school grounds, another mark of how far the family has fallen from paradise.) If that weren't bad enough, shortly after arriving at home, Alex informs Matt that the reason she and her mother had been fighting lately is that Alex had discovered Elizabeth was cheating on Matt. Like the figure of Gomer in the biblical book of Hosea, an unfaithful wife who symbolizes the infidelities and betrayals of the people of Israel, Elizabeth King's infidelity comes to stand for the failed expectations of paradise as well as for the betrayal of the birthright that is about to take place through the sale of the last King family land.

Feminist literary critic Annette Kolodny's account of the attitudes and expectations of Eden that European colonists brought to the New World resonate distinctly with Matt's description of the deluded notions about Hawaii held not just by mainland Americans but also by the members of his larger family:

> Eden, Paradise, the Golden Age, and the idyllic garden, in short, all the backdrops for European literary pastoral, were subsumed in the image of an American promising material ease without labor or hardship, as opposed to the grinding poverty of a previous European existence; a frank, free affectional life in which all might share in a primal and noncompetitive fraternity; a resurrection of the lost state of innocence that the adult abandons when he joins the world of competitive self-assertion; and all this possible, because at the deepest psychological level, the move to America was experienced as the daily reality of what has become its single dominating metaphor: regression from the cares of adult life and a return to the primal warmth of womb or breast in a feminine landscape.[8]

To be sure, all of this is myth. No adult may return to the womb or the breast; there is no real, sustainable way to escape the cares and responsibilities of adult life. And yet many of the members of the larger King family subscribe to a version of this myth. In the novel, Matt describes them as follows:

> I don't know what any of them do. To their credit, the cousins are not greedy or gaudy or ostentatious. Their sole purpose in life is to have fun. They Jet Ski, motocross, surf, paddle, run triathalons, rent islands in Tahiti. Indeed, some of the most powerful people in Hawaii look like bums or stuntmen. I think of our bloodline's progression. Our missionary ancestors came to the islands and told the Hawaiians to put on some clothes, work hard, and stop hula dancing. They made some business deals along the way, buying an island for ten grand, or marrying a princess and inheriting her land, and now their descendants don't work. They have stripped down to running shorts or bikins and play beach volleyball and take up hula dancing.[9]

These King cousins have abandoned the world of "competitive self-assertion." Insofar as they live off the proceeds of their inheritance, however, theirs is spurious "state of innocence," one predicated on a continual exploitation and depletion of the resources of their legacy.

As the quote above indicates, the King legacy itself is the result of the triumph of consent over descent: a Hawaiian princess and heiress who was supposed to have married a cousin decides instead to marry a white "haole"[10] banker from a missionary family named Edward King. Edward's surname clearly suggests a melding of native monarchical and white commercial/religious ruling interests. Indeed, for several generations, Matt's larger family has profited from the coming together of Hawaiian royal landowners and capitalist developers. As far back as Princess Margaret Ke'alohilani, the King family has been selling the land of its native Hawaii to white people and has made a lot of money in the process.

Like his father before him, however, Matt has chosen to live not on the proceeds of the trust but on his earnings from his (real estate) law practice. In marked contrast to his cousins, Matt has shown financial prudence and kept his eye on the future. Yet none of this has made him happy. Whatever hopes he may have had to experience familial or nurturing (feminine) warmth through his marriage to beautiful, charismatic Elizabeth have been dashed on the shores of his own workaholic habits and his wife's recklessness and infidelity. "What is it about the women in my life that they all seem to want to destroy themselves?" Matt asks himself, referring both to Elizabeth's self-destructive hobbies and his daughter Alex's alcohol abuse and sexual adventuring. In the face of all these disappointments, Matt seems quite ready to renounce his Hawaiian birthright with its false pretenses of Eden.

The journey depicted in the film, however, follows a meandering, circuitous route back toward some sort of reconstituted sense of descent and native belongingness. After finding out about Elizabeth's affair, Matt decides to go to Kauai to find Brian Speer, the man who slept with his wife, for the purpose of confronting him and informing him of Elizabeth's impending death so he too can say goodbye. To be sure, a major goal of this trip is for Matt to assert spousal privilege and right over the man who would threaten (with his own phallic "spear") Matt's masculine familial authority. That Matt discovers over the course of this trip to Kauai that real estate broker Speer is related to and works for the man to whom his family is planning to sell the land parcel only raises the symbolic stakes of this encounter.

But this is not all that happens during this Kauai sojourn. As it turns out, the land in question is also located on Kauai, and so the trip to trap and "spear" Speer also affords an opportunity for Matt and his two daughters (together with Alex's friend Sid) to tour the inherited site where so many generations of the King family, including Elizabeth and Alex in years gone by, have hiked and camped.

Figure 3.1. *The Descendants*, Looking at the Land in Kauai.

"What about me?" Scottie asks when Alex refers to these former camping trips. "I want to camp. I wished we lived in the old days."[11] It seems that in the seven years that separate Alex and Scottie a shift in parenting has taken place, with Elizabeth frequently off seeking thrills and Matt busy doing real estate deals. Scottie, who is named after Elizabeth's irascible father Scott but also bears an uncanny resemblance to Matt's Hawaiian princess ancestor, clearly has not been given the same access to the familial legacy that her older sister received. Recapturing some sense of that missing birthright will be one of the principal results of the story.

Over the course of Matt's search for Brian Speer, Matt, Alex, Scottie, and Alex's friend Sid visit a local bar/restaurant with native food and music and take walks along the beaches of Kauai, the camera lingering on gorgeous Kauai vistas. Walking on the beach and sharing familial stories, the Kings begin to bond and coalesce around a sense of familial narrative and shared experience.

A word about the presence of Alex's friend Sid in the midst of this familial bonding: a stranger who gets brought along by Alex to participate in an intimate family drama, Sid stands for the principle of consent, insofar as Alex wants him there even though he is a biological outsider, as well as for an element of comic relief in a time of great tragedy. When Elizabeth's demented mother, Tutu, responds to the announcement that they are going to see Elizabeth at Queen's Hospital by saying that she can't believe she is going to see "Queen Elizabeth," Sid indiscreetly laughs, earning himself a clout in the face by Elizabeth's father, Scott. Shortly thereafter, Sid is on the verge of getting another punch in the face from Matt when he suggests that Matt's discomfort with touching (Matt doesn't want Sid and Alex touching each other all the time in front of him) might be the reason why Elizabeth cheated on him. In a late-night conversation with Matt, Sid claims to be smart, whereupon Matt bluntly retorts, "You're about a hundred miles away from Smartville, no offense."[12] In the same conversation, however, Matt discovers that Sid's father died six months earlier in a drunk driving incident, and that Sid is more insightful and empathetic that one might initially think. Not just that: Sid's willingness to accompany Alex in this experience, despite being punched in the face by her grandfather and despite his own recent loss, models the kind of steadfast loyalty that will help Matt assume an invigorated paternal role. Together, Alex and Sid encourage Matt to reclaim his self-respect in the face of the humiliation of Elizabeth's affair. When Matt sets out with Alex to confront Brian Speer, Sid tells him, "Give 'em hell, boss," which Matt indeed does.

It is worth noting the absence of any cellphones during these Kauai scenes as well as during the later scenes in the hospital. (This contrasts starkly with an early scene in which Matt and Scottie go to the home of Lani Higgins to apologize for Scottie's rude and crude text messages to Lani.[13]) Matt makes a point of informing everyone of Elizabeth's impending death face-to-face. No mass emails or phone blasts go out. No screened forms of communication. Instead, the family adopts an old-fashioned, native, pretechnological approach to grieving and reconstituting the family unit, facing issues head-on rather than through type, recording, or other evasive media. Similarly, when Matt first hears about Elizabeth's affair, he runs full speed in his docksiders to the home of their best friends to demand that they tell him what they know. On Kauai, Matt finds Brian Speer by running on the beach. Later, he walks with his family over to the cottage where the Speers are staying to confront Brian about the affair. And when Matt decides to reject the recommendation of the majority of his King cousins to sell the land despite his prior commitment to follow the majority decision, he does so in person first by stating his convictions about his family's blood connection to the land to the leaders of the group and then by addressing the group as a whole.

It is only after facing his adversaries directly and reclaiming his connection to the metaphorical mother-island of Hawaii by refusing the sale that Matt is able to say good-bye to his wife, the literal, embodied mother of his children. Prior to this, both Matt and Alex had vented their spleen at the unresponsive Elizabeth, but now they manage to find a way to address her in a more resigned and loving manner, her impending death affording an opportunity for forgiveness and (imagined) reconciliation. As they say good-bye, the camera ranges over her body again, an effort to map out the human, emotional geography of their relationship.

Elizabeth's funeral at sea at sea, one of the most poignant and beautiful scenes in the film, marks the culmination of this process. First we see the lush, verdant landscape of the King family legacy on Kauai, a tribute to the birthright reclaimed, and then the funeral itself, which takes place at sea. Floating in a *wa'a* (Hawaiian canoe) and wearing leis, Matt, Alex, and Scottie each scatters Elizabeth's ashes in the ocean and then floats a lei in the water, the camera catching the leis from underneath as if from the point of view of Elizabeth's sinking ashes. Earlier in the film, on his way to pick up Alex at her boarding school on another island, Matt had

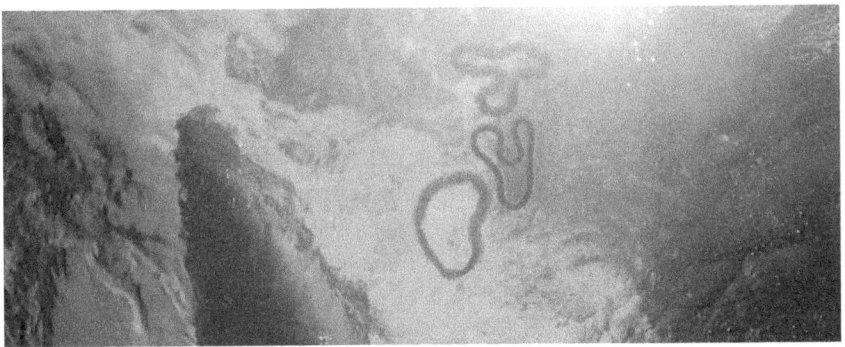

Figure 3.2. *The Descendants*, Archipelago.

lamented the disintegration of his family, saying, "My family seems exactly like an archipelago, all part of the same whole but still severed and alone and always drifting steadily apart." Forming the shapes of islands in an archipelago, however, the leis floating in the ocean after the funeral drift toward one another rather than apart, a visual/ritual representation of the strengthening of Matt King's family in the aftermath of this tragedy.

The screen then fades to white, a reversal of the opening, where the shot of Elizabeth waterskiing fades to black.

The scene immediately thereafter marks the final phase of their familial affirmation of legacy. Scottie is seen sitting alone on the couch, assuming a posture that is echoed physically by a painting hanging above the couch of a native Hawaiian woman.[14] Soon she is joined on the coach by Matt and Alex, and the three of them share bowls of ice cream under the yellow and white quilt that was previously draped over Elizabeth in the hospital. Together they watch *March of the Penguins*, narrated by Morgan Freeman, a stunning and poignant documentary about the yearly mating and breeding patterns of the emperor penguins, the last remaining natives of Antarctica.[15] Here is an ethnic family unit coming together to watch a film about generational continuity against all odds in a remote region and forbidding climate. In this scene, the King family "archipelago" becomes close and contiguous, a regular American family, but also newly marked by an awareness of their particular identity as native remnants. Though much has changed, the film concludes as it began, with the credits superimposed over batik paintings and the same song by guitarist-songwriter Gabby Pahinui, a circular structure characteristic of myth that suggests the enduring quality of stories passed as a legacy from generation to generation.

Descent/Consent, Jacob/Esau: Embracing or Renouncing the Birthright

In its concern with issues of consent and descent as well as ethnic and geographic birthright, *The Descendants* clearly evokes for the Jewish viewer the role of land and ethnic descent in the perpetuation of Jewish religious and national identity. Viewing the scenes where the King family visits Kauai, one cannot help but think of the mission of such organizations as Taglit/Birthright in taking thousands of young Jews on free trips to Israel: "We believe that the experience of a trip to Israel is a building block of Jewish identity, and that by providing that gift to young Jews, we can strengthen bonds with the land and people of Israel and solidarity with Jewish communities worldwide . . . Participants are introduced to key landmarks of historical, national, archeological and natural significance that have shaped, and continue to shape Jewish life."[16]

Along similar lines, Eugene Borowitz notes the role of a whole array of ethnic behaviors in shoring up Jewish identity, calling attention to the need to balance personal choice (or consent) with responsibility to the larger group:

> I am regularly exasperated by an American Jewry that, wallowing in its freedom, prates piously of the sanctity of personal choice and uses it mainly to sanction nonobservance and flabby ethics. I seek only to restore a proper tension between our autonomy and social responsibility, one the contemporary idolization of the self has grossly distorted. I too equate all human dignity with self-determination, but only within the context of a Covenant with God that gives us our personal significance and makes all God's covenant-partners an essential part of our selfhood . . . Being organized as an ethnic group also has a functional value in the Covenant. Israel must live in intense fealty to God amidst nations who will to ignore or spurn God's behests for them . . . The multiple ties that ethnicity engender help the imperiled people endure. Bound to one another and Covenant memories by land, language, customs, heroes, jokes, foods, gossip and other aspects of folk life, the Jewish people can defend itself from history's blows clothed in a many-layered ethnic armor. Infusing its folkways with

Covenant sensibility, it can powerfully transmit, reinforce and renew Israel's lasting purpose.[17]

The Descendants offers a powerful depiction of this very process: a family choosing to come together around ritual, food, music, and other aspects of Hawaiian folk life, sharing memories and experiences of land and ancestors, thereby reconfirming against prior attenuation bonds of familial descent.

The Descendants also sketches lines of physical as well as behavioral inheritance in the physical similarity of Scottie to Matt's princess great-great-great-grandmother and in the character similarities evinced by Alex and her impetuous, reckless, and strong-willed mother. Elizabeth herself is allied throughout the film with her prickly, combative father, Scott. The film makes clear the influences of descent, genetic determinism, and familial conditioning, but it also demonstrates the ways in which family members can choose to repudiate or embrace what has been passed down to them by their family members.

In this respect, *The Descendants* bears a strong thematic resemblance to Genesis 25, the story of the birth of Esau and Jacob and Esau's later relinquishment of the birthright. The beginning of the Jacob and Esau story places a heavy emphasis on inborn or inherited qualities. Rebecca, the mother, is infertile for twenty years and then has a tumultuous pregnancy with twins who "struggle within her," presaging the conflict that will unfold between the twins as they emerge into adulthood. Rebecca is led to a state of existential crisis by the deterministic nature of the pregnancy and declares, אִם־כֵּן לָמָּה זֶּה אָנֹכִי (Gen. 25.22; If this is so, why do I exist?)—an expression of suicidal despair that seems grounded in a sense of being trapped by biological destiny.

It is worth mentioning the almost obsessive repetition of the letter *mem* in the account of Rebecca's tumultuous gestation and birthing of the twins and in the prophecy that she receives when she goes to "inquire of the Eternal" (Gen. 25:22–24). God tells Rebecca that "*shenei le'umim mimei'ayikh yiparedu, u'le'om mile'om ye'ematz*" (two nations will be separated from your womb, and one *le'om* will overcome the other). Note how the splitting of these two nations as they emerge from their mother's womb (*le'umim* being the plural of *le'om*, the particular Hebrew word for nation that is etymologically connected to *eim* [mother]) is enacted, orthographically, in such phrases as *le'umim/mimei'ayikh yiparedu*, where one word ends with the same syllable as that which begins the next, separate word. The repetition of the "m" sound reinforces the maternal (mama) coding of this narrative; both of these sons will be connected in vital ways with their mother. One of them, in particular, will also be defined by the other common, cultural use of the "mmm" sound, that connoting delicious (yummy) food. Later in the chapter, the alliteration of "m" will recur specifically relating to famished Esau, who asks Jacob to give him *"min ha'adom ha'adom hazeh"* (from this red, red stew).

Much of the description of the twins seems fixed and inescapably determined. The first child, Esau, seems defined by the material and the tactile, by impulse and the immediate need to satisfy it. When he is born, he is described as אַדְמוֹנִי, כֻּלּוֹ כְּאַדֶּרֶת שֵׂעָר (ruddy and hairy) and is named עשו ('Esav), a name that calls to mind the word *'eisev* (עשב; grass) as well as the verb *'asah* (עשה; to make or to do). As his name and ruddy appearance predict, Esau becomes a red-blooded hunter, a wild sportsman, a doer, and a denizen of the outdoors. By contrast, the second child comes out holding the heel (עקב) of his older brother and is thus called יעקב (Jacob), suggesting a weak, lagging nature. As he grows up, this second child also confirms prior expectations. In marked contrast to his brother, Jacob is an *ish tam yoshev ohalim* (Gen. 25:27), an innocent, inexperienced in the hunt, who prefers hearth and home to the thrills of the outdoors.

As a hunter, Esau lives for the moment, while Jacob proves to be a planner, with his eye on the future. Familiar with Esau's hunting habits and his tendency to be famished after the hunt, וַיָּזֶד יַעֲקֹב נָזִיד—Jacob hatches a plan and prepares pottage, the words *vayazed* and *nazid*, calling to mind the word *vayazid* (to plot intentionally).[18] Upon his return from the hunt, Esau importunes Jacob to give him some of that red, red stew, a description that recalls Esau's ruddy appearance at birth as well as his appetite for the bloody hunt.

But this is where the story and the priority placed on descent and blood begin to shift. Jacob agrees to sell Esau the stew in exchange for the *bekhorah* (birthright of the firstborn), a preposterous, imbalanced exchange, the stew standing for the principle of instant gratification and the birthright standing for future power and privilege based on bloodline and birth order. Fixated on his hunger, Esau cannot see the point of the *bekhorah*:

וַיֹּאמֶר עֵשָׂו, הִנֵּה אָנֹכִי הוֹלֵךְ לָמוּת; וְלָמָּה זֶּה לִי, בְּכֹרָה.

> And Esau said: "Here I [*anokhi*] am going to die; what good is the birthright to me? (Gen. 25:32)

Esau's "*anokhi*" and "*lamah zeh li*" both directly recall Rebecca's questioning of her very existence [*lamah zeh anokhi*] in the wake of her troubled pregnancy, indicating a tendency on the parts of both mother and son to focus perhaps too much on immediate physical sensations and hence to despair about the future and brood about death. For Esau, the distant promise of birthright means so little that he agrees not merely to sell it but even to swear to its renunciation. Perhaps it is because she sees her own failings in her eldest son that Rebecca later favors Jacob (Gen. 25:28) and urges him to wrest from Esau not just the birthright (*bekhorah*) but also the blessing (*berakhah*).

As for Jacob, in concocting this plan, he attempts to overcome birth order and biological descent by getting Esau to consent to an exchange. There is something both loathsome and admirable in Jacob's decision to seize this imaginative, transactional opportunity to render himself the firstborn. Such temerity and gall! What if Esau really were dying of hunger? As a brother, shouldn't Jacob simply feed him and save his life, with no strings attached? As a result of all of this, Esau comes to despise not only the birthright but also Jacob himself, especially when later, at their mother's behest, Jacob poses as Esau to steal away his elder brother's blessing. Ironically, the very act of trying to bilk the blessing forces Jacob to flee his brother and wait several decades before he can claim any form of birthright.

At the same time, the text implies that, shenanigans notwithstanding, Jacob really deserves both birthright and blessing, and not just because God has already ordained to Rebecca that the elder child will serve the younger (Gen. 25:23). Though on paper a matter of biological descent, the concept of birthright depends on an ability to view life and legacy not just in immediate biological terms but also in a metaphorical, spiritual light, in terms of its impact on future generations. Esau seems to have no such ability. Even after he satisfies his dire hunger and slakes his burning thirst, he shows no compunction about what he has just given away. He simply gets up, leaves, and (in so doing) despises the birthright. Thus, in his commentary on Genesis 25:34, Nachmanides notes that "only fools care just about eating, and drinking and fulfilling their momentary desires, giving no thought to tomorrow."[19]

Returning for a moment to *The Descendants*, several significant analogies emerge between the film and the biblical text. Matt, like Jacob, is a tent dweller, a lawyer working in his office at a physical remove from the land as well as from the everyday goings on of his family. Again like Jacob, Matt will need to find a way to transcend nature, habit, and determinism to lay a claim to land and patrimony. By the same token, Matt's cousins, incapable of seeing beyond their immediate desires, recapitulate the mode of Esau.

Actually, there are several Esau-like figures in the film, all of whom Matt must counter: Elizabeth, the thrill seeker who continually courts death and danger without regard for her family and future; her father, Scott, who in the aftermath of the accident continues to scold Matt for saving his money and not gratifying Elizabeth's immediate desire to have her own boat or go on shopping sprees. And then there is long-haired (like hairy Esau) older cousin Hugh, always drunk and never working, except to promote the land deal with Holitzer. In the King family, cousin Hugh plays the lead role in enjoying the immediate profits of the land but despising the birthright.

Though seemingly committed before to selling the land, Matt comes to oppose this trend. We get an intimation of this when he arrives early at the lodge where the family vote will take place and spends a considerable amount of time perusing the wall of King family photographs, a kind of visual genealogy akin to the list of begats that punctuates the Genesis narrative. At the actual family meeting, Matt voices his opposition to the land sale in terms of historical, blood ties to the land:

> People will be relieved, Hugh, the whole state. I sign that document, it's over. End of the line. Something that was ours to protect will be gone. Even though we're haole[20] as shit and go to private schools and clubs and can't even speak pidgin, let alone Hawaiian, we still carry Hawaiian blood, and we're still tied to this land. And our children are tied to this land. It's a miracle that for whatever bullshit reason 150 years ago, we own this much of . . . paradise, but we do. And for whatever bullshit reason now, I'm the trustee. And I'm not signing.[21]

Matt's reference once again to the term "haole" points to the King's family's mixed, colonial lineage and its interloper status, which also recalls Isaac and Rebecca's mixed line, given Rebecca's Aramean origins. (Rebecca is identified as an Aramean three times in the opening verse of chapter 25.) What distinguishes Jacob is that despite this connection through his mother to Mesopotamia, and despite Jacob's tendency to stay indoors, he still insists of prioritizing his connection to Canaan and to the birthright.

According to Rashbam (R. Samuel ben Meir, Troyes, 1085–1158) in his commentary on Genesis 25:32, Esau's readiness to sell off the birthright directly relates to his occupation as a hunter and his daily encounter with death:

> *And Esau said: Here I am going to die*: Every day I go to hunt beasts in the forests where there are bears and lions and wild beasts and I am in constant danger of dying. Why bother waiting for the death of our father for a portion of the birthright? And this is the meaning of *And Esau despised the birthright*.[22]

For some, awareness of mortality breeds a sense of futility about the future and a determination to live only in the present. For others, a consciousness of mortality has the opposite effect: a renewed commitment to make one's life matter not just for present but also for future generations. Matt King's encounter with mortality as a result of Elizabeth's accident produces precisely this renewed commitment to land and familial tradition.

According to Nathan Rotenstreich,

> traditions are beliefs with a particular social structure: they are consensus through time . . . No receiving generation is ever totally immersed in past generations whose heritage is transmitted, because generation is to be understood as a historical reality not a biological transmission. The process of acceptance undertaken by the receiving generation implies an activity whereby it consents to subdue itself in order to authenticate the authority of the transmitted.[23]

Once again, we see the interplay of consent and descent. The notion of tradition, a set of shared beliefs or convictions, depends on a structure of descent, where practices, affiliations, and identity pass down or descend from generation to generation. At the same time, no tradition can endure if it remains static and inert. Traditions necessarily take on new forms depending on historical context. And to remain vibrant, they rely on the consent of the new generation to participate either in safeguarding or revising their structure. Familial or communal continuity depends on fidelity, presence, and participation. What enables Matt to re-embrace and pass down his birthright is both an affirmation and a revision of tradition.

Re-embracing the Motherland

I mentioned at the beginning of this chapter that *The Descendants* investigates the problematic implications of traditional, patriarchal figurations of family, birthright, and inheritance, and gestures toward a more complicated and nuanced feminist conception. Where does one see this? Might one not make a completely opposite argument: that as a whole, the film shores up patriarchal power? After all, the entire system of relations in this film is that of conquest, both of land and of woman, a classic masculine struggle.[24] That Matt's re-embrace of the motherland requires a casting off his actual, embodied wife, the literal mother of his children, only reinforces this patriarchal reading.

Indeed, one cannot deny the paternal focus of the film. To find the feminist message of the film, then, one needs to examine the paradigm-altering centrality of Matt's daughters in the unfolding plot. In contrast with the biblical story of Jacob and Esau, a battle for birthright fought between two sons, *The Descendants* is ultimately concerned with a father's transmission of birthright to two daughters. That these daughters happen to have conventionally masculine names, Alex and Scottie, highlights their role in blurring conventional gender roles.

Alex's position as the *bekhorah* in the film—the eldest daughter rather than son—is absolutely crucial to the unfolding story and to the film's revision of patriarchal tradition. It is Alex who dispels her father Matt's last lingering, deluded notions of marital paradise and compels him to face the fact of Elizabeth's infidelity. It is Alex who reaches out to the unlikely Sid for support in confronting the death of her mother. Likewise, it is Alex who consents to take the lead in tracking down Brian Speer and who insists on accompanying her father to Kauai. Alex's mother, Elizabeth, whom Alex clearly takes after, was a kind of femme fatale: living on a razor's edge, courting sex, thrills, and death. (In the novel, Elizabeth is a former model who urges her daughter to act older and pose for racy postcards of Hawaii.) By the end of the film, however, Alex has embraced and repurposed her gutsy, Elizabeth-like nature for the sake of aiding her father, supporting her younger sister, and facing her own future. Like her father, she too has rediscovered a certain sense of power, pride, and ethnic/familial solidarity. Repeatedly in the film, Elizabeth's father, Scott, obnoxiously berates both Matt and Alex for their treatment of Elizabeth, insisting (quite wrongly) that Elizabeth deserved more from each of them because she "was a good girl." Despite Scott's wrongheadedness, Matt and

Alex allow this tragedy-stricken old father and devoted husband to a demented wife to maintain his delusions about his daughter—a true act of *ḥesed shel emet*—of altruistic lovingkindness, the label given to acts of respect paid to the dead. Matt and Alex know things about Elizabeth that Scott does not know. They use this knowledge, however, not to take down Scott but to shore up their own immediate family.

Ultimately, both the film and the biblical text are about the preservation and transmission of enduring, unchanging truths in the face of dramatic life changes. In the film, that which endures above all is the landscape. As one critic notes, "[m]ontages of the lush landscape not only offer rhythmic punctuation to the narrative, but gather cumulative power as emblems of eternity itself."[25] One could go so far as to say that the landscape is a God figure in the film, a figure of solidity, eternality, a bulwark against the many vicissitudes and ephemera of human experience. In the biblical text, where Jacob is forced to flee home to Haran, the eternal is physically embodied in the stone monument that Jacob erects in Beit El after he dreams of a ladder reaching the sky with angels going up and coming down (Gen. 28:18). In Laban's household in Haran, Jacob will need to work seven years and then seven more years for his beloved Rachel, and then for six more years still before he can return to this same spot at Beit El, erect a sanctuary, and claim his birthright in Canaan. All along, he will harbor a great fear about returning home lest he be killed by his older brother, Esau. Likewise, Matt King has seven years to figure out how to restructure the family trust so as to allow the family to maintain its birthright. His cousin Hugh vows to fight him every step of the way: "We'll come after you. Just because you're a lawyer doesn't mean the rest of us would be afraid to come after you." But Matt remains resolved: "I'm not signing. And if you sue me, it'll only make us closer."[26] The film never tells us whether cousin Hugh and his cronies actually come after Matt, and if so, how Matt fares in the face of this familial opposition.

The biblical text, however, does tell us what happens when Jacob and Esau finally meet again. If, earlier in Genesis 25, Esau had shown a tendency to disregard the future, when he and Jacob meet again, Esau demonstrates a corresponding tendency to let go of the past. Indeed, Esau never tries to kill Jacob for buying the birthright from him and stealing his blessing. On the contrary: "Esau, though, ran to meet him, and embraced him, and fell on his neck, and kissed him; and they burst into tears" (Gen. 33:4). Both brothers consent to forget and reconfigure the past, to move on, to live and let live.

4

On *Memento*

Remaking Memory from the Outside In

Modern Jewish Learning in Reverse: Inner Remembering

The previous chapter explored the notion of generational transmission, a form of familial or collective remembering. This chapter follows this thread by looking even more closely at the role of memory in Judaism and some of its contemporary challenges.

In my discussion on method in the introduction to this book, I refer to Franz Rosenzweig's notion of "learning in reverse." Rosenzweig articulates this idea in a draft essay written "Upon the Opening of the Jüdisches Lehrhaus," a new experimental program of adult Jewish education that anticipated many of our contemporary American efforts to impart Jewish learning to secularly educated Jewish adults. In this talk, Rosenzweig calls for a new learning method, in which outside secular learning would be used to return to and strengthen one's Jewish core. Arguably, there is no value more central to Judaism than memory. Rosenzweig thus closed his remarks on the opening of the Lehrhaus with the hope that the Jewish intellectual return to Jewish learning become an experience of "inner remembering":

> May the hours you spend here become hours of remembrance, but not in the stale sense of dead piety that is so frequently the attitude toward Jewish matters. I mean another kind of remembrance, an inner remembering, a turning from externals to that which is within, a turning that, believe me, will and

must become for you a returning home. Turn into yourself, return home to your innermost self and your innermost life.[1]

Following Rosenzweig's lead, this chapter looks at a secular film that deals with the implications of remembering and memory loss as a way of reimagining Jewish memory for the contemporary moment. The film is Christopher Nolan's *Memento* (2000).[2] Viewing this film quite literally involves a process of learning and viewing in reverse, as much of the film proceeds backward rather than forward in time. As such, the film highlights a number of issues concerning the malleability and construction of memory on a personal as well as a collective level. In fact, *Memento* throws into serious doubt the very notion that it is possible, via memory, to locate or return to the past or to identify an "innermost self," as Rosenzweig envisions. The self, necessarily rooted in memory, is as unstable as is memory and therefore vulnerable to manipulations and changes. A wide gap yawns, it would seem, between Rosenzweig's call for memory and the postmodern condition of memory loss and destabilized interpretation, which the film *Memento* so aptly represents. Yet the absence, instability, or malleability of memory as presented in *Memento* also has its salutary aspects. While our culture, secular and Jewish alike, may have lost its sense of certainty surrounding collective and personal memory, it has come to embrace the idea of memory as story that we actively reconstruct, reimagine, and retell, thereby endowing our lives with some coherence and meaning.

Reading *Memento*

An acknowledged technical and narrative masterpiece, avidly studied not just in film schools but also by scholars of literature, narrative theory, and philosophy, *Memento* is the story of a former insurance investigator named Leonard Shelby, who, as a result of a blow to the head, suffers from profound anterograde amnesia. Since his injury, which occurred simultaneously with his wife's rape and [supposed] murder, Leonard has lived outside the regular flow of memory and time. While he can summon memories from before the assault, he cannot store and integrate any new memories. Painfully aware of the absence of his wife but unable to recall how much time has elapsed or what has transpired since the trauma, Leonard cannot move on with his life and thus lives for the sole, detached purpose of finding and killing "John G," the man who allegedly raped and murdered his wife and took away his memory.

Leonard's prior training as an insurance investigator has equipped him with skills of detection and deduction, which he hopes to employ in his search. Yet these skills are rendered almost useless by his inability to remember anything or construct a narrative in time. He claims to have learned how to observe body language in context and "see through people's bullshit."[3] Repeatedly, however, we see his marked inability to place details in context and to discern body language and telltale clues because of his lack of short-term memory. Leonard attempts to impose order on the chaos of his anterograde mind by employing a system of mnemonic devices. He writes notes, takes Polaroid photos of places and people, which he labels for future reference, and inscribes tattoos on his body with what he believes to be key "facts" of the case. But because he cannot remember anything for longer than ten minutes, he cannot integrate, internalize, and utilize these memory aids in any reliable way. Leonard's condition also makes him vulnerable to the nefarious manipulations of others, including a rogue cop named Teddy, who lures Leonard into killing a drug dealer named Jimmy Grantz (on the false pretense that the latter is Leonard's John G) so that Teddy can steal Jimmy's drug money, and Jimmy's girlfriend, Natalie, who ultimately helps Leonard kill Teddy.

All this seems fairly comprehensible and straightforward, though it is not so at all when one actually watches the film. Instead of taking the viewer from point A to point B in Leonard's story, the film radically breaks up the time, order, and even the color of Leonard's story, so that the viewer shares no small measure of Leonard's disorientation and confusion. The film begins in color with a shot of Leonard taking a Polaroid photo of the dead Teddy, that is shown in reverse. Rather than watching the image of the prostrate Teddy develop on the Polaroid, the audience watches it disappear back into the camera, which becomes symbolic both of Leonard's memory loss and the viewer's immediate and increasing loss of certainty with regard to the trajectory and meaning of the story.

The film proceeds with two alternating storylines that coincide only toward the movie's end. The first is shown in color and moves in reverse chronological order, from Teddy's murder to the immediate aftermath of Jimmy Grantz's murder. The other appears in black and white and moves forward in time, beginning with Leonard's conversations with a police officer, their eventual meeting, and the carrying out of the murder of Jimmy. To stitch together the pieces of the colored strand, each of the color sections ends with a repetition of an image from the end of the color section that preceded it, suggesting a stutteringly fragmented process of reconstruction, what Stephen Owen refers to in his book *Remembrances,* as "a 'pointing,' an index of absence."[4]

In the black and white sequence, which takes place sometime before the aforementioned murders, Leonard sits in a nondescript motel room, trying to figure out exactly where he is. "So where are you? . . . It's kind of hard to say; it's just an anonymous room."[5] Leonard's description of his surroundings and condition is provided in a voice-over that represents not only his inner thoughts but also our own confusion over where we are in the sequence of the narrative. Leonard then talks on the phone—we are not sure to whom, though Teddy seems the most likely candidate—about a man named Sammy Jankis. This black and white sequence covers a brief short period of time, a day at most, but because it is broken up and stretched out over much of the movie, it seems far longer, accentuating the distortions of time and memory that characterize Leonard's anterograde life.

The choice in a contemporary film to use black and white instead of color often evokes a nostalgic past or conveys a sense of documentary truth. The first element seems to obtain for *Memento,* as the black-and-white sections of the film antedate the serial experiences of violence and corruption that characterize the colored portions. Instead of providing a linear documentary account, however, the black-and-white sections take on an almost mythic, ritual quality, with Leonard repeatedly invoking Sammy Jankis, whose name is inscribed in a handwritten tattoo on his hand. Leonard refers at the very beginning of the black and white sequence to the Gideon Bible that he finds in the motel room night table and that he claims (somewhat flippantly) to "read religiously." (At one point in the film, he opens the Bible to Leviticus 24, which includes the Lex Talionis "eye for an eye" verse, pointing to his obsession with measure-for-measure justice and revenge). It is not the Bible, however, that Leonard reads religiously but his "Remember Sammy Jankis" tattoo, the story of which he tells as a kind of pseudo-biblical credo or prayer, a guiding text for his life.

According to Leonard, he repeatedly tells Sammy Jankis's story because it helps him understand his own situation. It turns out that Sammy was at the center of Leonard's first big case as an insurance investigator. Like Leonard's current circumstance, Sammy, too, had suffered an injury, making the storage of new memories impossible. Leonard was sent by his employer to determine whether Sammy's memory problems were due to

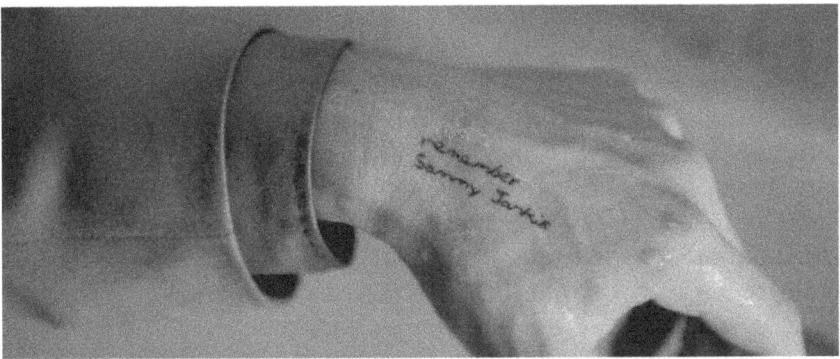

Figure 4.1. *Memento*, Remember Sammy Jankis.

a physical injury or were a symptom of psychosis (which would not be covered by his insurance policy). According to Leonard's understanding of the neuroscience of memory, even with damage to his hippocampus, Sammy should have been able to demonstrate habit memory and achieve some learning through conditioning.[6] But when tested, Sammy proved unable to make new habit memories, leading Leonard to the conclusion that Sammy's problem was psychological, not physical, and that he lacked the discipline or resolve to overcome it.

Saddled with medical bills and anxious to determine the true nature of Sammy's condition, his wife gives him her own test, repeatedly telling him that she needs her insulin shot, even though Sammy has already given it to her. She hopes that if Sammy's condition is psychological, the seriousness of her medical condition will jog him out of his memory loss before he repeatedly (and fatally) injects her with insulin. It does not, however, and she dies of an insulin overdose. Sammy's story, as Leonard tells it, is an object lesson on the mortal dangers of memory loss in the absence of a self and system to overcome it. Though Sammy had kept notes, they ultimately confused him. Leonard, by contrast, uses habit, repetition, and routine to bring order to his life. And he has a reason to make his life work—revenge.

Sammy's story is painful to Leonard because of the part he played in rejecting Sammy's insurance claim and in the sad demise of his wife, and because it ironically foreshadows Leonard's own condition. Nevertheless, Leonard seems to recount Sammy's story not so much to punish as to remind and admonish himself not to repeat Sammy's mistakes.

Consequently, throughout most of the film, Leonard proffers the imperative "Remember Sammy Jankis." But as Yosef Hayim Yerushalmi writes in *Zakhor*, "[m]emory is always problematic, usually deceptive, sometimes treacherous."[7] Leonard's ritualized personal injunctions to remember prove unreliable in their own, complicated way.

Indeed, everything asserted or demonstrated in *Memento* is subsequently questioned, challenged, or undercut. As William G. Little notes, the film's "disruptiveness is not limited to making problematic the viewer's desire to put events in 'proper' order. Equally unsettling is the fact that no character's point of view can be considered reliable."[8] For example, Natalie is initially presented as a somewhat sympathetic character until she is shown mocking and taunting Leonard with the knowledge that he will not remember anything ten minutes later. From the very beginning of the film, Teddy is presented as a smarmy, untrustworthy figure. But at the film's end, the possibility emerges that Teddy may be the only truth teller in the lot. According to Teddy, who claims to be the police officer assigned to Leonard and his wife's case, Sammy Jankis didn't even have a wife. Rather, it was Leonard's wife who was the diabetic. Leonard's wife actually survived the attack that robbed Leonard of his memory; and it was the anterograde Leonard, not Sammy, who unwittingly killed his wife by insulin overdose. Teddy avers that Leonard's repeated invocation of "Remember Sammy Jankis" is merely an attempt to repress the truth of his own deeds and exculpate himself. Deborah Knight and George McKnight thus argue that in killing Teddy, Leonard "kills the only person who could afford him any self-understanding because he kills the only person who challenges his own narratives about the past."[9]

There are plenty of reasons, scientific and otherwise, not to take Teddy at his word. While researchers of memory loss have indeed found evidence of anterograde patients' ability to form new habit memories,[10] Teddy alleges that the brain-damaged Leonard produced an entirely new episodic or declarative memory about Sammy Jankis to transfer his own guilt onto Sammy, which, though not inconceivable, would seem highly unlikely for a total amnesiac.[11] And, as I discuss below, Teddy's revelation occurs against a backdrop of other overarching lies that make him an unlikely arbiter of truth.

Still, there are several visual clues spliced into the film that support Teddy's contention: there is a brief tableau of Leonard sitting in a chair in a mental hospital in the same pose as Sammy Jankis, suggesting that Sammy's story is somehow really Leonard's. Leonard rejects Teddy's account on the grounds that his wife was not a diabetic. And yet the film includes split-second images that belie Leonard's view: (1) Leonard's preparation of an injection; (2) his injecting insulin into his wife's thigh; and (3) his wife lying in bed, first blinking and then with eyes rigidly open, as if she is suddenly comatose (from an overdose). A whole subfield within psychology, dating back to Hippolyte Bernheim in 1889, deals with the way in which therapists, law enforcement personnel, and others can manipulate the memory of others and/or plant memories in other people's minds.[12] Do these images constitute "facts," then, or are they simply ideas that appear in Leonard's mind as a result of Teddy's bullying suggestions? The film teases us by constantly juxtaposing competing interpretations. All of this, as Michael McKenna observes, places us in an interpretive quandary, emblematic of the postmodern condition: "Given the available evidence, there simply is no settled, proper interpretation of reality. As between competing and inconsistent interpretations, we are completely ill-equipped to settle on which, if any, is veridical."[13]

Memento and (Post)modern Jewish Memory: The Meaningfulness of Partial Truths

On the most basic level, *Memento* suggests that in the absence of memory and a functioning sense of narrative time, one has no coherent sense of self, no working interpretive framework, and no ethical system. Jewish tradition presages this attention to the urgent ethical importance of memory, both personally and collectively. In the Decalogue, the commandment to "Remember the Sabbath and keep it holy" immediately precedes the ethical commandments to honor your parents and not to murder, commit adultery, steal, or bear false witness, suggesting that ethics are entirely contingent on remembering God's role in creating the world in six days and resting on the seventh. As Yosef Hayim Yerushalmi famously notes in his book *Zakhor*, the Bible's "injunctions to remember are unconditional, and even when not commanded, remembrance is always pivotal. Altogether the verb *zakhar* appears in its various declensions in the Bible no less than 169 times, usually with either Israel or God as the subject, for memory is incumbent upon both."[14] If one has no memory, like Leonard, however, the entire structure risks collapse.

Most of us are not thoroughgoing amnesiacs. Or are we? Though pathological, Leonard's condition can also be viewed as an extreme version of the kinds of routine memory lapses and distortions that we all experience. "Like the amnesiac lead character in the 2000 film *Memento*," writes Jonathan Gottschalk in his book, *The Storytelling Animal* (2012), "we all go through life tattooed with indelible memories that didn't happen the way we remember them . . . Our memories are not precise records of what happened, and many of the details—small and large—are unreliable."[15]

And on a collective level, as intellectual historian David Ellenson writes in an essay titled "History, Memory and Relationship," our contemporary world is one "seemingly afflicted with amnesia. Many Jews and Christians either forget or ignore their history . . . The pluralism offered by the modern world makes tradition and the weight of tradition and memory an unattractive option for many people."[16]

That said, Jewish forgetfulness is not necessarily new or unique to the (post)modern condition. Regarding the issue of memory lapses or competing values, the Bible acknowledges that we all have a tendency to forget our core principles; hence the need for a system of ritual reminders. Deuteronomy 6, for example, commands us to love the Lord our God, insisting that this credo be taken to heart and taught diligently to one's children through repetition [*veshinantem*] that instills memory.

As if assuming that this learning by heart will not stick on its own, the passage further enjoins us to employ visual memory prompts as reinforcement: "Bind them as a sign on your hand and let them serve as a symbol on your forehead; inscribe them on the doorposts of your house and on your gates" (Deut. 6:8–9). Ritual/visual reminders appear in Numbers 15:38–39 in the commandment to place a fringe on one's garments so that one can look at and recall all of God's commandments and "not follow your heart and eyes in your lustful urge."

The Bible thus presents memory as a necessary and stabilizing element and a means of preserving one's self and one's central tenets. And yet even in the Bible, memory is presented as ephemeral, elusive, and unpredictable. As Adriane Leveen notes in her study of memory in the book of Numbers, in Numbers 11, memory introduces havoc rather than stability into the camp, as a collective, public remembering of the Egyptian delicacies triggers a series of disastrous events that ends up undermining the otherwise preserving influence of remembrance.[17]

In the Biblical world and in our own, then, memory is critical and necessary but also disruptive and unreliable. As Leonard Shelby avers in *Memento*:

> No, really. Memory's not perfect. It's not even that good. Ask the police, eyewitness testimony is unreliable. The cops don't catch a killer by sitting around remembering stuff. They collect facts, make notes, draw conclusions. Facts, not memories: that's how you investigate. I know, it's what I used to do. Memory can change the shape of a room or the color of a car. It's an interpretation, not a record. Memories can be changed or distorted and they're irrelevant if you have the facts.[18]

Leonard, out on his own trying to find the truth, might be regarded as a kind of modern empiricist collecting facts, not memories, determined to discover hard data through careful, ground-up, present-tense investigation. One simply has to know the right method for arriving at the truth, or so Leonard claims.

Of course, it suits Leonard to make an argument here against the efficacy and reliability of memory, because his no longer works. But at what cost does one uphold "facts" and eschew memory? Leonard's faith in "the facts"—given the way they are manipulated and falsely adduced throughout the film—is naïve in its own right.

All this calls to mind, once again, Yosef Hayim Yerushalmi's *Zakhor*. As memory and facts are to Leonard, so collective memory and history are to the great scholar. As mentioned earlier, Yerushalmi presents his vocation as a Jewish historian in search of hard data (like Leonard) as diametrically opposed to the traditions and habits of Jewish collective memory:

> Memory and modern historiography stand, by their very nature, in radically different relations to the past. The latter represents, not an attempt at the restoration of memory, but a truly new kind of recollection. In its quest for understanding it brings to the fore texts, events, processes, that never really became part of Jewish group memory even when it was most vigorous. With unprecedented energy it continually recreates an ever more detailed past whose shapes and textures memory does not recognize. But that is not all. The historian does not

simply come to replenish the gaps of memory. He constantly challenges those memories that have survived intact.[19]

The opposition presented here between memory and history was anticipated many years earlier, albeit in a different form, by French sociologist and anthropologist Maurice Halbwachs in his writings on the social context of collective memory. In recent years, however, scholars have challenged or attempted to modify both Halbwachs's and Yerushalmi's opposition of memory and history.[20] As Yael Zerubavel has argued, "Halbwachs's desire to highlight the unique qualities of collective memory appears to have led him to overstate its contrast to history. He therefore portrays them as two polar representations of the past." Nowadays, however, historians commonly acknowledge the constructedness not just of memory but also of history. "In fact, historians not only share the basic premises of collective memory but also help to shape them through their work, as the history of national movements has shown."[21]

So, as Leonard Shelby might say, where are we? I have thus far presented the relevance of *Memento* to a discussion of the necessity and the slippery nature of memory, as well as to the supposed opposition between modernist (empiricist) and postmodern (subjective, less stable) approaches to Jewish history and collective memory. We have shown that while memory is selective and constructed, the supposed realm of facts—historiography—shares, at least in some measure, these same features. With regard to the film itself, if we, the viewers, are detectives in our own right, attempting to discern the truth of this story, our conclusion may well be nihilistic, that is, that there are no "true facts" to be found. And yet, as Gene Borowitz noted once toward the end of a class discussion of *Memento*, a logical contradiction arises from that premise: if there is no truth, then this supposed "truth" about the lack of truth itself needs to be toppled (or so goes the "liar's paradox"). For decades, Borowitz had been making a plea for a middle ground between the Enlightenment faith in human reason with its abrogation of collective memory as a form of irrational myth and the nihilism of postmodernism: "Against the teaching of so much present-day philosophy and science," Borowitz wrote in 1974, "we find that we do not consider the universe empty of values and man thus free to adopt any form of behavior whatsoever."[22] In a similar vein, Borowitz warned the students in our Reel Theology class against the potential nihilistic message of *Memento*: "You cannot leave it at that."

Turning to me before departing to catch his train home, his charge to me was, pointedly, "I trust you will not leave it at that."

In response, I would like to argue that the film itself does not "leave it at that"—at least, not in any simple or straightforward way, which is why it serves as such an effective catalyst for discussion about current understandings of [Jewish] memory.

To this end, let's return to the film and consider its climax. In the denouement, Leonard murders Jimmy Grantz and realizes, traumatically (when he hears Jimmy refer to Sammy [Jankis], indicating that Jimmy knew him) that the latter was not his John G, after all. When Leonard confronts Teddy with the realization that he has just killed the wrong man, Teddy attempts to evade the truth and convince Leonard that Jimmy really is his John G. Against this backdrop of lies, Teddy rolls out his supposedly "true" version of Leonard's past, including the revelation that more than a year ago, Teddy helped Leonard track down the real John G—they even took a picture after that event, which he shows to Leonard—but Leonard could not remember this event. Over the course of this conversation, Teddy dissolves the few remaining memories and principles by which Leonard has lived, alleging that is was Leonard's wife who was a diabetic and that it was Leonard, not Sammy Jankis, who caused his wife to overdose on insulin. In addition, Teddy lets on that he used his knowledge of Leonard's disability to his own crass advantage—to make some money off a drug deal by having Leonard kill drug dealer Jimmy. Given this "reality," Leonard consciously decides to "forget" Teddy's would-be "truths" and to "remember" only his lies. Leonard thus burns the Polaroid photo of the dead Jimmy, labels the Polaroid shot of Teddy with the words "DO NOT BELIEVE HIS LIES," and tattoos Teddy's license plate number to his thigh—clues that, with Natalie's help, will lead him eventually to kill Teddy, as if he were John G.

One student asked: Why doesn't Leonard simply kill Teddy right there and then when he realizes what Teddy has done to him? Why does he delay by inserting Teddy into the story of his ongoing quest for his wife's rapist and murderer? Doesn't Leonard's manipulation of the "facts" here represent the worst kind of betrayal both of memory and "truth"?

Philosopher Michael McKenna would respond to my student that, at this point in the film, Leonard's "desire for revenge has outstripped what is true . . . In this moment, Leonard forsakes his allegiance to the truth as he cynically says to himself, 'Do I lie to myself to be happy? In your case, Teddy, yes I will.'"[23]

Perhaps. And yet one might also argue that this moment of cognitive fabrication on Leonard's part represents the only assertion of meaningfulness and agency in a life otherwise stripped of it. Leonard, desperately seeking justice and truth but suddenly aware of the extent to which his injury has mired him in the opposite, chooses to forget some things and "remember" others because of his tenacious desire to believe that his actions still have meaning. In the context of this film, where many views are presented but all are challenged, Leonard makes a pluralistic claim for the partial truth[24] of his grievance against Teddy and for the larger abiding truth of his quest for justice in the face of his wife's and his own suffering. Leonard's decision to fold Teddy's misdeeds into the memory of what John G did to him and his wife represents a reassertion of the ongoing meaningfulness of his own personal story.

Let me be clear: I am neither advocating that one murder and lie, nor am I attempting to justify the wholesale, self-conscious invention of one's past. Leonard is an extreme case: a flawed and pathetic hero whose pursuit of justice, truth, and meaning is sorely compromised and whose agency is woefully limited; he is, at best, an extremely weak illustration of Rosenzweig's call to the inner self.

That said, given a choice between competing truth claims, between a version of the past touted by one exposed as a greedy murderous manipulator and another version that, though potentially faulty or partial, allows one to seek the punishment of a wrongdoer while at the same time maintaining one's dignity—is the latter not preferable? Teddy dismissively says to Leonard, "So you lie to yourself to be happy. Nothing wrong with that—we all do."[25] But this—our tendency to fictionalize or to construct our past—is itself an important truth. "We are all tellers of tales," writes psychologist Dan P. McAdams in his book *Stories We Live By*:

> We each seek to provide our scattered and often confusing experiences with a sense of coherence by arranging the episodes of our lives into stories. This is not the stuff of delusion or self-deception. We are not telling ourselves lies. Rather, through our personal myths, each of us discovers what is true and is meaningful in life. In order to live well, with unity and purpose, we compose a heroic narrative of the self that illustrates essential truths about ourselves.[26]

What this means is that each of us emphasizes selective details from our personal as well as collective past so as to construct a narrative that propels our lives forward, generatively. Given Leonard's compromised state, resolving to construct a narrative that will lead him to kill his current aggressor, Teddy, is probably the best he can muster. And the moral consequences are quite unsettling, to say the least.

Torah she-be'al peh: Memory and the Imagination

Throughout the film, when Leonard attempts to conjure up details from his distant past or to fix an image in his mind, he is shown either looking up and away from the camera or closing his eyes. In one scene, Natalie asks him to tell her about his wife: "Close your eyes and remember her," she says. Leonard closes his eyes and, consequently, is able to call forth and describe a past memory of his wife that is textured, emotional, and commanding:[27]

> You can only feel details. Bits and pieces, which you didn't bother to put into words. And extreme moments you feel even if you don't want to. Put it together and you get the feel of the person, enough to know how much you miss them, and how much you hate the person who took them away.[28]

Here the amnesiac Leonard "remembers" not by using the externalized memory aids of his written notes, photos, and tattoos, but by looking inside himself and insisting on what he sees in his own mind's eye—a preference shared by the ancient Greeks. Tony Jackson explains as follows:

> As Plato prophesied long ago, the importance of memory in human affairs changes drastically with writing. Over time, writing usurped the place of what we may call public or communal memory, the oral means of handing on the past that is the only kind of history accessible to non-literate community. Plato charged that writing is unnatural, in that if you ask questions of it, it cannot respond; said another way, with writing, our words are no longer a function of the body. Because writing

removes our words from our voices and our histrionics and some specific flesh and blood communicative context, we cannot be as sure of the success of our linguistic intentions as we typically can be in speech.[29]

Leonard is exceptional. Yet, as mentioned earlier, we all share something of his problematic dependence on externalized, written-down (or, in our day, digitized) memory. Our reading practices, which consign learning to written form, abet this. As Robert Darnton describes, a reading revolution took place in the West around 1800. Before then, men read "intensively":

> They had only a few books—the Bible, an almanac, a devotional work or two—and they read them over and over again, usually aloud and in groups, so that a narrow range of traditional literature became deeply impressed on their consciousness. By 1800 men were reading "extensively." They read all kinds of material, especially periodicals and newspapers, and read it only, then raced on to the next item.[30]

Rosenzweig seems to register an awareness of the Jewish version of this phenomenon. In the beginning of his essay on the opening of the Lehrhaus, he argues: "It is to a book, the Book, that we owe our survival—that Book which we use, not by accident, in the very form is has existed for millennia ... Everything was really within the learning of the Book ... Then came the Emancipation."[31] Rosenzweig's educational project, described at the beginning of this essay, aims to reverse the process and thereby return Jews to an intensive reading of the Book, though not merely in an atavistic or an externalized sense. His hope is that this new form of learning, influenced by our extensive outside reading, will result in "inner remembering." But what might inner remembering look like?

What comes to my mind in this context is Judaism's insistence on the importance not only of *Torah she-bikhtav* [the written Torah] but also of *Torah she-be'al peh*, what Martin Jaffee refers to as "Torah in the Mouth." According to Jaffee's research on writing and oral tradition in Palestinian Judaism,

> [t]he written texts of the Torah in the mouth, that is to say, are not *Torah* at all as long as they remain merely written on

inscribed material surfaces; the real inscription of Torah in the mouth must be in memory, as memory is shaped by the sounds of the teacher's own rendition.[32]

Jaffee describes an ancient learning community where one studied, memorized, and shared aloud the teachings of one's master for the purpose of being imaginatively transformed by them. "The privileged path to such transformation lay in emulating the living embodiment of that knowledge in the writings and deeds of one's teachers, and their teacher's teachers. In the person of the philosophical Sage, the instructional text came alive."[33]

We are unlikely to return to those premodern days of remembering; our sense of what constitutes learning has forever changed. We are similarly unlikely to revive the ancient tradition of memorization, though if contemporary Jewish literature is any indication of our current disposition, our community is evincing a renewed interest in engaging Jewish memory in new and creative forms. In a *Tikkun* magazine symposium on the New Wave in American Jewish literature, nearly all the critics and writers included noted the centrality of Jewish memory in the work of the current wave of Jewish American writers.[34] One writer of this New Wave, Jonathan Safran Foer, whose debut novel *Everything Is Illuminated* tells the story of a young American writer who journeys to the Ukraine to recover the story of his family's pre-Holocaust past, claims that "Jews have six senses: Touch, taste, sight, smell, hearing . . . memory."[35] It is significant to note, however, that a good deal of his novel's investigation and evocation of the past involves the creation of a fictional[ized] *shtetl*, populated by imaginary "Slouchers" and "Uprights."

Even in the time of the Rabbis, Jewish remembering required a commitment not only to memorization but also to acts of the imagination. And forgetting this commitment posed special kinds of risk, as Rabbi Dostai ben Yannai says in the name of Rabbi Meir in Pirkei Avot, chapter 3:

> He who forgets a single word of his studies, Scriptures considers it as if he were liable for his life; for it is written (Deuteronomy 4:9) "But take care and watch yourselves closely, so as not to forget the things [that your eyes have seen].[36]

This Mishnah functions as a kind of Jewish *memento mori*—in the sense of being a reminder not of one's mortality, but of the potential danger to one's integrity should one lose one's memory. Note that in the Mishnah the very proof-text adduced for the notion that one's life depends on remembering what one has learned hangs on an act of the imagination. When Moses speaks to the people in Deuteronomy 4 and admonishes them not to forget what "your eyes have seen," he is speaking to that postwilderness generation of Israelites who didn't actually see the Exodus with their own eyes. As the Tiferet Yisrael[37] explains, it couldn't possibly be that the text is referring here to actual sight, as the Torah was written for all of Israel, and the latter generations, of which we are a part, did not witness any of the miracles. Rather, the biblical text seems to be referring to "the eye of one's intellect,"[38] adjuring that one ought not forget the formative ideas and stories that one sees—dare I say, invents?—in one's own mind.

At the ordination ceremony for the 2012 graduating class of rabbis and cantors at HUC-JIR, New York, Rabbi Cantor Angela Buchdahl delivered an address in word and song that offered a contemporary take on this ancient teaching about our need to imagine or invent memory anew:

> They say, "You can't change history." But here's the radical thing—you can change memory. In every generation, as we remember anew—we actually *re-form* Jewish memory itself. We come out of a new Egypt, we change the faces of those who stood at Sinai, we add new leaders who received authority from the very hands of Moses. . . . You who have been studying these letters, interpreting the words and decorating the text with your own understanding . . . You will become memory makers.[39]

Buchdahl offered her notion of memory making to commemorate two historic events that occurred the very year she was born (1972): the ordination of Sally Priesand as first woman rabbi in the American Reform movement and the release of Debbie Friedman's *Sing Unto God*, a landmark occasion in terms of the history of Jewish feminist liturgy and song. Within a single generation (according to the forty-year reckoning in the book of Exodus), these watershed events brought about a radical reimagination or reremembering of synagogue leadership and practice, forever changing, as if retrospectively as well as for generations to come, the nature of the rabbinate and of Jewish prayer leading.

Might Franz Rosenzweig have had something like this in mind when he envisioned the new enterprise of "learning in reverse?" A reading of a secular film about memory that itself resists easy explication as a means of reencountering and re-imagining the tradition of Jewish memory as storytelling or imaginative recollection? A reading of the current state of Jewish leadership and prayer as a way of creatively re-envisioning the notion of Jewish tradition? An embrace of "inner remembering," not in some naïve, romantic, anti-intellectual way; not without awareness of amnesia, alienation, rupture, and change, but with a brave willingness to reshape the familiar in light of the alien, and the past in light of the present? "In being Jews we must not give up anything," writes Rosenzweig, "not renounce anything, but lead everything back to Judaism. From the periphery back to the center; from the outside, in."[40]

5

Crimes, Misdemeanors, and Sin

The Wages of Sin

If memory becomes a slippery concept in the postmodern age, the idea of sin proves similarly elusive. "Woody Allen Counts the Wages of Sin"[1]—so reads the title of a Sunday *New York Times* article that appeared shortly after the 1989 release of Woody Allen's *Crimes and Misdemeanors*. The article, which enlisted commentary on the film by "three specialists on religious issues and their presentation in art and wider culture," including my senior colleague Eugene Borowitz, set the stage for an ongoing, theologically oriented response to the film. Borowitz's praise of the unexpectedly positive portrayal of Jewish life in *Crimes and Misdemeanors*—"A synagogue—better, a shul—a rabbi, a seder, a Jewish wedding, all receive respectful, even loving, treatment"[2]—was especially noteworthy and has been quoted repeatedly in later interpretations of the film.[3] It was not common, after all, for Woody Allen to receive such commendation from a rabbi.

Rereading that article now, however, what stands out most for me is the title referring to "the wages of sin." Curiously, the word "sin" appears nowhere in the article. Nor does it figure particularly prominently in *Crimes and Misdemeanors*. In fact, the word sin figures only twice in the movie, both in contexts where the very notion of sin is in some way dismissed or downplayed. In the first instance, a guilt-ridden Judah Rosenthal, having first committed adultery and then murder, repeats to his brother Jack the age-old adage that "one sin leads to a deeper sin"—*'aveirah goreret 'aveirah*, as the old rabbinic saying goes.[4] But the streetwise Jack dismisses this adage as sounding too much like their deceased, pious Papa and thus of no relevance to current reality, where religion has no real force. By the end of the film, Judah shows that he has come around to Jack's way of thinking when he concedes to Clifford Stern that people "carry sins" or "awful deeds" around with them yet manage to move on; they rationalize them away or ignore them most of the time and thus continue on their merry ways, unencumbered by guilt.

Sin is a value-laden, theologically grounded word, one that assumes that God witnesses and judges what we do and that religion has a valid and enduring role to play within the sphere of human action. Woody Allen's secular film, however, directly challenges these assumptions.[5] Throughout the film, Allen calls attention to the seeming absence in the world of divine providence and justice and thus questions the relevance of conventional ethics. In the absence of God, justice, and morality, how relevant is it, really, to speak of sin?

"We are a society that shies away from the use of the word 'sin,'" writes Rabbi Danny Zemel:

> We leave this word to such figures as colonialist preacher Jonathan Edwards (1703–1758), whose sermons (such as "Sinners in the Hands of an Angry God") have been made famous by history. We content ourselves instead with "mistakes" and "errors." Even when human lives are lost, families torn apart, and countries destroyed because we went to war over false intelligence, misinformation, and disinformation, we prefer terms like "policy misjudgment" or "misguided decision." No one sins anymore.[6]

The title of the film, *Crimes and Misdemeanors*, anticipates and supports Zemel's observation, showing how terminology alters the perception and significance of wrongdoing. Referring to the misdeeds, both large and small, of the protagonists of his film, Allen's title conspicuously omits all reference to sin. Instead, it presents two legal terms, the first referring to major and the second to minor infractions. To speak of crimes or misdemeanors instead of sins is to look at actions not in terms of how they are perceived by God but rather by how they are processed by a secular legal system. But what if, as in the case of Judah Rosenthal, one's crimes or misdemeanors are never detected? If one commits a crime or misdemeanor but is never caught and therefore never punished, does the wrongdoing lose its weight, consequence, or reality? In the absence of evidence of a God who sees all, do actions lose all meaning?

Category Confusion

Already at an early phase of his filmmaking career, with such films such as *Sleeper* (1973) and *Love and Death* (1975),[7] Allen was posing these kinds of questions, but *Crime and Misdemeanors* "raises the inquiry into the human condition to a new level of seriousness. His Jewishness no longer provides merely a source of humor, but it supplies the religious language for . . . agonizing questions."[8] This is not to say that *Crimes and Misdemeanors* is all high seriousness. On the contrary: it is a mixed-genre film composed of two interwoven narrative strands, one tragic and the other comic, each of which ends against the grain of generic expectations. The would-be tragic strand—the story of ophthalmologist Judah Rosenthal, who has his former mistress murdered to keep their affair and his financial improprieties a secret—ends "happily" at a wedding, its hero having escaped punishment. The comic strand—the story of documentary filmmaker Clifford Stern—ends sadly with Cliff losing his bid for Halley Reed's heart to his archnemesis, Lester. Allen's decision in this film to blur genres and narrative expectations is hardly incidental to the film's philosophical and theological stance. As Greg Bachman notes, *Crimes and Misdemeanors* subverts the conventional structure of cause and effect so as to expose "the impotence of the classic story structure"[9] and, by extension, the moral structure of the world.

The category confusion in this film works applies not just to art but also to character and behavior, where Allen consistently presents a mixed bag. Judah Rosenthal appears on the surface to be an ideal husband, family man, professional, and community leader—the kind of man, Eugene Borowitz used to say to our students, a rabbi might want as synagogue president. In reality, Judah is an adulterer, a swindler, and a murderer, yet no one, save the dead Dolores; his brother Jack, who arranges the "hit" on her; and we, the screen audience, sees or knows the real Judah. Just about all the other characters in the cast evince a complex combination of traits that defy ready categorization. Judah's brother Jack demonstrates a code of loyalty and a frank honesty that belie his otherwise shady doings. Cliff Stern fancies himself a serious filmmaker, yet he squanders a good deal of his time watching old-time Hollywood movies with his adolescent niece, whose adulation he craves.¹⁰ In the documentary that Cliff makes about TV producer Lester, Cliff attempts to expose Lester's philandering, yet Cliff himself pursues an affair with Halley while still married to Lester's sister, Wendy. Lester is an arrogant womanizer who nevertheless gives generously to his family and to others. Cliff deems Lester a *lesser* artist, a producer of "sub-mental" TV sitcoms. Yet over the course of the film Lester offers certain wise and true teachings about comedy and life. His definition of comedy—"Comedy is tragedy plus Time," though ridiculous in context, proves to be an apt and intelligent way of explaining how it is that people manage, with the passage of time, to derive humor from tragic experience. And, as Mark Roche notes, the Judah Rosenthal plot line appears to prove Lester's theory,¹¹ as Judah himself relates to Cliff at the end of the film when he tells his own story in the guise of a suggested plot for a movie. A man commits a murder:

> And after the awful deed is done, he finds that he's plagued by deep-rooted guilt. Little sparks of his religious background, which he'd rejected are suddenly stirred up. He hears his father's voice. He imagines that God is watching his every move. Suddenly, it's not an empty universe at all, but a just and moral

Figure 5.1. *Crimes and Misdemeanors,* Comedy is Tragedy Plus Time.

one, and he's violated it. Now, he's panic-stricken. He's on the verge of a mental collapse—an inch away from confessing the whole thing to the police. And then one morning, he awakens. The sun is shining, his family is around him and mysteriously, the crisis has lifted. He takes his family on a vacation to Europe and as the months pass, he finds he's not punished. In fact, he prospers. The killing gets attributed to another person—a drifter who has a number of other murders to his credit, so I mean, what the hell? One more doesn't even matter. Now he's scot-free. His life is completely back to normal. Back to his protected world of wealth and privilege.[12]

Judah's own experience suggests that time can turn tragedy into comedy. A man burdened with a sense of guilt becomes freed of his burden not as a result of confession or punishment, but simply because time passes and guilt fades. And he lives happily ever after.

All of this takes us back again to the film's title, *Crimes and Misdemeanors*, an adaptation, of course, of the title of Fyodor Dostoevsky's classic 1866 novel *Crime and Punishment*, the story Raskolnikov, a student who murders and steals from an old woman pawnbroker in part to test his hypothesis that some extraordinary people are entitled, by virtue of extraordinary daring, to defy conventional morality.[13] In the end, Raskolnikov succumbs to the same system of morality he had hoped to transcend, while Allen's Judah overcomes it. As David Landry notes with regard to Woody Allen's Judah Rosenthal and Dostoevsky's Raskolnikov,

both are murderers, both are tremendously adept at persuading themselves of the justice and necessity of their actions. And both are subsequently tormented by guilt. In both cases, one could argue that the hell that they put themselves through is a kind of "punishment" apart from any official or divine sanction. However, while Raskolnikov descends into madness and ultimately feels compelled to confess, first to his prostitute lover and then to the authorities, Judah does neither.

In the film, as indicated by the title, there is "Crime" but no "Punishment."[14]

Raskolnikov had aspired to create a new law for himself, as he attempts to explain to Sonia, his prostitute lover:

Anyone who is greatly daring is right in their eyes. He who despises most things will be a law-giver among them and he who dares most of all will be most in the right! So it has been till now and so it will always be. A man must be blind not to see it!¹⁵

Judah Rosenthal has no such vaunted aspirations, making his act of hired murder to cover up his affair and embezzlement at once more brazen and more banal. Unlike Raskolnikov, Judah does not initially set out to make himself a "law-giver." His decision to hire a hit man to kill Dolores is merely pragmatic. In the imagined nighttime conversation with Ben, Judah insists that God "is a luxury he cannot afford," which is to say, he needs to deal with the muck of reality rather than to hew to some religiously ordained moral ideal. For a while, Judah is haunted by the religious teachings of his youth, but this too passes. In the absence of any repercussions, then, Judah manages to rationalize his deeds and live with his guilt in a way that Raskolnikov never manages to do, in effect becoming an everyday, American version of Dostoevsky's nihilist superman.

(Not) Seeing and (Not) Being Seen

Raskolnikov's declaration to Sonia, "A man must be blind not to see" the relativistic nature of law and morality, calls to mind the many motifs of vision and blindness, both actual and metaphorical, that appear in *Crimes and Misdemeanors*. The film famously opens with eye doctor Judah Rosenthal's speech on the occasion of the opening of the new ophthalmology wing:

> I remember my father telling me, "The eyes of God are on us always." The eyes of God. What a phrase to a young boy. What were God's eyes like? Unimaginably penetrating, intense eyes, I assumed. And I wonder if it was just a coincidence I made my specialty ophthalmology.¹⁶

An eye doctor; the eyes of God; Rabbi Ben's failing eyes; the open eyes of Dolores Paley as she lies on the floor after her murder; Judah looking to the left and to the right before he burns Dolores's letter and when he runs with Dolores on the beach; Aunt May's call to Sol in the Seder scene to open his eyes to the realities of the world—all these images of sight accrue and press the central theological question: Does God see what we do? What do we make of the notion of divine providence when empirical reality seems to contradict it?

These are just the most obvious, immediately apparent examples of vision motifs in the film. But Allen does not stick to the obvious. As a filmmaker, he is in the business of visual representation, and as such the film is filled with subtle, metafilmic considerations of the nature of seeing and being seen, the relationship between appearance and reality, the role of the filmmaker and audience as seers of all in terms of the film's story, and the interplay of light and darkness, both visually and morally speaking.

Crimes and Misdemeanors is thus filled with scenes of people looking at illuminated images in the darkness, each meaning something else. In a dark office, Judah examines Rabbi Ben's eyes, asking him to identify points of light, a symbolic representation of Ben's enduring faith and moral "insight" even as he descends into physical blindness. Clifford Stern watches movies in the dark with his niece and with Halley Reed, a repeated effort on his part to inhabit the softly lit world of Hollywood romance, even as he stubbornly repudiates the sham nature of Hollywood success. Judah sits in his living room in the middle of the night, his face half-lit, conducting an imagined moral debate with a now barely visible Ben, lit up momentarily by a flash of lightning, a representation of Judah's steadily darkening conscience. The repeated visual play of light and dark in such different contexts complicates conventional symbolic associations and overturns assumptions about how we see, how we are seen, and the meaning of our actions.

Figure 5.2. *Crimes and Misdemeanors*, Judah Talks Morality with Rabbi Ben.

Critic Sam Girgus notes the design of Dolores Paley's apartment, which includes direct lines of sight but also many visual obstructions, symbolic of the obstructed or distorted lines of moral vision in the story.[17] He also observes the way in which Allen uses close-ups and flashbacks as a way of portraying not just the hidden truths of Judah Rosenthal's life but also the potential of film, in general, to look inward at human nature:

> For him [Allen], the metaphor of vision into the unknown concerns not only the examination of the moral dimension of human experience. It also becomes a metaphor for the artistic process behind his entire filmmaking project. The "eyes of God," a phrase from *Crimes and Misdemeanors*, describes precisely how he wants the cameras and his filmmaking to look within and bring out that world for art.[18]

Other critics such as Greg Bachman examine the various classic film excerpts that Allen splices into the Clifford Stern plot strand, showing how these excerpts add a metafilmic aspect to the film, enlarging its treatment of the themes of watching and being watched and of appearance versus reality.[19] For example, the first movie that Cliff and his niece watch together is *Mr. and Mrs. Smith*, a Hitchcock film about a husband and wife who discover that, despite all appearances and prior assumptions, they were never legally married. The issue of legality recalls our earlier discussion of the legal terminology employed in the film's title, *Crimes and Misdemeanors,* and how this language alters the substance and meaning of actions.

David and Bathsheba

Still other critics have noted the way in which the Judah Rosenthal plotline, with its many images of eyes and sight, alludes and responds to the biblical story of David and Bathsheba in 2 Samuel 11–12. The name Judah, after all, calls to mind the biblical tribe of Judah from which David descends. And the biblical story, like the film, tells the story of a powerful man who tries to get away with adultery and murder. As David Landry sums up:

Both stories emphasize how one sin leads to another. . . . [First] David shirks his duty as king, and thus is able to see Bathsheba bathing from the roof of his palace, after having lazily arisen from his couch "late in the afternoon." When he sees her, instead of averting his glance . . . he lets his gaze linger on her long enough to notice that she was "very beautiful." This leering glance leads him to inquire of her, and despite having learned that she the wife of Uriah the Hittite, one of David's own soldiers, he sends for her. Even if she does not come he has coveted his neighbor's wife. But she does come, as she must, and he lies with her. He has added adultery to coveting, and he will soon add murder when his lies and deceptions do not enable him to cover up having impregnated another man's wife.[20]

Landry specifically highlights the role of David's gaze in his descent into sin. But David is not the only one in the story who looks and sees. Meir Sternberg contends that in 2 Samuel 11, "the chain of events is presented in a neutral manner, as it were, without comment or judgment."[21] Yet moral evaluation does enter into this chapter by way of images of divine light and sight. The text specifies that Bathsheba's husband's name is Uriah, meaning "My light is God" or "God's Light," suggesting that in having him murdered, David has put out God's light. When David receives word of Uriah's death and sends a message back to Joab, he attempts to downplay the event as part and parcel of warfare: "*Al na yera hadavar be'einekha, ki kazo vekhazeh tokhal heḥarev*" (2 Samuel 11:25; Let this thing not be evil in your eyes for the sword devours in one way or another, my translation). The expression *yera hadavar be'einekha* enacts a suggestive and ominous play on the words ראה ra'ah (he saw) and רעה ra'ah (evil) that is replayed and recast only two verses later when David takes widowed Bathsheba as his wife and God's view of the deed is made known. If David had attempted in his message to Joab to downplay the significance of Uriah's death, the final verse of the chapter turns David's words on their head and pronounces direct, divine judgment against David's sin: "*Vayera hadavar asher 'asah David be'einei YHVH*" (2 Samuel 11:27; But the thing that David had done was evil in God's eyes).

All this is held up clearly to the light of day in the next chapter, where God sends the prophet Nathan to David to expose David's contemptible behavior. Nathan tells David a parable about a rich man who steals a poor man's lamb, to which David responds with righteous indignation, pronouncing the man who perpetrated this theft a *"ben mavet"* (one deserving of death).[22] Normally theft does not merit a death sentence, but clearly David has murder on his mind (like Judah Rosenthal in the Seder scene in *Crimes and Misdemeanors*, when he unwittingly asks his imagined family members their view of the man who kills). "You are the man!" declares Nathan, outing David as the real *"ben mavet,"* a man himself guilty of a capital crime. In response, David immediately confesses his sin: "And David said to Nathan: 'I have sinned against the LORD.' And Nathan said to David: 'The LORD has put away your sin; you shall not die. . . . The child that is born unto you surely shall die'" (2 Samuel 12:13–14).[23]

The contrast between the Judah Rosenthal plot and the biblical account thus emerges starkly. Recalling Judah's confession of wrongdoing with respect to his daughter-in-law, Tamar, in Genesis 38 (see chapter 2), David directly confesses his sin to God's messenger and repents. Note that in marked contrast to the biblical Judah, Allen's Judah Rosenthal makes several indirect confessions in the film but neither atones nor accepts punishment. When Judah Rosenthal first learns that the murder has been committed, he distractedly says to his wife and their assembled guests at a dinner party, "I think I have done a terrible thing," only to spin out a new lie: that he left some papers that he needs at his office and has to leave mid-party to get them. (What he actually does is go to Dolores's apartment to remove incriminating evidence.) For a while thereafter, Judah is tortured with guilt and is on the verge of confessing. In one scene at a restaurant, he declares to his wife that he believes in God because "without God life is a cesspool." One expects Judah to spill it out right then and there before his wife and daughter. But that is as far as it goes; Judah goes outside to cool down and keeps his secrets to himself. At the end of the film, a newly composed and once-again stable Judah makes another, more extended, elliptical "confession" in the form of the movie plot he shares at the wedding with filmmaker Clifford Stern. According to some interpreters who look at Judah's serious expressions as he tells the story, this scene proves that Judah continues to be plagued by guilt for what he has done.[24] Yet others, Woody Allen included, claim that at this point in the film, Judah harbors no guilt whatsoever.[25] Whereas the biblical David, king of Judah, confronts God's providential eyes and judgment, Judah Rosenthal ignores them entirely.[26]

Then again, does David not also escape, at least with his own life? The moral difficulty arising from the biblical story is that in place of guilty David, his innocent baby becomes a *ben mavet*, a son of death or a dead son.[27] At the end of *Crimes and Misdemeanors*, Judah's would-be confession details how the killing in question gets attributed to a drifter who had other crimes to his credit, allowing the real killer to go scot-free. In the biblical story, guilt gets similarly transferred, but to an innocent child rather than to a seasoned criminal. Nathan outs David as *"ha'ish,"* the guilty man or the mortal, proclaiming that David's punishment will be meted out *"le'einei hashemesh hazot"* (verse 11; in sight of the sun). But when David confesses and repents, God renders David's baby son mortally ill (ויאנש, *vayei'anesh*, verse 15), a play on the word ʿ*onesh* (punishment) and *ish* איש that signals the shifting or spreading of David's sin and punishment to the next generation.

To be sure, David has become undone. As Shmuel Herzfeld notes, "the David and Batsheva narrative stands at the turning point in David's fortunes. Prior to David's sin with Batsheva, his life is enchanted. He is a success. After the sin, his kingdom falls apart. His children rebel against him and his life becomes a punishment.[28] Amy Kalmanofsky extends this observation by noting the way in which the motif of sexual violation figures both in the David and Bathsheba story and its punitive aftermath:

> David jeopardizes the security of his own home when he commits adultery by sleeping with Uriah's wife Bathsheba and then plotting to have Uriah killed. Furious at David, God sends the prophet Nathan to condemn David's behavior and to deliver the prophecy that David's house will never again experience peace. Immediately after this, the rape of Tamar by Amnon fulfills Nathan's prophecy of doom to David in 2 Sam 12:11: "Thus says YHVH: 'I will make calamity rise against you from within your house.'"[29]

Indeed, one of the results of the sins committed by David in 2 Samuel 11 is the retributive replication of David's sins by his children—a form of ʿ*aveirah goreret ʿaveirah* (one sin leading to another) that is marked by the textual repetitions of certain key words. When David has intercourse with Bathsheba, for example, the verb used to designate their sexual relations is "*shakhav.*" Tellingly, in the account of Amnon's rape of Tamar in 2 Samuel 13, the verb *shakhav* appears five times, suggesting a widening circle of sexual abuse. Robert Alter similarly observes the repetition of the verb "*shalaḥ*" (to send), which occurs eleven times in 2 Samuel 11; "David, now a sedentary king removed from the field of action and endowed with a dangerous amount of leisure, is seen constantly operating through the agency of others."[30] Significantly, after he rapes Tamar, Amnon uses the same verb, albeit with a different connotation; overcome with revulsion for Tamar after raping her, Amnon commands his servants to expel Tamar from his room: "*Shilḥu na et zot me'alai haḥutzah une'ol et a delet aḥareha*" (Send this one outside away from me, and bolt the door after her).[31] Here Amnon not only emulates David's action but raises the familial stakes, indicating how David's habit of using others to do his dirty work is now resulting in the expulsion of members of his own family from the royal home. Thus, when Tamar protests Amnon's treatment of her, she refers to "*hara'ah hagedolah hazot*" (this great evil), recalling Nathan/God's judgment of David's wrongdoing as evil (*vayera*) in God's eyes, as well as Nathan's promise to "raise up *ra'ah*" (calamity, as translated above, or evil) against David's house (2 Samuel 12:11). Following the rape incident, David's son Absalom moves to have Amnon and all of the king's other sons murdered at a sheep shearing (2 Samuel 13:28–29). (Amnon is killed, but the other sons escape.) Significantly, David's name is absent from this part of the story, indicative of the erasure of his identity, agency, and power, as his sins bleed into or blend with those of his sons. The story of David's sin thus becomes a matter not merely of life but also of legacy. His familial descendants, and indeed the entire Jewish people, bear the consequences of his sins.

The Many Metaphors of Sin

How does Jewish tradition visualize or conceptualize sin? In the story of David and Bathsheba, we encounter sin as a generalized "*ra'ah,*" an evil that God can see and also as something that can be transferred onto others. The word "sin" (*ḥet*) itself appears only twice in the story and in the same verse, that is, when David confesses his sin, and God (through Nathan) immediately promises to put David's sin away. Paradoxically, it is David's use of the verb "*ḥatati*" to describe his behavior that allows him to escape death if not other forms of punishment. By saying "I have sinned before God," David effectively renounces his prior attempt to keep his behavior hidden and holds his deeds up to the divine light.

Jewish tradition, of course, employs a variety of words and metaphors for sin. These metaphors include visual, tactile, directional, and relational aspects. As Marc Zvi Brettler notes,

> The Bible is rich in sin and sin terminology. It is said that some native peoples in the Arctic have many words for snow; similarly, the Bible has many words for sin, including, most commonly *avon* (appearing 233 times), *pesha* (93 times), and *chet* (34 times). The words are often used interchangeably, however, making it difficult to know whether each expressed a different nuance. Etymologically, each comes from its own metaphorical sphere:[32] *avon* is related to words for "twisting, erring"; pasha, "to rebel," and *chet*, to miss the mark.[33]

From these terms alone, sin emerges as an action that unfolds in time and space, with physical as well as relational implications. Something tangible happens, changes, or results from sin. It has an effect that can be weighed or visualized. Things become bent or misshapen. An entity misses its target or strays from a path—an intention, a life. A relationship is violated.

In the Bible, sin is often a verb but also a thing with heft. This understanding of sin as a massive thing undergirds the use, throughout the Bible, of the verb נשא (*nasah*, to bear or to carry) to refer both to punishment of sin and to divine forgiveness. As Gary Anderson explains,

> Even in our own day we are prone to characterize the cares of the world or the guilt of sin as pressing down on one's shoulders. One frequently sees this illustrated by a figure walking around hunched over. The metaphoric weight with which the person is burdened is more than mere metaphor; it has all the appearances of being something real. In the process of forgiving sin, God picks up and carries away our weighty sins.[34]

Anderson explains that the idea of sin as weight undergirds the biblical Yom Kippur ritual of the scapegoat (Lev. 16:21–22), where a pack animal is designated by the High Priest to bear away the sins of the people to a place beyond human habitation and divine view.[35] "The weight of iniquity, our text presumes, cannot be annihilated after it has been created, but it can be banished."[36] Marc Brettler identifies the same notion in 2 Samuel 12:

> The careful reader will observe that the same physical understanding of sin as something concrete that can be transferred, removed, or otherwise dispelled as something no longer present stands behind the David and Bathsheba episode in 2 Samuel 12. The text there says after his adulterous union with Bathsheba, David's sins are *"he'evired"*—"moved," or "transferred," to the guiltless offspring that results.[37]

The weightiness of sin is reflected in David's attempt to stay the decree against his newborn child. David fasts and lies "all night on the earth" and refuses to be raised up from the ground (1 Samuel 12:16–17), as if to bear and maintain the weight of the sin on his own person.

According to the logic of this particular metaphor, sin can never move or lift itself of its own accord; it needs to be assumed, in the form of punishment, or borne away in the form of forgiveness.

Herein lies another major distinction between the biblical or Jewish worldview and that of Woody Allen's *Crimes and Misdemeanors*. When

Figure 5.3. *Crimes and Misdemeanors*, Judah's Confession.

Judah Rosenthal "confesses" his story to Cliff Stern, he describes how his guilt-ridden murderer wakes up one morning: "The sun is shining, his family is around him and mysteriously, the crisis has lifted."

Like the prophet Nathan in 2 Samuel 12, Judah refers to the light of the sun not as a witnessing eye, rather as proof of how passing time attenuates the significance of human deeds. Judah also uses the metaphor of lifting or carrying, but in marked contrast to the biblical text, the lifting here occurs involuntarily, without any form of action on God's or man's part. Instead of sin, Judah speaks of a "crisis," an otherwise inert, impersonal state that suddenly and unwittingly alters, leaving Judah free to evade responsibility for what he has done.

Because the biblical David confesses and faces his sinfulness, Jewish tradition anoints him a paragon of penitence, as is evident in Psalm 51, where David's curt, unelaborated confession in Samuel 12:13 ("I have sinned against the Lord") is transformed into an extended penitential script:

> 1) For the Leader. A Psalm of David;
> 2) When Nathan the prophet came unto him, after he had gone in to Bathsheba.
> 3) Be gracious unto me, O God, according to Your mercy; according to the multitude of Your compassions blot out my transgressions (*pesha'ai*).
> 4) Wash me thoroughly from my iniquity (*'avoni*), and cleanse me from my sin (*ḥatati*).
> 5) For I know my transgressions (*pesha'ai*); and my sin (*ḥatati*) is ever before me.
> 6) Against You, You only, have I sinned (*ḥatati*), and done that which is evil (*hara*) in Your sight; that You may be justified when You speak, and be in the right when You judge.
> 7) Behold, I was brought forth in iniquity (*'avon*), and in sin (*ḥet*) did my mother conceive me.
> 8) Behold, You desire truth in the inward parts; make me, therefore, to know wisdom in my inmost heart.
> 9) Purge me with hyssop, and I shall be clean; wash me, and I shall be whiter than snow.
> 10) Make me to hear joy and gladness; that the bones which You have crushed may rejoice.

11) Hide Your face from my sins, and blot out all my iniquities.
12) Create me a clean heart, O God; and renew a steadfast spirit within me.
13) Cast me not away from Your presence; and take not Your holy spirit from me.
14) Restore unto me the joy of Your salvation; and let a willing spirit uphold me.
15) Then will I teach transgressors (*poshʻim*) Your ways; and sinners (*hataʼim*) shall return unto You.
16) Deliver me from bloodguiltiness, O God, God of my salvation; so shall my tongue sing aloud of Your righteousness.
17) O Lord, open my lips; and my mouth shall declare Your praise.
18) For You delight not in sacrifice, else would I give it; You have no pleasure in burnt-offering.
19) The sacrifices of God are a broken spirit; a broken and a contrite heart, O God, You will not despise.
20) Do good in Your favor unto Zion; build the walls of Jerusalem.
21) Then will You delight in the sacrifices of righteousness, in burnt-offering and whole offering; then will they offer bullocks upon Your altar.[38]

Psalm 51 includes the three most common biblical Hebrew words for sin—*pesha*, *het*, and *ʻavon*—and beseeches God to forgive these sins through cleansing, purification, or erasure. Verse 7 even goes so far as to refer to the speaker as having been conceived in sin, indirectly recalling the sinful conception of the child born to David and Bathsheba.[39] At the same time, the Psalm omits all reference to the verb *nasa*, with its implications of sin as a massive weight that needs to be borne or lifted away. Instead, the Psalm seems to focus on sin as a visual mark, stain, or pollutant that can be cleansed and/or ritually purified. The speaker of the Psalm petitions God to "blot out" his transgressions (Psalm 51:3) and "wash" him "thoroughly of his iniquity" (verse 4);[40] "Hide Your face from my sins" (verse 11), he pleads, and "Cast me not from your presence" (verse 13). In exchange for this forgiveness, the speaker announces a readiness to serve as a symbolic exemplar, to "teach transgressors Your ways" and "sing aloud of Your righteousness" (2 Samuel 12:15, 16).

What underlies this metaphorical shift away from sin as "thing of weight" to a stain or impurity that needs laundering, purification, or blotting out by God? What is the relationship between this figuration of sin and the speaker's anxious desire to remain in God's presence? According to Edward Dalglish, "with reference to Israel, Judah, and Jerusalem, the phrase 'to be cast out form the face of Jahweh' is synonymous with the end of national existence."[41] To what extent should we consider this fear of being cast away from God's presence, then, as an expression of collective anxiety about the future of the nation?

The speaker's call to God in the second last verse of the Psalm to "build the walls of Jerusalem" suggests a possible post-Temple context for the Psalm. As Edward Dalglish again suggests, this verse represents the walls of Jerusalem as requiring rebuilding, suggesting an exilic date for the Psalm.[42] Rather than representing sovereignty and power, then, the David-like speaker of this poem appears to be speaking for Jews who lack both visual signs of God's presence and the ritual means of bearing away the weight of sin and of purification afforded by the Temple. The speaker mentions cultic details such as purging with hyssop but seems to be dependent on God, rather than the Temple cult, to carry out an imagined or yearned-for ritual. The visual nature of sin and forgiveness in this Psalm paradoxically offers an imaginative way to expunge the everyday evidence of punishment in exile and to visualize a return to God's providential precincts. If God can simply do away with the sign of sin, the sinning psalmist can be born again spiritually. As James Kugel writes, "Psalm 51 is about this 'sense of sin,' the feeling of being stained with impurity that will not go away and that now threatens everything . . . What he needs, what he asks for, is a fresh start."[43]

But David Never Sinned!

According to Amos Hakham, the absence in the Psalm of specific references to David's actual sins as described in 2 Samuel 11, despite the opening tag that connects it with the story of David and Bathsheba, suggests that this Psalm is not meant to be construed as David's prayer alone, but rather as a prayer "for the mouths of all of Israel in every generation."[44]

To be sure, adducing King David as the paradigm of sin and penitence carries its own risks and anxieties, as made evident in a famous and perplexing Talmudic passage from BT Shabbat 56a:

> R. Samuel b. Nahmani said in R. Jonathan's name: Whoever says that David sinned is merely erring, for it is said, And David behaved himself wisely in all his ways: and the Eternal was with him (1 Samuel 18:14). Is it possible that sin came to his hand, yet the Divine Presence was with him? Then how do I interpret, How have you despised the word of the Eternal, to do that which is evil in His sight? (2 Samuel 12:9). He wished to do [evil], but did not. Rab observed: Rabbi, [Judah the Prince] who is descended from David, seeks to defend him, and expounds [the verse] in David's favor [*mehapekh vedareish*]. [Thus:] The "evil" [mentioned] here is unlike every other "evil" [mentioned] elsewhere in the Torah. For of every other evil [mentioned] in the Torah it is written, "and he did," whereas here it is written, "to do": [this means] that he desired to do, but did not. You have smitten Uriah the Hittite with the sword (2 Samuel 12:9): you should have had him tried by the Sanhedrin, but did not. And you have taken his wife to be your wife: you had marriage rights in her. For R. Samuel b. Nahmani said in R. Jonathan's name: Every one who went out in the wars of the house of David wrote a bill of divorcement for his wife, for it is said, and bring these ten cheeses unto the captain of their thousand, and look how your brethren fare, and take their pledge ["*arubatham*"]. What is meant by "*arubatham*"? R. Joseph learned: The things, which pledge man and woman [to one another]. And you have slain him with the sword of the children of Ammon: just as you are not [to be] punished for the sword of the Ammonites, so you are not [to be] punished for [the death of] Uriah the Hittite. What is the reason? He was rebellious against royal authority, saying to him, and my lord Joab, and the servants of my lord, are encamped in the open field [etc].[45]

On the face of it, this Talmudic passage seems absurd, even nihilistic in its implications. How is it even conceivable to assert that David did not sin? The whole point of 2 Samuel 11–12 is to "out" David as a sinner who did evil in the eyes of God. David himself confesses as much, and Psalm 51 memorializes this confession, asking God to blot out and cleanse him of his acknowledged sin. What, then, would compel R. Samuel b. Nahmani and R. Judah the Prince along with him to be *mehapeikh vedareish*, to overturn the plain meaning of the text and reinterpret it in such a countertextual manner? Does he mean to suggest that, in repenting, David was so successful that he managed to erase and blot out all previous evidence of his cardinal sins?

Or is this text simply meant to be read figuratively? After all, R. Samuel bar Nahmani's assertion appears as part of a string of similarly constructed statements, all of which attempt to deny or reinterpret the accepted sins of biblical figures, including Reuben, the sons of Samuel, and the sons of Eli. According to a nonliteral reading, R. Samuel b. Nahmani's statements reflect a concern that such fallible biblical figures not become sources of moral disillusionment or objects of derision. Of course David, Reuben, and the sons of Eli and Samuel sinned! R. Samuel bar Nahmani simply wishes to issue a homiletic warning against jumping to hasty judgments of prominent personages, especially since everybody sins.[46]

That said, viewing this Talmudic passage in context also gives rise to a very different and in fact more literal interpretation, one that calls attention to the difference between Samuel Bar Nachman's assertions about David and those about Reuben or the sons of Eli. There is not much at stake in a debate about the sins of Reuben and the sons of Eli and Samuel. The biblical text sidelines all of them in any case and curtails their future influence. David, however, is another matter. His influence and legacy are meant to endure. "*David melekh Yisra'el ḥai vekayam*" (David King of Israel is alive and well) was the watchword that R. Judah the Prince instructed his disciples to use in when sending the message that it was time to sanctify the month, the waxing moon serving as a symbol for the future redemption of Israel.[47] Messiah is supposed to issue from David's seed, and thus the future redemption of the people depends on the House of David being "alive" in our imagination and worthy of occupying that place of pride.

It is for these reasons, I would argue, that R. Judah the Prince, identified in the Talmudic passage as "descended from David," suddenly makes an appearance in this last homily of the string for the purpose of reinterpreting the verses of 2 Samuel 11–12 in David's favor. The extreme nature of David's sins, the sense that they might be too weighty to be forgiven or for the people ever to be given a fresh start, seems to provoke serious anxiety in this sage and leader, scion of David's own Judean house. This anxiety in turn drives an effort to turn over David's sins through legal rationalization and textual manipulation.

In a world where rabbinic learning and authority come to replace both Temple ritual and sovereignty, one way to counter the effect of sin is to overturn it imaginatively, thereby facilitating a kind of hermeneutical atonement or compensation. To be sure, Rabbi Judah the Prince's reinterpretation of David's behavior is brazen, willful, even disturbing. It comes not to negate the idea of sin, however, but to uphold its reality and its dire implications. It also comes as a way of maintaining an imagined, hoped-for ideal of future redemption in the face of weighty, seemingly intractable sin and punishment.

What We Might See: Real and Imagined Worlds

According to film and religion scholar John Lyden, "the ritual function of religion is to unite the conception of how the world is with the conception of how it ought to be."[48] In this sense, according to Lyden, *Crimes and Misdemeanors* constitutes a religious work, insofar as the "the relationship between the ideal and the real is a major subject" in the film.[49]

As Gary Commins argues, "It would be foolish to say Allen's works function to bring the world to faith in God. But by setting before our eyes something of the absurdity of life, he does make faith in God, where it exists, more faithful to human experience—truly an appropriate act of loyal opposition."[50]

If so, the ending of the film calls out for interpretation. Is it not remarkable that despite the overall pessimistic message of the film, Allen chooses to end the film the way he does? The blind rabbi Ben dances with his daughter to "I'll be Seeing You in All the Old Familiar Places," as if to defy the reality of his blindness.[51] All the while, the voice-over of the existentialist Professor Louis Levy plays in the background:

> We're all faced throughout our lives with agonizing decisions, moral choices. Some are on a grand scale; most of these choices are on lesser points. But we define ourselves by the choices we have made. We are, in fact, the sum total of our choices. Events unfold so unpredictably, so unfairly. Human happiness does not seem to be included in the design of creation. It is only we, with our capacity to love, that give meaning to the indifferent universe. And yet, most human beings seem to have

the ability to keep trying and even try to find joy from simple things, like their family, their work, and from the hope that future generations might understand more.[52]

How does one process this statement? At this point in the film, we already know about Professor Levy's suicide; clearly his existentialist philosophy proved insufficient to sustain him in his own life, bringing to mind the suicides of such other Holocaust survivor intellectuals as Primo Levi and Bruno Bettelheim.[53] All this notwithstanding, do we not still feel some note of optimism at the end of this film? Are Professor Levy's words not remembered as an enduring ideal? Does the blind rabbi not still evince a more laudable point of view and way of life than that of Judah and Cliff? And do we not continue to find hope in future generations that, rather than carry on our sins and mistakes, they will learn, do better, and know more? And so we have it, an unlikely pair: Rabbi Judah the Prince and Woody Allen, creator of villain Judah Rosenthal, yearning together for a closing of the gap between the real world and the ideal, longing together, against all evidence to the contrary, for a restoration of virtue and hope.

6

Forrest Gump

Cleverness and Simplicity

Holy Fools

Our discussion of *Crimes and Misdemeanors* introduced us to an array of clever bur corrupt people and to the frequent gap, in both biblical and modern sources, between intellectual, professional, and worldly attainment, on the one hand, and moral virtue, on the other. Given all that, one wonders: what religious value does Jewish tradition attach to cleverness and, conversely, to simplicity? What happens when a virtuous or innocent simpleton sets out on the "road" of personal and historical experience?

The runaway hit of 1994, *Forrest Gump* is the story of Forrest Gump of Greenbow, Alabama, a supposed "fool" or "gump" who bumps up against all the major events and traumas of his generation but demonstrates the kind of virtue, moral intelligence, and success that defy his low IQ.[1] The Winston Groom novel that serves as the basis of the film begins with the first-person narrator both declaring and repudiating his identity as an idiot along the lines of I. B. Singer's "Gimpel the Fool": "I been an idiot since I was born. My IQ is near 70, which qualifies me, so they say. Probly, tho, I'm closer to bein' an imbecile or maybe even a moron, but personally, I'd rather think of myself as like a *halfwit*, or something—and not no idiot . . ."[2] In the film, this simultaneous acceptance and rejection of Forrest's status as an idiot finds expression in Forrest's frequent use his mother's phrase "Stupid is as stupid does." On the one hand, Forrest's pronouncement of this aphorism—meant as a retort to those who ask him, "Are you stupid or something?"—reinforces his idiot status insofar as Forrest seems to parrot his mother unthinkingly. On the other hand, this aphorism rejects the idea of Forrest as idiot, saying that a person ought to be measured not by his words but by his deeds. A supposedly intelligent person, like President Nixon or George Wallace, can render himself stupid by acting meanly or being ethically idiotic. And a supposed fool like Forrest can render himself wise by acting kindly, that is, by being ethically wise.

To be sure, Forrest's character type has considerable precedent in Western literature. In Christian tradition, the type of the wise or holy fool can be traced to St. Paul's teaching in 1 Corinthians 4:10 that the Christian is a fool in the eyes of the world.[3] In the Middle Ages and the Renaissance, the idiot was regarded "as being under the special protection of God. He was also often regarded as an 'innocent' or a 'natural,' a child of nature who lived without thought of the past or the future and was consequently happier than the supposedly wise man."[4] In Shakespeare's plays, the fool hardly comes across as a fool, but rather as a marginal social figure of considerable intelligence who is given license in the court to defy social convention and identify people's foibles, thereby conveying deep wisdom. In Voltaire's *Candide* (1759), the credulous optimism of the fool becomes the target of satire; at the same time, the sufferings endured by the itinerant, bumbling Candide occasion a critique of the cruelty of human nature. On balance, in much of this literature of the fool, the whole question of who is wise and who is foolish is thrown into question, the purported fool often emerging as a preferred alternative to the corrupt cleverness of the worldly or the "wise."

The same pattern obtains in *Forrest Gump*. As said previously, Forrest may not be intellectually gifted, but he does good works, often in stark contrast to the fickleness and malevolence of others. He is devoted and constant to those he loves. Over the course of his life as depicted in the film, which coincides with the Civil Rights movement; the Vietnam War and the anti-War movement; the assassinations of JFK, RFK, Martin Luther King Jr., and John Lennon; the Watergate scandal; the sexual revolution; the hippie counterculture with its promotion of psychedelic drug use; and the AIDS epidemic, Forrest grows up, becomes a star football player, decorated soldier, champion ping-pong player, shrimp boat captain, and millionaire businessman, but he never loses his sense of commitment to his close friends and family members regardless of their race, gender, or disabilities. The world may have become more complicated, jaded, and disillusioned, but Forrest maintains his emotional and moral compass. Styles and mores change many times over, but Forrest retains nearly everything about himself, including his style of dress and his crew cut. Only once, during his cross-country running trip back and forth across the United States (four times), does he ever let his hair grow, but more about that later.

Forrest Gump not only highlights Forrest's kindhearted constancy and simple virtue but also links it causally with stupendous wealth and achievement in ways that some intellectuals and scholars of American culture have found deeply problematic. According to critic Dave Kehr, Forrest survives and succeeds in the film precisely "because he isn't very smart," suggesting a reactionary bias against intellectualism or even ambition:

> He reacts, he runs, he remains magnificently blank, allowing those around him to read whatever they want into him (as do the crowds he attracts to his late guru phase, running aimlessly across the country). He is the feather presented in Zemeckis's magical opening, buffeted by the breeze, carried along by fate and luck.... But while this is a lovely image (and certainly one of the most sublime creations of modern special effects technology), it is not a comforting or a complacent one. Only by going along, by surrendering your will and identity, by refusing to see the horror around you, can you make it in America. Those near Forrest who try to stand up, to register a protest or to alter their fate, are soon struck down. Ambition is fatal: Jenny wants to become famous as a singer. Bubba wants to succeed as a businessman. But it's Forrest who achieves both fame and success, by the purest of chance, while Bubba and Jenny die pointless, early deaths, victims of war and disease respectively.[5]

Along similar lines, Thomas B. Beyers describes *Forrest Gump* as a conservative, Reagan-era film. According to Beyers's scathing critique, *Forrest Gump*

1. distorts and flattens out history
2. fantasizes idiotically about racial reconciliation (through Forrest's relationship with Bubba and his family and his "role" in the experience of desegregation), but in reality co-opts black aspiration for the cause of white entrepreneurship

3. erases feminism (it is one of the only movements important to this period that is not represented in the film) yet elevates Forrest as a sensitive new-age husband and father
4. punishes political opposition (the antiwar movement) and countercultural experimentation to death, as evidenced so clearly in the death of Jenny to HIV.[6]

Kehr and Beyers are not unique in their opposition to what they perceive as the right-wing message of the film. In spite of, or perhaps because of its stupendous popularity and commercial success, *Forrest Gump* has become the film that American intellectuals love to hate.

I'd like to go on the record, though, as an intellectual who thinks that the meaning of *Forrest Gump* is not that simple. Rather than celebrating anti-intellectualism and simplemindedness, I'd like to suggest that the feather sequence highlighted by Kehr, and by extension much of the film, hermeneutically buffets us as "readers," carrying us up and along its interpretive road, sliding us off the shoulder of one interpretation and onto the sidewalk of another. There are moments, as when Forrest picks up the feather that has fallen by his feet and places it securely into his copy of *Curious George*, when we feel, like Kehr and Beyers, that we have trapped the meaning of this film between the pages of our critical "book."

And there are other moments, when the feather slides out from inside the book, when we become unsettled by this prior reading and curious about other potential interpretations.

We consider the film's immense appeal and popularity and wonder: is it fair to dismiss and deny the power that Forrest's goodness and constancy have had on all these viewers? Are they all hopeless dupes? When Bubba and Forrest's mother die and Forrest tersely encapsulates his feelings of despair in the words "And that's all I have to say about that," do we not perceive great wisdom in his restraint? When Forrest watches Jenny throw rocks at her father's old house and says, "Sometimes there just aren't enough rocks," do we really feel, in our verbal sophistication, that we could say it any better?

To be sure, there are times when we raise our eyebrows at Forrest's cluelessness. When, at the opening of the film, Forrest calls attention to the seemingly comfortable shoes of the black nurse sitting next to him on the bus stop bench, and the nurse replies that her feet hurt, we wonder whether Forrest has the capacity to understand what it means to walk

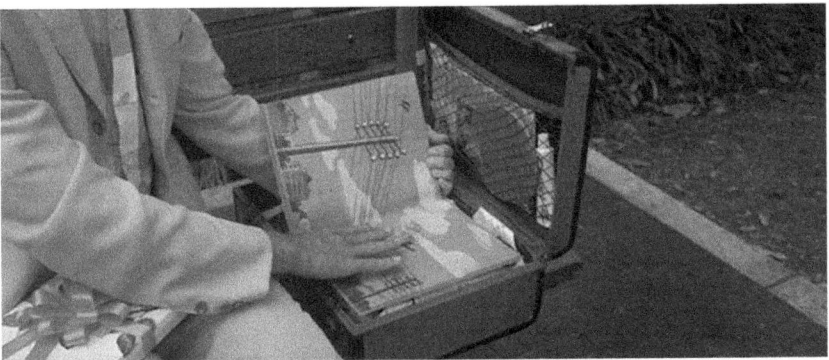

Figure 6.1. *Forrest Gump*, Forrest Traps a Father in his Copy of *Curious George*.

around in other people's shoes. When he names his shrimp boat *Jenny* and hopes "that whatever she is doing is making her happy," while at that very moment a drug-addled Jenny is on the verge of hurling herself over the edge of a balcony, we wonder if he is just too hopelessly naïve. We find it difficult to see him, with his IQ of seventy-five, his literalism, his unthinking meteoric speed, and his accidental fortune, as representing us.

Then again, to understand and appreciate this film, do we have to assume Forrest represents us? Is the film really advocating a universal dumbing down of American culture? Isn't that itself an idiotic reading, one that entirely misses the point of this long-standing Western trope of the holy or wise fool, a clever invention meant to satirize those who pretend to virtue while practicing vice, who use the human tool of cleverness to dubious ends?

And what about the self-conscious and satirical use of technology in the film? If the message of the film is backward and retrograde, what does one make of the fact that the film demonstrates such advanced technical wizardry, including the feather sequence and the frequent insertion of Forrest's image into historical political footage from the 1960s, 1970s, and 1980s? Indeed, a self-consciousness pervades the way in which this technique is employed, which supports a more ironic counterreading. As Steven D. Scott observes, "Gump himself flaunts the techniques, waving to the camera, for example, before he disappears into the University of Alabama after picking up Vivien Malone's books in the George Wallace sequence."[7] In fact, the very first instance of the use of this device—the sequence that places an image of Tom Hanks/Forrest in a scene from D. W. Griffiths' famously racist classic film *The Birth of a Nation* to explain the origin of his name—typifies the complex, postmodern uses of this technique. Forrest tells the black nurse sitting next to him on the bench that his mother named him after an ancestor, Nathan Bedford Forrest, a supposed Civil War hero who helped found the Ku Klux Klan. Watching this scene, we gasp at Forrest's obliviousness in choosing to tell this story to a Southern black woman. As the scene progresses, however, we discover that Forrest was given this name not out of veneration for this racist ancestor, but as an object lesson on the effects of moral idiocy. "Mama said the Forrest part was to remind me that sometimes we all do things that, well, just don't make no sense."

What exactly doesn't make sense? Forrest's mother's choice of this name? Nathan Bedford Forrest's decision to found the Ku Klux Klan? Forrest Gump's decision to talk about it? According to Steven D. Scott, this statement itself is hard to interpret in any straightforward way: "In fact, Gump's naming continues the kind of double (or multiple) coding that I have begun to point out as nearly ubiquitous in the film, and which Linda Hutcheon has claimed is the essence of postmodernism."[8]

Forrest himself experiences many historical events that "just don't make no sense," and his reactions to these experiences provoke contradictory interpretations. These contradictory or mixed meanings, I would argue, are especially evident in the film's many references and representations of the American road. Though not typically seen in this way, *Forrest Gump* is a road movie, but of an unconventional sort. In the American road movie tradition, the road is often presented as weightless, fast, automated, transforming.[9] Road imagery proliferates in this film, but despite his late twentieth-century context, Forrest is never associated with an automobile. On several occasions in the film, Forrest boards buses, but, contrary to the idea of bus and train travel as fast, free, accessible, and democratic, these bus journeys are never unencumbered or unfettered for Forrest. The first time he rides a school bus as a child, no one, with the exception of one child at the back—the abused, impoverished Jenny—agrees to sit next to him. The second time he boards a bus (as a soldier in the US Army), only Bubba, Forrest's black counterpart, agrees to have Forrest share his seat. At the end of the film, Forrest waits for a bus, and it is in this waiting, rather than in boarding the bus, that his story unfolds. And Forrest never gets on that bus. Instead, he runs the few blocks to Jenny's apartment, reinforcing the film's association of Forrest with a simpler, nonmechanized form of road travel.

Forrest's distance from the mechanized American road casts a shadow on the idea of American mobility and the American Dream. The road motif plays a significant role in Forrest's Vietnam experiences, but again with a satirical result. The army may advertise itself as a context where you can "Be all that you can be," but in the case of Forrest's buddy Bubba, a young man obsessed with the entrepreneurial dream of being a shrimp boat captain, all that he can be is dead. Many of the Vietnam scenes in the film take place along roads, and although the trip to Vietnam has expanded the road map of Forrest's life, the roads on this map are filled with hidden mines and buried traps. According to the logic of its road imagery, one of the ostensible messages of *Forrest Gump* is the late twentieth-century end of the American dream, the closing down of its roads and opportunities.[10]

And yet again, that is only one possible interpretation. For while buses in this film fail to deliver on the promise of a meaningful or transformative ride (see, for example, the scene where Jenny joins her abusive boyfriend in boarding a bus back from Washington, DC, to Berkeley, a moment when it is clear she is on the road to absolutely nowhere), and while unchanging Forrest represents the very opposite of the Jack Kerouac hipster on the road, the film is built around images of Forrest running down the various roads, each time with spectacular success. The first time Jenny exhorts Forrest to run away from his tormentors ("Run, Forrest, Run!"), he miraculously bursts out of the restraints of his braces and outruns his bike-riding pursuers, even though they have the advantage of wheels and gears. Fast forward a number of years, and a teenaged Forrest manages to outrun the same bullies who are chasing him in a truck. Forrest's ability to command the road on foot simultaneously deflates and reinflates the ideological wheels of American freedom and mobility on the road.

The same mixed message emerges when one attempts to chart the course of Forrest's various journeys. On the one hand, Forrest's running reinforces the idea of linear movement and progress. When properly directed, Forrest knows how to run a straight line, from Jenny or from his Shrimp boat named *Jenny*, all the way home to his (ailing) mama or from one end of the football field to another. On the other hand, Forrest often seems to be running in circles, as represented linguistically by the circular, repetitious structure of Jenny's exhortation: "Run, Forrest, Run!"

In Vietnam, Forrest achieves distinction as a soldier not because he knows how to run a straight line and get from point A to point B, but because he runs back and forth, doubling back to save his friend Bubba. Bubba dies, of course, but Forrest manages to save Lieutenant Dan, a victory born of virtue and speed that is tempered or undercut by the amputation of Lieutenant Dan's legs. Forrest achieves fame as a ping-pong player, taking him further along the Asian road to China. Of course, ping-pong is not a game of getting from point A to point B, but rather of back and forth, of rally and return.

"It used to be," Forrest says, sitting at that bus stop bench in Savannah and reflecting on his running prowess, "I ran to get where I was going; I never thought it would take me anywhere." There is a tautological quality to this statement, of course, which I think encapsulates the workings of road imagery and directionality in this film.

Consider, for example, the road sequence in Forrest's long stint of cross-country running. In the absence of an explanation for his running, people elevate Forrest (like Jerzy Kosinski's Chance the Gardener in *Being There*[11]) to the level of spiritual guru and project their own meanings onto his running. Their over-cleverness about why Forrest runs becomes an occasion of satire, mocking American pretensions to understanding as well as the yawning spiritual void that their embrace of Forrest's running seems to fill, albeit temporarily.

In recounting his story, Forrest supplies two possible interpretations for why he ran, the first unthinking, the second more considered. On the one hand, he says that he just felt like running; on the other, he invokes the wisdom of his mother and says that he was running to put his past behind him. Neither of these explanations appears entirely correct. After all, Forrest only begins running after the shock of Jenny's departure; when she leaves, one might say, he suffers an experience of abandonment and loss that he cannot bear standing still. As for the claim that he is running to put the past behind him, Forrest never really achieves that, for all of his roads lead back to home and to his past—to his mother and to Jenny. On a geographical level, the back-and-forth quality of this cross-country journey suggests that Forrest's running is not really about leaving the past (point A) to arrive at the future (point B), but about a literal mixing of the two.

During this running sequence, Forrest changes—at least, he seems to change—indicating an emergent, progressive attitude. For the first time, he lets hair and beard grow; as such, he begins to look like one of Jenny's hippy friends or Lieutenant Dan. In the Southwest of the United States, a visual setting evocative of the Western and of the American frontier, he sees rock formations, sunsets, and natural wonders that leave a deep impact.

But after three-plus years, when he finally tires of running, he simply stops and turns in the opposite direction, toward home. Before we know it, he is back in Greenbow, his hair cut short and his old clothes back on. The road for Forrest thus proves to be a means of escape and also the way back home. It is a path to success, yet he gives up the road in its various incarnations to become a gardener, referencing Voltaire's foolish *Candide*, with his message of "Let us cultivate our garden," as well as the innocence of Adam and Eve in the biblical Garden of Eden.

And so, as in the case of the elusive feather flight that begins and ends the film, we have yet another visual sequence that doubles back on itself, another quest for meaning that returns us to where we began.

Toward the end of film, Forrest, who has already married and buried Jenny, now talks to her by her graveside. Until this point in the film, Forrest has told his story while sitting on a bench at a bus stop and much of this storytelling suggests that despite all that he has experienced, he is still very much the naïf he was as a boy. He snacks on a box of chocolates meant as a gift; he talks without regard for whether his bench mates are actually listening; he refers, as a child might, to the wisdom of his mama. Often when he describes an event in his life, the visual account of the story that accompanies his narration exposes the gap between Forrest's innocent view and that of the "real" world around him.

By the time Jenny dies, however, and Forrest stands speaking to her before her grave under their tree, he has fully assumed the role of father, which includes not only feeding little Forrest and reading with him, but also pretending that he doesn't know how to play ping-pong very well so that little Forrest can be less intimidated and learn how to play himself—a kind of benign adult duplicity that Forrest, with his childish literalism and straightforwardness, has never before demonstrated. His announcement that he bulldozed Jenny's father's house shows his understanding of symbolism as well as his fierce loyalty. With regard to the larger questions of personal destiny, Forrest confesses to Jenny that he does not know "if Mama was right or if it was Lieutenant Dan," that is, if each of us has a destiny or "we're all floating accidental-like on a breath but I think maybe it's both. Maybe both happening at the same time." With this, Forrest displays not just constancy and virtue but also some awareness of life's complexities and mixed messages. *Forrest Gump* thus chronicles the progress of time as well as an instance of nostalgic return. It puts to great effect the tools of irony and satire, but also offers a paean to the values of enduring innocence and simplicity.

The Fool in Jewish Tradition

What does Jewish tradition tell us about simple men like Forrest? To what extent does it embrace them as sources of wisdom or as models of virtue? The earliest origins of the notion of the holy fool in Jewish literature, and the reputed source for Paul's New Testament evocation of the holy fool, are in the Hebrew Bible. As Sandra Billington notes, there are two Hebrew words for fool. The Hebrew word *tam* conjures up notions not so much of foolishness as of innocence or blamelessness in the context of worldly depravity and sin. Noah, for example, is designated as an "*ish tzaddik tamim bedorotav,*" a righteous and blameless man in his generations (Gen. 6:9). The other "is the root *ksl*, and contains the willful, evil meanings of folly . . . St. Paul meant the first. The mode of [his] thinking is Hebrew-Aramaic; it arouses pleasant associations of completeness and integrity."[12]

Elsewhere in post-biblical Jewish literature, the fool is commonly referred to as the "schlemiel," literally, *shlomi-el*, meaning "my well-being is God," as in "God watches over fools" (Psalms 116:6). *The American Heritage Dictionary of the English Language* (fourth edition, 2000) defines schlemiel as a "bungler or a dolt," but Jewish literary tradition portrays him much more lovingly. According to Sanford Pinsker, for an often persecuted and powerless Jewish Diaspora community, Jewish humor about the schlemiel constituted an important cultural strategy of self-mockery. Indeed, the schlemiel served as a kind of metaphorical stand-in for the Eastern European shtetl Jew:

> In the face of world's injustice—and, at times, even God's—the shtetl Jew solidly maintained his innocence . . . At the same time, however, they [shtetl Jews] also saw the schlemiel's ineptitude in socioeconomic matters as an extended metaphor of their own. . . . Because he was a character of ineptitude, a bumbling misrepresenter of reality, his comic victimhood helped to sustain those who were only partially schlemiels.[13]

In addition to providing comic relief from the woes of shtetl life, the schlemiel or Jewish simpleton figures prominently in Jewish literary representations of the modern conflict between reason and faith. A good example of this is "A Tale about a Clever Man and a Tam" (*a mayse mit a khokhm un a tam*) (1805) by the Hasidic master Rebbe Nachman of Bratzlav (1772–1810). The story tells of a *khokhm* (clever boy) and a *tam* (simple boy) who grow up as neighbors. The *khokhm* (clever man) goes out on the road, travels from place to place, achieves success in every city and in every endeavor, yet is never satisfied, finding fault with each of his achievements. By contrast, the *tam*, a poor shoemaker, stays home but is happy with his lot. The king of the land hears about these two young men, who, having grown up next door to one another, nevertheless demonstrate widely divergent abilities and dispositions. Curious about this, the king invites them both to his palace. The *tam*/cobbler immediately responds to the king's invitation, travels to the palace, and the king, tired of the intrigue and corruption of his current governor, appoints the *tam* in his stead. By contrast, the *khokhm* responds skeptically, doubts the king's existence, and rejects his invitation. As a result, a role reversal occurs, with the *tam* ascending to prominence while the *khokhm*, so wracked by doubt and dissatisfaction, becomes wholly incapable of any positive action or feeling.

For Rebbe Nachman, himself an intellectually gifted scholar, but one who was worried about the negative spiritual effects of both European rationalist philosophy and rigidly traditional forms of Talmud study, this story upholds the value of faith in the face of stultifying intellectualism and empiricism.[14] Hassidism in general and Rebbe Nachman's brand in particular brought about many innovations, including the use of secular storytelling—reminiscent of the rabbinic mashal—for spiritual purposes. This particular story typifies this kind of inventiveness but also takes a conservative position with regard to the Jewish Enlightenment as an assault on wholehearted, simple faith. According to Rebbe Nachman, "One must believe in God in the way of faith not proof. God says to the one who approaches him: 'Serve me simply and without cleverness, but serve me constantly.'"[15]

Note that in this story, it is the *khokhm* rather than the *tam* who qualifies as a true denizen of the road; until the king beckons him to the palace, the *tam* is perfectly happy to live within the confines of his native village. In part, it is a question of purpose. When the clever man travels the road, he does so restlessly, skeptically. Thus, he gains little in the way of satisfaction or spiritual wisdom. When the *tam* finally travels, he does so with the purpose of meeting the king—a barely veiled metaphor for meeting God—and as a result gains wisdom, as indicated by the end of the story, where the *tam* reprimands the wandering *khokhm* for failing to receive "the grace of simplicity."[16] As Ruth Wisse notes, "the story puts the clever and simple men to a basic pragmatic test, the criteria of which are worldly success, happiness and healthy psychic survival. The simple man is not a natural saint; in fact his reliance on faith seems no more than a compensation for his lack of a power to reason. Nevertheless, and whatever its origins, his trust brings him the trust of others and enables him to take full advantage of opportunities."[17] As we saw above, the personality and career of Forrest Gump follow this model.

The best-known modern American Jewish tale of a *tam* is I. B. Singer's classic story "*Gimpl tam*" (published in Yiddish in 1945 and in an English translation by Saul Bellow in 1953, effectively launching Singer's American career). Singer's Gimpel is a fabulously gullible baker who is repeatedly tricked by his community and cheated on by his wife, yet somehow, in the face of all this, he maintains his faith both in human beings and in God. Bellow translated the title of Singer's Yiddish story as "Gimpel the Fool," but this translation does not quite capture the meanings of the Hebrew/Yiddish word *tam* as used in both the Rebbe Nachman tale and this story. *Tam* variably means complete or unblemished, as in the many Biblical uses of this word to describe animals brought as ritual sacrifices or in Solomon's repeated description of the Shulamite in the Song of Songs as *yonati tamati* (my dove my perfect one); mild, as in Genesis 25:27, where the patriarch Jacob is described as an *ish tam* (a mild man, a dweller in tents); or righteous and wholehearted, as in the description of Noah in relation to his wicked generation as an "*ish tzaddik tamim*," or of Job as *tam veyashar*, as a wholehearted and upright man, Job 1:1). Singer's protagonist (like Winston Groom's Forrest) introduces himself at the start of the story not as a fool but as a *tam*. "I am Gimpel *tam*. I don't consider myself an idiot . . . On the contrary. But that's what folks call me."[18] Gimpel's neighbors shower him with mocking epithets and strive to make a fool out of him by taking advantage of his trust. He is good and kind to those around him, even as they cheat and trick him, which renders him ever more idiotic and gullible in their minds. Gimpel is devoted to his family, even though his wife constantly betrays him. He claims to be aware all along that he is being betrayed, which renders him divided in consciousness if not in deed. When Gimpel consults with the rabbi about how he is being treated by the townspeople, the rabbi shores up Gimpel's position, advising that "it is better to be a fool[19] all your days than for one hour to be evil. You are not a fool. They are the fools. For he who causes his neighbor to feel shame loses Paradise himself."[20]

Though foolishly credulous, Gimpel is ethically blameless. That is, until his wife confesses her unfaithfulness and an evil spirit seizes him, telling him that there is no such thing as God and urging him to urinate into the dough for the next day's bread so as to punish all those who have deceived him. Gimpel takes steps to execute this plan but is ultimately prevented from completing it by none other than his dead wife, Elka, who appears to him in a dream and scolds him for betraying his nature as a *tam*. "Because I was false, was everything else false too? . . . I'm paying for it all, Gimpel. They spare you nothing here."[21] So shaken is Gimpel by all of this that he resolves that he must leave his native village and go out on the road, becoming a kind of archetypal Jewish wanderer/sage: "I wandered over the land, and good people did not neglect me. After many years I became old and white; I heard a great deal, many lies and falsehoods, but the longer I lived the more I understood that there were really no lies. Whatever doesn't really happen is dreamed at night."[22]

What does one make of Gimpel's wise assertions at the end of the story? Given his personal experiences and the post-Holocaust publication date of the story, his abiding faith strikes the reader both as both perspicacious and preposterous. After all, who, before the death camps, could ever imagine such horrors coming to pass, yet here they are in the historical record. Who in their right mind could believe in God after all of this, yet is the alternative so appealing and exalted an option? The ambiguity of the story's end is crucial to its power and to our mixed assessment of Gimpel's character. On the one hand, his abiding goodness and faithfulness render him a model to which to aspire; on the other hand, he knows he is being duped and nevertheless allows it all to happen, a nod perhaps to those Jews who continued to believe in the goodness of God and the glory of European civilization right up to the gas chamber. The example of Gimpel can be marshaled to make a traditionalist argument that given all this, what our benighted world needs now is neither intellectualism nor Western sophistication but the steadfast belief and constancy of a Gimpel, for tomorrow we shall die. At the same time, Gimpel's story also reads as a subversive object lesson against accepting whole cloth any philosophical doctrine or religious dogma, especially after the Shoah.

Singer himself seemed to have embodied the contradictory meanings of this story. His father, a Hassidic rabbi, was a great and staunch believer. His mother was something of a skeptic. "The net result," said Singer, "is that I remained both a doubter and a man of faith."[23] According to biographer Paul Kresh, "Singer often said that he himself was Gimpel, a statement that should not be taken too literally. Gimpel is everything that Isaac [Bashevis Singer was] not—a victim, cuckold, shnorrer, butt of the world's jokes."[24] Perhaps in identifying himself as Gimpel, Singer was pointing to the wiser Gimpel of the ending of the story, the storyteller, who like Singer himself, left his hometown for the United States, and went out "into the world" to spin yarns. Or perhaps Singer identified within himself that paradoxical mix of critical awareness and gullible faith that characterizes his lovable protagonist?

One way to understand the paradoxical nature of Gimpel is by way of Paul Ricouer's theory of "second naïveté."[25] In his book *The Symbolism of Evil*, Ricoeur writes the following about faith in the modern age:

> In every way, something has been lost irremediably lost: immediacy of belief. But if we can no longer live the great symbolisms of the sacred in accordance with the original belief in them, we can, we modern men, aim at a second naïveté in and through criticism. In short, it is by interpreting that we can hear again.[26]

For those of us who live in and embrace the modern world and who accept the challenges of history, science, philosophy, and the academic study of religion, Ricoeur suggests that there is no easy way back to the garden of original innocence or faith. We cannot really emulate the simplicity of a Forrest or Gimpel, at least not according to the simplest reading of their stories. Of course, as I have attempted to show in this chapter, their stories prove to be not that simple after all. They, like we, embody all kinds of contradictions. Each of them stands for steadfast, homegrown simplicity, but at crucial junctures, each of them must leave home, wander the world, and find a way to reconstitute himself. As readers of these stories, we ourselves become interpretive wanderers, straying from one interpretation to another in an effort to arrive at an ever-elusive hermeneutic conclusion. According to Ricoeur, that itself—the enterprise of interpretation—is a way of hearing the sacred. We embrace the task and take to the road of reading religiously in an act of willed innocence or wholeness, in the hope of discovering some new, even clever understanding. We do not play the part of the fool. Nor do we assume that tradition is merely the province of the simpleton. We go back to the sources, plant our new gardens of learning, and hope they will grow and prosper.

7
───

The King's Speech

Speaking God's Word

If *Forrest Gump* demonstrates the possibility of attaining wisdom despite apparent intellectual limitation, *The King's Speech* (dir. Tom Hooper, 2010), winner of several Academy Awards, including Best Picture, tells a paradoxical story about the continuity of royal tradition through its disruption and about the power and significance of speech as demonstrated by a man with a speech defect.

The film opens in 1925 at the closing ceremonies of the Empire Exhibition at Wembley Stadium in England, where, for the first time, King George V's second son, Albert, the Duke of York, is scheduled to deliver a radio message on behalf of his father. Before the scene begins, titles inform us that King George rules over an empire that includes one-quarter of the people of the world. Instead of offering a visual representation of empire, however, the film opens with several close views from various directions of the BBC announcer's broadcast microphone: from the right, where it has an almost ballistic appearance; from behind; and from the front, as if to suggest that this new, multidirectional broadcast medium is the very tool and weapon of worldwide rule. Throughout this opening sequence, the camera moves back and forth from the warm, calm, light-brown interior of the broadcast room to the cold, gray stairwell of the stadium, ironically marked above with the sign "WAY OUT," where the Duke waits anxiously to deliver his speech, his breath visible in the cold. Various people attending the Duke, including the unctuous archbishop of Canterbury, offer him blandishments and encouragements, which only intensify his worry. As the Duke awaits his turn at the microphone, the

BBC announcer inside the warm and brightly lit broadcast room performs various ritualistic, preparatory vocal exercises consisting of gargling, vocal spraying and repeated (stuttered) consonants, a foreshadowing of the stuttering that the Duke will not be able to control. These vocal drills also anticipate the regimen of exercises that the Duke/eventual King will have to undertake to overcome his disability. Much of the film is structured in this way, introducing motifs or actions that are repeated and amplified in subsequent scenes, adding meaning and interpretive resonance.

The BBC announcer begins his broadcast by telling his audience that fifty-eight colonies and dominions have participated in this exhibition, making it the largest exhibition staged anywhere in the world. The Duke of York's broadcast, his inaugural appearance on the radio, is thus being made before a geographically vast audience—an announcement that further intensifies the gravity of the moment. As the Duke/Prince approaches the microphone, he, too, like the microphone in the opening scene, is presented from various angles, many of them oblique, blurry, and distorted, highlighting the pressure and scrutiny that he feels. In the background is a large number 2, marking the zone in the stadium but also calling attention to Albert's secondary status, both as a younger brother and as the second (less able) prince to make such a broadcast.

Figure 7.1. *The King's Speech*, The Duke's Speech at Wembley Station.

Everyone in the stadium stands in respect, but this offers no comfort. A horse whinnies, calling to mind such talking equines as the biblical Balaam's she-ass in Numbers 22 and foreshadowing Albert's impending humiliation; even a horse can speak more naturally, more fluently, than Albert, Duke of York.[1] Albert is able to get out only the first half-sentence of his message before he is blocked by his stammer: "I have received a message from his majesty the K—," he says, stumbling of the hard consonant at the beginning of the word "King," the echo from the microphone further accentuating the stammer. Bertie's difficulty pronouncing the word "King" points to the larger drama of speech that will unfold over the course of this film: the eventual need for Bertie to receive and process the mixed messages of his family about his (un)fitness to be king and to assume the responsibility of royal speech.

The next scene occurs in 1934, a full nine years later, marking the end, it would seem, of a series of efforts to cure the Duke's speech problem. The Duke and Duchess have been visited this time by a stuffy, aristocratic, and imperious speech therapist who advocates cigarette smoking to achieve relaxation and open the lungs and who employs the classical method of Demosthenes as his method of treatment. The Duke is instructed to place several glass marbles in his mouth and then is commanded by the therapist, who is photographed from a low angle and very close up so as to evoke a monstrous, looming presence, to read out loud, concentrate, and enunciate. Elizabeth, Albert's ever-supportive wife and a barometer of correct thinking in the film, questions the purpose of using a method that dates back to ancient Greece, asking, "Has it cured anyone since?"[2] The only result of this session, representative of a hyperbolic adherence to tradition and royal protocol, is that Albert, known by his family members as Bertie, swears off all future efforts at speech therapy. That is, until his wife goes to Harley Street and finds him a very different sort of therapist, a failed Aussie actor named Lionel Logue.

From the get-go, Logue, whose office is situated on 146 Harley Street, represents the antithesis of royal etiquette and protocol. The Duchess, having made her appointment under an assumed name, arrives late at the therapist's office, only to find him "just in the loo." When he emerges from the WC, Mr. Logue calls attention to her lateness as well to the absence of the patient, Mr. Johnson—"not a very promising start." Logue says he needs her "hubby" to "pop by" and give his personal details, to which the Duchess replies that she does not have a "hubby," that they never "pop," nor do they discuss their private lives, and that Logue will need to come to them. Logue rejects these conditions forthwith: "My game, my turf, my rules," he says, and then walks away into another room. "And what if my husband is the Duke of York?" calls out the Duchess, causing Mr. Logue himself to be momentarily tongue-tied, signifying, on the one hand, a recognition of their difference in station, and, on the other, a leveling of the playing field between the therapist and the royal stutterer. Logue refers to the Duchess as "Your Royal Highness," but once again insists that for his method to work, the treatment has to occur under conditions of absolute equality, in the safety of his consultation room, no exceptions. The Duchess is on the verge of leaving his office when she shakes his hand and says, "When can you start?"

I have gone to the trouble here of detailing this interaction between Elizabeth and Lionel Logue, conjured up by screenwriter David Seidler in the absence of actual documentation of the Duke/King's meetings with Logue,[3] because it depicts an attempt to strengthen the capacities of the Duke and eventual King through a departure from regular royal practice and an embrace, however reluctant and partial, of liberal, egalitarian values. The pivotal part played by Bertie's wife, Elizabeth, in helping him find and pursue treatment is but one indication of this liberal strain in the film and a harbinger of Elizabeth's celebrated role in shoring up British morale during the German bombing of England during World War II. Note that tradition is hardly abrogated in the film. Rather, it is shored up through a willingness in certain crucial instances to reinterpret protocol and assume a more flexible, more familiar, and less hierarchical approach. A sign of this approach can be seen in the scene immediately thereafter, where a tuxedo-clad Duke gets down on his knees for his daughters and walks like a penguin, as he tells a story of his own devising about a prince who is turned into a penguin by an evil witch and sent to the South Pole, but who manages to swim back to Buckingham Palace and claim his position. This scene emphasizes the Duke's likability, his powers of imagination, and his willingness to laugh at himself. It points to the Duke's sense of being impeded or imprisoned by forces beyond his control but also to his potential, like the penguin in the story, to find his way to the palace of the King should he resolve to get off his high horse and do what it takes.

To be sure, the Duke does not recognize all of this right away. When the Duchess first tells him about Logue, he rebuffs her. The film then cuts to a scene in which Logue auditions for the part of Richard the III (the story of Richard of Gloucester, one of two sons of the Duke of York who is determined to take over the throne of his brother, Edward IV). Logue is quickly dismissed from the audition, told that in his (Australian-accented) reading he does not adequately convey the regal image of a deformed man yearning to be king, a comment that speaks both to Logue's failed thespian aspirations and to Bertie's reluctance to claim the role of king. Immediately thereafter, we see the Duke and Duchess en route to Logue's office for an appointment. At the session, the Duke objects vociferously to Logue's calling him Bertie and to his inquiries about his private life. He evinces a quick temper as well as a combination of haughtiness and insecurity. Logue attempts to prove to Bertie that he can indeed speak by recording Bertie reading Shakespeare's "To Be or Not to Be" soliloquy from *Hamlet* while listening to Mozart's Overture to *The Marriage of Figaro*. Logue operates here on the assumption that stutterers generally do not stammer if they are listening to music or singing. With the earphones on his ears, Bertie manages to read the soliloquy brilliantly but decides, even before hearing the recording, that therapy is not for him. To be in therapy or not be in therapy—and later, to be king or not to be king—these are the two questions either addressed or foreshadowed by this scene and by the choice of this soliloquy.

Only later, at the King's Christmas broadcast, when King George browbeats Bertie into reading out loud, resulting in a terrible bout of stuttering, does Bertie acquiesce to listening to the recording of his fluent reading and henceforth to be treated by Logue. A montage chronicling this therapy, set this time against Mozart's Clarinet Concerto in A Major[4] and interspliced with scenes from various speaking engagements, culminates with Bertie practicing the pronunciation of the word "father," suggesting that Bertie's place in relation to his father, the King, is at the heart of his struggle.

Indeed, by the time we see Bertie practicing the words "father," we have already gained a clear sense of his anxiety with respect to his royal father and his own place within the family line. We also know that his older brother, Edward/David, has been seeing a twice-married woman and that all of this may have implications for the succession. In the Christmas broadcast scene mentioned above, King George refers angrily to his son David's lies about his amorous affairs, as well as to the impending crisis in Europe, with Stalin on one end of the political spectrum and Hitler on the other. The King declares rather intimidatingly that Bertie had better practice speaking into a microphone, however demeaning the show-business aspects of the radio thing may be, because with David shirking his duties, Bertie most likely will have to do a lot more of it.

David's disinterest in living up to his responsibilities to his family and the throne are clearly demonstrated in the various scenes surrounding the King's illness, dementia, and death, where he absents himself from dinner and other duties so that he can whisper telephonic sweet nothings to his lover, Wallis. When George V dies, David bursts into tears on the shoulder of his cold and impassive mother, not because of grief about the passing of his father but because being king means he is now "trapped" and cannot marry Wallis. The remarkable coldness displayed between mother and son contrasts markedly with the warm interactions depicted in the scenes featuring Logue and his family. The rare instances of warmth in the family all occur between Bertie, his wife, and his children. George V's last words before his death (albeit not to Bertie's face) were "Bertie has more guts than the rest of his brothers put together," indicating George's awareness, dementia notwithstanding, of Bertie's superior qualities of character in comparison to the frivolous and selfish David. All this is borne out even more dramatically at a party at David's residence after David is crowned king. When Bertie attempts to talk to David about David's need to fulfill his royal duties, including "to sort out Herr Hitler," David bullies Bertie about his stutter, mocking his efforts to overcome it by way of "elocution lessons," and accuses him, the younger brother, of trying to push him off the throne. Bertie is completely unnerved and silenced by David's aggressive, derisive treatment; his stutter prevents him from eking out any sort of reply. Scenes like this mount the argument that Bertie actually deserves the throne more than David despite or even because of his stutter, insofar as it instills within him a sense of humility and an appreciation for the weight of words.

Still, to carry out the basic duties of kingship, Bertie must learn how to speak serviceably, and for this, he turns to Logue, who represents another way. Bertie's work with Logue involves elements of the Freudian talking cure,[5] physical exercises, and the exploitation of open pathways of speech.

Anger is one such pathway that plays a particularly fascinating role both in blocking and unlocking Bertie's ability to speak. In the session after Bertie is intimidated into silence by David, Logue notes to Bertie, "You don't stammer when you swear," leading to a humorous scene where Bertie unleashes a torrent of profanity, all without stuttering. For Bertie, anger and passion serve as potent tools to help him relax and claim his voice, but when mixed with fear they also lead to outbursts of temper, such as when Logue suggests to Bertie that he would make a good king himself. Bertie becomes so incensed that he breaks off all communication with Logue, only to come back to him when David abdicates and Bertie still cannot adequately discharge his speaking duties. In the aftermath of a disastrous, stutter-marred meeting at the House of Lords, filmed from a variety of distorted and blurred angles so as to underscore Bertie's disorientation and inadequacy, Bertie breaks down to his wife, saying, "I'm not a king, I'm a naval officer, I'm not a king." All this reveals, in poignant but certain terms, Bertie's humility and humanity and at the same time the need for him to finally claim his voice.

Here, too, anger and passion serve a crucial function. During preparations for the coronation ceremony, the Archbishop of Canterbury reveals to the King that his trusted Logue has no proper academic or medical credentials. Bertie confronts Logue in a rage, accusing him of abusing his trust to get a star patient. But Logue turns all of this back on Bertie, brazenly sitting down on the coronation chair, questioning Bertie's qualifications to be king given his reticence to take on the job in the first place, and provoking him to defend both royal tradition and his right to the throne. Bertie's anger and defensiveness climax with the words "I have a voice," marking his readiness at last to assume his regal position and speaking responsibilities.

At the same time, the connection between anger and fluency of speech is shown to be extremely dangerous when released on the world stage. In one memorable scene, the royal family watches a newsreel of Bertie's coronation that is immediately followed by a tape of Hitler speaking at Nuremburg in front of thousands of goose-stepping and saluting Germans. Bertie's eldest daughter, Elizabeth (the present-day Queen), mesmerized and frightened by the spectacle, asks: "Papa, what is he saying?" "I don't know, but he seems to be saying it rather well," answers the King, pointing to the dangers of charismatic, passionate speech when yoked to territorial aggression and genocidal racism. Insofar as Bertie's climactic speech in the film—a rejoinder to his failed speech at Wembley—is an announcement that Britain is now at war with Germany, Bertie's disfluency becomes symbolic of opposition to Nazism and Hitler's fanatical, hate-filled, murderous rhetoric.[6] More specifically, stuttering, a speech impediment that often involves the constriction of breathing and the labored repetition of sounds in a way that blocks fluency, becomes a metaphor for practice, growth, careful intention, and a respect for the gravity of speech.

Figure 7.2. *The King's Speech,* Watching Hitler.

Going back to the title of the film, then, *The King's Speech* takes on multiple meanings, referring to the two speeches that open and close the film, the first halted and unsuccessful and the second successful in spite of its practiced, coached "heaviness." In addition, the title refers to the grave responsibilities of royal speech. Translated into a theological context, *The King's Speech* also hints at the challenge of transmitting the speech or word of God, the divine King, into the human context.

Moses's Speech

All of this brings to mind the story of Moses, the first leader of the Israelites, who demonstrates a similar disposition and reluctance to assume the mantle of leadership because of a general sense of unworthiness as well as a speech impediment. In spite or perhaps because of all of this, Moses rises to become the emblematic speaker of God's word and teacher of the people of Israel.

When God speaks to Moses from the burning bush and asks him to return to Egypt to take the Israelites out of slavery (Ex. 3:10), Moses repeatedly demurs, saying, "Who am I that I should go unto Pharaoh?" (Ex. 3:11). Unlike Pharaoh (and David, prince of Wales), whose claim to power and authority were ordained by birth, Moses sees himself, as Bertie does in *The King's Speech*, as a pretender or interloper, an alien to the natural order. Born a Hebrew slave, raised an Egyptian prince, and now a shepherd in Midian, Moses seems to belong to no people. Within his own Levite family, Moses is second in line to his older brother Aaron and therefore is unqualified by birth to be the leader of his clan. Moses insists that the people will not believe that he has been sent by God and will not heed his voice, prompting God to demonstrate the miraculous power of Moses's staff—a kind of extension or incarnation of God's own long and strong redemptive "arm." Of course, one's arm is no replacement for one's birth order or one's mouth. Moses thus continues to resist the call on the grounds that he cannot speak: "Oh Lord, I am not and have never been a man of words, neither yesterday, nor the day before, nor since You spoke to your servant; for I am *kevad peh ukh'vad lashon*, heavy of mouth and heavy of tongue."[7] Later in Exodus 6, Moses will reiterate his sense of unfitness to speak before Pharaoh on the grounds that he is *'arel sefatayim* (uncircumcised of lips), his speech pathways somehow closed and unconsecrated. Moses's protestations about his uncircumcised lips provoke consideration of the connection between speech and circumcision, given that in Hebrew the word for "word" and "circumcision" is identical: *milah*. According to Ella Shohat, "Judaic culture is thoroughly predicated upon concepts having to do with 'word' and 'hearing.' Central to the 'covenant' (*brith* in Hebrew) between God and the Jewish people is the duty of male circumcision . . . known as *brith milah*, or the covenant of the word."[8] Impeded of speech, Moses thus considers himself an unfit vehicle for words of freedom and covenant.

What exactly is Moses's speech problem? Some commentators, such as the Rashbam (Rabbi Samuel ben Meir, 1085–1158), categorically reject the idea that a prophet who spoke face-to-face with God could have had an actual speech defect, maintaining instead that Moses lacked proficiency in the Egyptian language, having fled Egypt as a young man.[9] Most commentators disagree, however, and conclude that Moses suffered from a speech impediment.[10] A famous midrash from Exodus Rabbah even provides an etiology for this impediment, linking it to an injury that occurred when Moses was a toddler:

AND SHE BROUGHT HIM UNTO PHARAOH'S DAUGHTER. Pharaoh's daughter used to kiss and hug him, loved him as if he were her own son, and would not allow him out of the royal palace. Because he was so handsome, everyone was eager to see him, and whoever saw him could not tear himself away from him, and he [Moses] used to take the crown of Pharaoh and place it upon his own head, as he was destined to do when he became great. . . . The magicians of Egypt sat there and said: "We are afraid of him who is taking off they crown and placing it upon his own head, lest he be the one of whom it is prophesied that he will take away the kingdom from thee." Some of them counseled to slay him and others to burn him, but Jethro was present among them and he said to them: "This boy has no sense. However, test him by placing before him a gold vessel and a live coal; if he stretch forth his hand for the gold, then he has the sense and you can slay him, but if he make for the live coal then he has no sense and there can be no sentence of death upon him. So they brought forth these things before him, and he was about to reach for the gold, when Gabriel came and thrust his hand aside so that he seized the coal, and he thrust his hand with the live coal into his mouth, so that his tongue was burnt, with the result that he became slow of speech and of tongue.[11]

As if to counter charges of genetic inferiority linked to his heaviness of mouth, the midrash quoted above imagines the toddler Moses as so precocious and handsome that he captivates not just Pharaoh's daughter but also Pharaoh himself. The magicians, however, guardians of Egyptian tradition and lore, look with suspicion at the admiration and affection being showered on this outsider/stepchild; when toddler Moses takes Pharaoh's crown and places it on his own head, they view his playfulness as an act of proto-usurpation, punishable by death. The intercession of Jethro at this point collapses time and space, bringing together Moses's childhood in Egypt and his adulthood in Midian. In the same way that Jethro gives sanctuary to the adult Moses when he flees Egypt to Midian, he engages here in an effort to save the baby Moses from harm by the magicians.

Still, the test devised by Jethro to prove young Moses's innocence places Moses in a precarious position with no real way out. If Moses reaches for the gold, which cannot physically harm him, he'll be killed. If he reaches for the coal, he'll be saved but irreversibly injured. That the angel Gabriel participates in the story, compelling the toddler to reach for the burning coal instead of the gold,[12] points to God's role in keeping Moses alive as well as in making him a *kevad peh*. In the same way that God closes and then opens the wombs of the (barren) matriarchs, so as to allow for the continuity of the Abrahamic line, God seems here to be sealing or encumbering Moses's mouth to enable a divine opening or easing.[13]

In contrast to this midrash from Exodus Rabbah, which identifies in Moses an unspecified speech defect as a result of physical injury to his mouth, Rashi interprets the words *kevad peh* (heavy of mouth) specifically as stuttering, citing the old French word for stutterer (*bulbo*).[14] It is this interpretation that his grandson the Rashbam seems to have in mind when he rejects the idea of Moses as *gamgeman*—the rabbinic Hebrew word for stammerer. In employing this onomatopoetic term, the Rashbam indirectly points to the threefold repetition of the word *gam* in Exodus 4:10, where Moses insists that he has never been an *ish devarim* (man of words), "neither yesterday, nor the day before, nor since You spoke to Your servant"[15] (*gam mitemol, gam mishilshom, gam me'az dabrekha el 'avdekha*). The notion that Moses was afflicted with the sort of speech impediment that often presents in the form of multiple repetitions of the same sound or syllable is further intimated by the fourfold repetition of the word "*seneh*" (bush) at the beginning of the burning bush scene (Ex. 3:3–4), the twofold repetition of the word "*kevad*" (*kevad peh ukh'vad lashon*, Ex. 4:10), and Moses's opaquely repetitive request to God—*shelaḥ na beyad tishlaḥ* (Ex. 4:13). This latter sentence especially, often understood as a plea to send someone else in Moses's stead, illustrates Moses's heaviness of speech, as he is unable even to make clear exactly whom he would like God to send instead of him.

The idea of *gimgum* as a form of (traumatic) repetition figures in yet another fascinating midrash, which supplies an alternative etiology for Moses's encumbered speech. Here, instead of imagining a scene in Pharaoh's palace, the midrash delves into the trauma of Hebrew slavery, especially that experienced by Israelite babies in the wake of Pharaoh's decree that they be thrown after birth into the Nile River. According to this midrash, the Egyptians developed a strategy for ferreting out hidden Israelite boy-children:

> When an Israelite woman would give birth to a boy and hide him from the Egyptians to avoid him being slaughtered, the

> Egyptian women would come to the homes of the Hebrew women, and their Egyptian babies [whom they carried with them on their backs] would babble/stutter [*megamgem*] in their language and the Hebrew babies hidden in their mother's beds would answer back in their language, at which point the Egyptian women would go back and tell their husbands who would report it to their king, and Pharaoh would send officers to take the hidden boys."[16]

And so it was with Moses, but before the Egyptians could return to take him away, Yocheved placed him in a basket on the Nile, averting his death. According to this midrash, *gimgum* represents not merely a speech defect but a formative traumatic betrayal that reverberates in Moses's consciousness—recall Bertie's recollection of how he was abused by his nanny in *The King's Speech*—and fates him to labor on behalf of freeing the Israelites. Moses's twice-pronounced complaint, even after accepting God's call, that he is of "fore-skinned lips," itself an echo of the mysterious circumcision scene in Exodus 4:24–26, further emphasizes this notion of stuttering as form of recurrent or traumatic repetition.

All of these sources point to Moses's heaviness of tongue as an actual defect or impediment. In Exodus 4, God reassures Moses that he can discharge his duty despite this impediment, first by telling him that He will teach Moses what to say, and second that his brother Aaron will serve as his spokesman. Why then doesn't God simply send Aaron himself? Aaron would be a far more practical choice, given his speaking skills and his credibility with the people. And yet God prefers Moses. Given this, as Brian Britt observes in his study of modern rewritings of the Moses story, any interpretation of this Exodus 4 must "understand Moses' inability not as a regrettable circumstance to be overlooked but rather as an inherent and positive feature of Moses' role as a prophet and a leader . . . YHWH's decision to keep Moses despite his protests suggest that that Moses and his handicap are necessary to the process of revelation and salvation."[17]

But why? What is it about heaviness of speech that recommends itself, given that public speaking plays such a central role in leadership in general and in Moses's errand in particular? More broadly speaking, given Moses's own objections to his election, what explains God's insistence that Moses assume the leadership of Israel? This former Egyptian prince turned Midianite shepherd knows little about the people he is meant to lead. His speech defects seem to go hand in hand with a tendency, like that of Bertie in *The King's Speech*, toward hotheadedness and anger, as evidenced by his killing of the Egyptian overseer in Exodus 2:11–12, a crime to which he never 'fesses up, electing simply to bury his victim out of sight. Popular film reimaginings of the Exodus story, such as Cecille B. DeMille's *The Ten Commandments*, provide various reasons for Moses's election as part of an imaginative presentation of Moses's earlier life in Egypt. Ramses, Pharaoh's firstborn son, is depicted as power-hungry, lustful, and ambitious, whereas Moses, the younger stepbrother prince, is industrious, guileless, and upright (like Bertie in *The King's Speech*). DeMille completely sidesteps the whole subject of Moses's speech impediment, rendering him an eloquent speaker so as to make him more appealing to a screen audience. Spielberg's animated film *The Prince of Egypt* (1998) similarly omits any depiction of Moses as stutterer, offering background on Moses and Ramses's relationship as a means of fleshing out their later conflict when Moses asks his stepbrother to let his people go. Of course, no such backstory is provided by the biblical text. And yet God's choice of Moses as the one to plead the cause of Israel's liberation indicates that there is something about his heavy or uncircumcised speech that is beneficial or generative. If so, what is it?

One way to understand Moses' election is to examine the way in which the verb *kvd* serves, in Martin Buber's terminology, as a *leitwort* or key word in these early chapters of Exodus.[18] This verb first appears in Moses's self-description in Exodus 4 ("I am heavy of mouth and heavy of tongue," Ex. 4:10) but thereafter proliferates throughout the account of the Exodus from Egypt. In Exodus 6, we learn the name of Moses's previously unnamed mother, Yokheved, a name that inscribes the root *kvd* into Moses's own family lineage and that Buber translates as meaning "YHVH is weighty."[19] As the story progresses, the same verb appears alternately in relation to Pharaoh and God, as Pharaoh bears down ever more heavily on the enslaved Israelites (Ex. 5:9) and hardens (or makes heavier) his heart with respect to Moses's demand for deliverance (Ex. 7:14, 8:28). God, in turns, claims responsibility for this hardening (or rendering heavy) so as to enable a greater show of divine *kavod*/honor. In Exodus 10:14, the plague of locusts is described as exceedingly heavy ("*kaved me'od*"). The scene of the splitting of the Red Sea is twice depicted as an occasion for God's powerful weight and honor to be displayed before Pharaoh (Ex. 14:4; *Ve'ikabdah befar'o*; and Ex. 14:18; *behikabdi befar'o*), while Pharaoh's pursuing chariots ride with encumbrance (Ex. 14:25; *bikhveidut*) and, ultimately, are hurled into the sea.

Read in conjunction with these other uses of the word *kvd*, Moses's heaviness of mouth becomes part of a plan to debunk Pharaoh's pretensions to divinity and thus reveal the weight and truth of YHWH's word. Moses is meant not to be the charismatic focus of this revelation, but rather a medium or tool for its transmission. His heaviness of mouth, like the heaviness of Pharaoh's heart, becomes a pretext for divine intervention and consequently a manifestation of God's honor.

But again: what is it exactly about Moses's stammering that makes it the best vehicle for the transmission and honoring of God's word? If the point is simply to downplay the human vehicle so as highlight the divine origin of the speech, why not choose someone who is entirely mute? Or cure Moses's stammering outright, in the same way that God makes the barren matriarchs fertile? According to Martin Buber, there is a tragic, lonely element to the fact that "[i]t is laid upon the stammering to bring the voice of Heaven to Earth," insofar as it raises a barrier between Moses and the human world.[20] But is there no way to assign affirmative content or theological value to Moses's stuttering? Can we offer an interpretation of Moses's heavy mouth that grants him greater agency and acknowledges his journey over the course of his life toward becoming an *ish devarim*, a man of divine words?

Comparative literature professor and former stutterer Marc Shell notes the astonishing fact that in the burning bush scene, God also presents as a stutterer. Moses asks for God's name, and God replies, "*Eheyeh asher eheyeh*" (Ex. 3:14; I am that I am, or I shall be what I shall be).[21] In Exodus, then, stuttering serves as a metaphor both for the closeness of God and Moses as well as for the eternal, necessary gap between divine and human language. Moses's stutter, with its halts, repetitions, and substitutions, reminds us that there is no way to communicate God's complex, sublime, eternal message in a fluent, straightforward, definitive way. Conjoined with God's own stutter, which presents itself as "*Eheyeh asher eheyeh*," a name-state of eternity or ever-becoming, stuttering also becomes a figure for ongoing invention, substitution, improvisation, and interpretation.

We have already seen, in our discussion of Buber's *leitwörter*, the way in which repeated—stuttered—words in the Torah provide an interpretive key to the text. Might Moses's stammer be seen, then, as a model for speech/Torah as dynamic, provisional, and open, given to an ongoing process of exegesis and commentary? Might the forty years of Moses wandering with the Israelites in the *midbar*, a word that includes the Hebrew verb *dbr* (to speak), be seen as a metaphorical representation of landscape as speech, the wilderness being gapped and desolate as well as blessed with miraculous, oft-repeated phenomena?

By extension, can the various gaps, hiatuses, silences, and irregularities of stuttered speech be seen as an overarching metaphor for the kinds of gaps, silences, curious repetitions, parallelisms, and anomalies that appear throughout the Bible and continually give rise to new understandings? As Daniel Boyarin writes, "[t]he heterogeneity—the multivocality of the biblical text itself, its hiatuses and gaps, creatively but not open-endedly filled in by the midrash—allows it to generate its meanings—its *original* meanings—in ever new social and cultural situations."[22] Might this not be seen, therefore, as a kind of textual representation of "*Eheyeh asher eheyeh*"?

Scholars of rabbinic midrash/aggadah often call attention to the historical context that gave rise to its development. As Joseph Heinemann notes,

> Aggadah represents a creative reaction to the upheaval suffered by Israel in their land during this long period [Second Temple]. It also represents an attempt to develop new methods of exegesis designed to yield new understandings of Scripture for a time of crisis and a period of conflict, with foreign cultural influence pressing from without and sectarian agitation from within. . . . This complex of spiritual, political, and national challenges required constant grappling with problems and taking new stands suited to present needs. To achieve this, it was necessary that the Torah remain dynamic and open to varying interpretation in order to meet the challenges of drastically varying circumstances.[23]

One can make similar observations about the role of stuttering in Exodus, a story that takes place against a backdrop of the great oppression of slavery and threatens to erase the very names, traditions, and bodies of Jacob's descendants. The Hebrew name of this second book of the Bible is *Shemot*, referring to the names of all those from Jacob's family who went down to Egypt. Yet, by the second chapter of the book, almost all proper names disappear from the text.[24] Moses's own name is not so much a proper name as a suffix, connoting birth or becoming.

Sholem Asch notes in his novel *Moses* the sharp contrast between the Egyptian obsession with death and the Hebrew notion of God "as eternal being, of creation, of becoming, of life, of all that there was, of all presentness."[25] Indeed, part of Moses's burgeoning consciousness in Asch's novel involves a developing hatred of Egyptian culture, in which "the living work for the dead."[26]

The tyrannical context of all of this is hardly incidental. According to Martin Buber, who wrote his own study of Moses in 1944 against the backdrop of Hitler's Reich, ancient Egypt was a sinister, impersonal bureaucracy, characterized by fixed, immovable, routine and form. God and Moses as stutterers stand against this mode, presenting a view of life, interaction, and speech that is open, dynamic, and covenantal.[27]

All this brings to mind that scene in *The King's Speech* where Bertie and family watch Hitler's speech at Nuremburg. In this scene, disfluent Bertie (like Moses for Buber) is presented as the antithesis to maniacally fluent Hitler. Oratorical acumen is viewed in the film as suspect, manipulative, coercive, and demonic.

Eventually, of course, both Moses and Bertie become men of words. Moses's transformation into an *ish devarim* is evidenced by the Hebrew title of the fifth book of the Pentateuch and the many instances—too numerous to list—where Moses serves as a *medabber*, a speaker of God's word (*davar*) to the people. If Moses is presented at the beginning of his journey to leadership as heavy of mouth and tongue, by the time we read the book of *Devarim* (Deuteronomy), he has become fully and breathtakingly fluent.

In *The King's Speech*, Bertie's pathways of speech are widened when he listens to music on earphones or sings about his difficult childhood to the tune of "Swanee River." Moses's speech pathways similarly open when he sings his famous "Song of the Sea" (Ex. 15:1–21). Note that unlike the preceding chapter (Ex. 14), where the verb *kvd* recurs conspicuously, Moses's song makes no mention of this Hebrew verb. From its very beginning, the song strikes a chord of lightness, describing the Lord as "*ga'oh ga'ah*" (highly exalted), carried aloft as if weightlessly, while, on the Egyptian side, "*sus verokhvo ramah bayam*" (Ex. 15:1; God hurls the Egyptian horses and riders into the sea).

Renowned speech therapist Dr. Phil Schneider refers in his documentary film *Transcending Stuttering* to the way in which his patients, over the course of their treatment, travel "from places in their lives, where they're stuck in fear and isolation, to places of freedom of speech and fulfillment."[28] Schneider's documentary, which tells the story the therapeutic journeys of seven different stutterers, portrays certain emblematic stuttering experiences, including that dreaded first day of school where a stutterer is asked to say his or her name. That names—their absence, their substitution, their formal and more intimate forms—play such a significant role both in *The King's Speech* (Mr. Johnson, Your Royal Highness, the King, Bertie, Lionel) and in the book of Exodus/*Shemot* (Names) only supports the connection between all of these materials. According to Schneider, the pain of stuttering becomes a very important motivator. More than others, stutterers grow up with goals and hopes for the future, with a need to move forward beyond obstructions of speech. Fascinatingly, a great number of them go on specifically to become orators, actors, and teachers of others. Viewed through the lens of stuttering, Moses's journey of speech becomes a similar story, a gapped, halted, or open-ended "telling" that "begets retelling"[29] and thus becomes a paradigm for the eternal speech and ongoing teaching of God's word.

8

Stranger than Fiction

God as Author

From our consideration of the spoken word, we now move to a discussion of writing and authorship. For centuries, Judeo-Christian tradition has generated versions of the God-as-author metaphor. A recent satirical article in *The Onion* takes on this long-standing theological model, depicting God as a celebrated but reclusive writer, one whose entire reputation rests on one highly influential and interpreted holy Book but who now seems to be suffering from major writer's block:

> Leading writers, scholars, and publishers gathered this week at Fordham University for a literary conference and panel discussion on God, the widely praised but reclusive deity who has not published a book since His landmark debut 2,000 years ago.
>
> Hailed by critics as one of the most important authors in recent millennia, the eccentric divinity is said to have long ago retreated from the public eye, eschewing a life of celebrity for one of solitude and quiet. To this day, experts confirmed, His artistic reputation rests exclusively upon His bestselling and highly acclaimed first work, the Bible.[1]

This *Onion* satire addresses the vexatious issue of God's seeming absence from our troubled world and also makes clear the absurdity of taking too literally the God-as-writer metaphor. As Abraham Joshua Heschel warns, the "cardinal sin in thinking of ultimate issues is *literal-mindedness*.[2] Not only does literal mindedness limit and close down the many possibilities for understanding religious truth, but it also threatens to reduce God to an anthropomorphic caricature. For this reason, Maimonides, in *Hilkhot yesodei hatorah*, insists on the nonliteral nature of such corporeal or anthropomorphic references in the Bible to "God's hand," "God's eyes," or to the two tablets having being "written with the finger of God" (Ex. 31:18): "Man can think only in terms of bodies and the Torah speaks the language of human beings. Lest one take this all literally, Maimonides concludes, '*Ela hakol mashal*'—All of this, rather, is parable or metaphor."[3]

To be sure, there is very little that any of us can say with certainty about the nature of God, and no "back of the book" to which we can refer to check if we've gotten our formulation right. Everything we advance is perforce inadequate and proximate, relying at best on prior texts, on narrative and imagination. As Christian feminist theologian Sally McFague notes, "admitting that theology is mainly fiction, mainly elaboration, we claim that some fictions are better than others . . . So we try out different models and metaphors in an attempt to talk about what we do not know how to talk about."[4]

Stranger than Fiction (2006), directed by Marc Forster and written by Zach Helm, subtly tries out the God-as-author "fiction" and dramatizes its various implications. As in *The Truman Show*, this film too features a zany comedic actor (Will Ferrell) in a tragicomic role. The title of the film calls to mind Mark Twain's famous pronouncement that "Truth is stranger than fiction, because fiction is required to stick to possibilities, but Truth isn't."[5] A conventional reading of this epigram points to the ways in which real-life experience sometimes outstrips even our wildest imaginings. A theological reading of this same quotation suggests that Truth both partakes of but also exceeds the fictions that we devise around it. The metaphors and fictions that we invent for God inevitably fall short. The film *Stranger than Fiction* advances this notion by having the (divine) Author's fiction collide with the facts of a character's "real" life.

Harold Crick, the protagonist of the film, is an internal revenue service agent, a rational, mathematical, routine-bound but lonely man who counts brush strokes when he brushes his teeth and seconds as he ties his tie or walks to the bus stop for his morning commute. The GUI interface images that accompany the narration and visual depiction of Harold's daily routine only underscore this mathematical, schematic orientation.

One morning, while getting dressed for work, Harold starts hearing a voice that narrates his life and interrupts his routine, a disruption that is marked on the screen by the shattering of the GUI interface marks that fall like broken glass onto the road as Harold runs to catch his bus. Soon thereafter, the voice predicts his imminent death. Harold yells at the voice, as if at heaven, inquiring why he has to die imminently and when. He asks other people if they can hear the voice. At home, Harold rails and rants against the voice in the hope of provoking the narrator to divulge more information, but to no avail. Eventually he lands in the office of a psychiatrist, Dr. Mittag-Leffler, where the following conversation takes place

>MITTAG-LEFFLER
>Mr. Crick, I hate to sound like a broken record, but that's schizophrenia.
>HAROLD
>You don't sound like a broken record, it's just not schizophrenia.
>(She just looks at him.)
>HAROLD (CONT'D)
>Okay. What if what I said was true. What if, please . . . just, hypothetically. If I was part of a story . . . a narrative, even only in my own mind . . .
>(pause)
>What would you suggest I do?
>MITTAG-LEFFLER
>I would suggest that you take prescribed medication.
>HAROLD
>Other than that.
>MITTAG-LEFFLER
>I don't know . . . I would . . . I'd have you speak to someone who knows about literature . . . I suppose.[6]

That Harold actually favors his narration theory over Dr. Mittag's-Leffler's medical diagnosis marks a major departure from his former mathematical obsessions, an opening up to new kinds of knowledge. Not that this film leaves the world of math and science behind. Virtually every character in the film is named after one famous modern scientist or mathematician or another. The psychiatrist Dr. Mittag-Leffler, for example, is named after Swedish mathematician Magnus Gustaf Mittag-Leffler (1846–1927). The author of Harold's life story, Karen Eiffel, is named after

Alexandre Gustave Eiffel (1832–1923), the engineer and architect who designed the Eiffel tower, while her assistant, Penny Escher, evokes the mathematically oriented graphic artist M. C. Escher (1898–1972). Harold Crick himself is named after Francis Crick (1916–2004), co-discoverer with James Watson in 1953 of the structure of the DNA molecule, the building block of life.

Indeed, in choosing character names from the world of modern math and science for this story about fiction, the film insists on a connection rather than a conflict between math and storytelling and between science and religion. There are many who view science and religious experience as inherently antithetical modes. As Eliezer Berkovitz writes,

> Science deals with events as they occur in the external world of "objects"; the [religious] encounter, on the other hand, is an event that occurs on the most intimate level between one subject and another. Science, in order to succeed, must eliminate all personal and conscious elements from the field of observation, for the personal and the conscious are threats to the validity of the scientific method. Thus the scientist is an observer; he must never be a participant in the event he investigates. If he does not remove himself from the field of observation, he interferes with and upsets the data. In the [religious] encounter, however, the opposite is true: the more intense the personal presence and the richer the conscious element, the more valid the experience. In scientific study, we deal with events in their objective relatedness to the outside world; in the encounter, we establish the relationship in the inner world of personal reality.[7]

Stranger than Fiction suggests, however, that these modes need not be strictly opposed. Fittingly, Harold's love interest is named Ana Pascal, after Blaise Pascal (1623–1662), a scientist, mathematician, and philosopher who experienced a religious conversion and is best known for Pascal's wager, an argument that posits that even though we cannot prove the existence of God, given the potential benefits or losses associated with belief or unbelief, a rational person should live as though God exists and endeavor to believe. Of all the above-mentioned mathematicians and scientists, Pascal is unique for having merged a commitment to scientific inquiry with religious devotion. Ana is Harold's Pascal, an artistic and articulate baker who strives to improve the quality of social life through baking cookies, thereby exposing Harold to notions of beauty, interconnectedness, and meaningful work hitherto absent from his life. Harold's IRS work friend Dave, who harbors a lifelong fantasy to go to space camp, serves a similar function in that he represents childlike receptiveness to awe and wonder at the created world.

Christian theologian Gene C. Fant notes in his book *God as Author* that "[f]or the ancients, authorship was tied directly with divine Creation."[8] The opening of *Stranger than Fiction* draws a similar connection between cosmology and authorship, beginning with a God's-eye view of the heavens, then zooming ever closer to earth, and then providing an establishing shot of the particular neighborhood, building, and apartment of a particular man named Harold Crick. On the morning we meet Harold, he is wearing a dark business suit and carrying a green apple in his mouth as he runs to make his bus, a direct visual reference to *The Son of Man*, an iconic painting by French surrealist painter Rene Magritte (1898–1967). Later on, as Harold becomes increasingly plagued by the narrator's voice and is called in for a "convo" with the IRS human resources manager, Dr. Cayley (a reference to British mathematician Arthur Cayley, 1821–1895), he is pictured sitting on a couch in front of a wall mural of blue sky and clouds that mimics the cloud-and-sky background of Magritte's painting. In the painting, as in the first scene, where Harold runs for his bus with a green apple in his mouth, the human face is almost entirely obscured, suggesting a form of modern, white-collar anomie or self-effacement. In the Christian Bible, "Son of man" frequently carries a Christian messianic connotation, an idea that some see reflected in the film where Harold knowingly steps in front of a bus to save a young boy on a bicycle; for Christian viewers, Harold's survival after this accident is perceived as a Christological evocation of martyrdom and resurrection. In the Hebrew Bible, however, the phrase *ben Adam* (son of Adam), or the first man, refers first and foremost to the descendants of the first created human being, the apple featured in the Magritte's painting and in *Stranger than Fiction* symbolizing the knowledge of good, evil, and ultimately mortality. Elsewhere in the Bible, the moniker *ben Adam* features prominently in the book of Ezekiel as God's repeated form of address to the prophet. It is as *ben Adam* that Ezekiel is asked by God to present the vision of the dry bones, a prophecy of regeneration and rejuvenation, which Harold actually manages to achieve for himself by the end of the film.

To arrive at this new life, the apple must fall away from his face. In other words, Harold needs first to undergo a journey of emotional self-discovery that begins with Dr. Mittag-Leffler's recommendation that he go see someone "who knows something about literature." This line, of course, is a literature professor's fantasy: the idea that knowing literature somehow constitutes a lifesaving capacity. That lives depend on what we teach. That if someone called out, in the middle of a flight, "Is there a doctor on the plane?," I could answer: *Yes! I am ready and waiting to provide services for anyone stricken with an interpretive emergency or a literary-critical quandary!*

Harold does indeed go to see a literature professor—Dr. Jules Hilbert, named after German mathematician David Hilbert (1862–1943) and played by Dustin Hoffman—who provokes him to consider whether he is the hero of a tragedy or a comedy and subjects him to a hilarious survey so as to determine what specific storyline he inhabits. When Harold expresses skepticism about Hilbert's bizarre line of questioning ("Has anyone recently left any gifts outside your home . . . anything: gum, money . . . a large wooden horse?" . . . "Are you the King of anything?" . . . "Was any part of you now at one time part of something else?"[9]), Hilbert explains:

> Odd as it may seem I've just ruled out half of Greek literature, seven fairy tales, ten Greek fables, and determined conclusively that you are not Hamlet, Scout Finch, Ms. Marple, Frankenstein's monster or a golem. [pause] Aren't you relieved to know that you're not a golem?"[10]

No mere joke, the above golem reference points to serious and real issues of determinism versus autonomy in the conduct of one's life. In Jewish folklore, a golem, like Adam in Genesis 2, is a creature made of mud, subjected to the will and commands of his maker. Before he begins to hear the narrator's voice in his mind, Harold himself is golem-like, an office automaton who never veers away from the expected. When he begins to hear the author's narration of his life, however, Harold begins to shed his golem-ness and play an active, independent role in his own life story. In exposing Harold to a variety of literary plots, only to discover that Harold's plot doesn't easily fit into any premade template, Hilbert ultimately prods Harold to live the life he always wanted—to learn to play guitar, to pursue a love interest with Ana Pascal, and ultimately to track down the narrator of his story so as to avert imminent death.

The specific narrator of Harold's life actually turns out to be a woman writer, Karen Eiffel, a feminine version of the divine author metaphor, familiar to us from Exodus 31:18 ("And He gave unto Moses, when He had made an end of speaking with him upon Mount Sinai, the two tables of the testimony, tables of stone, written with the finger of God"), as well as from the High Holiday *Unetaneh tokef* prayer, where God yearly inscribes and seals our lives in the book of life or the book of death.[11] As such, *Stranger than Fiction* affords an opportunity for feminist scholars to consider what happens when a long-standing masculine God metaphor is recast in feminine form.

One might hope, in a somewhat utopian feminist moment, that, in rendering feminine the God-as-writer metaphor, the theological paradigm would be altered or improved in some fundamental way. As it turns out, however, this woman writer-as-God reinforces rather than undermines conventional, patriarchal stereotypes. She is miserable, narcissistic, obsessive, and removed from the world—a caricature of the solitary, hierarchical Creator God. Add to this the fact that she is in the throes of a ten-year writer's block, suggesting impotence rather than authority. She lives by herself in a spare apartment and strives in vain to turn sentences around. She sleeps on a table and harbors a morbid fascination with death, as evidenced by her tendency to kill off every one of her protagonists—a sly nod at the fact of human mortality. She chain-smokes but has the quirky habit of snuffing out her cigarettes—like her protagonists!—when only half-smoked, spitting into a tissue and then extinguishing the cigarettes in the crumpled, damp wad. Throughout the film, we see Karen Eiffel imaginatively inhabiting various death scenarios—jumping off a building, driving off a bridge in the rain—suggesting both homicidal and suicidal inclinations. In one particularly memorable scene, Eiffel and her assistant, Penny Escher, sit out in the rain by the side of highway, as Eiffel smokes one cigarette after another and imagine car wrecks. When Eiffel starts coughing, Escher, a tough-minded ministering angel, hands her literature about the nicotine patch and suggests that it might save her life, at which point Eiffel ripostes, "I'm not in the business of saving lives, in fact, quite the opposite."[12] Clearly this version of the divine author demonstrates none of the strength of the transcendent, authoritative God. Nor does she exemplify any of the aspects of a revised feminist model of interconnectedness and maternal care.

In her book *Models of God*, Sally McFague sketches out the implications of a theology based on God as artist as opposed to a theology based on God as parent: "An artist upon completion of a work makes a judgment whether it is good or bad; . . . But a child, the product of our bodies is not judged this way . . . Rather, it is the quality of the relationship between parents and child that is most important; we judge then, in categories of love, not art."[13]

Love NOT Art. Art NOT love. At the beginning of *Stranger than Fiction*, these categories, like science and religion, seem inexorably opposed. By the end of the film, however, we are presented not with an opposition but with a combination: a model of art PLUS love.

Over the course of the film, both Karen Eiffel and Harold Crick move from a strict, detached practice of their professions or crafts to a life of love and empathy. In narrating the myriad details of Harold's life and in predicting his imminent death, author Karen Eiffel provokes lonely, routine-bound, numerically obsessed IRS agent Harold to reconsider the quality (not just the quantity) of his life—to pursue authentic love and music, as represented by the various punk rock songs that he plays and that play in the soundtrack of the film. At the same time, Harold Crick precipitates change in Karen Eiffel when he comes to her apartment and pleads with her not to kill him off at the end of her novel just as she has finally figured out an aesthetically perfect way for him to die.

It is only when Karen Eiffel meets Harold and sees what kind of person Harold has become, when she puts a living face on the creature of her pen, that she rediscovers compassion, kindness, and authorial love. This woman Writer-as-God has to learn that *lo tov*—it is not good, neither for Harold, *ben Adam*, nor for her to be alone. She has to be brought to care about the effect her writing has on the world. She has to be reminded, in the most profound sense, of the world-making and life-breaking power of words. As the speaker of the biblical book of Proverbs reflects: "*Mavet vehayim beyad halashon* (Proverbs 18:21; The tongue has the power of life and death, and those who love it will eat its fruit).[14]

At the end of the film, as Harold lay injured in a hospital room, with Ana by his side feeding him cookies, narrator/author Karen Eiffel offers a gorgeous meditation on the importance of writerly detail in life and in relationships:

As Harold took a bite of Bavarian Sugar Cookie, he finally felt that everything was going to be okay. Sometimes, when we lose ourselves in fear and despair, in routine and constancy, in hopelessness and tragedy, we can thank God for Bavarian Sugar Cookies. And fortunately, when there aren't any cookies, we can still find reassurance in a familiar hand on our skin. . . . Or a loving gesture . . . Or a subtle encouragement . . . Or a loving embrace . . . Or an offer of comfort. Not to mention hospital gurneys . . . And nose plugs . . . And uneaten Danish . . . And soft-spoken secrets . . . And Fender Stratocasters . . . And maybe, the occasional piece of fiction . . .

And we must remember that all these things, the nuances, the anomalies, the subtleties, which we assume only accessorize our days, are in fact here for a much larger and nobler cause. They are here to save our lives."[15]

As writers, teachers, and students of Judaism and Torah alike, we need to believe that these things matter, but not in some detached aesthetic or scholarly sense. We need to believe that stories and texts and Torah are here to save our lives.

I am reminded in this context of the famous Talmudic story from Tractate Menahot 29b, in which Moses ascends on high to receive the Torah and sees God busy tying crowns ("*kosher ketarim*") to the letters of the text. Typically the phrase *kosher ketarim* is understood as calligraphic embellishment. A more literary way to interpret this image, however, would be to imagine God as an author in her study, busily revising and refining the Torah, adding extra little nuances, details, and anomalies to unify, intensify, and deepen the work to earn the writing its crowns of praise.

Moses asks God: "*Mi me'akev 'al yadekha?*" (What's taking you so long to finish? Why all this seemingly superfluous, forty-day attention to detail?) God explains to Moses that all of this is necessary because at the end of many generations, a man named Akiva Ben Joseph will arise who will expound on every *kotz*, every jot of text heaps and heaps of laws. Moses then asks God if he can see this Akiva, at which point Moses finds himself sitting eight rows back, completely incapable of following anything being taught.

Typically, this story is adduced to support the idea of an unfolding legal tradition that begins at Sinai but continues to develop in every generation. I'd like to suggest another interpretation of the story, however, that builds on the lifesaving quality of writing and reading stories.

Recall, for a moment, our discussion in chapter 7 about what the Moses says to God in Exodus 4:10 in response to God's request that Moses speak to Pharaoh and demand that the Israelites be set free: "*Lo ish devarim anokhi, gam mitmol gam mishilshom.*" In that context, we interpreted this verse as referring to Moses's speech defect. I'd like here to consider another possible interpretation of that verse that relates to BT Menahot 29b, a reading in which Moses declares to God that he is not naturally talented with or interested in words, not given to caring—not today, not yesterday, not the day before yesterday—about the subtleties, nuances, anomalies, and details of writing and storytelling. According to this reading, only when Moses ascends on high and then time-travels to the future to Rabbi Akiva's *beit midrash* and humbly sits in the eighth row—the number eight connoting something outside the regular, seven-day cycle of nature—does he learn about the wondrous, interpretive possibilities inherent in every *keter* and *kotz*, every crown and thorn, of text. It is only when witnessing the work of Rabbi Akiva that Moses becomes an *ish devarim*—a writer, interpreter, preacher, and teacher of Torah.

Imagine his shock when later in this same story Moses discovers that Rabbi Akiva's reward for his Torah is to have his flesh weighed out in the Roman market—that his recompense for his interpretive attention to detail is not salvation but cruel martyrdom, a fate anticipated by the twin use of the words *keter* (crown) and *kotz* (thorn) to refer to the details that God adds to the letters of the Torah. For Akiva, the Torah becomes a crown of thorns. Moses questions God as to how this could be, but God tells Moses to be silent. "This is what arose ['*alah*] in my thoughts." In the same way that Moses ascends ['*alah*] on high to receive the Torah, thoughts arise in God's mind, though in the latter usage, the phrase seems to connote caprice or, at best, a divine plan to which no human beings have real access.

According to Talmud Professor Jeffrey Rubinstein, this story is so significant because it juxtaposes "two important theological questions: the expansion of Torah and the problem of theodicy . . . The greatest Torah scholar ever, perhaps even greater than Moses, suffers the cruelest death, and yet God gives no explanation. God takes great care for his Torah, meticulously adding crowns to each individual letter, but apparently cares less about those who dedicate their lives to it."[16]

In my view, the audacious, incisive, thorny brilliance of this story is that it depicts God honestly and demands, like the film *Stranger than Fiction*, that both we and God do better. What good is a perfect, exquisitely embellished Torah if the righteous people who uphold it are left to suffer so cruelly? What good is Karen Eiffel's aesthetically perfect novel if it allows good people like Harold Crick to die for the sake of delivering a good ending?

Man in Search of God the Author/God the Author in Search of Man

At the beginning of the film, both Harold Crick and Karen Eiffel are seen as living miserably alone, each in a colorless, sparsely decorated apartment. Eiffel's isolation is first interrupted by the unwanted arrival of assistant Penny Escher, a companionship that seems to do little at first to move Eiffel's writing along. Unbeknownst to Eiffel, however, her halted narration begins to propel Harold on his quest for his "author," ultimately resulting in an encounter that impacts and transforms them both.

First Harold meets and pursues his love story with Ana Pascal, the baker whom he has been sent to audit. Having had no previous experience with love and at a distinct disadvantage given the circumstances under which they meet, Harold breaks IRS protocol, which forbids the giving or accepting of gifts, and goes one night to the bakery to present Ana with "flours," a play, of course, on the conventional romantic gift of flowers that also acknowledges Ana's particular gifts as a baker.

In presenting this gift, Harold demonstrates a new capacity to be a man not just of "infinite numbers and endless calculations,"[17] but also of words, poetry, and story. As Harold presents Ana with the "flours," he enacts yet another wordplay. "I've been odd," he says. "I know I've been odd, but I want you." In his interactions with Ana, Harold has "audited," and has been odd as well as "awed," propelled into a very different kind of experience or encounter with infinity than his prior life as a man of infinite numbers had ever allowed.

This sense of odd/awed encounter is only amplified when Harold knocks on author Karen Eiffel's door to confront her with the facts of her fiction. As Harold walks into the apartment, we see a bronze sculpture on the right side of the frame of a tree with snake-like winding branches,

Figure 8.1. *Stranger than Fiction*, Flours.

evocative of the biblical story of the Garden of Eden. Unlike the earlier Adam reference, where Harold's face is obscured, Magritte-like, by the green apple, here he boldly and knowingly faces the author of his fate. "How did you find me?" Karen Eiffel asks in shock. Harold explains that ten years earlier, Eiffel had been audited by the IRS, an experience that seems to have prompted the idea of writing a novel titled *Death and Taxes*. Because this audit had occurred, when Harold finally discerns the name behind the narrating voice, he is able to track down her address and phone number in the IRS files, allowing him to present himself to her in person with and plead that she not kill him off in her novel, lest it kill him in real life.

The problem is that prior to Harold arriving at her apartment, Eiffel had finally devised a way to kill him and had committed the idea to paper, albeit only in handwritten form. Eiffel agrees to let Harold read the draft—to audit her, again, albeit in a literary rather than a numerical way—which Harold passes on to Jules Hilbert for his advice. Hilbert reads the draft and (tragicomically) declares to Harold that he must die; the novel is Eiffel's masterpiece. Harold musters the courage to read the novel himself and concurs with Hilbert that it is indeed a great work of fiction, a moment that marks the culmination of his transition from a man obsessed with numbers to one who can also appreciate and admit other values. As a result, Harold altruistically gives Karen Eiffel permission to type up the ending and kill him off as planned.

Earlier in the film, in an effort to help Harold discern the nature of his storyline, Professor Hilbert quoted a statement from the end of Italo Calvino's *If on a Winter's Night a Traveler*, which refers to the traditional endings of all stories:

> In ancient times a story could end only in two ways; having passed all tests, the hero and heroine married, or else they died. The ultimate meaning to which all stories refer has two faces: the continuity of life, the inevitability of death.[18]

Hilbert's invocation of Calvino compels Harold to analyze his life in terms of its plot. Is it a comedy? A tragedy? In our discussion of *Crimes and Misdemeanors*, we encountered a film that deliberately conflated and confused these generic categories so as to flout or expose as a lie the very idea of classical story structure and traditional morality. In *Stranger than Fiction*, we meet a protagonist who, although he never before considered his life in terms of story, begins to trace the plot patterns of his life in search of self-understanding. As the film nears its conclusion, Harold's story seems to be on a course defined by Calvino's second, tragic option, yet something very different occurs, and redemptive possibility is reaffirmed.

Because of his newfound capacity to be awed by love and literature, Harold discovers a greater capacity, when his story intersects with that of a bus driver and a little boy on a brand-new bicycle, to do generous and loving acts, a shift in orientation that also accords with recent scientific research. According to a report published recently in the *Wall Street Journal*, "[r]esearchers have found that 'awe experiences' increase our pro-social behaviors, making us more generous and more humble. They increase our 'empathic accuracy,' so we recognize another person's emotional expression and respond with concern. And they make us more willing to engage with trust and connect with others."[19]

Harold's "awedness," if you will, also provokes Karen Eiffel to experience radical, authorial empathy and thereby to reconsider her ending. "How many people do you think I've killed?" she asks Penny Escher in desperation. "I've killed eight people," she answers bleakly, deciding as a result of this newfound awareness to rewrite Harold's story and reject the inevitability of Harold's premature death. Written collaboratively by author and character, *Death and Taxes* thus becomes the story not of those inevitable, inexorable aspects of life—like dying and paying taxes, or being consumed by predators as in the grisly animal shows that Harold watches in an effort to arrest the plot of his own human story—but of those contingent elements of life, love, and religion that hinge on creative and affirmative choices, on genuine encounters with other human beings and with a God who also proves receptive to generative, qualitative change.

Moments of Awe and How a Wristwatch Saved Harold Crick

Our theological reading of *Stranger than Fiction* thus arrives at the two insights, both beautifully articulated by Abraham Joshua Heschel: 1) that transformative religious experience is constituted by moments of awe and 2) that not only does man seek God, but God also seeks out man.

According to Heschel,

> [t]he ultimate insight is the outcome of *moments*, when we are stirred beyond words, of instants of wonder, awe, praise, fear, trembling, and radical amazement; of awareness, of grandeur, of perceptions we can grasp but are unable to convey, of discoveries of the unknown, of moments in which we abandon the pretense of being acquainted with the world, of *knowledge by inacquaintance*. It is at the climax of such moments that we attain the certainty that life has meaning, that time is more than evanescence, that beyond all being there is someone who cares.[20]

Recalling Heschel's location of religious experience in "instants of wonder," *Stranger than Fiction* argues that what ultimately saves Harold Crick from his tragic fate is his wristwatch—that is to say, a renewed, qualitative appreciation of life stories as unfolding in time.

At the beginning of *Stranger than Fiction*, as the camera zooms in from outer space, we hear the ticking all over of watches and the sounding of a cuckoo clock, signaling that not just place but also time will figure prominently in this film. Indeed, as the voice-over narrative makes clear, Harold Crick is a man who adheres slavishly to his watch. Time as a quantity governs and deadens all aspects of his life. When God the author begins to narrate his life, however, Harold's watch begins to misbehave, and as a result, his prior approach to time is radically disrupted. He takes time off work. He enters into a relationship. He experiences his life as a detailed story that unfolds preciously in minutes and hours and days.

The commandment in the Torah requiring the Israelites to mark the month of Nissan as the first month of the year (*Haḥodesh hazeh lakhem rosh ḥodashim* [Exodus 12:2; This month shall be unto you the beginning of months; it shall be the first month of the year to you]) communicates a similar message. Exodus Rabbah 15:9 explains the significance of this commandment with a mashal:

> THIS MONTH SHALL BE UNTO YOU THE BEGINNING OF MONTHS. Another explanation: We may illustrate by the parable of a king unto whom a son was born, whereupon he made a joyous celebration; but the son was taken captive and spent a long time in captivity. On his release, the king fixed an anniversary. So, too, prior to Israel's descent into Egypt, they counted by years; but after they had gone down to Egypt and become enslaved there, God performed miracles for them and they were redeemed; and then did they begin to count the months, as it says "This month shall be unto you the beginning of months."[21]

According to this midrash, slavery, depicted here by way of a parable about the kidnapping of a prince, deprives the slave of any control over the details of time. Each day and month becomes identical to the one before it and the one that comes after. Therefore, the first mitzvah given to the kidnapped, princely Israelites when they are freed from slavery is to take ownership of their time, not just by counting and recording the seconds and minutes of their lives but by shaping them into a story and endowing it with meaning.

The shared Hebrew root of the verbs *lispor* (to count) and *lesapper* (to tell or recount, as in a story) seem to reflect this connection between counting or measuring units of time and shaping them into a story. The "*Unetaneh tokef*" prayer referred to earlier includes a similar combined description of God as *kotev vehotem vesofer umoneh*, writing, inscribing, counting, and totaling. BT Kiddushin 30a states that the earliest rabbinic scholars were called *soferim* because they used to count all the letters of the Torah. The same word *sofer* refers to a ritual scribe as well as a writer. In imagining God as a *sofer*, we call to mind notions of God as author of the universe, as creator and shaper of Time, as inventor of language and story as a medium of religious truth.

According to Exodus Rabbah, God's redemptive presence in our lives effects an awareness of time and story's true, sacred significance. In the presence of God and real human relationships, one's activity in time is transformed from slavish repetition and redundancy to a story worth telling and celebrating.

The second teaching attributed above to Abraham Joshua Heschel is that achieving this awareness and experiencing moments of awe matters not only to human beings but also to God. In fact, God pursues a similar quest:

> This is the mysterious paradox of Biblical faith: *God is pursuing man*. It is as if God were unwilling to be alone, and He had chosen man to serve Him. Our seeking Him is not only man's but also His concern, and must not be considered an exclusively human affair . . . All of human history as described in the Bible may be summarized in one phrase: *God is in search of man*.[22]

Note that while Heschel presents this image of God in search of man in exclusively masculine terms, *Stranger than Fiction* puts a feminine face on the image, suggesting that Karen Eiffel's change of heart, mind, ending, and disposition constitutes a recovery of *raḥamim* (compassion), a word related to *reḥem*, the Hebrew word for womb.

Throughout the film, Eiffel appears sickly and drab, dressed in shapeless, androgynous garb. When she appears at Jules Hilbert's office, though, after years of receiving letters from him and never deigning to answer a single one, Karen Eiffel has become feminine and stylish, dressed in a striking asymmetrical sweater, her face bright and her hair carefully combed. Everything in the way she comports herself during this meeting suggests a turn of heart and disposition. Radical empathy for her character, Harold Crick, opens up Karen Eiffel herself to awe, wonder, creativity, and productivity—experiences that seems to have eluded her in recent years. As Christian writer Anne Lamott reflects in terms of her own practice of writing:

I honestly think in order to be a writer, you have to learn to be reverent. If not, why are you writing? Why are you here? Let's think of reverence as awe, as presence and openness to the world. The alternative is that we stultify, we shut down. Think of those times when you've read prose or poetry that is presented in such a way that you have a fleeting sense of being *startled* by beauty or insight, by a glimpse into someone's soul. All of a sudden everything seem to fit together or at least to have some meaning for a moment. This is our goal as writers, I think; to help others have this sense of—please forgive me—wonder, of seeing things anew, things that catch us off guard, that break in on our small, bordered worlds.[23]

Read in terms of this notion of writerly awe, *Stranger than Fiction* compels us to consider not only our own human experiences of religious wonder but also God's relation and response to them. If God writes Torah and our lives, we comment and add and contribute to every aspect of the story. We work together to reach one another, reading and writing in collaboration to save our lives.

9
―――

A Serious Man

Parables of Jewishness

And now, in this book that looks at the Jewish engagement with film as a form of inverted midrash, in which film plays the role of mashal to the nimshal of Jewish text, comes a chapter on a film composed of meshalim within meshalim—parables within parables.

Larry Gopnik, the protagonist of *A Serious Man*, is a Jewish physics professor at the University of Minnesota whose life is suddenly thrown into disarray. First his wife, Judith, announces that she wants a divorce so that she can marry a dumpy and unctuous man named Sy Ableman. Within days Larry finds himself exiled from his own home, living miserably at the Jolly Roger motel with his misfit brother, saddled with mounting legal bills and other unanticipated expenses. Then Larry discovers that his application for tenure has been jeopardized by an anonymous denouncer—perhaps his wife's lover? At the same time, his professional and moral integrity is threatened by a Korean student who attempts to blackmail him for a better grade. All the while he is repeatedly (and comically) harassed by Dick Dutton of the Columbia Record Club for failing to pay for record albums that he neither ordered nor listened to. Larry cannot understand why all these bad things are happening to him, given that he didn't "do anything."[1] What, he wonders, is the meaning of it all?

Written and directed by acclaimed filmmakers Joel and Ethan Coen, *A Serious Man* is their most Jewish film to date. As such, it has provoked widespread responses from rabbis and Jewish academics, some irate, some adulatory. (In 2011, a major chunk of an issue of the journal of the Association for Jewish Studies, *AJS Review*, was dedicated to a symposium on the movie.) The film touches upon several of the themes explored in *Forrest Gump*—simplicity, faith, the meaning of life—but treats these issues within a specifically Jewish context and takes them decidedly in the direction of perplexity and the absurd. It deals with a number of sociological, educational, and theological issues—the banality of Jewish family life in a late 1960s Minnesota suburb; the failure of the Hebrew school movement to educate meaningfully,[2] and the seeming inability of religion and science alike to provide real and credible answers to life's major questions—and repeatedly approaches these issues or questions by way of parables. Like the rabbis[3] who attempt to explain a textual difficulty by using the phrase *mashal lemah hadavar domeh* (a parable: to what can it be likened?), the Coen brothers introduce several parables into their film, creating concentric rings of stories within stories.

Rather than offering any real answers or nimshalim, however, these parables only reinforce and sharpen the central questions of the film. Why do good people suffer? What role does God play in the workings of the world? What, if anything, can be known with certainty? If, at the conclusion of the Forrest Gump chapter, I turned to Paul Ricoeur's notion of second naïveté and argued that interpretation can serve as a means of reencountering the sacred, *A Serious Man* "sets interpretation itself as a problem."[4]

The Epigraph and the Prologue

The film begins with the words "Receive with simplicity everything that happens to you," a line taken from Rashi's commentary on Deuteronomy 18:13, which enjoins each Israelite to "be whole-hearted [*tamim*] with the Eternal your God." Rashi's commentary comes to explain the placement of this generalized call to simplicity or "whole-heartedness" within the context of a biblical discussion of prohibitions against soothsaying and necromancy:

> Walk with Him in simplicity/completeness, hope for Him/ expect Him and don't search for foretellings, rather receive with simplicity all that happens to you, and thus you will be with Him and with His portion. (my translation)

Based on this epigraph, one might expect the ensuing film to tell the story of a protagonist who receives (or refuses to receive) all that happens to him with simplicity. That doesn't exactly prove to be the case. In fact, the connection between the epigraph, the Yiddish prologue that immediately follows it, and the main body of the film that comes thereafter is hardly straightforward, requiring considerable reflection and interpretation.

Why do the Coen brothers begin the film with this call to simplicity? And why do they choose to follow this epigraph first with an image of falling snow (or whirling particles) and then with a Yiddish prologue set in the shtetl, featuring characters who have no clear connection to the rest of the film?

Perhaps the Yiddish prologue is meant to be a nostalgic gesture, an effort to transport the viewers back to simpler Jewish times, apropos of the epigraph. But this is no familiar or classic Jewish folktale, and thus it provides no easy route back to times of purportedly naïve faith. Rather, it is a narrative of the writer-directors' original devising, one that serves chiefly to introduce the problem of interpretive uncertainty that hovers over the film as a whole. Velvel, the hero of the prologue, is returning home on a snowy night after a wondrous experience. "*Mamesh a vunder*," he says, "*Emes a vunder!*" Upon reaching his house, he explains to his stony-faced wife, Dora, that he is late because the wheel broke off his cart. Miraculously, at this late hour, a droshky passed by, and out came an old man who helped him with the cart. Who was this old man? None other Traitle Groshkover, an elderly scholar whom Dora herself knows. Appalled, Dora retorts that Traitle Groshkover is dead! He died three years ago from typhus. Her cousin attended the shiva after his death, and so the man Velvel met must have been a dybbuk. Velvel laughs off this idea, but Dora sticks to her story. "Dybbuk" means "to cling" or "to stick" in Hebrew. So we wonder: is Traitle really a dybbuk, or is the real dybbuk Dora's clinging superstitions?

Suddenly there is a knock on the door: it is Traitle Groshkover himself, as Velvel had invited him over for a bowl of soup, a gesture of thanks for helping him out so on the road. Traitle greets Dora jovially with a string of compliments. Dora in turn greets the old guest with cold suspicion (underscored by her persistent act of chopping ice), accusing him outright, when he refuses to have any soup, of being a dybbuk, insofar as dybbuks don't eat. Velvel tries to excuse her behavior, explaining to Traitle what Dora thinks of him, but that he himself doesn't believe such *bobe-mayses* (grandmother's tales). He is a rational man, with his head *of'n ort* (in place). (One cannot help thinking, in light of this phrase, of the wheel that broke off Velvel's cart; perhaps Velvel is overly sanguine about his ability to avoid stories and keep everything in its rational place?) Tellingly, skeptical Dora ignores her husband's claims of rationalism and points to the supposedly uneven trim of Traitle's beard as further evidence of his dybbuk-ness, recalling that the beard of dead Traitle had also been uneven. Traitle himself attempts to counter Dora's tenuously argued story, saying that he gave himself a hurried shave this morning, and while he had formerly been sick with typhus, he had recovered. Mid-sentence, Dora leans forward and stabs him in the chest with her ice pick. As such, she evokes the biblical Yael in Judges 4, who turns an occasion of hospitality into an opportunity to impale the Canaanite commander, Sisera, with a tent peg. Is Dora a heroine or a criminal, a savior or a murderer? Are she and Velvel now destined for divine retribution? It is very uncertain.

Velvel is dumfounded and shocked, but Traitle responds with laughter. Dora observes this illogical laughter and deduces that Traitle's wound seems to be having no ill effect on him, proof again that he cannot really be human. It is only after Dora notes Traitle's seeming invulnerability that Traitle claims not to be feeling well and begins to bleed around the site of the wound, as if on cue. Perhaps it would be best, he says, for him to have a bowl of soup after all? Traitle then abruptly changes his mind; a man knows when he is not wanted. In an instant, he walks briskly out of the house, the ice pick still sticking out of his chest, his massive clown-like shoes plodding ahead into the winter storm. A dybbuk or not a dybbuk? That is the prologue's question. But what does any of this have to do with the rest of the movie?

The Coen brothers themselves speak of the prologue in generic terms as an introductory folktale:

> It [the film] felt like a folk tale, so it served implicitly as an introduction, to say, "Here's another folk tale, here's another Jewish story." I guess this is imposing an explanation after the fact, because we don't really think about it in these terms while we're doing it, but, yeah, it's part of the whole Yiddishkeit, part of the whole Jew storytelling thing. Jews are big on stories, you know?[5]

More specific terms, I would argue, are in order. Viewing the prologue not so much as a folktale but as a mashal or parable allows for a potentially deeper understanding of its relation to the rest of the film. The word parable derives from the Greek word meaning juxtaposition, analogy, or comparison. As scholar David Stern explains,

> A parable suggests a set of parallels between an imagined fictional event and an immediate "real" situation confronting the parable's author and his audience. In both parables and fables, though, the literary form tends to imply the parallel rather than explicate it. The task of understanding the parallel and its implications, or levels of implication, is left largely to the audience.[6]

Part of the point of a parable, then—and this clearly obtains to the structure of *A Serious Man*—is to provoke consideration of the significance of the parallel. Stern also notes the frequent presence in rabbinic parables of "inequalities and inconsistencies between the mashal and the nimshal,"[7] allowing for ambiguity or dynamism in interpreting the midrash as a whole. Sometimes the analogy is not entirely clear or immediately obvious. There are gaps or incomplete correspondences that suggest the need for yet another comparison to complete the picture. There are riddling elements that require further consideration.

If the prologue of *A Serious Man* is a mashal, then the main body of the film—which itself contains other meshalim—is the nimshal or analogous "real-life" event. How so? What exactly are the parallels that draw together these otherwise very different stories, one taking place in the shtetl in Yiddish, the other in Minnesota in English?

We begin with the similarities between Velvel and Larry. Both men fall victim to the deeds of their cold, stonyhearted wives. Both, in their own contexts, claim to be men of reason but are faced with problems that do not lend themselves easily to rational explanation or resolution. Both are decent men, wholehearted and grateful, until trouble comes their way and undermines their certainties. As it turns out, both succumb to misfortune just as they attempt to do good. Velvel invites Traitle to his home to repay him for his kindness, inadvertently luring him to his death (that is, if he is human after all). Almost every time Larry attempts to do someone a kindness, he ends up in trouble. He lets his hapless brother move in with his family and ends up having to live with him at the Jolly Roger and pay his legal expenses. He gets on the roof to fix the TV antenna for his son, only to see his next-door neighbor sunbathing naked and be lured into her house. Larry wants to return the bribe money to Clive but then finds himself threatened by Clive's father with a defamation suit. Rather than serving as a shield or a source or merit, goodness renders these men a target for evil.

One cannot help but think of Job, that famous biblical *tam veyasher*, who does good but in doing so makes himself vulnerable to the denunciation of the Satan and thus to suffering and, even so, accepts everything that happens to him with simplicity. "Naked I came from my mother's womb and naked I return there. Yahweh has given and Yahweh has taken, Blessed be the name of Yahweh (Job 1:20–21),[8] says Job after he is afflicted by the Satan with boils and his children are killed—all a ploy by the Satan to test his wholeheartedness and uprightness. In spite of his suffering, Job neither sins nor blames God. In contrast to his cynical wife, Job "'*odenu maḥazik betumato*"; Job continues to cling (dybbuk-like?) to his innocence or wholeheartedness. That is, until his friends start pestering him, insisting that no one suffers this way unless they deserve it. Only then does Job begin cursing his days and eloquently expressing his rage over all that has unfairly befallen him.

Is Larry Gopnik a modern-day Job? It has become something of a commonplace among critics and scholars to read *A Serious Man* in light of this biblical book.[9] What I would like to add to this commonplace interpretation is a sense of how the book of Job serves as an ironic proof-text for the meshalim within meshalim that constitute this film. The rabbis of the Talmud themselves debated how to read the story of Job, that is, whether to view the book as historical or as a mashal.[10] This rabbinic uncertainty as to how to label Job's story is itself intriguing and resonates with the themes of uncertainty or interpretive ambiguity that are represented in *A Serious Man*.

There are several more specific parallels to be drawn between Job and *A Serious Man*. Like Job, who suffers illness and familial loss and then is subjected to diatribe and harangue from would-be friends Eliphaz, Bildad, Zoar, and Elihu, trouble-struck Larry is subjected to hollow speeches by friends and rabbis alike. The book of Job climaxes with God's retort to Job from the whirlwind, and *A Serious Man* similarly ends with the image of an impending tornado.

Job's divine whirlwind, however, is far more articulate and communicative than the Coen brothers' mute tornado. In response to the divine whirlwind, the otherwise loquacious Job finally acquiesces to the will of

God the Creator and holds his peace. "I see how little I am," says Job. "I will not answer you. I am putting my hand to my lips" (Job 40:4).[11] According to translator Raymond P. Scheindlin, though,

> Job is never reconciled, his heart demands meaning, even though intellectually he intuits (and we know) that he cannot have it . . . Job's anger helps tame ours and bring it into manageable compass; this itself is a kind of consolation. We read Job not because it provides answers to our questions, consolation for our grief, or redress for our anger, but because it expresses our questions, our grief, and anger with such force.[12]

Both the book of Job and *A Serious Man*, it seems, "demand meaning." At the end of the biblical book, however, God restores Job's fortune and blesses him with new children, while *A Serious Man* provides no such resolution or restitution. (The closest one gets to restitution in the film is the return of Danny Gopnik's radio by Rabbi Marshak, a character who fits a childish conception God-as-Old-Bearded-Man; but all that happens before the tornado.) The fate of Larry and his son Danny hangs in the balance as the movie comes to a close. If *A Serious Man* is a contemporary Job story, then it is one that raises similar theological challenges, but without the easy fix of the biblical ending. The book of Job is a story about a serious man with serious troubles and grievances. By contrast, none of the characters or institutions in *A Serious Man* can be taken entirely seriously: not Larry, not his department chair, not the rabbis, and certainly not Sy Ableman, Rabbi Nachtner's eulogy about him as a "serious man" notwithstanding. The biblical book attempts to assuage doubt and nihilism by voicing Job's complaints and "rewarding" him in the end. *A Serious Man*, however, offers no such rewards. What it does provide, however, is the alternative consolation of laughter. The film raises serious questions and laughs at all the silly answers that people like to give to them. The ironic juxtaposition of Job and Larry Gopnik serves this theological-comic cause.

More (on) Parables

Comedy in *A Serious Man* also comes from the mock, moronic mini-parables that are stitched together throughout the main body of the film. First there is the parable proffered to the insight-seeking Larry by the junior rabbi of the synagogue. Informed that Rabbi Scott is covering for the more senior rabbi, Rabbi Nachtner, Larry reluctantly tells young Rabbi Scott about his marital separation and his wife's desire to get a *get* (a Jewish divorce). Young, inexperienced Rabbi Scott (we're not sure whether Scott is his first name or his last, reinforcing our sense of his childish obtuseness) responds with an exhortatory parable about the empty synagogue parking lot—"Look at the parking lot, Larry!"—a fatuous attempt to convince Larry that his problem is that he has lost track of Hashem and needs to rediscover his sense of perspective and his capacity for wonder. Taken in the abstract, Rabbi Scott's enthusiastic embrace of wonder echoes Abraham Joshua Heschel's notion of radical amazement as a precondition for religious experience.[13] The problem, of course, is that none of this has anything to do with Larry's real problem, which is that Judith has been seeing Sy [sigh!] Ableman and is asking for a Jewish divorce. Rabbi Scott also suggests that Larry has been treating Judith as a thing—a reference, it seems to Martin Buber and his discussion of I-It relations in *I and Thou*.[14] But Larry has not treated her as a thing; he has not "done anything," which itself might be the problem, for in doing nothing, he enabled Sy Ableman to do quite a bit. Rabbi Scott's parable is a mock parable because it is neither relevant nor apposite nor analogous. Not to mention the fact that an empty parking lot is hardly the best staging ground for radical amazement. In the context of his meeting with Larry, Rabbi Scott's parable turns out to be as vacant as its central image.

Larry doesn't have much better luck with the senior rabbi. When Larry finally meets with Rabbi Nachtner, it is after Sy Ableman has been killed in a car accident. So demeaned and unmanned is Larry by his wife, Judy—her name brings to mind the New Testament story of Judith and Holfernes—that she expects him to pay for her lover Sy's funeral. (Later they are seen sitting shiva for Sy in Larry's home, as if Sy were a close relative.) Larry presents all of this to Rabbi Nachtner in the scene the scene excerpt that follows:

> **LARRY:** I don't know where it all leaves me, Sy's death. Obviously it's not going to go back like it was.
> **RABBI NACHTNER:** Mm. Would you even want that, Larry?"
> **LARRY:** No, I—well yeah! Sometimes! Or—I don't know; I guess the honest answer is I don't know. What was my life

before? Not what I thought it was. What does it all mean? What is Hashem trying to tell me, making me pay for Sy Ableman's funeral?
RABBI NACHTNER: Mm.
LARRY: And—did I tell you I had a car accident the same time Sy had his? The same instant, for all I know. Is Hashem telling me that Sy Ableman is me, or we are all one or something?[15]

Larry wants Rabbi Nachtner to tell him whether he should treat the story of Sy Abelman as a parable for his own life. He wants the rabbi to identify correspondences between things, to suggest that there is an order and design behind the way things happen. In response to this questioning, Larry is told another mock-parable, this time a story about a dentist named Sussman (itself a kind of ironic joke, since Sussman means "sweet man," not very apt for a dentist). Sussman the dentist discovers the Hebrew word הושיעני (help me, save me!) mysteriously engraved on the back of the teeth of a "goy's teeth."

Completely mystified and obsessed by this vision, Sussman recontacts the "goy" in question (Rabbi Nachtner uses this derogatory term throughout his recounting of the story), goes in search of other such messages on the

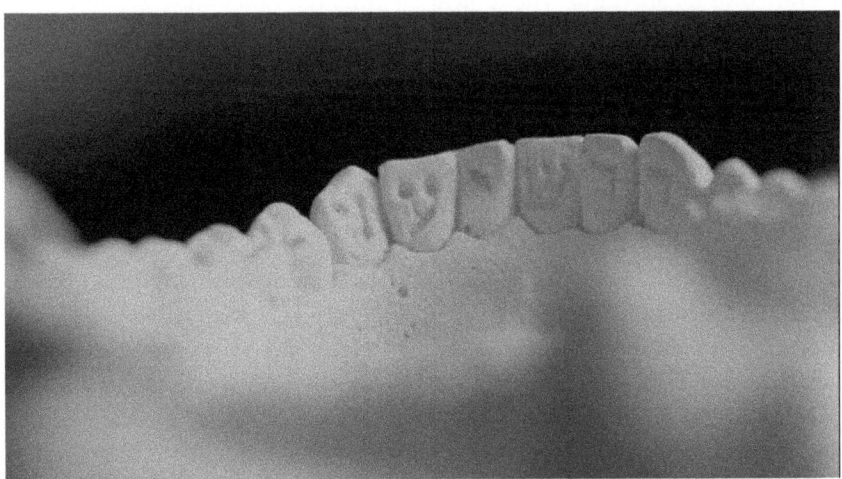

Figure 9.1. *A Serious Man*, Sussman's Teeth.

backs of other people's teeth, and even attempts to see if the inscription can be decoded using Hebrew numerology. He comes up with nothing. Eventually, Sussman (like Larry) goes to Rabbi Nachtner for guidance:

> What does it mean, Rabbi? Is it a sign from Hashem? Help me. I, Sussman, should be doing something to help this goy? Doing what? The teeth don't say. I should know without asking? Or maybe I'm supposed to help people generally—lead a more righteous life? Is the answer in cabalah? In Torah? Or is there even a question? Tell me, Rabbi—what can such a sign mean?[16]

Rabbi Nachtner recounts all of this to Larry but stops short of offering any commentary. Larry asks him what he told Sussman in response, assuming that his response to Sussman's questions might shed light on some of his own predicament and questions. The rabbi, so caught up in the telling, so immersed in the mashal that he cannot remember the nimshal, is surprised by Larry's question. It is even relevant? Reluctantly, at Larry's urging, the rabbi recounts his response to Sussman: "The teeth, we don't know. A sign from Hashem, don't know. Helping others, couldn't hurt."[17] Building on the dentistry imagery, he then tells Larry that the questions that are bothering him are like a toothache. "We feel them for a while, then they go away. . . . We all want the answer. But Hashem doesn't owe us the answer, Larry. Hashem doesn't owe us anything. The obligation runs the other way."[18]

Chauvinism aside, Rabbi Nachtner's parable, like Rabbi Scott's, includes a few obvious, indisputable truths. First, none of us can identify a "sign from Hashem" with any certainty, and "we can't know everything." Second, helping others cannot hurt. It is not true, however, according to our covenantal tradition, that God owes us nothing. And Larry's problems and questions are not like a toothache, as most toothaches do not actually go away when left untended. Typically, they get worse. As for the parable of the goy's teeth, again: what does that have to do with anything? Rabbi Nachtner's decision to guide Larry via a story in which a Jewish dentist marvels over the very idea of a gentile being marked for salvation—this, when Jesus's Hebrew name (Yehoshua) means just that—shows us that glib Rabbi Nachtner really has very little to offer Larry other than bigotry and boiled-down Noachide ethics. Doing good can't hurt. Then again, isn't the problem here that Larry keeps on getting hurt in the process of trying to do good?

Where Physics and Theology Meet

Larry is a physicist, a man of science. One might think, then, that he would gain some sense of certainty from his own scholarly discipline. From what we see during the film, however, the field of quantum mechanics, meant to provide a picture how things work in the world on the smallest possible scale, yields its own share of uncertainty. There are two scenes in the film that show Larry teaching physics—one where he is seen explaining the paradox of Schrödinger's cat, the other where he is detailing the equations related to Heisenberg's uncertainty principle, both of which call out for interpretation.

In 1935, Erwin Schrödinger published his famous thought experiment, one of the most celebrated paradoxes in quantum theory, written in critical response to Heisenberg's uncertainty idea. As John H. Lienhard explains:

> The riddle of the cat begins with Heisenberg's Uncertainty idea: the most precise measurement we could ever make would be to shoot one photon of light at a moving object. But even so delicate a peek will change the position and motion we're trying to measure. At best, you always measure with some uncertainty.
>
> That's easy enough to understand. But an awesome subtlety turns it into a new tenet of scientific faith. It makes precise measurement unthinkable. And that means we no longer have reason for thinking the world has any ultimate precision to measure.
>
> So we take the last terrible step. We admit the world is indeterminate. We admit that electrons have fuzzy edges. When one collides, it may bounce one way. It may bounce the other.
>
> Schrödinger said that if that's the case, let's seal a cat, a Geiger counter, a fragment of radioactive material, and a bottle of poison gas into a box for one hour. There's a 50-50 chance that radioactive decay will trigger the Geiger counter, activate a mechanism that breaks the bottle, and poison the cat. He asks if we'll find a live cat or a dead one when we open the box.[19]

Within the context of the film, the paradox of Schrödinger's cat serves as yet another parable. Is the cat in the box dead or alive? In quantum theory, we can speak only of probability, not certainty. And so it is with many of the scenarios in the film. Is Traitle Groshkover a dybbuk or a human being? Does he live (forever) or die? In leaving Velvel and Dora's house and exiting into the snowy, particle-strewn night, Traitle metaphorically enters the dark box of Schrödinger's experiment. And we are left wondering.

Then there is Larry's predicament with his student, Clive Park. Early on in the film, Larry has a conversation with Clive in which Clive raises objections to his failing grade on the physics midterm, saying that, equations aside, he understands [the parable of] "the dead cat." Larry retorts: "You can't really understand the physics without understanding the math. The math tells how it really works. That's the real thing; the stories I give you in class are just illustrative; they're like, fables, say, to help give you a picture. An imperfect model. I mean—even I don't understand the dead cat. The math is how it really works."[20] Here Larry presents "the math," perhaps misleadingly, as a realm of certainty or comprehension, as opposed to the stories or fables that remain elusive or riddling. Ironically, Larry's "story" with Clive itself becomes impossible to interpret definitively. Did Clive leave that envelope full of money on Larry's desk after their first conversation to bribe Larry for a better grade, or did he not? Larry insists later that in his office, "actions have consequences." But Clive denies that he did anything or that he is missing anything: "Mere surmise, sir; often uncertain." The later intervention of Clive's father, with threats of a discrimination lawsuit should Larry accuse Clive of bribery, only intensifies the predicament, placing Larry, so to speak, in the position of Schrödinger hypothetical scientist, unable to open the box to prove one thing or another.

The classic rabbinic literary response to riddling texts or issues of this sort is that of Ben Bag Bag (whose repetitive name itself suggests to need to try and try again): "Turn it and turn it over, for everything is in it" (Pirkei Avot, 5:25). Fittingly, the Coen brothers include several images in the film of objects turning around. In the prologue, a wheel falls off Velvel's cart, initiating the action of the film. Visually echoing this image, the main body of the film begins with the image of a circular opening that gets ever larger as the camera zooms in, turning into the opening of Danny's ear as he listens to the words of Jefferson Airplane's psychedelic classic "Somebody to Love." Later Danny listens repeatedly to a phonograph record playing the opening verse of his bar mitzvah Torah portion, which refers to God speaking to Moses on Sinai and commanding the laws of the sabbatical and jubilee years (Leviticus 25), including the return of land and property to their previous owners despite their having fallen on hard times. The record turns around and around, returning Danny again and again to the original site or uncertainty of divine revelation. Larry himself listens over and over to a record of a Yiddish folk song by Mark Warshawsky (1848–1907) called "The Miller's Tears," the lyrics of which depict a cycle of exile and woe:[21]

O how many years have passed by since I've been a miller here The wheels turn, the years go by I'm already growing old and grey.	אוי וויפֿל יאָרן זענען פֿאַרפֿאָרן זינט איך בין אַ מילנער אָט אָ דאָ די רעדער דרייען זיך, די יאָרן גייען זיך, איך בין שוין אַלט און גרויס און גרא.
There are days I want to remember if I ever had a bit of luck. The wheels turn, the years go by, I get no answers back.	ס'איז טעג פֿאַראַנען, כ'וויל מיך דערמאָנען צי כ'האָב געהאַט אַ שטיקל גליק. די רעדער דרייען זיך, די יאָרן גייען זיך, קיין ענטפֿער איז ניטאָ צוריק.
I heard it said they want to drive me out of my village and from the mill. The wheels turn, the years go by without an end, without a goal.	כ'האָב געהערט זאָגן, מען וועל מיך פֿאַריאָגן, אַרויס פֿון דאָרף און פֿון דער מיל. די רעדער דרייען זיך, די יאָרן גייען זיך, אוי, אָן אַן עק און אָן אַ ציל.
Exiled from happiness, I'll remain without a wife, children, all alone. The wheels turn, the years go by And I am lonely like a stone.	פֿון גליק פֿאַרטריבן, בין איך געבליבן, אָן ווײַב, אָן קינד, אַ דו אַליין. די רעדער דרייען זיך, די יאָרן גייען זיך און עלנט בין איך ווי אַ שטיין.
Where shall I live? Who wants me? I'm already old, already tired. The wheels turn, the years go by and with them too goes the Jew.	וווּ וועל איך וווינען? ווער וועט מיך שוינען? איך בין שוין אַלט, איך בין שוין מיד. די די רעדער דרייען זיך, די יאָרן גייען זיך און אויך מיט זיי גייט אויס דער ייִד.

As it turns out, this Yiddish folk song itself is a parable, one that uses the story of a miller and the image of revolving millstones as a metaphor for the recurrent expulsions of the Jews from the lands of their exile. Within the context of the film, the song also echoes Larry Gopnik's situation, cast out, as he is, from his home, at a remove from his wife and children. In the same way that classic rabbinic parables are meant to lament as well as allay Jewish anguish, this song, which Larry listens to over and over, seems to offer him comfort as well as an opportunity to vent about his sense of unfair suffering. Where is the providential God in this recurring scheme? Where is the sabbatical calm or the Jubilee restitution for the modern Jew?

Together these stories within the story, the ridiculous alongside the sublime, form a litany of filmic parables, with each story adding something to the overall narrative but remaining insufficient on its own. Turn it and turn it again, the film seems to say. Bring on more and more stories! Indeed, the plethora of parables in this film suggests that the parable is not simply a device in the film but a meta-subject in its own right.

The idea of composing a litany of meshalim on the subject of the mashal also falls squarely within midrashic tradition, as in this famous midrash from Song of Songs Rabbah, which lavishes praise on Solomon for creating the parable by piling up one parable on top of another. Only with the creation of the parable, says this midrash, was anyone able to gain access to Torah:

> [B]efore Solomon, there was no model of the parable. R. Nahman told two parables: It can be likened to a large palace that had many entrances. Everyone who entered got lost from the entrance. A certain clever man came who took a skein of thread and hung it along the way from the entrance. And everyone came and went by means of the skein of thread. Likewise, before Solomon arose, no one was able to learn words of the Torah; but after Solomon everyone began to comprehend Torah. R. Nahman gave a second parable: It is like reed thicket, which no one was able to pass through. A certain clever man came along, took a scythe and cleared it away, and everyone began to enter and leave through the clearing. So it was with Solomon. R. Yose said: It can be likened to a large basketful of fruit, which did not have a handle, so it couldn't be carried. A certain clever man came along, who made handles for the

basket, and so the basket could from now on be moved with its handles. Likewise, before Solomon arose, no one was able to learn words of the Torah; but after Solomon everyone began to comprehend Torah. R. Shela said: It can be likened to a large pot full of boiling water, which did not have a handle to be moved. A certain clever man came along, made a handle for it, and it could now be moved with its handle. R. Hanina said: It is can be likened to a deep well full of water whose waters were cold, sweet and delicious, but no creature could drink from it. Then a certain man came along, and supplied the well with rope upon rope and cord upon cord, and used these to draw the water from the well and drink from it. Everyone thereafter drew and drank. Likewise, from one matter to another, from one parable to the next, Solomon arose and arrived at the secret of Torah, as it was written: "The proverbs (*Mishlei*) of Solomon, the son of David, king of Israel" (Prov. 1:1-2). This means: By means of his parables, Solomon understood Torah. Our rabbis say: Let not the mashal [parable] be made light of in your eyes, for by means of the parable one can understand Torah. A parable [to what can it be likened?]: To a king for whom gold or a precious pearls have gone missing from his house. Does he not find it by means of a wick worth a small Roman coin? In the same way the parable should not be made light of in your eyes, for by means of the parable one takes hold of the words of Torah.[22]

In this midrash, parables are adduced to explain the merits of parables. If the Torah is like a labyrinthine palace, the parable is a spool of thread that allows one to find one's way through without getting lost. If the Torah is a thicket, the mashal is a scythe that allows you to cut a path through it. It Torah is a basket of fruit or, more dangerously, a pot of boiling water, the parable allows one to get a handle on it, so that one can either taste it or avoid getting scalded by its message. If the Torah is a well of water, the parable—or, more precisely, the litany of parables—is a series of strings that, tied together, allow one to draw up the water and quench one's thirst. According to this image, one parable will not suffice, as Solomon himself needed a series of them to gain access to Torah.

After all this unqualified, variegated praise of the mashal comes the strange reversal, in the form of a rabbinic admonition quoted in the introduction in this book, not to regard the parable as something trivial. This last mashal likens the parable form to a cheap wick used to find a missing jewel. As David Stern notes, this closing section, in relying on the image of the easily snuffed wick, "radically qualifies, even overturns, the praise that preceded it,"[23] implying doubt. What then is the real value of the parable? Is it really an indispensable implement, one that enables access, nourishes, protects, quenches, eases, and illuminates? Or is it merely a fleeting, readily extinguished, dime-store tool? Is it something serious or silly? Is the cat dead or alive? Or both?

Both, of course. But let me explain what I mean by way of a parable, one of the last parables in the film, the core narrative, it seems, from which the rest of this film script grew.[24] There's this boy named Danny Gopnik who has only three aspirations: to listen to music, watch *F-Troop*, and get stoned. Because he likes to listen to music so much, he brings his radio to Hebrew school, where it gets confiscated by his teacher, together with a twenty-dollar bill he owes to a boy named Fagle (his pot dealer). He likes smoking pot so much that he gets stoned even on the morning of his bar mitzvah. Somehow, he manages in his pot-induced haze to get up before the congregation and chant his Torah portion about the sabbatical year and the Jubilee, bringing his estranged mother and father back together, if only for a moment, in their shared pride—itself a moment of Sabbatical respite and restitution. As a reward for his performance, Danny is given the privilege, untendered to his father, of meeting with the elusive Senior Rabbi Marshak, a man so secluded and otherworldly that he does not even set foot (heaven forbid!) in the sanctuary of this Conservative synagogue. Rabbi Marshak's office is a surreal lair, adorned with paintings depicting dramatic and violent biblical scenes and filled with objects floating in formaldehyde. The old, hoary rabbi is a fantastic mix of old-world sage, modern scientist, art curator, curiosity shopkeeper, and wizard. Danny's meeting with Rabbi Marshak, undertaken when he is still in a drug haze, stands for his own access to Torah. But what sort of access? And what sort of Torah?

The scene of Danny's meeting with Rabbi Marshak is outlandish and hilarious, but also serious and loving. Here is this ancient rabbi, a quasi-mythical character. Approaching him, Danny, still drug-stupefied, is genuinely terrified. But what does the rabbi do when Danny approaches his desk? He gives him back his radio, even though it's the Sabbath, and touching a radio on the Sabbath is forbidden by Jewish law. The typical Orthodox rabbi likely would not do such a thing, but this artistically and

Figure 9.2. *A Serious Man*, Marshak.

scientifically inclined rabbi seems willing to meet all Jews where they are. In considering the image of Marshak, one cannot help but think of Rabbi Menachem Mendel Schneerson, the seventh and last Lubavitcher Rebbe (1902–1994), a prodigious Torah scholar who studied math and science and at the University of Berlin and the Sorbonne, became an advisor to religious and secular leaders alike, and created a massive Jewish outreach network predicated on one central idea, namely "the love of every Jew."[25]

As if to say, I love you as you are and I want to know what you care about and meet you there, Marshak goes on to recite the lyrics of Jefferson Airplane's "Somebody to Love," the song that Danny had been listening to when his radio was confiscated by his dullard Hebrew teacher. Somehow, miraculously, in this pre-Walkman, pre–MP3 player moment, R. Marshak knows exactly what Danny was listening to when the radio was confiscated. Somebody to love: that is what's important. Marshak then begins to recite, as if detailing a holy lineage, the names of the members of Jefferson Airplane, stumbling only on Jorma Kaukonen, a difficult name, to be sure, which Danny attempts to help him pronounce—a kind of mock Torah reading, with Danny serving as *gabbai* and the old Rabbi as novice reader. On this day of Danny's bar mitzvah, Danny and the old rabbi manage together to "study" a name and a central insight. Danny gives the rabbi the gift of new cultural exposure. The rabbi in turn tells Danny to be good and offers him the gift of old-world authenticity combined with an openness to contemporary spirituality—and here is the nimshal—a way of approaching Judaism that becomes representative, indeed, of Chabad and of such rabbis as Shlomo Carlebach and Zalman Schachter Shalomi. If Danny, like many of his peers, is ever going to attend shul regularly, this is the sort of rabbi he will likely seek out. The glib slickness of a benighted Nachtner (*nacht*, in Yiddish/German, means night) will not pass muster. Marshak will be Danny's parable, his penny candle.

That is, if he makes it out of the tornado alive. As the film draws to a close, Danny has gotten his radio back and is once again to listening to music in Hebrew class when the teacher disrupts the illusion of Hebrew "conversation" about planting trees in the Land of Israel to announce the evacuation of the class to the synagogue basement because of an impending tornado. (The fact that the movie takes place in 1967 adds an additional political dimension to the mix, pointing to a post-1967 political tornado that continues to storm and rage in the Middle East.) Standing outside with the other students as the inept teacher fumbles with the keys to the basement, Danny calls out to Fagle so that he can finally give him the twenty dollars he owes him for the pot. But Fagle, looking in the dark direction of the approaching twister, indicates that at the present moment even he has bigger worries. Danny has "done nothing" to deserve this, unless one takes into account that he pilfered the twenty dollars he needed to pay Fagle from his sister. Now that he is a bar mitzvah, is he being held to account for this petty crime?

At the very same time, Larry, who has just received mazel tov wishes on Danny's bar mitzvah and unofficial good news from his department chair that he has been granted tenure, opens up a letter from his lawyer that includes a $3000 legal bill. Until this point in the film, Larry hasn't "done anything" wrong, but the sight of this whopping figure propels him finally to change Clive Park's failing physics grade to a C minus and thus to claim the money left in the envelope on his desk to pay his bill. And now, after all of this, Larry has "done something" wrong. Immediately thereafter, as if in retribution, the phone rings with a call from his doctor telling him to come into the office immediately to discuss the results of his recent chest X-ray, an ominous call to be sure. Larry, like Danny, now faces mortal danger. His story has suddenly become that much more serious.

What consolation can parables really offer in the face of this Jobian scenario, minus the happy ending? Aren't all stories merely trivial talk when one stares at the tornado of illness and death? Perhaps, but if shelters are locked and medicine fails, what else can we rely on? The book of Job is itself one such literary shelter in hard times, a paradoxical text about protest and capitulation, which, as Dermot Cox argues, teaches us acceptance of the absurd: "The whole meaning of human life is that at its most basic level it is contingent, it is absurd. Faced with this fact man must learn to accept existence as it is, not to seek to change it (for he cannot), and yet strive to understand it without ever expecting to fit it into a fully rational pattern."[26]

A parable: to what can this chapter be likened? To the ongoing effort on the part of religious groups and scientists alike to interpret the world and discern its broader workings in the absence of certainty. To the practice of reading human experience as a series of parallel stories. To the man who drops a precious gold coin in the dark and goes searching for it with a flimsy wick—with no assurance that he will find what he has lost before the flame goes out. Such practices are often unsure, inconclusive, and part of parcel of religious life. As Sally McFague acknowledges:

> A theology that is informed by parables is necessarily a risky and open-ended kind of reflection. It recognizes not only the inconclusiveness of all conceptualization when dealing with matters between God and human beings (an insight as old as religion itself), but also the pain and skepticism—the disease—of such reflection. Theology of this sort is not neat and comfortable; but neither is the life with and under God of which it attempts to speak. The parables accept the complexity and ambiguity of life as lived here in this world and insist that it is in *this* world that God makes his gracious presence known. A theology informed by the parables can do no less—and no more.[27]

10

Exam

Test, Trials, and Attachments

The book of Job, touched upon in the previous chapter, begins with God subjecting Job, at the Satan's behest, to a series of difficult trials of faith. There, a Satanic antagonist instigates the test, but elsewhere it is God who tests a leader and the people, or the people who test God.[1] Tests abound in our culture, both mundane and monumental, marking stages of life and development and establishing criteria for acceptance to many different institutions, but for what purpose? To what pragmatic, social, spiritual, and moral ends do we test our children, our students, our employees, and our loved ones? Are the tests meant to exclude or include, to teach or reveal something to those tested, those who test, or both? Do tests mark the culmination or end of a learning process, or do they constitute a vital, formative stage of learning in and of themselves? Are tests designed to separate or join individuals? To single out the elect or to forge connections between people?

Testing for the Elect

The British film *Exam* (2009, written and directed by Stuart Hazeldine) provides an opportunity to consider these questions. Eight finalists for a high-level position at an unspecified company are called together for a final examination to determine who among them will get the job. These eight finalists constitute a racial, ethnic, and intellectual microcosm, each one representing a different group and/or excelling at a different skill set.

There are two white men: one with glasses who rarely speaks and is thus dubbed Deaf by the other white man, who calls himself White. There is a white woman with blonde hair (Blonde), and there are two white women with brown hair, one with glasses (Dark) who is a psychologist and another without glasses (Brunette). There is a man of South Asian extraction (Brown), a man of African descent with a scientific disposition (Black), and an assiduous Chinese woman who is seen in the opening sequence outlining her eyes with eyeliner, suggesting circumscribed vision, and taking deep breaths to calm herself down. Deaf is first seen in this opening sequence, preceded by an image of water running from a faucet, suggesting a need or capacity to cleanse; he then washes his eyes, places a small bandage above his eye, and puts on glasses—actions that suggest a sense of woundedness and highlight the motif of vision, which, as in *Crimes and Misdemeanors*, will play an important role in the film. White is seen in this same sequence taking a blue pill and tightening a black and white tie. Brown flips a coin, indicating a gambler's temperament. Black, who has bloodstains at the edge of his sleeve, wears a necklace with a large cross on it, which he clutches as he intones the words "I can do all things. *All things.*" All of this forges an early connection between Black and the notion of blood sacrifice. This entire opening sequence is composed of extreme close-ups, signaling to the viewer the importance of minute attention to detail. For the watcher of this film to pass the test of attentive or "re-creative" viewing, it will be important to look closely and remember what he or she has seen.

Next we see the eight candidates assembling in a spare, windowless exam room with eight desks, the door guarded by a uniformed security guard. A black man dressed in a black suit walks in and makes the following speech:

> I am the Invigilator. Listen carefully, for there will be no repetition.
>
> I won't apologize for the hardships you've endured to reach this room because the pressures and pains were necessary. Resilience is a key attribute in these troubled times and if you can't survive our selection process you won't survive in the job. Many highly qualified candidates tried to get this far and failed. You have succeeded—and now the final stage lies before you. One last hurdle separates you from your goal: which is

to join our esteemed ranks. The test is simple in comparison, yet it will determine who leaves this room with a contract of employment and who leaves . . . with the bus fare home.

Through your trials you have gained some idea of the power of this organization, so believe me when I tell you that there is no law in this room but our law. And the only rules in here are our rules.

There is one question before you, and one answer is required. If you attempt to communicate with myself, or the guard, you will be disqualified. If you spoil your paper, intentionally or accidentally, you will be disqualified. If you choose to leave the room for any reason, you will be disqualified.

Any questions?[2]

The invigilator then announces that the candidates will have eighty minutes to complete the exam: "Eighty minutes to convince us you have what it takes to join us. . . . Eighty minutes to determine the next eighty years of your lives."[3] The reference to eighty years raises the stakes of the exercise significantly, linking success on this eighty-minute exam not just to an offer of employment, but to longevity itself.[4]

The problem that each of the candidates discovers as the exam begins is that his or her paper is completely blank. The invigilator's declaration that "the only rules in here are our rules" had already wiped away law and social convention, and now they find this blankness. The film's audience faces a similar blankness as well. Unlike the typical film, which moves from location to location, *Exam* unfolds entirely in this one spare room, evocative of both a black box theater and a police interrogation room. The screen that is mounted at the front of the room indicates that someone is on the other side of the screen (like us, the audience), observing and evaluating what is taking place, but who is it? Most of the film from this point on is composed of close and medium shots, underscoring a sense of limited space and time and mounting pressure.

The Chinese candidate, the first to cave in under the pressure, picks up her pencil and begins to write, "I believe, I deserve . . . " Immediately and rather brusquely, she is ushered out of the room. "This isn't a proper test!" she protests, thus violating not just the rule against spoiling her paper, but also of communicating with the invigilator and the guard.

The Chinese candidate earns her disqualification twice over. Still, she has a point about the exam lacking a proper format. What, after all, is the question that the examinees are meant to answer?

This is the question that recurs throughout the eighty minutes of the exam, with the candidates alternatingly collaborating and turning against one another in the process of trying to find it. White, a swaggering, bullying type, with respect neither for the female and minority candidates in the room nor for intellectual or philosophical inquiry, takes the lead at the beginning, disturbing the quiet and detecting that the things the invigilator didn't say are just as important as his articulated instructions. "Is this the ultimate mind-fuck, or what???" he says to the group, noting that, while they are not allowed to speak to the invigilator or guard, they have not been prohibited from speaking with one another, moving around the room, or collaborating. True, they are competing against one another, but, to begin with, they ought to cooperate over what they need to answer.

And so, for some time, with White at the head, the group works together, exposing the test paper to different kinds of light (ultraviolet and infrared) and to various liquids as well. None of this works, though, prompting White to begin a campaign to get others disqualified so as to narrow the field of competition. First he tricks Brunette into burning (spoiling) her own paper, then prods the seemingly unstable Deaf into ripping and eating his test paper. White's cutthroat tactics unleash the latent racial and gender tensions in the room: Black versus White, Brown versus Dark, Man versus Woman. Black slugs White, ties him to a chair, and refuses to give him his pill when he needs it, causing White to pass out. Meanwhile, Brown, who suspects psychologist Dark of being a company "plant," subjects Dark to harsh physical interrogation as a way of forcing her to divulge the exam question. White eventually seizes the guard's gun and turns it on the various candidates in the room to intimidate them into leaving, shooting Black (seemingly dead) in the process. The devolution of the exam from cooperation to violence recalls William Golding's *Lord of the Flies* (1954), where Jack Merridew turns his "tribe" of hunters on the wise Piggy and democratically elected Ralph with appalling and tragic results.[5]

The only candidate in the room who remains above the fray throughout is Blonde, who frequently stands quietly on the sidelines, listening to and assessing the various arguments and stepping in occasionally to diffuse a conflict, dispel a misconception, solve an urgent problem, or aid a fellow candidate. When Brown interrogates Dark and slashes her with a piece of paper on her already cut thigh, Blonde gives Dark the Band-Aid she had placed on her own heel to prevent a blister from her high-heeled shoe. When White's medication is thrown across the room and lands inside a metal grate on the floor, Blonde uses her hairpin—a conventionally feminine accessory—to extract the pill from the grate and save White's life. Dark disqualifies herself in this same scene, unable to figure out how to address White's health emergency without breaking the rules and calling out to the invigilator for help. By contrast, Blonde seems to possess unique problem-solving skills as well as a caring disposition. She demonstrates an ability not just to follow the instructions but also to think contextually in ways that benefit not just her but the group as a whole. While White attempts to bully his way to the top, Blonde actually figures out the exam question without sacrificing any of her fellow candidates. By using the broken glass from the lights together with Deaf's glasses, she examines the paper and sees a "1." without any question following it. Recalling the last two words of the invigilator ("Any questions?"), she walks up to him, the exam period having just ended, and says: "No." In other words, there are no questions, at least none spelled out on paper. Blonde alone manages to provide this answer.

Figure 10.1. *Exam,* Blonde Looks Through Deaf's Glasses.

Life as a Blank Sheet

The blankness of the test paper, save for the number 1, serves as key plot twist in the film. More importantly, it opens the film up to a symbolic moral or religious interpretation, namely that each of us has but one life with which to make a mark, and it is up to us to decide what it should be. The exam administered in this film serves as a compressed test case of how these character types might make this mark on the blank sheet and in the limited time that is their lives. Will they spoil it? Will they work together with the others or turn against them? Will they be human beings or savages? Will they demonstrate selfish or altruistic purpose?

Theologian and geologist Pierre Teilhard de Chardin presents a similar image in his book *The Divine Milieu* (1960), where he exhorts his readers to consider life as a test or exercise presented in the form of a blank sheet:

> Try to grasp this: the things which are given to you purely as an exercise, a "blank sheet" on which you make your own mind and heart. You are on the testing ground where God can judge whether you are capable of being translated to heaven and into his presence. You are on trial. So that it matters very little what becomes of the fruits of the earth, or what they are worth. The whole question is whether you have used them in order to learn how to obey and how to love.[6]

Most of the candidates taking this exam fail to see the deeper significance of the test. Viewing the exam as nothing more than a Darwinian exercise, they spend the eighty minutes that stand for their eighty-year lives trying to triumph and survive. They are unable to see beyond the immediate goals of the test to any higher symbolic purpose.

Teilhard's repeated use of images of sight in the paragraph above corresponds with the repeated invocation of such imagery in *Exam*: first in the apparent blankness of the page, then in the candidates' efforts to coax out a visual image of a question by exposing their papers to different kinds of light, and finally in the various images of sight associated with Deaf (who turns out in the end to be the CEO of the company). Before being ejected from the exam room, Deaf mumbles in French about the ability of the shards of glass from the broken lights to reflect our image. Later he declares, "*Toujours y voir clairement est primordial*" (To see clearly is all).[7] For Deaf, identified in the exam room as Candidate 1, this is a primary value. When he is brusquely ushered out of the exam room after eating his exam paper, he leaves behind his eyeglasses, which later are taken up and used by Blonde. The centrality of Deaf's abandoned eyeglasses in this part of the plot recalls the importance of Piggy's eyeglasses in *Lord of the Flies*, insofar as Piggy stands for the principle of wisdom and social/democratic order in that novel, and Deaf turns out in the end to the be CEO of the company administering this exam. In *Lord of the Flies*, the theft of Piggy's glasses by Jack's savages will lead to the collapse of the last semblance of moral order among the boys on the island. The pejorative nature of both of their nicknames, despite their wisdom/brilliance, is another element that draws Piggy and Deaf together. These are characters deserving of emulation rather than denigration.

In taking up Deaf's eyeglasses, Blonde thus becomes the only figure in the exam room capable of answering the exam question as well as implementing Deaf's wise values and "vision." Prior to her decoding the non-question and "no" answer to the exam, White also had already deduced that there was no question, at least not the kind they were all looking for. Despite his correct deduction, White fails to "to see clearly" the moral implications of this deduction, namely that it is up to each of us to identify a constructive purpose and ethics for our lives. Whereas White remains blind, Blonde sees what Deaf Candidate 1—a semi-mute stand-in for God—would like her to see. As Teilhard de Chardin writes of the significance of "seeing" in the test that is life:

> To try to see more and better is not a matter of whim or curiosity or self-indulgence. *To see or to perish* is the very condition laid upon everything that makes up the universe, by reason of the mysterious gift of existence.[8]

Kohlberg/Gilligan/Noddings and the Moral Dilemma as Test

Given the twin interdictions against spoiling one's paper and communicating either with the invigilator or the guard, even if Blonde had been able to see the question and discern the "no" answer before the end of the eighty minutes, she would not have been able to submit this answer before the end of the eighty-minute exam period. All this suggests that is that in this exam the process of arriving at an answer is just as important as the answer itself.

Indeed, much crucial information comes to the fore over the eighty-minute process of the exam. White shows himself willing to commit murder to get what he wants. Brown demonstrates a penchant for gambling as well as for terrorism and intimidation. Black displays a similar willingness to resort to violence in protecting the interests of the group, implicating his Christian commitments along the way. Dark participates with Black in the effort to "deal with" and disqualify White, though later in the film she will disqualify herself in an effort to save his life. Blonde wins the job not merely because she is able to answer the question but also because of the tough-minded but caring way she comports herself throughout the test and thereafter, protecting herself and the rest of the group at the same time. Her moral compass is so unwavering that when offered the position, she refuses to accept until she is able to challenge the company about its willingness to sit by and watch as White shoots Black dead.

"What makes you think he's dead?" the invigilator responds, explaining that the guard's gun had been loaded with a "magic bullet" containing a drug that enables rapid cell regeneration:

> Such a breakthrough creates unanticipated dilemmas. A lot of people are going to need this product, but we can only make so much of it so quickly. Tough decisions will have to be made by a wise administrator: someone who combines a listening disposition . . . (holds up her sheet) with attention to detail . . . (nods toward Deaf) . . . and compassion toward her fellow man.[9]

This revelation that the company is looking for a leader with the capacity to make difficult decisions regarding the dispensing of a revolutionary new medication immediately brings to mind the psychologist Lawrence Kohlberg's use of moral dilemmas in the teaching and testing of the stages of moral development. According to Kohlberg,

> [t]he way to stimulate stage growth is to pose real or hypothetical dilemmas to students in such a way as to arouse disagreements and uncertainty as to what is right. The teacher's primary role is to present such dilemmas and to ask Socratic questions that arouse student reasoning and focus student listening to one another's reasons.[10]

The Heinz dilemma, the most famous such moral dilemma employed by Kohlberg and his colleagues, was one that specifically concerned the dispensing of medication. Kohlberg summarizes the dilemma as follows:

> In Europe, a woman was near death from a very bad disease, a special kind of cancer. There was a drug that the doctors thought might save her. It was a form of radium that a druggist in the same town had recently discovered. The drug was expensive to make, but the druggist was charging ten times what the drug cost him to make. He paid $200 for the radium and charges $2000 for a small dose of the drug. The sick woman's husband, Heinz, went to everyone he knew to borrow the money, but he could only get together about $1000, which was half of what it cost. He told the druggist that his wife was dying, and asked him to sell it cheaper or to let him pay later. But the druggist said, "No, I discovered the drug and I'm going to make money from it." Heinz got desperate and broke into the man's store to steal the drug for his wife.[11]

In Kohlberg's research, students/examinees were exposed to this dilemma and then asked to comment on whether or not Heinz should have done what he did, providing moral reasoning for their answer. In *Exam*, no such specific dilemma is directly posed to those being examined. Instead, a series of interpersonal dilemmas present themselves over the course of the eighty minutes, some of them explicitly related, as in the Heinz dilemma, to the administering of medication.

Early on in the exam process, conversation among the examinees reveals that a strange new virus has overtaken Europe and that the company conducting this job search/exam manufactures the only available virus suppressant. Brunette confesses that her husband has been stricken with this disease and cannot afford the medication, hence her desire to get this job; White passes out because of his need for the antiviral pill, as he too has been infected; Black admits to being a carrier and to his wife having died as a result of this illness. Indeed, the awareness and experience of this illness as a personal and communal problem permeates the exam experience and thereby alerts the audience to view the exam as a kind of extended, multipartite Kohlbergian dilemma.

According to Kohlberg's testing, there are three distinct development stages of moral thinking, each of which has two stages:

1. The Preconventional Level, in which a person responds egocentrically to the notions of good and bad in terms of what he or she stands personally to gain or lose.
2. The Conventional Level, in which moral thinking is linked to familial or group expectation and aims to uphold social conformity.
3. The Postconventional, Autonomous, or Principled Level, where an individual is seen as asserting and defining moral values that have authority and validity beyond that of a social group, including abstract or universal ethical principles.[12]

Most of the characters in the film exam demonstrate moral thinking that conforms to Kohlberg's first two levels. White's unbridled egocentrism places him at the Preconventional Level. Brown and Black's fidelity to the group clouds their moral vision, leading them to resort to immoral behavior toward individuals and confining them to the Conventional Level. The opening sequence that shows Black holding his cross necklace and stating, "I can do all things," announces a form of confident Christian identity that ultimately fails, however, to find highest moral expression in the exam process.

Some viewers with whom I have discussed this film take offense at the seeming passivity of Blonde. From a feminist point of view, they criticize her tendency to sit back and watch while others argue and act. Viewing Blonde's behavior through the lens of Kohlberg's stages of moral development only strengthens this critique, insofar as Blonde's often reactive, contextually based and caring behavior, like many of the women tested by Kohlberg, locks her into the third "good boy–good girl" stage.

However, Kohlberg's theory demonstrates a clear masculine bias that calls out for feminist critique. As Kohlberg's colleague and later critic, Carole Gilligan notes:

> Prominent among those who thus appear to be deficient in moral development when measured by the Kohlberg scale are women, whose judgments seem to exemplify the third stage of his six-stage sequence. At this stage morality is conceived in

interpersonal terms and goodness is equated with helping and pleasing others. This conception of goodness is considered by Kohlberg and Kramer (1969) to be functional in the lives of mature women insofar as their lives take place in the home. Kohlberg and Kramer imply that that only if women enter the traditional arena of male activity will they recognize the inadequacy of this moral perspective and progress like men toward higher stages where relationships are subordinated to rules (stage four) and rules to universal principles of justice (stages five and six).[13]

That Blonde evinces a caring, contextual orientation even within the workplace highlights the blind spot in Kohlberg's theory, insofar as it privileges autonomy, separation, and the articulation of abstract universal principles and completely ignores female patterns of development through interaction. As Gilligan further explains,

> Herein lies a paradox, for the very traits that traditionally have defined the "goodness" of women, their care for and sensitivity to the needs of others, are those that mark them as deficient in moral development. . . . When one begins with the study of women and derives developmental constructs from their lives, the outline of a moral conception different from that described by Freud, Piaget or Kohlberg begins to emerge and informs a different description of development. In this conception the moral problem arises from conflicting responsibilities rather than from competing rights and requires for its resolution a mode of thinking different from that is contextual and narrative rather than formal and abstract.[14]

I'd like to suggest, then, that in lauding the leadership model of Blonde, the film *Exam* supports Gilligan's efforts to inject an interconnected perspective into the concept of moral stages. Blonde's is a singular but not an isolated triumph. The end of the film proves that it is not her beauty or sex appeal that enables her success, as White chauvinistically charges, but rather her ability to work with and listen to people, including the brilliant but socially awkward CEO of the company (Deaf). Blonde is able to look out for both herself and the group, all the while preserving the ability to raise an independent voice of conscience if necessary. This is what enables her to pass the test: attachment rather than detachment or isolation, collaboration rather than stubborn individuation.

In addition, Blonde plays something of an iconoclastic role in the film, insofar as she defies the feminine film stereotype, as feminist film theorist Laura Mulvey has written, of "the woman as icon, displayed for the gaze and enjoyment of men, the active controllers of the look."[15] While White may stand for the conventional, masculine filmic gaze, repeatedly ogling Blonde and intimating a desire to get together with her sexually, *Exam* negates White's capacity to see by elevating that of Blonde. The opening sequence that introduces all the candidates represents Blonde in ways that might typically be associated with masculine viewing pleasure—the tying of her blonde hair with a hairpin, the placing of a bandage a the back of her heel and the slipping of her foot into a high-heeled shoe. Blonde's gray suit and white shirt also directly evoke the screen persona of an iconic, dangerously seductive blonde: Kim Novak as Madeline/Judy in Alfred Hitchcock's *Vertigo* (1958).[16] Against the grain of viewing expectations, however, the hairpin and bandage both prove irrelevant as sexual objects even as they become useful tools for Blonde in problem solving and dispensing care. Rather than being defined by the male gaze, Blonde herself spends most of the film observing, taking stock, learning, and listening, indicating not passivity (in the sense of woman as passive object of the active male gaze) but the assumption of a feminist prerogative to view, interpret, and do good.

Jewish Testing of the Elect

Many of the issues raised in the film concerning the role of tests in discerning the elect and their capacity for exemplary actions are anticipated by rabbinic sources on the testing of the righteous. In the film, only the most skillful or worthy candidates are invited back for the final leadership test. Genesis Rabbah 32:3 offers a similarly elitist perspective, albeit one centered on moral rather than intellectual or vocational excellence:

> *The Lord tests the righteous; but His soul hates the wicked and him who loves violence* (Ps. 11:5). R. Yonatan said: a potter

> does not tests defective vessels, because he cannot give them a single blow without breaking them. Similarly, the Holy Blessed One does not test the wicked but the righteous: thus *The Lord tests the righteous*. R. Yose b. Hanina said: When a flax worker knows that his flax is of good quality, the more he beats it the more it improves and the more it glistens; but if it is of inferior quality, he cannot give it one knock without it splitting. Similarly the Lord does not test the wicked, only the righteous, as it says *The Lord tests the righteous*. R. Eleazar said: When a man possesses two cows, one strong and the other feeble, upon which does he put the yoke? Surely upon the strong one. Similarly, the Lord tests none but the righteous.[17]

This midrash is presented as commentary on a verse from the book of Psalms, which speaks about God's practice of testing the righteous as opposed to the wicked. One might consider this unfair: why should the righteous, whose good deeds themselves attest to their merit, be subjected to difficult trials? What more can be revealed about their goodness? The developmental trajectory of the midrash, where trials first prove durability, then a capacity for improvement, and finally an ability to bear the yoke of leadership, associates trials and tests with a pattern of continuing moral growth and responsibility. Like Kohlberg's theory, which uses dilemmas to move students to further stages of moral growth, the rabbis envision a series of lifelong tests that hone and perfect virtue.

According to this midrash, tests are conducted not to reveal information to the already all-knowing God, but rather to those being elected so that they can develop their righteous vocation. In his commentary on Genesis 22:1, Nachmanides, also invoking Psalms 11:5, similarly emphasizes that God tests the righteous not to learn anything new about them but to afford the righteous an opportunity to learn about themselves. According to Nachmanides, God "does not test the wicked, who disobey. For all the tests in the Torah are for the sake of those who are tested."[18]

In many classical Jewish sources, being tested emerges as a privilege accorded only to the (Jewish) elect, a dubious honor, perhaps, given the history of Jewish suffering and persecution. As if anticipating objections to the idea of Jewish suffering under the guise of "tests," Pirkei Avot 5:3–4 suggests a connection between trials and divine miracles:

3. Our father Abraham, peace be upon him, was subjected to ten tests[19] and he withstood them all—in order to make known how great was our father Abraham's love, peace be upon him.
4. Ten miracles were performed for our forefathers in Egypt, and another ten at the sea. Ten afflictions were wrought by God upon the Egyptians in Egypt, and another ten at the sea. With ten tests our forefathers tested God in the desert, as is stated (Numbers 14:22), "They tested Me these ten times, and did not hearken to My voice."

According to Mishnah 3, even though the Bible uses the verb "*nissah*" (tested) only once with respect to Abraham, the founding patriarch actually underwent ten separate trials. Why was he subjected to this ongoing examination? (The repetition of the honorific "'*alav hashalom*"—peace be upon him—bespeaks a certain rabbinic anxiety about this disruption of Abraham's peace as a result of these many trials.) The answer provided by the Mishnah is that Abraham was put through these tests to show "*ḥibato shel Avraham*," a somewhat ambiguous phrase in that it can be construed as referring to either God's love of Abraham or Abraham's love of God. While the latter interpretation makes the most sense grammatically, Mishnah 4, which refers to God performing ten miracles and bringing about ten plagues in Egypt, suggests a measure-for-measure relationship between the miracles and the tests, the ten miracles and plagues serving as God's (loving) reward to Abraham and his descendants for having loved God and withstood repeated examination. The proximity between the Hebrew words *nisim* (miracles) and *nisyonot* (tests) reinforces this connection.

R. Simeon ben Zemah Duran (1361–1444), known as Rashbatz, expands this list of "tens" even further. In his commentary on Mishnah Avot, Rashbatz lauds Abraham for enduring his ten trials without expressing any misgivings about "God's attributes." He further links Abraham's ten trials to "the ten sayings with which the world was created" (Avot 5:1), suggesting that the whole world was created as if in anticipation of Abraham's great righteousness: "And this is why Abraham was subjected to ten tests: so that the world, which was created with ten sayings, would be sustained because of his merit, and correspondingly, God brought ten plagues upon the Egyptians, and ten miracles were done for our forefathers in Egypt and by the Sea, and God gave the people ten commandments."[20] This commentary sets up a mathematical as well as a moral correspondence between all these events, suggesting that the merit accrued by Abraham by passing his tests sustains the entire world.

The conclusion of Avot 5:4, however, complicates and undermines these numerical equivalences, insofar as the people respond to God's miracles and plagues not with thankfulness and compliance but with ten challenges to God's authority. To be sure, the proof-text quoted from Numbers 14:22 ("They tested me these ten times, and did not hearken to my voice"), occurring as it does within the context of the story of the twelve spies, does not cover the Israelites in glory. The Mishnah suggests that the people's ten tests of God effectively overturn Abraham's legacy of lifelong obedience and faith.

And yet one wonders: Is disobedience necessarily bad? To what extent should one test or measure the excellence of a leader or a generation based on their qualities of strict compliance? Do we not expect our religious leaders or spiritual elect to have the ability, as Kohlberg suggests, to think on their own, take a stand, and oppose that which they consider unjust or unfair? Given Abraham's own previously demonstrated abhorrence of injustice, as seen in his discussion with God over the possibility that innocent people might perish in Sodom (Gen. 18:25), what do we make of his silent submission to God's will in Genesis 22? Might we not have expected him to question God with respect to the morality of binding and sacrificing his innocent, unsuspecting son? While many classical commentaries, written against the backdrop of Roman or medieval persecutions of Jews, laud Abraham's unquestioning willingness to offer up Isaac, some even going so far as to reimagine Genesis 22 as a consummated rather than a thwarted sacrifice,[21] many modern readers reject the notion that willingness to commit violence or murder in the name of God constitutes the highest level of faith.

Of course, God doesn't ultimately demand Isaac's blood; at the very last moment, Abraham is instructed not to lay a hand on Isaac and to sacrifice a ram instead. That said, God's intervention through an angel raises a red flag.[22] If the whole point of the Akedah exercise is for Abraham to demonstrate his devotion to and union with God, what do we make of this mediated communication, especially given that the initial command to sacrifice Isaac seems to come directly from God rather than through an angelic intermediary? Perhaps the whole point of this test is to prompt a reaction from Abraham, to have him voice an objection, take a stand, or disobey?[23] If so, does Abraham's failure to object constitute a failure of the test?

An interesting comparison can be made, for example, between God's testing of Abraham in Genesis 22 and another important instance in the Pentateuch where the verb *n.s.h* appears specifically in conjunction with the verb *a.h.v.* (to love). In Deuteronomy 13:2–4, the people are enjoined not to heed the prophet or dreamer who urges them to "go after other gods," even if he provides signs to prove his prophecy, "for the Eternal your God is testing you [*menasseh etkhem*] to know whether you do love the Eternal your God with all your heart and with all your soul."[24] In this verse, the people are instructed not to hearken to the words of this prophet, even if he marshals sign and wonder as proof, as God is merely testing their devotion. Is it not possible, then, that in hearing the call to sacrifice his son, Abraham actually misinterprets and thus fails the test, thereby halting all future, direct communication with God?

Along these lines, I would like to suggest that Abraham passed a test of fear but failed a test of love. I say this because the episode of the Akedah begins with love; in fact, the Hebrew verb root *a.h.v* makes its first biblical appearance at the beginning of the chapter, when God tells Abraham to "take your son, your only son, the one that you love (*asher ahavta*)" and raise him up as an offering. In verse 12, however, God says to Abraham, "Lay not thy hand upon the lad, neither do thou any thing unto him; for now I know that you are a God-fearing man."

Indeed, if Genesis 22 begins under the sign of love and connection, it concludes under the sign of fear and awe, the verb *ahv* entirely disappearing from the text along with Isaac. At the beginning of the chapter, in verses 6 and 8, Abraham and Isaac are repeatedly described as walking together (*yaḥdav*). At the end of the chapter, however, Isaac is nowhere to be seen, with Abraham walking *yaḥdav* not with his son, but with *neʿarav*, his servants, a chilling rhyme to be sure. Abraham's willingness to sacrifice Isaac clearly precipitates a rupture in their relationship: when Sarah dies in the next chapter, Abraham is pictured mourning for his wife alone, without his son. It also seems to bring about an estrangement of Abraham and Sarah, as she dies in Kiryat Arba (Gen. 23:2), whereas Abraham seems to be located in Beersheba (Gen. 22:19). If these estrangements were not enough, the Akedah episode also seems to result in a distancing of Abraham from God, as, after the Akedah episode, they never again speak to each other. If read as a test of divine awe, predicated on separation from all other earthly attachments, then Abraham clearly passes. If read as a test of love and attachment, however, he fails on all scores.

Testing for Connection:
Toward a Feminist Theology of Attachment[25]

I'd like to return for a moment to the feminist critique of Kohlberg introduced above. Over the past several decades, feminist theorists of psychological and moral development, such as Nancy Chodorow, Carol Gilligan, and Nel Noddings, have written about the differences between masculine and feminine development and insisted that greater merit be assigned to the conventionally feminine mode than has been previously the case. According to Chodorow, girls, having been mothered by mothers, have a different disposition with respect to the developmental process of individuation. Girls come out of the Oedipal phase

> with a basis for "empathy" built into their primary definition of self in a way that boys do not. Girls emerge with a stronger basis for experiencing another's needs or feelings as one's own (or of thinking that one is so experiencing another's needs and feelings). Furthermore, girls do not define themselves in terms of the denial of preoedipal relational modes to the same extent as boys. From very early on [. . .], girls come to experience themselves as less-differentiated than boys, as more continuous with and related to the external object-world and as differently oriented to their inner object world as well.[26]

In direct response to the value assigned to autonomy and hierarchical preference by Kohlberg in his theory of moral stages of development, Carol Gilligan explores and compares the moral choices made by boys and girls. In assessing these differences, Gilligan considers the contrast between two models of selfhood: "between a self defined through separation and a self delineated through connection, between a self measured against an ideal of perfection and a self-assessed through particular activities of care."[27] To elucidate this contrast, she refers to two different biblical moral dilemmas that play out along opposing gender lines:

The blind willingness to sacrifice people to truth, however, has always been the danger of an ethics abstracted from life. This willingness links Gandhi to the biblical Abraham, who prepared to sacrifice the life of his son in order to demonstrate the integrity and supremacy of his faith. Both men, in the limitations of their fatherhood, stand in implicit contrast to the woman who comes before Solomon and verifies her motherhood by relinquishing truth in order to save the life of her child.[28]

Nel Noddings raises a similar objection to the conventional reading of Genesis 22 in her book *Caring: A Feminine Approach to Ethics and Morality*:

> God used Abraham and Isaac to teach His People that human sacrifice was unacceptable to Him, and henceforth forbidden. This interpretation will not satisfy the mother. The mother in Abraham's position would respond to the fear and trust of her child—not to the voice of abstraction. The Mother-As-God would not use a parent and child so fearfully and painfully to teach a welcome lesson to her other children. The Mother-God must respond caringly to Abraham as cared-for and to Isaac as cared-for, and she must preserve Abraham as one caring in relation to Isaac.[29]

To be sure, not all feminists take the same tack with respect to Genesis 22. There are those feminist Bible interpreters such as Phyllis Trible who see value in Abraham's role in the Akedah test and see Sarah's absence therefrom as a form of chauvinist exclusion. According to Trible,

> [i]n view of the unique status of Sarah and her exclusive relationship to Isaac, she, not Abraham, ought to have been tested. The dynamic of the entire saga, from its genealogical preface on, requires that Sarah be featured in the climactic scene, that she learn the meaning of obedience to God, that she find liberation from possessiveness, that she free Isaac from maternal ties, and that she emerge a solitary individual, non-attached, the model of faithfulness.[30]

Trible, like Kohlberg and so many traditional interpreters of the Akedah, values the principle of detachment; as a feminist seeking equal spiritual access for women, she only wishes that Sarah had been put through this test together with or instead of Abraham. Contrary to Trible, however, and in accordance with the theories of Gilligan and Noddings, I do not want "in" on this narrative. I do not want Sarah to be the protagonist of the Akedah. I need her to be absent from Genesis 22 so that she can be present elsewhere in the text as an alternative to Abraham's trial and God-encounter through detachment. I need her to serve as a model of love and connection rather than fear. Fittingly, the next time that the verb *a.h.v* appears in the Bible, in Genesis 24, it does so with reference to the departed Sarah, for she is the one who keeps the notion of love alive in the text, even as she herself dies.

Genesis 24, which follows the death and burial of Sarah, begins with Abraham sending his servant [*ha'eved*] to Aram Naharayim to bring home a wife for his son. Recall that Abraham's sacrifice of Isaac had been prevented by an angel. Here, too, the only way that Abraham can play a role in his son's life is through an intermediary. Abraham, it seems, has disqualified himself from future direct involvement in Isaac's life and thus must depend on someone else to perform this intimate task of seeking a mate for his son; the servant is left to petition Abraham's God for assistance too. At the end of this very long chapter, when the servant finally returns to Canaan with Rebecca, Isaac is seen alone, strolling in the field in Be'er Lahai Roi (Well of the Living Who Sees Me). Abraham is nowhere to be seen. As in the Akedah narrative, which is rife with images of sight (Gen. 4, 8, 13), culminating in Abraham espying the ram as substitute for Isaac (v. 14), the scene of Isaac's meeting Rebecca climaxes with sight, the place name Be'er Lahai Roi invoking the God who sees and the reciprocal images of Isaac looking up to see the approaching camels and Rebecca espying her husband. Then comes the account of their marriage: "And Isaac brought her into the tent of his mother Sarah; he took and she became his wife and he loved her. Thus did Isaac take comfort after [the death] of his mother" (Gen 24:67).

Significantly, at this very important juncture, when Isaac sets out to create a family of his own in a place named for a well and a God who sees us, the text invokes not the living father, Abraham, but the dead mother, Sarah, and her legacy of love and attachment. Abraham fails the test of love, but Sarah, who does not participate in or witness the Akedah, passes this test and passes on this posthumous legacy of love to

Isaac and Rebecca. To arrive at this interpretation, however—to see all of this clearly—one has to examine the text differently, seeking out attachment and union rather than detachment and autonomy. As Theilhard de Chardin once again writes:

> *Seeing:* We might say the whole of life lies in that verb—if not ultimately, at least essentially. Fuller being in closer union: such is the kernel and conclusion of this book. But let us emphasize the point: union increases only through an increase in consciousness, that is to say, in vision. And that, doubtless, is why the history of the living world can be summarized as the elaboration of ever more perfect eyes within a cosmos in which there is always something more to be seen.[31]

11

The Hunger Games

In God's Image

We move now from the need to see and interpret differently so as to arrive at a different moral conclusion to a discussion of a novel/film trilogy that is packed with images and image making, with film spectacle and costumes, but also with brutal, amoral violence. We thus come full circle, returning to issues raised at the end of the introduction of this book concerning the relationship between film and idolatry and the need, in the case of film re-creation, to adopt of a stance of *re-creative alienation.* The ruling culture in Suzanne Collins's *Hunger Games* trilogy is all about televised images, flash and flamboyant color, and visual and real effects on-screen and in life. Ritual and recreation conjoin in this culture, but to entirely sordid effect. According to film and religion scholar S. Brent Plate, "[t]he result of both religion and film is a re-created world: a world of recreation, a world of fantasy, a world of ideology, a world we may long to live in and a world we wish to avoid at all costs."[1] The latter, of course, obtains to the world of the *Hunger Games*, where carnage is promoted as entertainment and where the trappings of religious ritual abound, albeit devoid of moral content and the slightest tinge of God.

Duty and Dignity in the Absence of Religion

"The Hunger Games Snubs Religion"—so reads a headline in the *Star Tribune* about the first *Hunger Games* film.[2] The headline calls attention to the conspicuous absence in the popular *Hunger Games* series of any trace of religiosity. No churches, synagogues, or mosques. No religious holidays, recognizable liturgy, or customs. No scriptural references, and nary a mention of the divine.[3]

Instead, we are introduced to a dystopian country called Panem located in the former territory of North America, which consists of twelve industrially defined, largely impoverished Districts and one flamboyant, wealthy Capitol that rules the Districts through a system of deprivation, fear, film and television propaganda, and reality horror-show diversion. As a punishment for a rebellion that took place in the Districts more than seventy years ago, the Capitol requires that the Districts hold an annual, ritualistic lottery called the "Reaping" for the purpose of selecting two "tributes"—one girl and one boy—to fight to the death in an annual televised "pageant"/gladiatorial event called the Hunger Games. The pomp and ceremony surrounding the Hunger Games come replete with rites and ceremonies and religiously reminiscent terminology—words such as "tribute," "courage," "repentance," "thanks," and "sacrifice"—albeit emptied of theological/moral content.

This, after all, is a society where parents are forced to send their children off to kill one other for no purpose other than to entertain the wealthy, indulged citizens of the Capitol, while the Districts are kept in a continual state of frightened deprivation. To fend off deadly hunger, children in the Districts can sign up for tesserae (tokens), entitling them to additional grain, but only by increasing the number of times their names appear in the "Reaping." The everyday, post-Edenic struggle to reap one's bread (in Latin, *panem*) is thus linked inextricably with the risk of being selected for the Hunger Games (reminiscent of the Roman gladiatorial competitions, or *circuses*), locking every adult and child of the Districts into a political structure and mind-set as closed and monitored as the arena where the Hunger Games are fought. "Two things the people of Rome anxiously desired," writes Abraham Joshua Heschel in his magisterial essay *The Sabbath*: "Bread and circus games. But man does not live by bread and circus games alone. Who will teach him how to desire anxiously the spirit of a sacred day?"[4]

The people of Panem have no vocabulary with which to conceptualize such a day. They see no way out of Panem, no power to appeal to other than chance. Hence the pseudo-liturgical phrase *"May the odds be forever in your favor,"* recited over and over with regard to the Reaping and the Hunger Games, which encapsulates the sense of being governed by an eternally random force over which one has no real sway and to which one must simply acquiesce. To be sure, this phrase only serves to mask the power and control wielded by the Capitol over every District resident.

Along comes Katniss Everdeen,[5] a teenager from coal-mining District 12, whose sense of duty and self defies the norms of the Capitol and eventually galvanizes an uprising. The story begins on the morning of one particular Reaping, when Katniss's beloved twelve-year-old sister, Primrose, is chosen as tribute, and Katniss volunteers to take her place. No one from District 12 has ever volunteered before. In general, volunteering occurs only in those wealthier districts where children are trained from a young age to be "careers" (professional Hunger Games contestants), and where participation (and triumph) in the games is promoted as a perverse honor. Not so in poorer areas like Districts 11 and 12, where everyone struggles every day not to starve to death.

The system of the Capitol depends on the twin principles of Hunger and Games, hence the title of the "pageant" and of the first novel/film: if you continually deprive people of what they need to survive so that all they can afford to hope for is mere animal subsistence; if you pit them against one another, even members of the same community, in a perpetual battle to stay alive; if you bombard them, through the televised broadcast of the Games, with images of brutality and submission, they will never muster the moral vocabulary, imagination, and self-image necessary to oppose the regime.

Katniss Everdeen defies this logic. By putting her young sister's well-being above her own and volunteering to take her place at the Reaping, she publicly exhibits a countercultural ethics of altruism and care. Even before the Reaping, in the wake of her father's death in a tragic mining accident and her mother's catatonic reaction, Katniss privately demonstrates this ethics of care by assuming the responsibility to provide food for her family. Together with friend and fellow-orphan Gale Hawthorne, Katniss adopts a daily morning practice, in defiance of Capitol rules, of sneaking under the occasionally electrified District 12 fence to hunt in the woods. "The woods became our savior,"[6] Katniss reflects, indicating a determination to look beyond the similarly spelled "odds" for salvation. Even on the morning of the Reaping, Katniss goes to the woods to hunt with Gale; Prim asks Katniss where she is off to, and Katniss answers simply, "I have to go but I'll be back,"[7] articulating without fanfare an unswerving sense of duty to provide for her family. That morning in the woods, when Gale suggests that they simply run away, Katniss demurs, saying, "I have Prim. You have your brothers." In the absence of adult role models or formal teaching, Katniss quietly embodies the principle of humanistic duty famously articulated by Hillel, a rabbi who lived in the time of Herod and the Romans and therefore was no stranger to imperial cruelty: *Bemakom she'ein anashim, hishtadel lihyot ish* (In a place where there are no men, strive to be a man),[8] or, in this case, a strong, capable woman.

At the Reaping, Katniss's private bravery and altruism suddenly become a public affair. Until this point, the Capitol had managed to fend off dissent by denying the value of the individual and by separating individuals from community. Katniss's decision to volunteer in Prim's place threatens the status quo by communicating at once a sense of selflessness and self-worth. By definition, the act of volunteering implies volition: personal freedom, will, capacity, dignity, and agency—ideas that the Capitol has worked assiduously to root out. At the same time, Katniss's willingness to place her own life at risk to protect her sister suggests that there is more to one's life than one's self.

The first-person narrative point of view of the novels underscores these mixed notions about the self. To be sure, the first person offers a restricted, individual perspective. In contrast to the films, which give us access not just to Katniss's point of view but also to the machinations of those around her, Katniss's first-person narrative in the novels is limited by what she knows and what she is thinking at each moment of the tense, suspenseful story. At the same time, Katniss's freely articulated inner voice and thoughts point to a potent, individual way out of the pervasive control of the Capitol. Moreover, the first-person depiction of Katniss's ever-growing consciousness proves the immense possibilities that reside within each individual.

The film adaptation of the first novel, the screenplay of which was also written by Collins, does not attempt to reproduce this distinctive, first-person voice. Instead it depicts Katniss's point of view through close-ups of her subtle facial expressions, and through a series of visual contrasts that oppose Katniss's world with that of the ruling elite of the Capitol. Unlike the novel, the *Hunger Games* film begins not in District 12 but with a scene from a glitzy, pre–Hunger Games interview with game maker Seneca Crane conducted by telecast host Caesar Flickerman. From the flickering, propagandistic absurdity of this interview clip, the film cuts to the realistic, somber, blue-gray, early-morning tones of Katniss's home in District 12, where she maternally soothes her screaming sister Prim, who has just had a pre-Reaping nightmare-premonition that she is going to be chosen as tribute. At various, crucial moments in the film, these color contrasts recur: at the Reaping, where the garishly colored hair, makeup, clothing, and mannerisms of Effie Trinket stand out luridly against the blue-gray tones of the homes and clothing worn by the children and parents of District 12, reminiscent of the Depression-era documentary photography of Dorothea Lange (1895–1965); in the train

Figure 11.1a. Dorothea Lange, Migrant Mother.

Figure 11.1b. *Hunger Games*, Dorothea Lange–like Portrait.

to the Capitol and the transport to the arena, where for a few brief shots Katniss is filmed in blue-grays before the camera returns to full color depiction; and when Katniss is under the influence of the tracker-jacker venom and hallucinates in blue-gray images about her father's tragic death in a mining explosion.

Katniss's perspective is depicted visually in the film not only through contrasts but also through similarities and symmetries. Note how the film both begins and ends under the visual specter of the Reaping, with an early and a concluding scene in the District 12 town square, indicating Katniss's sense of limitation, fear, and emotional confusion even after winning the games. Note as well the striking resemblance between the Hunger Games arena and the woods in District 12. The woods is the "arena" where Katniss exercises some measure of autonomy, ingenuity, and human capacity to rule over her natural surroundings, climbing trees and hunting with her bow and arrows to support her loved ones. It will be Katniss's task to somehow bring her know-how and her autonomy to the Hunger Games arena as well so as to model a moral, caring self.

To be sure, Katniss's voluntarism and altruism reveal not only the powers of the self, but also those of the self in relation to community. If the Capitol presents a twisted notion of community, cynically promoting the Hunger Games, as in the opening interview with Flickerman and Crane, as a ritual that "knits us all together," Katniss's decision to volunteer provokes a genuine communitarian response, as signified by the three-fingered salute offered to Katniss by all the citizens of District 12 when she steps forward to take Prim's place. Later, in the arena, Katniss allies herself with Rue, a twelve-year-old, dark-skinned District 11 tribute, who reminds Katniss of her sister Prim and shares Katniss's experience of class-based deprivation. When young Rue falls prey to the careers, Katniss extends this same three-fingered salute to the viewers from District 11 as a show of solidarity in their time of sorrow (or rue). In response to Katniss's kindness to Rue, the people of District 11 send Katniss a gift of bread (panem), the first time that members of one district have ever helped a member of another district in the games. Insofar as the French word "rue" means roadway or street, Katniss's experience with Rue and her district members establishes a precedent or pathway for future interdistrict solidarity and care.

As previously discussed in relation to the film *Memento*, memory is essential to any concept of ethics or self. "This is how we remember our past; this is how we safeguard our future," says President Snow in the movie version of the *Hunger Games* in the clichéd propaganda film that is screened every year before the Reaping, reflecting an ongoing campaign on the part of the Capitol to colonize and control memory. The propaganda film is slick and inauthentic in both form and message, a fact that is underscored by the contrasting, handheld, documentary filming style used to depict the children of District 12 as they assemble in the town square for the Reaping and are "processed" by the Peacekeepers. Later, as the ceremony begins and the Reaping "trailer" is screened, Gale and Katniss mockingly mouth President Snow's words, indicating their refusal to be "snowed" by his propagandistic version of the past.[9]

Over and against the Capitol's efforts to colonize memory, Katniss cultivates her own set of memories. She recalls what her father taught her about hunting and foraging as a tool to help herself and her family survive. She replays in her mind her late father's songs and sings them to those she loves. When the baker's son, Peeta Mellark, is chosen to be her fellow District 12 tribute in the games, Katniss remembers Peeta's gift to her of bread (pita?) from years ago, when she almost collapsed from starvation behind his family's bakery, and frets over how she will ever stand against him in the games given this act of charity. Katniss has a tough veneer, but inside she is fiercely principled and loyal. And Peeta, who has always loved Katniss from afar, remembers what she wore on their first day of school and how she sang her father's songs in front of the entire class. After their joint victory in the first Hunger Games, Katniss and Peeta start assembling a scrapbook that chronicles their memories of the people they have loved and lost as a result of the Games. Together, Katniss and Peeta safeguard a set of authentic memories that serve the cause of personal and interpersonal dignity.

In the decadent Capitol, which valorizes artifice and denigrates the natural human form, people routinely alter and disfigure their faces, hair, and bodies. Culture, art, technology, creativity, and the capacity to heal all are harnessed here to the machine of the Hunger Games. Deadly animals are genetically and digitally created to serve as physical and psychological predators in the arena. Images are designed and projected to the Districts with a murderous mock-divine purpose.

By contrast, Katniss and Peeta use art and beauty as a means of dignifying individual human life. When Katniss is unable to protect Rue from the careers, she sings the Valley Song to Rue to usher her to her death with respect and care. She then bedecks her in natural wildflowers as a show of love and an act of protest.[10]

Figure 11.2. *Hunger Games,* Laying Rue to Rest in a Bed of Flowers.

Peeta's talent for decorating cakes—the stuff of happy human occasions—helps camouflage and save him in the arena, allying him with the habits of nature and humanity rather than pitting him against them. After surviving the Hunger Games, Peeta becomes a painter, portraying on canvases his memories of his Hunger Games experience as a way of chronicling the horror and humanizing the experience. In the second book/film, *Catching Fire,* during the Quarter Quell—the 75th Hunger Games, where the tributes are drawn from the existing pool of Hunger Games victors, throwing both Peeta and Katniss back into the arena—Peeta strokes the hair of the dying morphling who saves his life and engages her in a conversation about color and the mixing of paint: "With my paint box at home," he tells the morphling, "I can make every color imaginable. Pink. As pale as baby's skin. Or as deep as rhubarb. Green like spring grass. Blue that shimmers like ice on water" (*Catching Fire,* 312–13). It is no accident that all of Peeta's color similes refer to nature and growth, while the Capitol's world of outlandishly artificial hair coloring, tattooing, and body modification serve the cause of dehumanization and death.

In *The Varieties of Religious Experience,* William James defines the "saintly character" as "a feeling of being in a wider life than that of this world's selfish little interests." Saintliness, says James, usually includes a conviction regarding the existence of an Ideal Power; a shifting of one's emotional center that may lead to self-surrender, even asceticism, and an increased habit of purity, charity, and tenderness toward others.[11]

Even in the absence of a religious framework, Katniss and Peeta demonstrate many of these saintly traits. While neither of them makes any reference to God or any other conventional notion of Ideal Power, Katniss's devotion to her family and Peeta's loving and tender commitment to Katniss each points to love as that sort of power.[12] Katniss exemplifies an attitude of purity in her reluctance to feign emotion and act the part of Peeta's lover to curry favor with those in power in the Capitol; Peeta embodies a similar purity of character when he tells Katniss before the games of his hope "to die as myself . . . I don't want them to change me in there. Turn me into some kind of monster that I'm not" (*Hunger Games*, 141).

Peeta's virtuous determination to live and die as "himself" in the arena recalls Holocaust survivor and logotherapist Viktor Frankl's observations about the quest for meaning and dignity even in the face of the dehumanizing conditions of the concentration camps: "If the man in the concentration camp did not struggle against this in a last effort to save his self-respect, he lost the feeling of being an individual, a being with a mind, inner freedom and personal value."[13] In the "living laboratory" of the camps "we watched and witnessed some of our comrades behave like swine while others behaved like saints."[14] Likewise, in the gladiator ring of the arena, Katniss and Peeta manage to triumph over the "swine" and comport themselves like saints.

Toward a Theological Reading of the Trilogy

It is perhaps because of these proto-saintly qualities that Christian interpreters tend to impose on the trilogy a Christian, typological framework. According Diana Butler Bass, "when Katniss volunteers for the games, she saves her sister's life by offering to die in place of another. This echoes the Christian teaching of Jesus's death as a sacrificial substitution for another."[15] "There are only a handful of books besides the Bible that have really made me love Jesus more," says Laura Snider in *Christianity Today*, "but I've added the *Hunger Games* to that list. When I read about Peeta, I feel Christ—not because Peeta is divine or has any special power to save the world, but because he exemplifies sacrificial love."[16] In a book that claims to explore the secular political lessons of the trilogy but actually assumes a Christian scriptural orientation from the outset, author Jamey

Heit[17] likens President Snow of the Capitol to King Herod, the Roman client king of Judea, who, according to the Gospel of Matthew, murdered children for political ends and persecuted Jesus.[18] Other Christian readers refer to the many Roman references in the trilogy—names such as Cornelius, Plutarch, Seneca, Cato, and of course Panem[19]—as an opportunity to recall Jesus's crucifixion at the hands of the Romans and the fact that in the Roman era "crowds would gather to watch Christians getting torn apart by wild animals or burned alive."[20] Still others point to Katniss's cruciform pose when being lifted out of the arena at the end of the film version of *Catching Fire* as evidence of an overarching Christological interpretation.[21]

One can certainly appreciate the draw of the Christological reading for the devout Christian reader/viewer. As a Jew, however, I remain keenly aware of the ways in which images of Jesus's crucifixion have been used over the centuries to justify the persecution of Jews and other nonbelievers. And I am equally troubled by the ways in which notions of martyrdom and sacrifice continue to undergird appalling acts of religious violence all over our world to this day. I need to look elsewhere, therefore, to bring the *Hunger Games* trilogy into conversation with my religious beliefs.

Might it be better to avoid the religious reading of the trilogy altogether? Perhaps the most honest interpretation of the trilogy would be to maintain a secular humanistic approach, as I have been doing thus far, one that celebrates the individualistic achievement of Katniss and Peeta in discerning a moral code, a sense of loving commitment and personal dignity, without recourse to a recognizable theology or communal religious practice. This approach seems to accord with Collins's own decision to scrub her story clean of any reference to God or church.[22]

And yet one cannot ignore the major difficulties that Katniss and Peeta face in deriving and maintaining a sense of dignity and morality all on their own. Given the violent culture of Panem and the tendency for violence to breed more violence, Collins's protagonists are continually placed in compromising, confusing, and almost impossible moral situations. In *Catching Fire*, when Katniss is airlifted out of the arena of the Quarter Quell to join the rebels of District 13 in their campaign against the Capitol, and Peeta is taken prisoner by the Capitol, these difficulties only intensify. In *Mockingjay*, Katniss ultimately has to go so far as to assassinate the District 13 rebel leader, President Coin, to save her own life and finally break the cycle of violence.

It appears that even in the best of times, secular individualism can prove a flimsy structure on which to build and safeguard morality and dignity. As sociologists Bellah, Madsen, Sullivan, Swidler, and Tipton write with respect to the inherent limitations of the ideology of individualism in the American social context:

> In times of economic prosperity, Americans have imagined individualism as a self-sufficient moral and political guide. In times of social adversity such as the present, they are tempted to say that it is up to individuals to look after their own interests. Yet many of us have felt, in times both of prosperity and adversity, that there is something missing in the individualist set of values, that individualism alone does not allow persons to understand certain basic realities of their lives, especially their interdependence with others. These realities become more salient as individual effort alone proves inadequate to meet the demands of living . . . The biblical tradition, a second language familiar to most Americans through a variety of communities of faith, teaches concern for the intrinsic value of individuals because of their relationship to the transcendent. It asserts the obligation to respect and acknowledge the dignity of all . . .[23]

All this presses me more urgently in the direction of a Jewish reading of the trilogy, a need that becomes even more urgent in light of the analogy with the Holocaust that is visually signaled in the Reaping scenes of the *Hunger Games* film.[24] Here are grim, gray pictures of people standing in rows in a town square, of children being rounded up, registered, and

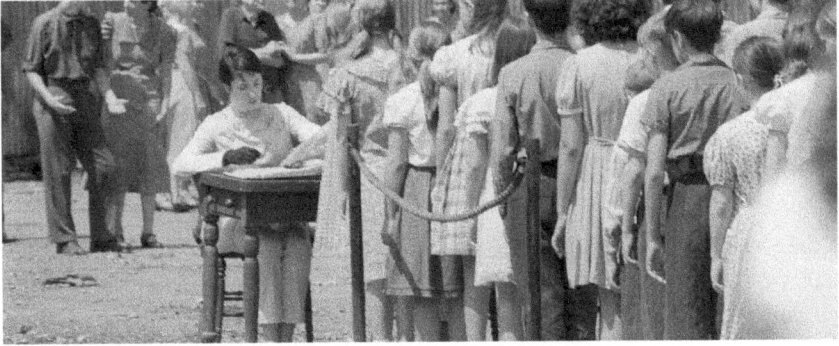

Figure 11.3. *Hunger Games*, Registering the Children at the Reaping.

selected for almost certain death—images painfully reminiscent of black and white photos of the concentration camps or the ghettos.[25]

When I watch these scenes, I cannot help recalling that in the nineteenth and early twentieth centuries, Germany represented the apex of secular Western humanistic culture, boasting titans of music, literature, and philosophy, and yet this same culture failed to furnish a moral bulwark against genocide.

Jewish theologian Irving Greenberg offers a fierce indictment of secular culture in light of the Holocaust in a famous essay titled "Cloud of Smoke, Pillar of Fire":

> In this [modern] culture the primary alternative to religion is secular man in a world closed off from any transcendence, or divine incursion. This world grows out of the intellectual framework of science, philosophy, and of social science, of rationalism and human liberation, which created the enterprise of modernity. This value system was—and is—the alternative faith which Jews and Christians joined in large numbers in the last two centuries, transferring allegiance from the Lord of History and Revelation to the Lord of Science and Humanism. In so many ways, the Holocaust is the direct fruit and will of this alternative. Modernity fostered the excessive rationalism and utilitarian relations, which created the need for and susceptibility to totalitarian mass movements and the surrender of moral judgment. The secular city sustained the emphasis on values-free sciences and objectivity, which created unparalleled power but weakened its moral limits . . . Mass communication and universalization of values weakened resistance to centralized power, and served as a cover to deny the unique danger posted to particular, i.e., Jewish existence . . . In light of Auschwitz, secular 20th century civilization is not worthy of this transfer of our ultimate loyalty. Nothing in the record of secular of secular culture on the Holocaust justifies its authority claims.[26]

Greenberg's reference above to the "secular city" brings to mind Harvey Cox's insistence in *The Secular City* that one need not lament the secularization process that is part and parcel of modernity; according to Cox, "God can be just as present in the secular as in the religious realms of life, and we unduly cramp the divine presence by confining it to some specially delineated spiritual or ecclesial sector."[27] In principle, I agree with Cox's assertion; in writing this book, which identifies content for religious conversation in secular popular film, I share Cox's conviction that there is ultimate and enduring value to secular culture. Yet there are limits to what the secular city can offer if it is completely and utterly detached from core religious and ethical values. Note that Cox himself presents his argument about the value of secularization by presenting it as an offshoot of biblical faith. According to Cox, the disenchantment of nature that is a necessary precondition of modernity and secularization begins with the biblical Creation story, which rejects the magical view of nature.[28]

According to Greenberg, the Holocaust exposed the moral limits of secularization. More than that: "it destroyed the meaning of the categories 'secular' and 'religious' by virtue of the fact that there were many so-called religious people who helped carry out the systematic murder."[29] Yet Greenberg clings to one fundamental testimony, that of human life itself: "There is one response to such overwhelming tragedy: the reaffirmation of meaningfulness, worth and life—through acts of love and life-giving. The act of creating a life or enhancing its dignity is the counter-testimony to Auschwitz."[30]

According to Greenberg, the historical experience of the Holocaust calls on Jews, Christians, and others to resist the authority of the secular cultural moment and to insist instead on a renewed religious and ethical code based on the fundamental dignity of each human life as created in the image of God (see Genesis 1:26–27). According to this notion, human dignity inheres not in some humanistic or individualistic achievement but in an awareness that each human being shares and therefore ought to represent something of the divine. As James Orr argues, the notion that human beings are created in the image of God "is the conception, tacit or avowed, which underlies all revelation" and is "the presupposition of the history of God's dealing with man from the first to the last.[31]

Created in the Image of God

What does it mean to be created in God's likeness and image?[32] What does this expression convey about the distinctiveness of every human self and the centrality of humankind in God's design for creation? We first encounter this concept in Genesis 1:26, where God declares an intention after creating the rest of the animal kingdom to make *ha-Adam* (humankind) "*betzalmeinu kidmuteinu*" (in our image and after our likeness); "and let them hold sway over the fish of the sea, and over birds of the sky, over the beasts, over all the earth, overall that creeps upon the earth." According to biblical scholar Nehama Leibowitz, the creation of the first human "qualified for a special preamble," indicative of human "preeminence" and "difference in kind from the rest of the animal world whose creation was announced in the immediately preceding passage."[33] Not just that: the preamble suggests that in addition to speaking, distinguishing, creating, seeing and evaluating, and naming, God imagines, designs, and makes similes or metaphors, drawing connections between the divine and human realms. In imagining humans *kidmuteinu* (like our image), God in effect becomes the originator of the simile and the metaphor; we in turn activate our Godly image by speaking, evaluating, naming, and imagining a sense of self that connects us to God as well as other human beings.[34]

The preamble of Genesis 26 is followed by a description of the actual creation of the first humans, male and female in God's image, as well as by a divine blessing and directive to be fruitful and multiply, to fill the earth and dominate it. Another meaning, then, of being created in the image of God inheres the ingenuity and creativity to assert dominion over other living things and over the natural world. As Rabbi Joseph Soleveitchik observes,

> Man's likeness to God expresses itself in man's striving and ability to become a creator. Adam the first who was fashioned in the image of God was blessed with great drive for creative activity and immeasurable resources for the realization of this goal, the most outstanding of which is the intelligence, the human mind, capable of confronting the outside world and inquiring into its complex workings.[35]

Biblical scholar Randall Garr does an in-depth, book-length consideration of Genesis 1:26–27 as well as other biblical references to *demut* and *tzelem* and thus provides an even more detailed, philological, and intercultural analysis of their significance. According to Garr, the use of the term *demut* in Genesis 5:1, which tells of *toldot Adam* (the generations of Adam) and of humankind's having been created "*bidmut Elohim*," refers to a feature of God's self-disclosure:

> Stated generally, human beings imitate God in this respect, representing God in the world. To the extent that they imitate God in perpetuity, they register his everlasting presence in the world. They are, then, a theophany. Specifically, Adam, Seth and his descendants share a God-given ability/capability to generate תולדות and populate the world with human beings. More God-like than godlike, they engender, produce and sustain human life.[36]

In terms of the meaning of the term *tzelem Elohim*, which occurs in Genesis 1:26–27 and then in Genesis 9:6, Garr contends that "God 'gives dominion to the human race' (Gen. 1:26b). Through its 'image' [*tzelem*], the human race will ultimately represent divine rule."[37]

As the story progresses, however, Adam and Eve exercise this theophanic, ruling agency in various problematic ways. Indeed, not long after creating Adam in the divine image and urging them, male and female, to be fruitful and multiply, God begins to regret ever having created humankind. First, man and woman eat the fruit of the Tree of Knowledge of Good and Evil against God's explicit directive and consequently are driven from Eden. Then their eldest son, Cain, murders his younger brother, Abel, betraying a jealous disposition in addition to an excessive will to dominate. Alas, God's charge to the first humans had been to rule over the birds and fish and other animals, not to prey on other *benei Adam*. After the murder of Abel, Adam and Eve give birth to another son, Seth, but the downward moral spiral continues; both the biblical text and rabbinic commentary thereon elaborate on the spiritual degeneration of the human line after Adam. Genesis Rabbah 23:6 asks why Genesis 4:26 refers to Adam begetting a son named Seth and Seth begetting a son named Enosh but then offers the names of no other progeny. The midrash answers that "[h]itherto they were created in the likeness and the image [of God] . . . but from then onward Centaurs were created"[38]—a mythological/metaphorical explanation suggesting a greater proximity, on the part of Enosh's descendants, to the animal kingdom than to the divine realm, an ironic state of affairs to be sure, given that the Hebrew word "*enosh*" literally means "man" or "human." As the text continues, Adam's descendants multiply both in their numbers and predatory tendencies. God thus concludes that "the wickedness of man was great in the earth, and that every imagination of the thoughts of his heart was only evil continually" (Gen. 6:6), and resolves to "wipe humans whom I have created from off the face of the earth" (Gen. 6–7).

That is, with the exception of righteous Noah. The drowning of everyone in the world except for Noah and family wipes the land-slate clean and renders Noah a second Adam. Thus, after the Flood subsides, God reiterates to *benei Noah* the Adamic notion of human creation *betzelem Elohim* (in the divine image) so as to provide them with an opportunity to get right what *benei Adam* had gotten so terribly wrong.

As such, the reiteration of the notion of human creation *betzelem Elohim* in Genesis 9:6 comes with important clarifications and elaborations. God blesses Noah and his generations; bids them to be fruitful and multiply and to "replenish the earth"; and informs them that from now on they will be permitted to eat the meat of other animals and not just plants. If the broad license to dominate the earth given to Adam and his descendants had engendered a culture of intrahuman violence without limits, Noah and his descendants are now told that while they may hunt animals for food, they may not eat animals while their lifeblood still courses within them (see Gen. 9:4). And they are expressively forbidden from preying on other human beings. As Genesis 9:6 poetically declares: "The shedder of human blood / that person's blood will be shed by [another] human / for human beings were made / in the image of God."

With the giving of this code, the meaning of the concept of *tzelem Elohim* becomes at once more expansive and clearer. As biblical scholar Nachum Sarna explains, the notion of being created in the image of God now comes to encapsulate everything that distinguishes humankind from the rest of the animal kingdom, including "intellect, free will, self-awareness, consciousness of the existence of others, conscience, responsibility, and self-control. Moreover, being created 'in the image of God' implies that human life is infinitely precious,"[39] hence the explicit prohibition in Genesis 9:6 against shedding human blood. According to Sarna, "the Bible's concept of the divine image in man thus constitutes another revolutionary break with the contemporary world. The pagan bond between man and nature had been severed once and for all. No longer is man a creature of blind forces, helplessly at the mercy of the inexorable rhythms and cycles of nature. On the contrary, he is now a being possessed of dignity, purpose, freedom and tremendous power."[40]

Abraham Joshua Heschel explains that the prohibition against making symbols or images of God teaches that the world is not a symbol of God—in other words, that "God is not and cannot be localized in a thing":

> And yet there is something in the world that the Bible does regard as a symbol of God. It is not a temple or a tree, it is not a statue or a star. The symbol of God is *man, every* man . . . How significant is the fact that the term *tselem* which is frequently used in a defamatory sense for a man made image of God, as well as the term *demuth*, of which Isaiah claims (40:18), no *Demuth* or likeness can be applied to God—are employed in denoting man as an image and likeness of God.[41]

Along similar times, Yair Lorberbaum outlines the teaching of the school of Hillel and later of R. Akiva with respect to the notion of *tzelem Elohim*. Hillel and Akiva taught that "the human being is an *eikon*," an image or augmentation of God's presence on earth.[42] As Lorberbaum explains, "God's desire to augment and magnify himself leads him to create man 'in His image and likeness'—that is an extension of Himself. This was the motivation for the creation of man in the divine image and the source of the great severity involved in the prohibition on bloodshed in tannaitic literature, on the one hand, and of the obligation to procreate and multiply, on the other."[43] R. Akiva thus teaches, invoking Genesis 9:6, that "[w]hoever sheds bloods is regarded as though he had annulled the [divine] image, as it says, 'Whoever sheds the blood of man, by man shall his blood be shed [for in the image of God did he make man].'"[44] The seriousness with which R. Akiva takes the notion of *tzelem Elohim* as an extension of God also explains his resistance to the application of capital punishment, as we read in Mishnah Makkot 1:10:

> The Sanhedrin that puts to death one person in seven years is deemed tyrannical. R. Elazar ben Azariah says One person in seventy years. R. Tarfon and R. Akiva say, If we had been on the Sanhedrin, no one would have ever been put to death.[45]

Indeed, if one truly takes seriously the idea that every human being embodies the image of God, how can one allow a court to shed human blood, even that of a murderer? Would that not merely perpetuate the very diminishment of God's presence that the biblical interdiction against murder had hoped to prevent?

What if one of God's functions, however, is to kill? In his book *God: A Biography*, Jack Miles makes the disturbing observation, with regard to Genesis 9:6 and the reiteration of the *tzelem Elohim* idea, that the "prohibition of human bloodshed comes just after the Lord/God shed a great deal of human blood, or at any rate, taken a great deal of human life."[46] According to Miles, the image of God that emerges from the Noah story is not just of Creator but also of Destroyer. If so, what does this do to our concept of what it means to be created in the image of God? Does the prohibition against murder come specifically to limit that destructive human power that is inherent in being created in the image of a murderous God?

Holocaust survivor and Hebrew poet Dan Pagis seems to imply as much in his chilling poem "*'Edut*" (Testimony), which specifically identifies the Nazi murderers as "*benei Adam*," having been created "*betzelem*." In contrast, says the speaker-victim who offers testimony in the poem, "I was a "*tzel*" (shadow). I had another Creator."[47]

In this poem, which grapples with how it was that human beings committed the atrocities of the Shoah and a supposedly omnipotent God allowed it all to happen, Pagis presents two divergent views of what it means to be created "in the image": one solid, embodied, identified with uniforms, boots, and *bnei Adam*; the other clipped (*tzel* versus *tzelem*), weightless, and blue like air, a soul rather than a body, equated with impotent smoke rising from the crematoria. To be sure, the testimony offered by Pagis authorizes neither theological model. The Destroyer God is a travesty. The "omnipotent smoke" is a mere shadow version of the idea of a God who has no bodily form—a faceless theological absence.

Fittingly, Pagis lops off the word "*Elohim*" from *tzelem Elohim*, the biblical expression referring to creation in the image of God. The omission of any reference to God in the poem reflects God's glaring absence from this chapter of human history. It also highlights the fact that it was human beings, not God, who perpetrated the horrors of the Shoah.

A similar observation can be made with regard to Miles's description of God as Destroyer. After all, in the biblical text, it is not God but a human being who creates murder: Cain, *ben Adam*, son of Adam. (Pagis makes this point in his poem, actually, by identifying the booted, uniformed Nazis as "*bnei Adam*.") And it is the sons of Cain and Seth, culminating with the generation of Noah, who turn violence and murder into a perverse, ever-multiplying efflorescence that overtakes all aspects of their civilization. The ubiquity of this violence becomes explicit in Genesis 6 in the repetitious descriptions of corruption filling every part of the earth: "the earth was filled with violence" (Gen. 6:11); "God saw how corrupted the earth was" (Gen. 6:12); and "The earth is full of violence on their account" (Gen. 6:13).

Panem and the Flood Generation

Returning for a moment to the story of the *Hunger Games*, it is hard not to notice the parallels between the ubiquitous corruption of Noah's generation before the Flood and that of the Capitol. Noah's world is singled out as a culture of "*ḥamas*"—of violence and murder—hence the need after the Flood to explicitly forbid murder as well as the eating of meat whose "lifeblood" is still in it. Similarly, when President Snow appears at Katniss's home at the beginning of *Catching Fire*, Katniss notices that while Snow (whose name cynically masks his own blood-red sins) bedecks and perfumes himself with roses, his breath nevertheless reeks of blood: "*What does he do?* I think. *Drink it?*"[48] This detail about Snow (hinted at in the film adaptations in the recurrent scenes of Snow tending his garden of white roses) subtly links Snow with the bloodthirsty behavior of the Flood generation.

Noah's generation had lost sight of the notion and moral implications of human creation in the divine image. The people of Panem demonstrate a similar moral and spiritual malaise. Early on in the *Hunger Games* novel, as Katniss prepares to board the train for the Capitol to fight in the Hunger Games, her friend Gale reminds her that she already knows how to hunt and therefore to kill: "How different can it be?" says Gale grimly. "The awful thing," Katniss admits, "is that if I can forget they're people, it will be no different at all" (*The Hunger Games*, 40–41). Survival in the arena is thus shown to be contingent on hunting people as one would hunt an animal, that is, on an erasure of any concept of human distinctiveness and sanctity. Ultimately, it becomes Katniss's and Peeta's task to eschew this attitude and exemplify another way.

Katniss's disinterest, confessed at the very beginning of the trilogy, in ever having children (*The Hunger Games*, 8)[49] also brings to mind the connection, as explicated by Garr, between created *bidmut Elohim* and having the capacity to procreate and thus carry on the divine act of human creation. After the Flood, God feels the need to reiterate the blessing of "be fruitful and multiply" to Noah and kin. The repetition of this blessing of fecundity suggests a new beginning but also points to the reluctance on the part of Noah and his family to embrace the project of repopulating the world after witnessing so much human carnage.

Along similar lines, both the Noah story and *The Hunger Games* trilogy reflect the temptation, when confronted with such a ruined world, simply to escape and evade the challenge of trying to fix it. Shortly after leaving the ark and seeing the rainbow, a sign of a new covenant with God (Gen. 9:15–16),[50] Noah plants a vineyard and drinks himself into a stupor (Gen. 9:21). Likewise, in the *Hunger Games* trilogy, we meet such victors and survivors of the Hunger Games as the dying morphling addict in *Catching Fire* and the alcoholic victor Haymitch Abernathy, who spends most of his days dead drunk, that is, until he takes it upon himself to mentor Katniss and Peeta and, subsequently, help lead a rebellion against the Capitol.

As previously observed, the rabbis (particularly R. Akiva, who continued a tradition dating back to Hillel the Elder[51]) enlisted the concept of *tzelem Elohim* as reiterated in Genesis 9:6 to inculcate a reverence for the human body as an image of God. Leviticus Rabbah 34:3 teaches:

> *The merciful man doeth good to his own soul* (Prov. XI, 17). This applies to Hillel the Elder who once, when he concluded his studies with his disciples, walked along with them. His disciples asked him: "Master, whither are you bound?" He answered them: "To perform a religious duty." "What?" they asked. "To wash in the bathhouse." Said they: "Is this a religious duty?" "Yes," he replied: "if the statues of kings, which are in theatres and circuses, are scoured and washed by the man who is appointed to look after them, and who thereby obtains his maintenance through them—nay more, he is exalted in the company of the great of the kingdom—how much more I, who have been created in the Image and Likeness: as it is written, '*For in the image of God made He man.*'" (Gen. IX, 6)[52]

Targeted for critique in this midrash is the Roman cultural tendency in their theaters, circuses, and sculptures to venerate man-made images of the kings at the expense of the dignity of plain, ordinary human beings. Compare this to the habit, on the part of the "stylists" of the gladiatorial Hunger Games, to hose down and scour the bodies of the tributes so thoroughly as to denude them of all body hair and even layers of skin. The Capitol residents harbor revulsion for the natural human body and a preference for the false body presentations generated by their artificial culture. The teaching of the modest and poor Hillel the Elder comes to criticize the Roman aristocratic culture of self-aggrandizement through physical icons and to teach veneration for the common human body and being as created in the image not of a flesh-and-blood king, but of God, the true King/Creator. The use of a proof-text for humanity's creation in the image of God not from Genesis 1:27 but from Genesis 9:6, with its concomitant prohibition of murder, serves to criticize the culture of murder on display at these same theaters and circuses.

With the power that attends to being created in the image of God comes great responsibility. Referring to the structure set up in Genesis 9:5–6 of capital punishment for capital crimes, the Mishnah in Sanhedrin carefully warns witnesses against abusing this power by bringing false testimony:

> Mishnah: How were the witnesses warned in capital cases? Witnesses in capital cases were brought in and warned in this way: Perhaps what you say is based on supposition, or is evidence from other witnesses, or heard even from a trustworthy person? Perhaps you are unaware that we would test you by cross-examination and inquiry? Know that capital cases are not like monetary cases. In monetary cases, one gives money and effects atonement but in capital cases the executed person's blood and the blood of his potential descendants hang on you until the end of time. For thus we find in the case of Cain, who killed his brother, that it is written: The bloods of thy brother cry unto me [Gen. 4:10], not the blood of thy brother but the bloods of thy brother, i.e., his blood and the blood of his descendants . . . For this reason man was created alone, to teach that whoever destroys a single soul in Israel, Scripture imputes [guilt] to him as if he had destroyed the whole world; and whoever preserves a single soul in Israel, Scripture ascribes [merit] to him as if he has saved the whole world.[53]

The problem with murderous cultures such as those of Cain's descendants or of the Capitol is that they render human life very cheap. In a world rife with death, how does one come to believe that individual lives matter? That destroying one life is a world-destroying act, while saving one life is equivalent to saving the entire world?

One way to inculcate this belief is by showing the benefits and effects of a single well-lived life. Noah's is one such well-lived life, and by saving him, God preserves the future of all humanity going forward. Similarly, Katniss and Peeta exemplify the kind of individual will, agency, and commitment to others that helps achieve *tikkun olam*, the repairing and salvation of their entire world.

Irving Greenberg uses the term *"tikkun ha-adam"* (the repair of Adam), an amalgam of the concepts of *tzelem Elohim* and *tikkun olam*, to refer to the project of repairing the world on the basis of a belief in the "infinitive value, equality and uniqueness" of every *ben Adam*. "Since every human being is in the image of God," says Greenberg, "there is no preferred image—God is neither white nor black, male nor female, Jew or non-Jew."[54] This is an important statement, one that builds on the egalitarian account of human creation offered in Genesis 1:27 and serves as a corrective to the notion that one might derive from the end of the Mishnah from Sanhedrin that only Jewish lives matter, insofar as the Mishnah specifically refers to "a single soul of Israel" rather than to just any ordinary human soul. Greenberg is careful to insist that *Tzelem Elohim* not be construed as an exclusively Jewish or masculine concept; it appears in biblical sources not in reference to Abraham or the people of Israel, but in the stories of Adam (who was created simultaneously male and female) and Noah and his wife, the progenitors of all of humankind thereafter. As such, it undergirds not just Jewish or masculine value, but a universal conception of human dignity. At the same time, the reference at the end of the Mishnah, coming as it does in the context of a discussion of the workings of a Jewish court, insists on the dignity of Jewish particularity and its potential contribution to the best unfolding of the human self.

The ending or epilogue to the *Mockingjay*, the third book in the *Hunger Games* trilogy, presents a set of images that gesture in the direction of Greenberg's notion of *tikkun ha-adam*. The rebellion against the Capitol is finally over. The Hunger Games arenas have been dismantled. Katniss and Peeta, married and living back in District 12, now have two children: a girl and a boy, who play, like Adam and Eve, in the (Edenic)

Meadow, free of the fears and violence that characterized their parents' upbringing.⁵⁵ Katniss, however, continues to have nightmares about her horrific past and to worry, perhaps like Noah's descendants after the Flood, that her world might once again be taken away. "That's when I make a list in my head of every goodness I've seen someone do," Katniss says. "It's like a game. Repetitive. Even a little tedious after more than twenty years. But there are much worse games to play" (*Mockingjay*, 390).

Katniss's therapeutic "game" calls to mind Viktor Frankl's insistence on the "will to meaning" as the primary motivation of human life and a means of coping with suffering. According to Frankl, one way of finding meaning is "by experiencing something—such as goodness, truth and beauty—by experiencing nature and culture, or last but not least, by experiencing another human being in his very uniqueness—by loving him."⁵⁶ Restated in religious terms, one finds meaning by experiencing those aspects of human life that symbolize or emulate God. For, as Mark Mangano shows, the experiences that Frankl enumerates—goodness, truth, beauty, and love—all appear in the Bible as characteristic of the divine.⁵⁷ As Psalm 118 enjoins, "Give thanks unto God, for God is good, God's kindness endures forever." Katniss's list of "every goodness" she's ever seen anyone do is thus a kind of catalogue of human behavioral images or imitations of God.

Katniss's list includes not just one or two acts of goodness, but many—so many in fact that compiling the list in her head becomes a tedious exercise or repetitive "game"—one endowed, nevertheless, with real ritual meaning, in marked contrast to the meaningless cataloguing of the fallen and the victors of the Hunger Games. Would that this were the case in our world as well: that the business of cataloguing human kindness could become an extensive, tiresome form of recreation! For that would mean that God's image had finally become truly manifest in all aspects of human life; that goodness had finally triumphed over all the other murderous forces in the contemporary world, many of which masquerade as expressions of religious faith; and that the idea of being created in the "image of God" rather than some man-made idol had finally been projected, broadcasted, and shared with the entire world, a feat of religious image making to make any Reel Theologian proud.

Conclusion

Moonrise Kingdom: And the Youth Shall See Visions

We began our exploration in this book with *The Truman Show*, a film about an adult living in fake Seahaven who escapes his media-made ersatz Eden to pursue freely chosen love and find a true home. We conclude with Wes Anderson's *Moonrise Kingdom*,[1] a film about Suzy Bishop and Sam Shakusky, a girl and boy in love who run away from home and khaki scout camp, respectively, to set up their own home in the wilderness, a preadolescent Eden of innocent love and discovery. That is, until they are apprehended and separated, locked into a struggle with their elders over the future of Sam, an orphan whose foster parents have renounced him and who is about to be sent to an orphanage by a character-cum-Institution known as Social Services.

Of all the films discussed in this book, *Moonrise Kingdom* is the most visually distinctive. Wes Anderson is known for his idiosyncratic style, including offbeat humor, deadpan acting, and moments where characters in medium shot look directly at the camera, each a colorful miniature or visual tableau. Anderson tends to linger over the details of setting in his films, such as in the opening to *Moonrise Kingdom*, where the camera pans horizontally through the various yellow-hued, dollhouse-like rooms in the Bishop house. He likes to fill his scenes with nostalgic objects and details, such as the 1960s minidresses worn by Suzy Bishop throughout the film and the Davey Crockett hat worn by Sam Shakusky. Anderson commonly creates a cyclical structure in his films, ending them the same way they began, in this case with one of the Bishop boys setting up his portable record player to listen to Benjamin Britten's "Young Person's Guide to the Orchestra" and the other Bishop kids sitting down and listening along, Suzy sitting nearby on the window seat reading a book.[2]

Figure 12.1. *Moonrise Kingdom*, The Bishop Kids Listening to Benjamin Britten.

Anderson's visual style depicts but also transcends reality, gesturing in the direction of fantasy and parable, thus its particular relevance to the discussion in this book. *Moonrise Kingdom*, which imagines children pursuing new love in the primordial garden of the Chick-Chaw trail, which is interrupted by the encroachments of parents, civilization, law enforcement and Social Services, especially fits our discussion because of its evocation of the biblical book of Song of Songs, one of the primary parables of the Bible, insofar as it has commonly been understood in rabbinic literature as an allegory for the yet-unconsummated love story of the people of Israel and God.

It is not my intention here to engage in a full analysis of the film or the Song, but rather to highlight the theme of thwarted young love depicted both in film and in the biblical text. In the Song, the Shulamite is menaced and beaten by the watchmen in the city, when she sets out at night in pursuit of her beloved (Song 5:7), and by her older brothers, who threaten to wall her off in a tower and enclose her with boards of cedar (Song 8:9). But none of these forces of age and civility can quell the fires of her love. Instead, they only intensify the erotic attraction and mutual, egalitarian pursuit. Likewise in *Moonrise Kingdom*, Suzy Bishop and Sam Shakusky are flanked on all sides by adult figures representing Law, Order, and Society. Both of Suzy's parents (played by Bill Murray and Frances

McDormand) are lawyers; Suzy has discovered that her mother is having an affair with "that sad dumb policemen," the regional police officer, Captain Sharp (played by Bruce Willis), which suggests that neither of them is adhering to the law of faithfulness. Besides, none of these adults can seem to appreciate or get through to Suzy. Sam Shakusky is similarly misunderstood by Scout Master Ward (Edward Norton), a well-meaning but ineffectual leader who enforces the rules and teaches the skills of the military-sounding khaki scouts, but neither knows that Sam is an orphan nor notices how Sam is bullied by the other, more conventional campers. Only Sam and Suzy seem to understand each other.

The Bishops live on the Island of New Penzance in New England (evocative of Gilbert and Sullivan's *The Pirates of Penzance*) in a spot called Summer's End, connoting the waning of innocence and summer love. But camp season in this region continues well into September. And Suzy and Sam are hardly prepared to forego their innocence in order to conform. Instead of relinquishing their naïve love and commitment, Sam and Suzy come to influence the people around them to change their stance. First, the other khaki scouts band together to prevent Sam from being turned over to Social Services and make sure that Suzy and Sam can stay together. Then, in a climactic storm scene that takes place in the church that also serves as a theater for the production of Britten's one-act opera *Noye's Fludde*, Captain Sharp, not otherwise known for his sharp wit, grasps the urgency of the moment and volunteers to be Sam's new foster father. Note that Sam and Suzy first met when Sam came to see *Noye's Fludde* and noticed Suzy, who played the part of the raven in the opera. Mid-show, Sam went backstage to the dressing room to meet the girl he'd spotted and to ask her what kind of bird she was. And so the story comes full circle. Sam's initial attraction to dark-eyed Suzy is shown to be no mere silly crush, but an example of what the new generation can teach the old. Fear of the law gives way to the purifying compassion of an adult for a vulnerable child. In keeping with the Noah's Flood evocation, the historical storm that takes place that night on the Island of New Penzance wreaks physical devastation on the island, but, as the red-jacketed, green-hatted, elf-like narrator of the film explains, the crops the following year will be better than ever before. New beginnings are afoot.

Given the church setting of the climax, one can certainly imagine a Christian reading of the film based on the New Testament principle of love superseding law. But law does not get abolished in this film; rather, it assumes a new, loving face, as Sam trades in his khaki scout garb for a child's-size Island Police uniform. Like Song of Songs, which ends on the same note of amorous pursuit as it began, *Moonrise Kingdom* ends with the same record playing-scene, but this time, as the camera moves from room to dollhouse room, Sam is also there in the house, listening along as he paints on an easel. Everything is the same, yet everything is different, as Suzy has been reintegrated into her family, Sam has found a home with Sharp as well as with the Bishop clan, and everyone has learned how to love better.

A whimsical, offbeat story of generational estrangement thus culminates in a sense of newly shared vision. A parable: to what can it be likened? To the experience of watching film, one of the youngest of our visual artistic genres, and seeing the way it helps us see Jewish tradition differently. To the experience of bringing Jewish texts into conversation with contemporary narrative visuality and seeing what new interpretive light can be shed on both. Throughout much of Anderson's film, Suzy Bishop is seen peering through binoculars, looking for Sam and for what she has been missing. By the end of the film, both she and her elders have seen and understood something new. As the prophet Joel envisions, "And it shall come to pass afterward, that I will pour out My spirit upon all flesh; and your sons and your daughters shall prophesy, your old shall dream dreams, your youth shall see visions" (Joel 3:1).

APPENDIX I

On the Design of "Reel Theology," from e-mail archives

-----Original Message-----
From: Eugene B. Borowitz [eborowitz@huc.edu]
Sent: Monday, November 26, 2001
To: Wendy Zierler
Subject: Re: our course

Sorry for the long delay in responding. The bottom line is this: we'll do whatever you are comfortable with. My mantra is: since the students will get a great deal out of what we are trying to do, I assume that we will learn from this year's experience how we want to do it in the future.
That being clear, I hope, let me comment on specifics.

As to how many weeks we should set the content, eight, as you suggest, is fine with me. You pick what you think are the items for those sessions, though I would appreciate having one so I can help them get some sense of what seems to be a basic shift in thinking about people, the chief sense of the postmodern that impinges on our present religious sensibilities. As for that, I'd like to consider the films *Shrek* and *As Good as it Gets*, by contrast to *You've Got Mail*. Whatever movies you want to do are fine with me. It might be helpful to try to vary our sessions so that the long reading assignments, e.g., *American Pastoral* (a book I very much liked), are balanced by shorter assignments in between.

In the early sessions, we need to spend some time each week working out with the students what they'd like to consider in the student-led sessions toward the end of the semester. Since we have no idea how many people will be taking the course, this will take some working out.

In general, I think of this more as a course in gaining skills than in gaining content, though it would be silly to try to separate the two. Rabbis spend their lives, in their various roles, as what used to be called middle-"men," intermediaries between significant meanings and people who may read more than the average American but whose interests and concerns are increasingly not highbrow. Our job is to try to keep them from dumbing down more than they have to, but they want rabbis who can talk to them as they really are and where they really are. I do not know what your synagogue experience has been since being back in the United States or what it was before you left, but I have been quietly involved in synagogues and other institutions all my life and so am committed to trying to make it possible for my students to be able to talk to their people, and talk to them about serious things in ways they can hear and understand. So I hope that you will take it as two of your goals to help them learn how to read/see/hear in some depth and how the feminist vision needs to be a major part of the way they look at things. I have always learned a good deal from watching my students try to explain or apply what I have been doing with them, and while those skills need to be learned by continual doing and honed by a growing self-judgment, I feel I need to give them a start on that.

Enough, maybe more than enough. Please shape this as you think best, and I will be as helpful as I can and you will instruct me how best to be. Gene

-----Original Message-----
From: Eugene B. Borowitz
Sent: Wednesday, July 21, 2004 3:41 PM
To: Wendy Zierler
Subject: Pre-talk thoughts 2

Dear Wendy,

Let me meander over some of the untidy terrain of some thoughts I have about the reading I've done, thanks to your industry, and that will lead me to a practical matter, I hope.

The best thing about the readings was their clarification of the relation between popular culture and the "spiritual" realities/deep values it often contains. And there were some nice things about the way one can go about excavating these. I assume that you are more sensitive to this kind of "critical" reading than I am, so I will not say more about that except to say that I think a comparison with midrash-as-reading is very much in order for us. Of course, midrash works from the sacred text to the social-cultural explication/application, and this contemporary reading works in the opposite direction: from the secular to the sacred. Still, it is roughly the same process.

One issue that they didn't say much about but that seems important to me is the ephemeral quality of much of this material. Reading some of the enthusiastic analyses of this or that—and especially the side comments about works of a similar impact, though not further analyzed—I was continually saying to myself, "Do people still remember that and its depth impact?" Is it my advanced age and my having so many things already stuffed in my culture-kopf that I don't take them and don't see younger people taking last year's sensation that seriously?

Another way of talking about this is to focus for a moment on the way we are interested in what is NEW and how we take it for granted that there will be a flood of new TV programs, films, popular music, and personalities to appeal to us. Much of this is what's-hot/cool today—and the todays keep coming along. Lasting impact is the exception; something that's memorable is rarer in this onrushing flood than it was in a time where culture moved more slowly compared to our mass production. Or so it seems to me.

Thus, the problem of sounding critically nearly-out-of-date by the time one is finally in print. I think that the best response to this is to look at whatever we do less as a classic exemplification than as a pretty good example of what is likely to be coming along in another form.

Another matter that troubles me—at least as a template for us—is the way most of these writers talk about "religion." That is a useful construct for people at secular universities or whose discipline only "allows" people to speak in secular terms. It is a useful construct indeed to do what universities do best, speak about a great number of particularities in some universal understanding. And, for political reasons, I think that can be very useful. But as a believing Jew, I think that religion-in-general, the Noachides, is a second-order construct. It rests on what the university would call a first-order revelation, in our case, Torah (by which, of course, I mean the liberal Jewish construct I write about and practice).

I am mostly interested in teaching Torah out of culture only because our people often come to us with a lack of knowledge of Torah but with a strong immersion in culture and what it communicates. So my goal is mostly what theologians call "apologetic," I want to teach them not about religion-in-general but, building or contrasting or whatever, I want to teach them about Judaism. I don't mind communicating what we believe in common with some other people these days, but that is a secondary concern for me. And I have only a light interest in teaching them about what our artists see as the problems with our culture, unless that leads on to some deeper Jewish prophetic lesson.

So in choosing my things, I try to figure out what Jewish truth can I get to from some contemporary production. At the moment, I think I can do that for my four selections for our course on these themes: human nature; ethnicity; God (the hardest one to get to); and tikkun olam. All of which leads me to ask you how you go about your selecting, though I quickly add that a number of the things you have mentioned, I could find quite congenial to my general approach. But it would help me a great deal if, at some point, you could briefly indicate what you think rabbis could get from the things that appeal to you (e.g., I think *Memento* is a good way of teaching the importance of history).

Sorry to go on so long, but I hope this is helpful for the ongoing conversation. Gene

-----**Original Message**-----
From: Zierler, Wendy
To: Borowitz, Eugene
Sent: 7/22/04 1:02 PM
Subject: RE: Pre-talk thoughts 2

Hi Gene,
Thanks so much for your thoughtful meanderings . . .

Yes, you are correct. There is indeed a problematic ephemerality to this material. I confess, that I am less interested in examining every single new pop cultural phenomenon than I am at examining really noteworthy, compelling examples, and in this regard, it is less important for me to choose the newest hottest sensation for my teaching or even for our book. Again, I assume that the students—at least some of them—will want to address some of these cultural moments.

I also concur that the books I have been sending you are most useful in the ways they point out the nexus between pop culture and spirituality/religious life. I see them as guidebooks as to how it can be done. There is a whole "genus" of these sorts of books that look at pop culture specifically in dialogue with Christianity and the New Testament. A notable example is two books by Robert Jewett called *Saint Paul at the Movies* and *Saint Paul Returns to the Movies*. Another such book is *Faith and Film* by Bryan P. Stone. One some level, these books offer a more pointed example of what we can do with this material, i.e., specifically connect it to Torah and Jewish teaching.

So, you wanted to know about my selections:

In the past, I have given a lecture that uses *Memento* as an occasion to examine Jewish notions of history and memory. It includes references to all the kinds of remembering that are prescribed in the Torah, and then modern attitudes toward memory. Essentially, the argument of this lecture is that if traditional Judaism requires us to remember, the modern Jewish experience, in many regards, has been a collective effort to forget. And yet, I show, through close reading, that even the most forgetful of the moderns tends on some level to enact a revival of Jewish memory.

Forrest Gump (and *The Frisco Kid*) are an occasion for me to consider the tension in Jewish sources between simplicity (the notion of the *Tam*, in all of its forms) versus cleverness (the *Hakham* in all its forms). In the past, I have had students read the Rabbi Nachman of Bratslav story "The Clever Man and the Simple Man." To that I would add sources about Jacob as an "*ish tam yoshev ohalim*," and the notion of a "whole, pure sacrifice" as well as statements from Kohelet about wisdom versus ignorance . . . Additionally, there are the four sons of the Haggadah and Singer's "Gimpel Tam." What attracts me to these materials is that they provide an opportunity to consider (postmodern) misgivings about Enlightenment and reason as paths to Truth, at the same time that they demonstrate the limitations of non-rational modes . . . (Some of this is explicitly addressed by you, of course, in your own work, i.e., your discussion of postmodern disappointment with modernity in *Renewing the Covenant*.)

Magnolia, which I haven't worked on yet, but which really fascinates me, is a film that highlights the role that the viewer has to play in piecing together and interpretation. I like films like that for courses such as ours. They help school the students in the practice of close reading. Beyond that, what moves me about this film is its treatment of the religious impulse to confess/repent and the role of death as a life-fact that catalyzes spiritual introspection . . . The film also treats the subject of human interconnectedness (*arevut*), which I think is a fundamental Jewish tenet—that we as a community are interconnected. Our paths cross, literally and figuratively.

God gives us opportunities to come together to help one another and also charges us with this responsibility.

I love the film *Smoke*, because it provides an opportunity to teach about the Jewish/religious centrality of storytelling. You mentioned that the practice of midrash is important to our course and our thinking. Here I'd add that Judaism encodes and communicates fundamental Jewish tenets in stories and requires us ritually to retell stories as a way of teaching, forging community. Ronald Dworkin's notion of law as a serial novel is relevant here. So is the Passover Seder, and the very practice of embedding stories in midrash: "*mashal lemah hadavar domeh.*" Also, it connects this theme of the religious dimension of storytelling to the image of smoke, which itself is very powerful as religious symbol in a Jewish context: the revelation of God through smoke, the smoke of sacrifices, and the smokestacks of the Holocaust as a challenge to all of this.

With regard to the film *The Hours*, I was interested in the question of the value of life (over suicide) in Jewish sources. *Whalerider*, another feminist film, speaks about feminist issues of inclusion in ritual and tribal intellectual life.

I hope all of this helps clarify my thinking. WZ

APPENDIX II

More Movies and Midrash

There is no end to the films that can be brought into meaningful conversation with Jewish tradition, and as such, the additional resources in this appendix do not attempt to be exhaustive. Rather, they are meant to inform readers of other films that were included over the years in the Reel Theology course but did not become full chapters in this book. The list is presented alphabetically by film title and includes brief discussion of the Jewish theological/textual theme discussed by way of "inverted midrash."

American Beauty (1999), written by Alan Ball and directed by Sam Mendes, is the story of a frustrated, middle-aged, suburban father who develops an infatuation for his teenage daughter's best friend. In the very first iteration of the Reel Theology course, we paired this film with Philip Roth's Pulitzer Prize–winning novel *American Pastoral* (1997) as a means of considering their common critique of the American way of life. The plastic bag sequence in *American Beauty* and the extended description of the construction of gloves in *American Pastoral* offer a fruitful comparison in terms of their representation of beauty as a matter of art and craft and as a source of value and meaning. Dr. Borowitz took the opportunity, as part of our discussion, to expatiate on the potential pitfalls of beauty and aesthetics as a replacement for faith, as seen in the Reform worship context. (See his remarks in the foreword to this book.)

Doubt (2008), written and directed by John Patrick Shanley and based on Shanley's successful stage play by the same name, is the story of a parish priest (Philip Seymour Hoffman) who is accused of child abuse by the nun who heads the parish school (Meryl Streep). While the film engages the issue of priests abusing children in the Catholic Church, its main concerns are with questions of faith, doubt, and interpretation. In class discussions, we analyzed some of the crucial scenes in which the priest and nun faced off against one another, noting her certainties as opposed to his clinging to the ineffable; her openness and frankness as opposed to his withholding; her willingness to subvert the patriarchal system as opposed to his conservatism. Was the film ultimately about faith and doubt, we asked, or about power? Jewish sources for discussion included Genesis Rabbah 39:1, a midrash that attempts to understand how it is that Abraham set out on his journey of monotheistic faith that includes a parable about a man who set out on a journey and came to a place where he saw a palace on fire/aglow and inquired after the master of the house. Interpretations of this theological parable that engage issues of faith and doubt were brought from Abraham Joshua Heschel's *God in Search of Man*, "The Problem of Evil," 367–81); Louis Jacobs, *We Have a Reason to Believe* (23–31); Jonathan Sacks, *A Letter in the Scroll* ("A Palace in Flames," 51–58)' and Norman Lamm's *Faith and Doubt* (1986).

Harry Potter and the Sorcerer's Stone, novel by J. K. Rowling (1997), the first in the *Harry Potter* series, which also resulted in a series of popular films. The first *Harry Potter* film was released in 2001, but our discussion in the first iteration of the Reel Theology course focused on the novel and what drew so many people, young and old, to its particular magic world. Some attention was paid to the religious controversies that swirled around the witchcraft elements of the story and its invocation of supernatural power outside the realm of God. Even more attention was given to the problem of evil, and in this respect, the novel was paired with the popular television show *The Sopranos*. Discussion also centered on the story of young Harry and that of the biblical Moses.

The Hours (2002), directed by Stephen Daldry and written by David Hare, based on the Pulitzer Prize–winning novel by Michael Cunningham by the same title, is composed of three interlocking narrative strands, all of which relate to Virginia Woolf's novel *Mrs. Dalloway* (1925): 1) the story of the life, work, and suicide of Virginia Woolf herself; 2) the story of a depressed, 1950s-era housewife and her attempted suicide; and 3) the story of Clarissa Vaughn, who like Clarissa Dalloway in Woolf's novel, is preparing for a dinner party. The question we engaged with respect to this film, together with a discussion of the television show *Six Feet Under* (2001–2005), which deals with a family that owns a funeral home, was

"Why live?" Having set before the people the blessings and the curses, life, and death, Deuteronomy 30:19 enjoins us to "Choose life." But why? Sources engaged included the episode of King Saul falling on his sword when the Philistines seem likely to capture him (I Samuel 31); the book of Ecclesiastes; Elliot Dorff, *Matters of Life and Death*; Nachum Amsel, *The Jewish Encyclopedia of Moral and Ethical Issues* (1996); and Neil Gillman, *The Death of Death* (1997).

Midnight in Paris (2011), directed by Woody Allen, depicts a writer (Owen Wilson) who is infatuated with the Paris of the 1920s modernists. On a trip to Paris with his fiancée, he has a series of fantastic midnight encounters with his modernist literary and artistic heroes, which sheds complicated light on his nostalgic yearnings. The religious discussion of this film centered on the twin ideas of loss and nostalgia. Readings included Psalms 126 and 137; Mishnah Sotah 9:12; Simon Rawidowicz, "Israel: The Every Dying People," in *Israel: The Ever Dying People and Other Essays* (1986, 53–63); and Haim Soleveitchik, "Rupture and Reconstruction," *Tradition* 28, no. 4 (Summer 1994), http://www.lookstein.org/links/orthodoxy.htm.

My Big Fat Greek Wedding (2002), directed by Joel Zwick, written by and starring Nia Vardalos, tells the story of a young Greek woman who falls in love with an American, non-Greek man. Dr. Borowitz chose this film because "ethnicity/history is significant to us in relation to God . . . *Big Fat Greek* is a very popular introduction to the role groups can have in people's lives. In this case, it's lovingly making fun of Greek insularity—ethnicity is not all good. But it does have much going for it as compared to the uptight, upper class apparently Protestant types that the guy comes from and while it is little too Zorba-ish for my tastes it makes its point" (e-mail correspondence, September 21, 2004). Discussion of the film included analysis of the intermarriage theme in important works of twentieth-century Jewish literature (Sholem Aleichem's *Tevye the Dairyman*, particularly "Chava," and Anzia Yezierska's *Hungry Hearts and Other Stories*), in addition to discussion of a theology of community, as seen in Eugene Borowitz, "The Social Side of Jewish Selfhood, *Renewing the Covenant* (170–81).

Smoke (1995), directed by Wayne Wang and written by Paul Auster, based on Auster's short story "Augie Wren's Christmas Story," follows a group of characters who frequent a Brooklyn tobacco store. At the center of the film is the idea of the Christmas story, a genre that has religious importance but is also very much the product of Hollywood, the American dream, and consumer culture. What happens when a postmodern writer confronts this genre? What do we do with the literary legacy of magic, of divine intercession, of angels meeting humans and helping them see how to live their lives? The story treats the difficulty of writing about cultural and religious occasions in a meaningful way, because they are so deeply imbued with personal expectations and nostalgia. In a sense, it is a story about how one finds originality amid triteness and endlessly reproduced images. The motif of smoke, identified in the film with the power of imagination and the cigar store camaraderie, provided an opportunity to analyze the image of smoke in Jewish culture: its ritual use in the case of the temple incense; its appearance in representations of God's protective powers (e.g., the Pillar of Smoke that accompanied the Israelites in the desert). Smoke is something you can see but cannot touch and thus engages notions of divine presence, wrath, revelation, or epiphany. Finally, there is the role of smoke in historical and literary representations of the Holocaust, as in the poetry of Dan Pagis, quoted in chapter 11.

Tuesdays with Morrie is a memoir by Mitch Albom (1997) and a TV movie (1999) starring Jack Lemmon and Hank Azaria. Dr. Borowitz and I used the book/film as the material for the first meetings of Reel Theology for the first few years that we taught the course, in part because of its popularity, in part because of its treatment of the teacher–student relationship, and in part because the course met on Tuesdays! Discussions examined Morrie as a countercultural, nonconformist teacher, his refusal to make money in an exploitative manner, his rejection of the cults of youth and noncommitment, and the encounter with Morrie's death that is part of Mitch's story. The Jewish application of this involved an analysis of the teacher–disciple relationship in the story of Elijah and Elisha and Elijah's death-ascent in a chariot of fire in II Kings 2.

Traffic (2000), directed by Steven Soderburgh, deals with the subject of drug trafficking and addiction via the story of a judge appointed to pursue the war on drugs, whose own daughter becomes a drug addict. The AMC series *Breaking Bad* (2008–2013) has since explored some of the very same issues to even more probing and chilling effect. Jewish religious exploration included discussion of what Dr. Borowitz called "the power of the forbidden," including readings from Proverbs 9 and BT Sanhedrin 75a. On the subject of addiction, we also looked at the episode of the *ben soreh umoreh* (the rebellious son) in Deuteronomy 21:18–21 and the related Talmudic commentary in BT Sanhedrin, chapter 8, 68b–75a.

Unforgiven (1992), directed by Clint Eastwood, is an unconventional Western that reverses many of the stock conventions of the genre. Instead of a black-and-white presentation of good and evil, this film depicts a villain who steps in to do justice and seek revenge for a woman who was cruelly disfigured. Discussion of this film dealt with the idea of love as a counterforce to evil, the ethics of revenge, and the connection between political and sexual dominance, as well as the role of family, community, and state in policing women's bodies. All of this was paired with an analysis of similar issues as seen in the Dinah story in Genesis 34.

Whalerider (2002), directed by Niki Carol, is a film about a Maori community in New Zealand stricken with various problems: dissolution of family, lack of male role models, economic hardship, erosion of tribal practices, and general ignorance. The leader of the community is obsessed with preserving the old ways, which include dynastic male leadership, and as such shuns the granddaughter who yearns to be taken seriously and even to lead. Jewish discussion of this film focused on issues of female leadership in Judaism and the feminist critique of patriarchy. Texts discussed included the story of Deborah (Judges 4–5) and such feminist theological works as Judith Plaskow's *Standing Again at Sinai* (1991), Rachel Adler's *Engendering Judaism* (1998), and Tova Hartman's *Feminism Encounters Traditional Judaism* (2008). In other iterations of the course, discussion of these issues took place around such feminist buddy films as *Thelma and Louise* (1991) and *Fried Green Tomatoes* (1991).

Notes

Introduction

1. Ruth Humleker, *New York for the Independent Traveler* (Saint Paul, MN: Marlor Press, 1997).

2. The one recent exception is Rabbi Herbert J. Cohen, *Kosher Movies* (Jerusalem: Urim Publishers, 2015), which includes two-page reviews/plot summaries of various popular films from a Jewish point of view, but offers little in the way of analysis either of the films or of relevant Jewish texts.

3. See, for example, Joyce Antler, *Talking Back: Images of Jewish Women in American Popular Culture* (Hanover, NH: University Press of New England, 1998); Omer Bartov, *The "Jew" in Cinema: From The Golem to Don't Touch My Holocaust* (Bloomington: Indiana University Press, 2005); Henry Bial, *Acting Jewish: Negotiating Ethnicity on the American Stage and Screen* (Ann Arbor: University of Michigan Press, 2005); Paul Buhle, *From the Lower East Side to Hollywood: Jews in American Popular Culture* (New York: Verso, 2004); Lawrence J. Epstein, *The Haunted Smile: The Story of Jewish Comedians in America* (Cambridge, MA: Perseus Books, 2001; Patricia Erens, *The Jew in American Cinema* (Bloomington: Indiana University Press, 1988); Neal Gabler, *An Empire of their Own: How Jews Invented Hollywood* (New York: Anchor Books, 1989); J. Hoberman and Jeffrey Shandler, *Entertaining America: Jews, Movies, and Broadcasting* (Princeton: Princeton University Press, 2003); and Joel Samberg, *Reel Jewish: A Century of Jewish Movies* (Middle Village, NY: Jonathan David Publishers, 2000).

4. Insofar as Jewishness figures at all in any anthologies of essays on religion and film, it is in the context of Jewish-themed films or in discussions about Jewish filmmakers. See, for example, Allison Smith, "Judaism and Jewishness in Film" and Guy Matalon, "Holocaust Movies," in *The Continuum Guide to Religion and Film*, ed. William Blizek (London: Continuum, 2009), 167–76, 231–41; and "Judaism," in *The Routledge Companion to Religion and Film* (New York: Routledge, 2009), 99–108. None of these essays attempts to define a Jewish theological or textual reading practice.

5. See, for example, Joel W. Martin, "Introduction: Seeing the Sacred on the Screen," in J. W. Martin and Conrad Oswalt, Screening the Sacred (Boulder: Westview, 1995); Terry Lindvall, "Religion and Film: Part 1: History and Criticism," *Communication Research Trends* 23, no. 4 (2004): 3–44, which also includes a comprehensive bibliography; Steve Nolan, "Understanding Films: Reading the Gaps," in Anthony J. Clarke and Paul Fiddes, *Flickering Images: Theology and Film in Dialogue* (Oxford: Regent's Park College Oxford, 2005), 25–48; and Jonathan Brant, *Paul Tillich and the Possibility of Revelation Through Film* (Oxford: Oxford University Press, 2012). See also the selective bibliography included in Eric Mazur, *The Encyclopedia of Religion and Film* (Santa Barbara: ABC-CLIO, 2011), 563–75.

6. Harvey G. Cox, "Theological Reflections on Cinema," *Andover Newton Quarterly* 3, no. 2 (1962), 31, 33. For an early twentieth-century essay advocating for the religious importance and uses of film, see Herbert A. Jump, "The Religious Possibilities of the Motion Picture (1910), in *Film History* 14, no. 2 (2002): 216–28. Excerpts included in Jolyon Mitchell and S. Brent Plate, eds., *The Religion and Film Reader* (New York: Routledge, 2007), 14–24.

7. Harvey Cox, *The Secular City* (New York: Macmillan, 1965), 15.

8. Paul Tillich, *Theology of Culture*, ed. Robert Kimball (New York: Oxford University Press, 1959), 41.

9. Carl Skrade, introduction to *Celluloid and Symbols*, ed. John C. Cooper and Carl Skrade (Philadelphia: Fortress Press, 1970), 1, 3. For another early book that seeks to enrich the church with the revelational potential of film, see James M. Wall, *Church and Cinema* (Grand Rapids, MI: William B. Eerdmans Publishing Company, 1971). Also see Neil Hurley, *Theology Through Film* (New York: Harper & Row, 1970). Another book published at this same time is Roger Kahle's and Robert E. A. Lee's *Popcorn and Parable* (Minneapolis: Augsburg Publishing House, 1971), which refers by title to the Christian parable, but includes no real discussion of the parable genre.

10. John May and Michael Bird, eds., *Religion and Film* (Knoxville: University of Tennessee Press, 1982); Robert K. Johnston, *Reel Spirituality* (Grand Rapids: Baker Academic, 2000), and *Reframing Theology and Film: New Focus for an Emerging Discipline* (Grand Rapids, MI: Baker Academic, 2007); Craig Detweiler and Barry Taylor, *A Matrix of Meanings: Finding God in Popular Culture* (Grand Rapids, MI: Baker Academic, 2003); and Anthony Clarke, "Gaining Fresh Insights," in Anthony J. Clarke and Paul Fiddes, eds., *Flickering Images: Theology and Film in Dialogue* (Oxford: Regent's Park College Oxford, 2005).

11. For an early example of this dialogic strain, see Malcolm Boyd, "Theology and the Movies," *Theology Today* 14, no. 3 (1957): 359–75. For later writings on the dialogue of film with Christianity, see Gerard Loughlin, "A Theological Introduction," in *Cinéma Divinité*, ed. Eric S. Christianson, Peter Francis, and William Telford (London: SCM Press, 2005), 1–14.

12. Bryan Stone, *Faith and Film: Theological Themes at the Cinema* (Saint Louis: Chalice Press, 2000), 4.

13. See Robert Jewett, *Saint Paul at the Movies* (Louisville, KY: Westminster/John Knox Press, 1993); Sara Anson Vaux, *Finding Meaning at the Movies* (Nashville, TN: Abingdon Press, 1999); Catherine M. Barsotti and Robert K. Johnston, *Finding God in the Movies* (Grand Rapids, MI: Baker Academic, 2004); Robert K. Johnston, *Reel Spirituality: Theology and Film in Dialogue*, 2nd ed. (Grand Rapids, MI: Baker Academic, 2006), and *Theology and Film: New Focus for an Emerging Discipline* (Grand Rapids, MI: Baker Academic, 2007); Richard Leonard, *Movies That Matter* (Chicago: Loyola Press, 2006). *The Religion and Film Reader*, ed. Jolyon Mitchell and S. Brent Plate (New York: Routledge, 2007), aims to be a global study of film and religion, but in some respects it too skews decidedly Christian.

14. Tom Beaudoin, *Virtual Faith: The Irreverent Spiritual Quest of Generation X* (San Francisco: Jossey Bass Publishers, 1998), 13. For a similar generationally focused exploration, see Craig Detweiler and Barry Taylor, *A Matrix of Meanings: Finding God in Popular Culture* (Grand Rapids, MI: Baker Academic, 2003); Gareth Higgins, *How Movies Helped Save My Soul: Finding Spiritual Fingerprints in Culturally Significant Films* (Lake Marie, FL: Relevant Books, 2003); and David Dark, *Everyday Apocalypse: The Sacred Revealed in Radiohead, The Simpsons, and Other Pop Culture Icons* (Grand Rapids, MI: Brazos Press, 2002).

15. See, for example, Clive Marsh and Gaye Ortiz, eds., *Explorations in Theology and Film* (Malden, MA: Blackwell, 1997); Christopher Deacy and Gaye Williams Ortiz, eds., *Theology and Film: Challenging the Sacred/Secular Divide* (Malden, MA: Wiley Blackwell, 2008).

16. John C. Lyden, *Film as Religion: Myth, Morals and Rituals* (New York: New York University Press, 2003). The idea of reading film for evidence of the numinous or the transcendent is also explored by screenwriter Paul Schrader in his now-classic work, *Transcendental Style in Film: Ozu, Bresson, Dreyer* (New York: Da Capo, 1988), originally published by University of California Press in 1972. For a beautiful, evocative essay about film transcendence by another filmmaker, see Nathaniel Dorsky, *Devotional Cinema* (Berkeley, CA: Tuumba Press, 2003).

17. Joel W. Martin and Conrad E. Oswalt Jr., *Screening the Sacred* (Boulder, CO: Westview Press, 1995).

18. Melanie J. Wright, *Religion and Film: An Introduction* (London: I.B. Tauris, 2007); Gregory Watkins, ed., *Teaching Religion and Film* (New York: Oxford University Press, 2008); and William L. Blizek, ed., *The Continuum Companion to Religion and Film* (London: Continuum, 2009).

19. Roy M. Anker, *Catching Light: Looking for God in the Movies* (Grand Rapids, MI: William B. Eerdmans Publishing Company, 2004); Wright, *Religion and Film: An Introduction*; Steve Nolan, "Towards a New Religious Film Criticism: Using Film to Understand Religious Identity Rather than Locate Cinematic

Analogue," in *Mediating Religion: Conversations in Media, Religion and Culture*, ed. Jolyon Mitchell and Sophia Marriage (London: T & T Clark, 2003), 169–78; Jonathan Brant, *Paul Tillich and the Possibility of Revelation Through Film*; and S. Brent Plate, "Religion/Literature/Film, "Toward a Religious Visuality of Film," *Literature and Theology* 12, no. 1 (1998): 16–38.

20. Brant, *Paul Tillich*, 23.

21. I do not include a full overview of film terms and film analysis in this book given that there are many good books out there that do that work. For more on film terminology and/or "how to read film," see James Monaco, *How to Read a Film* (New York: Oxford University Press, 2000); William H. Philips, *Film: An Introduction*, 4th ed. (New York: Bedford/St. Martin's, David Bordwell, 2009); *Film Art: An Introduction* (New York: McGraw Hill Education, 2012); and Louis Giannetti, *Understanding Movies*, 13th ed. (New York: Pearson, 2013). For an excellent lexicon of film terms, see the Brooklyn College Film department "Film Glossary," http://userhome.brooklyn.cuny.edu/anthro/jbeatty/COURSES/glossary.htm.

22. Introduction to John R. May, ed., *New Image of Religious Film* (Kansas City: Sheed & Ward, 1997).

23. Christopher Deacy's book begins with the following question: "How plausible is it to examine the medium of film through a Christian lens?" See Christopher Deacy, *Faith and Film: Religious Themes in Contemporary Cinema* (Burlington, VT: Ashgate, 2005), vi. Likewise, Clive Marsh and Gaye Oritz's *Explorations in Theology and Film* begins with references to Christians and churchgoers and then with the "concern throughout Christian churches in the West to foster lay training and theological education and to stimulate theological debate." See Clive Marsh and Gaye Ortiz, introduction to *Explorations in Theology and Film*, ed. Marsh and Ortiz (Malden, MA: Blackwell, 1997), 1. For another book that similarly equates faith with Christianity and diversity, with diverse Christian perspectives, see William D. Romanowski, *Eyes Wide Open: Looking for God in Popular Culture* (Grand Rapids, MI: Brazos Press, 2007).

24. William R. Telford, "Through a Lens Darkly," *Cinéma Divinité: Religion, Theology and the Bible in Film*, ed. Eric S. Christianson, Peter Francis, and William R. Telford (London: SCM Press, 2005), 26.

25. Robert Jewett, *Saint Paul at the Movies: The Apostle's Dialogue with American Culture* (Louisville, KY: Westminster/John Knox Press, 1993), and *Saint Paul Returns to the Movies: Triumph Over Shame* (Grand Rapids, MI: William. B. Eerdmans Publishing Company, 1998).

26. See Cox, *The Secular City*, 15–31.

27. Peter Ochs, "Postcritical Scriptural Interpretation in Judaism," in *Interpreting Judaism in a Postmodern Age*, ed. Steven Kepnes (New York: New York University Press, 1996), 55.

28. Eugene Borowitz, "Textual Reasoning and Jewish Philosophy: The Next Phase of Jewish Postmodernity," in *Textual Reasonings: Jewish Philosophy and Text Study at the End of the Twentieth Century*, ed. Peter Ochs and Nancy Leveen (Grand Rapids, MI: William B. Eerdmans Publishing Company, 2002), 157.

29. Franz Rosenzweig, "Upon the Opening of the Jüdisches Lehrhaus," in *On Jewish Learning*, ed. N. N. Glatzer (New York: Schocken Books, 1955), 96.

30. Some of the films and themes in the course were chosen and organized around the chapters and thematic foci of Eugene Borowitz's *Renewing the Covenant*. For several years we taught the film *My Big Fat Greek Wedding* under the thematic rubric of "The Self and the Folk: The Social Side of Jewish Selfhood." See Eugene Borowitz, *Renewing the Covenant* (Philadelphia: Jewish Publication Society, 1991), 170–81. Likewise, discussion first of the television show *The Sopranos* and later of the film *Crimes and Misdemeanors* dealt in part with ideas included in "What Can We Do About Our Will to Do Evil," in *Renewing the Covenant*, 155–69.

31. James Kugel looks at this early, prerabbinic exegesis in terms of the model of Joseph in Potiphar's house: "If Joseph was changed and, in the story, likewise tempted in Potiphar's house, he nevertheless remained in another sense, profoundly true to his origins." See James L. Kugel, *In Potiphar's House: The Interpretive Life of Biblical Texts* (New York: HarperSanFrancisco, 1990), 7. The study of the Dead Sea Scrolls has led to a much broader awareness of prerabbinic biblical exegesis, beginning with the later books of the Bible and continuing into the Second Temple period. In 1961, Geza Vermes coined the term "Rewritten Bible" to refer to "a narrative that follows scripture but includes a substantial amount of supplements and interpretative developments." See Geza Vermes, *Scripture and Tradition in Judaism* (Leiden: Brill, 1961), 95. On the question of the ongoing relevance or accuracy of Vermes's term, see Moshe Bernstein, "'Rewritten Bible': A Generic Category Which Has Outlived Its Usefulness?," *Textus* 22 (2005): 169–96; and Jozsef Zsengeller, ed., *Rewritten Bible After Fifty Years* (Leiden: Brill, 2014). See also Paul Mandel, "The Origins of Midrash in the Second Temple Period," and Steven Fraade, "Rewritten Bible and Rabbinic Midrash as Commentary," in Carol Bakhos, ed., *Current Trends in the Study of Midrash* (Leiden: Brill, 2006), 59–78 and 9–34, respectively.

32. Lesleigh Cushing Stahlberg, *Sustaining Fictions: Intertextuality, Midrash, Translation, and the Literary Afterlife of the Bible* (New York: T & T Clark, 2008), 133, 137.

33. Hebrew original from the Bar Ilan Responsa Project, version 14. Translation quoted in Cushing Stahlberg, 137.

34. Brad H. Young, *The Parables: Jewish Tradition and Christian Interpretation* (Grand Rapids, MI: Baker Academic, 1998), 3.

35. David Stern, *Parables in Midrash: Narrative and Exegesis in Rabbinic Literature* (Cambridge, MA: Harvard University Press, 1991), 9. Also see Michael

Fishbane, *The Exegetical Imagination* (Cambridge, MA: Harvard University Press, 1998), 3.

36. Ibid., 47.

37. Hebrew original of Shir Hashirim Rabbah 1:1:8 from the Bar Ilan Responsa Project, version 14. Translation mine. For more on this midrash, see chapter 9.

38. S. Brent Plate, *Religion and Film: Cinema and the Re-Creation of the World* (London: Wallflower, 2009), 8.

39. Ibid., 9–10.

40. Eugene Borowitz, *The Mask Jews Wear* (New York: Sh'ma, 1980), 209.

41. It is important to note that the issue of idolatry also figures in Christian discussions of theology and film. As early as 1959, William F. Lynch S. J. wrote a book called *The Image Industries* (New York: Sheed and Ward, 1959), in which he expressed concern over the manipulative power of television and movie images and expressed a need for "creative theologians." And Neil P. Hurley wrote the following in his book *Theology Through Film* (New York: Harper & Row, 1970):

> The very first commandments on the Tablets of the law given to Moses on Sinai proscribed the worship of graven images, whether of clay, wood, stone, ivory, silver, or gold. Today the images that influence man's memory, imagination, mind and will are more subtle. In the scientific age, we are less prone to worship totem poles, statuary carvings and temple figurines. Nevertheless the temptation is still with us to idolize, to believe that one is in touch with the supernatural through some visible or audible link with earth. Contemporary urban man is literally barraged with images. . . . While recognizing this danger, this primer on a cinematic theology has sought to establish the positive value of the "image" . . . If the temptation to idolatry has not been diminished by the advent of the camera, the motion picture screen and television set, there is still in these products of man's technical genius a yearning to give witness to the deepest aspirations of the human spirit and larger scheme of truth after which it thirsts . . . All images, therefore, have some relation to this Proto-Image, the matrix of the Eternal Plan of Providence. (191–92)

42. Translation from Tamara Eskenazi and Andrea Weiss, eds., *The Torah: A Woman's Commentary* (New York: Women of Reform Judaism, 2008), 417. All future translations from the Pentateuch are from this translation unless otherwise noted.

43. For more on idolatry and image making, see Moshe Halbertal and Avishai Margalit, *Idolatry* (Cambridge, MA: Harvard University Press, 1992), and

Leora Batnitzky, *Idolatry and Representation: The Philosophy of Franz Rosenzweig* (Princeton: Princeton University Press, 2000).

44. Marc Shell, *Stutter* (Cambridge, MA: Harvard University Press, 2006), 126.

45. Vivian B. Mann, *Jewish Texts on the Visual Arts* (Cambridge: Cambridge University Press, 2000), 4.

46. Yaron Eliav, "Roman Statues, Rabbis, and Greco-Roman Culture," in *Jewish Literatures and Cultures: Context and Intertext* (Providence, RI: Brown Judaic Studies, 2008), 99.

47. Ibid., 101.

48. Ibid., 114.

49. Translation from *Mishnayot: Seder Nezikin*, trans. Shalom Shraga Blackman (London: Judaica Press, 1963), 463.

50. Ibid., 115.

51. Jerusalem Talmud, Avodah Zarah 1:40, column 1, halakhah 7. Downloaded from Bar Ilan Responsa Project, version 14.

52. See, for example, Ovadiah Yosef, *Shut yeḥaveh daʿat* 4, siman 7. Downloaded from Bar Ilan Responsa Project, version 14.

53. As Joseph Marty writes:

> The conditions of "projection" amplify this even more. The spectator, comfortably seated in the dark, has his outer perceptions minimized while the screen comes to life and the sound wraps around him. His liberty and his consciousness are lulled because he is fascinated by the shadows, the lights, the rhythm, the actions or the passions presented. Other reactions set in. Emotion and sensibility are sharpened and he is as though hypnotized, in a sort of second state between waking and dreaming. He attributes his own feelings to the characters, identifies himself with their actions and empathizes with them all the more so, because he is passive.

Marty goes on to affirm, however, his sense of the potential of film to arouse sensibility and thus broaden "our outlook, our affectivity, our approach to the sacred," though his terminology and concerns are thoroughly Catholic. See Joseph Marty, "Toward a Theological Interpretation and Reading of Film: Incarnation of the Word of God—Relation, Image, Word," in John May, *New Image of Religious Film*, 135.

54. Lyden, 53.

55. Neil P. Hurley, *The Reel Revolution* (Maryknoll, NY: Orbis Books, 1978), 4.

56. Emmanuel Levinas, "Contempt for Torah as Idolatry," in *In the Time of the Nations*, trans. Michael B. Smith (Bloomington: Indiana University Press, 1994), 59.

Chapter 1

1. *The Truman Show*. Dir. Peter Weir. Paramount, 1998. Film.

2. *The Truman* Show was not the only 1998 film to communicate this idea. According to Linda A. Mercadante, both *The Truman Show* and *Pleasantville*, which came out the same year, "introduce questions of illusion and reality, control and freedom, viewing and being viewed. These two products of the media world themselves ask how much our own interpretations of reality are influenced by our culture's modern media." See Linda A. Mercadante, "The God Behind the Screen: *Pleasantville* & *The Truman Show*," *Journal of Religion and Film* 5, no. 2 (October 2001), http://www.unomaha.edu/jrf/truman.htm. Other films that came out around the same time that suggest a need to critique and oppose the cultural system include *Fight Club* (1999), *American Beauty* (1999), and *The Matrix* (1999). For a discussion of the dangers of popular culture and how this culture furnishes its own self-critique, see Gordon Lynch, "Can Popular Culture Be Bad for Your Health?," in *Understanding Theology and Popular Culture* (Malden, MA: Blackwell, 2005), 69–92. See also Theodor Adorno, *The Culture Industry: Selected Essays on Mass Culture* (London: Routledge, 1991), and Chris Edges, *Empire of Illusion: The End of Literacy and the Triumph of Spectacle* (New York: Nation Books, 2009).

3. For a reading of how *The Truman Show* recapitulates as well as reverses aspects of the story of Adam and Eve in the Garden of Eden and their eventual expulsion, see Adele Reinhartz, *Scripture on the Silver Screen* (Louisville, KY: Westminster Press, 2003), 5–23.

4. http://www.kafka-online.info/before-the-law.html.

5. For yet another modernist, philosophical approach to the film from the point of view of Cartesian epistemology, see Kimberly A. Blessing, "Deceit and Doubt: The Search for Truth in *The Truman Show* and Descartes's *Meditations*," in *Movies and the Meaning of Life: Philosophers Take on Hollywood*, ed. Kimberly A. Blessing and Paul J. Tudico (Chicago: Open Court, 2005), 3–16.

6. For more on this notion of *tzelem Elohim*, see chapter 11.

7. Richard Leonard, SJ, *Movies That Matter*, 76.

8. Penina Galpaz-Feller, *Yonah: masa el haḥofesh* (Jerusalem: Carmel, 2009), 16.

9. Bruce Vawter, *Job & Jonah: Questioning the Hidden* God (Ramsey, NJ: Paulist Press, 1983), 89. Vawter, like many other scholars, notes that there is actually another Yonah ben Amittai in the Bible, in 2 Kings 14:25, but that this other figure in the book of Kings "would have leaped at the opportunity to call down on Nineveh," concluding therefore that the book of Jonah offers a satire of prophets and prophecy. See Vawter, 89.

10. Aviva Zornberg, *The Murmuring Deep: Reflections on the Biblical Unconscious* (New York: Schocken Books, 2009), 81.

11. See Genesis 8:8.

12. All translations from Jonah are from http://www.mechon-mamre.org/p/pt/pt1701.htm unless otherwise noted.

13. For the full text of the poem, see A. M. Klein, "Jonah," in *The Collected Poems of A. M. Klein* (New York: McGraw Hill, 1974), 66–67.

14. Elie Wiesel, "Jonah," in *Five Biblical Portraits* (Notre Dame: University of Notre Dame Press, 1981), 133. Bruce Vawter sees Jonah's death wish as a satire of Elijah the prophet's call for his own death in 1 Kings 19:4–12. See Vawter, 113. See also Devorah Steinmetz, "Jonah: Son of Truth," in *Beginning Anew: A Woman's Companion to the High Holidays*, ed. Judith Kates and Gail Reimer (New York: Simon & Schuster, 1997), 308–24.

15. Translation from H. Freedman, trans., *The Soncino Talmud* (London: The Soncino Press, 1969), http://www.come-and hear.com/sanhedrin/sanhedrin_89.html#PARTb.

16. Yvonne Sherwood, *A Biblical Text and Its Afterlives: The Survival of Jonah in Western Culture* (Cambridge: Cambridge University Press, 2000), 117. Sherwood's book is especially fascinating in that it offers a survey of Christian, Jewish, and other literary interpretations of Jonah, noting how different readers adapt, and in a sense fix, Jonah's meaning according to a particular contemporary agenda, in effect missing the whole point of this lesson of indeterminacy.

17. For more on this theory, see Meir Sternberg, *The Poetics of Biblical Narrative* (Bloomington: Indiana University Press, 1985), 318–20.

18. Translation from Uriel Simon, *JPS Bible Commentary: Yonah* (Philadelphia: JPS, 1999), 36–38.

19. My translation, adapted from *The Torah: A Women's Commentary*, 510. Note that this translation does not actually translate the Hebrew tetragrammaton, but rather keeps it in Hebrew. Here I am translating it as LORD to conform with the Simon translation above.

20. Peter Ochs, "Truth," in *Contemporary Jewish Religious Thought*, ed. Arthur A. Cohen and Paul Mendes Flohr (New York: Free Press, 1987), 1017.

21. See Louis Jacobs, "Truth and Lies in Jewish Tradition," in *The Jewish Religion: A Companion* (Oxford: Oxford University Press, 1995), http://www.myjewishlearning.com/article/truth-and-lies-in-the-jewish-tradition/.

22. See for example, Genesis 24:49, 32:11, 47:29; Exodus 34:6; 1 Kings 3:6; Micah 7:20.

23. Simon, 45–46.

24. My translation.

25. See J. D. Eisenstein, "Midrash Yonah" in *Otsar hamidrashim* (New York: J. D. Eisenstein, 1915), 221. Translation mine.

26. See for example, Uriel Simon, *JPS Bible Commentary: Yonah*, xxi–xxii; Rachel Adler, "A Carnival at the Gates," *Beginning Anew; A Woman's Companion to the High Holidays*, 327–31.

27. Sigmund Freud, *Jokes and Their Relation to the Unconscious* (New York: W. W. Norton & Company, 1960), 10. Thanks to my husband, Daniel Feit, for this point about the comedy in Truman.

28. Adler, "A Carnival at the Gates," 328.

29. Ibid., 330.

30. John Morreall, *Comedy, Tragedy and Religion* (Albany: State University of New York Press, 1999), 151.

31. Meir Shalev, *Reishit* (Tel Aviv: Am Oved, 2008), 192. My translation.

32. Steinmetz, "Jonah: Son of Truth," 320.

Chapter 2

1. John Ellis, *Visible Fictions* (New York: Routledge, 2002), 127.

2. *Magnolia*. Dir. Paul Thomas Anderson. New Line Productions, 1999. Film.

3. Paul Thomas Anderson's own father, Ernie Anderson, died of cancer in 1997, an experience that apparently shaped the representation of Earl's illness and death in *Magnolia*. For more on father figures in Anderson's films, see Noel Murray, "The Five Types of Father Figures in Paul Thomas Anderson's Films," *The Dissolve* (April 9, 2015), https://thedissolve.com/features/movie-of-the-week/988-the-5-types-of-father-figures-in-paul-thomas-ander/.

4. Paul Thomas Anderson, *Magnolia: The Shooting Draft*, http://www.dailyscript.com/scripts/magnolia.html.

5. Robert K. Johnston takes another view of this and sees the theme of chance as related to the message of the book of Ecclesiastes and the notion that "time and chance happen to us all" (Eccl. 9:11). See Robert K. Johnston, "The Saddest Happy Ending: Paul Thomas Anderson and *Magnolia*," in *Useless Beauty: Ecclesiastes Through the Lens of Contemporary Film* (Grand Rapids, MI: Baker Academic, 2004), 78.

6. In this structure of interlocking stories, *Magnolia* follows in the tradition of director Robert Altman in such films as *Nashville* (1975) and his LA-based *Short Cuts* (1993).

7. Roy Anker refers to this interlocking story structure as a "Mosaic narrative" and argues that "Anderson pushes hard the notion that through what seems coincidence and chance, a mysterious supernatural presence pushes his characters . . . toward self-recognition and reconciliation." See Roy Anker, "Narrative," in *The Routledge Companion to Religion and Film*, ed. John Lyden (New York: Routledge, 2009), 347.

8. Note that in the original draft of the screenplay, both Marcie and Dixon's roles were much more developed. See P. T. Anderson, *Magnolia: The Shooting Draft*, http://www.dailyscript.com/scripts/magnolia.html.

9. It is worth noting that, in Jim's case, his instant negative reaction to profanity also prevents him from being able to listen to Dixon's "rap prophecy," which suggests that someone called "The Worm" committed the murder, because the victim had been his "longtime oppressor," perhaps his abuser. In the original shoot draft of the script, this Dixon/Worm storyline was more developed but was later deleted. See P. T. Anderson, *Magnolia: The Shooting Draft*, http://www.dailyscript.com/scripts/magnolia.html.

10. Irving Greenberg refers to the practice of reciting the *vidui* on Yom Kippur as simulating a deathbed confession. "The sense of imminent death is so strong that traditional Jews recite the Viddui, the deathbed confession of sins, during Minchah before the meal, lest they die during the meal and not make it to Yom Kippur." See Irving Greenberg, *The Jewish Way* (New York: Touchstone, 1993), 205–6. See also BT Yoma 87b.

11. Anderson, *Magnolia: The Shooting Draft*, sequence H.

12. It is important to note that while several confessions take place in the film, almost all of them occur through a third party, a form that most people identify as Christian rather than Jewish. Generally speaking, Jewish tradition stipulates that if one sins against one's neighbor, one must first confess one's sin and regret directly to the injured party. See Maimonides, *Hilkhot teshuvah*, 1:1. According to Louis Jacobs, however, it is incorrect to say that confession of sin to a third party is unheard of in Judaism. "In the circle of the 13th-century German pietists who produced the *Sefer Hasidim*, the idea is found of confessing sins to a spiritual mentor, a 'father confessor,' who would give the sinner a penance to perform," a practice that Jacobs notes might have been a Christian influence, although it is cast in a Jewish form. Louis Jacobs, "Confession," in *The Jewish Religion: A Companion* (Oxford: Oxford University Press, 1995), 91–92.

13. Apparently, Anderson did not intend originally to allude to the Bible, but rather included this element as a result of his reading into freak phenomena. Only later, when alerted to the Biblical passage, did Anderson choose to exploit the allusion, inserting 8's and 2's all over the film. For more on the significance of the frog rain as well as Christian elements in the film, see Adele Reinhartz, "*Magnolia* and the Plague of Frogs (Exodus)," in *Screening Scripture*, 24–38.

14. Reinhartz, 32. For a reading of *Magnolia* and the frog rain in terms of Christian Liberation Theology, see Mario DeGiglio-Bellemare, "Magnolia and the Signs of the Times: A Theological Reflection," *Film and Religion* 4, no. 2 (October 2000), http://www.unomaha.edu/jrf/magnolia.htm.

15. While the frogs are mentioned in Exodus 8:8, they first appear in Exodus 8:2, which is numerically referenced throughout the film.

16. Peter Travers, review of *Magnolia*, *Rolling Stone*, February 27, 2001, http://www.rollingstone.com/movies/reviews/magnolia-20010227.

17. See Elie Kaunfer, "Limmud on One Leg," http://limmud.org/publications/limmudononeleg/5771/vayeshev/.

18. For a discussion of this verse in relation to the "*Ashamnu*" liturgy, see Elie Kaunfer, "*Aval hatanu* ("But/In Truth We Have Sinned)," in *We Have Sinned: Sin and Confession in Judaism*, ed. Lawrence Hoffman (Woodstock, VT: Jewish Lights, 2012), 181–86.

19. Genesis Rabbah 99:8, ed. Theodor Albeck, accessed through the Bar Ilan Responsa Project, version 14. My translation.

20. Individuals are also commanded by the Bible to make their own confessions of wrongdoing as well as to make monetary restitution. See Numbers 5:6–7.

21. See Maimonides, *Hilkhot teshuvah* 1:1.

22. Translation from http://www.mechon-mamre.org/p/pt/pt3409.htm. See also Ezra 10 and Nehemiah 9 for similar communal prayer confessions.

23. Tzvi Luz, "Repentance," in Cohen and Mendes-Flohr, *Contemporary Jewish Religious Thought*, 786.

24. It is worth noting that the prophetic book of Malachi closes the Christian Old Testament and therefore furnishes a different, eschatological understanding of the role of Elijah and the notion of fathers returning to sons. Also, Christians commonly conflate Elijah with the figure of John the Baptist. For more on this, see Reverend Lawrence Frizell, "Elijah the Peacemaker: Jewish and Early Christian Interpretations of Malachi 3:23–24," Institute of Judeo-Christian Studies: Seton Hall University, https://www.academia.edu/3376942/Elijah_the_Peacemaker_Jewish_and_Early_Christian_Interpretations_of_Malachi_3_23-24.

25. For any article that explores this idea, see Rabbi Will Berkowitz, "Forgiving God," in *We Have Sinned: Sin and Confession in Judaism*, 146–49.

26. See, for example, Leviticus 16:21.

Chapter 3

1. Werner Sollors, *Beyond Ethnicity: Consent and Descent in American Culture* (New York: Oxford University Press, 1986), 6.

2. *The Descendants*. Dir. Alexander Payne. Fox Searchlight, 2011. Film.

3. Kaui Hart Hemmings, *The Descendants* (New York: Random House, 2008).

4. Alexander Payne, Nat Faxon, and Jim Rash, *The Descendants*, shooting script, http://www.imsdb.com/scripts/Descendants,-The.html, #8.

5. In the novel, Hart Hemmings makes clear that Matt does not relish this position of being trustee and considers it, in a sense, un-American. "I have inheritance issues," he says. "I belong to one of those Hawaii families who make money off of luck and dead people. My great grandmother happened to be a princess. A small monarchy decided what land was theirs, and she came into a lot of it." *The Descendants*, 22.

6. According to a YouTube post by "naffera," the lyrics to this opening song can be translated as follows: "I love the Famous wind of this land Mine to cherish / The wind named Love-snatcher. Chorus: "My flower, my lei, mine to cherish / My lei that I adore above all others / You are my favorite and precious to me / A lei forever for my body / Beloved is this home / This home so delightful to visitors / Where I stayed many years / With my love that was once snatched by the wind." See https://www.youtube.com/watch?v=2PfUFEf2ais. All of the music in the film is composed and played by local Hawaiian artists.

7. Payne et al., *The Descendants* script, #3, #4.

8. Annette Kolodny, *The Lay of the Land: Metaphor as Experience and History in American Life and Letters* (Chapel Hill: University of North Carolina Press, 1975), 6.

9. *The Descendants*, 157.

10. A derogatory Hawaiian name for the white upper crust.

11. Payne et al., *The Descendants* script, # 87. The words "I wished we lived in the old days" appear in the script but not in the actual film.

12. Payne et al., *The Descendants* script, #101.

13. In the novel, the lesson that Matt imparts to Scottie with regard to Lani Higgins is that "you have to speak to people to their face." *The Descendants*, 33.

14. Thanks to Nicole Auerbach for this astute observation.

15. It is noteworthy that *March of the Penguins* has itself garnered a good deal of religious commentary, particularly from the Christian religious right, which sees this documentary as a paean to old-fashioned family values. For a summary of this reading and some counter-commentary, see David Smith, "How the Penguin's Life Story Inspired the US Religious Right," *The Guardian* (Sunday, September 18, 2005), https://www.theguardian.com/uk/2005/sep/18/usa.filmnews.

16. About Birthright Israel, http://taglitww.birthrightisrael.com/TaglitBirthrightIsraelStory/Pages/About-Birthright-Israel.aspx.

17. Eugene Borowitz, *Renewing the Covenant*, 222, 231–32.

18. See, for example, Exodus 21:14: "And if a person schemes [*vayazid*] against another and kills him through treachery, you shall take that person from my very altar to be put to death."

19. Nachmanides, commentary on Genesis 25:34, *Torat ḥayyim* (Jerusalem: Mossad HaRav Kook, 1986), 10. My translation.

20. A derogatory Hawaiian term for white person.

21. Payne et al., *The Descendants* script, #122. In the novel, Matt frames his opposition to the sale as a form of rebellion that echoes that of his princess ancestor, who married against her parents' wishes. "Kekipi [the name of the princess in the novel] rebelled, and so will I" (230). Of course, this time the rebellion marks an embrace rather than a repudiation of descent and inheritance.

22. Rashbam, commentary on Genesis 35:32, *Torat ḥayyim* (Jerusalem: Mossad HaRav Kook, 1986), 8.

23. Nathan Rotenstreich, "Tradition," in Cohen and Mendes-Flohr, *Contemporary Jewish Religious Thought*, 1008. Emphasis added.

24. Alona Nir, reflection assignment on *The Descendants*, Reel Theology, February 2015. Cited with permission from the author.

25. Elbert Ventura, "Palm Tree of Life: The Sneaky Profundity of The Descendants," *Slate* (February 23, 2012), http://www.slate.com/articles/arts/culturebox/2012/02/the_descendants_alexander_payne_s_movie_is_as_profound_as_terrence_malick_s_tree_of_life_.html.

26. Payne et al., *The Descendants* script, #121–22.

Chapter 4

1. Franz Rosenzweig, "Upon the Opening of the Jüdisches Lehrhaus," in *On Jewish Learning*, ed. N. N. Glatzer (New York: Schocken Books, 1955), 102.

2. *Memento*. Dir. Christopher Nolan. Newmarket, 2001. Film

3. Christopher Nolan, *Memento*, shooting script, http://www.imsdb.com/scripts/Memento.html, scene 28.

4. Stephen Owen, *Remembrances* (Cambridge, MA: Harvard University Press, 1986), 66.

5. See Christopher Nolan, *Memento*, scene 2.

6. For more on the difference between declarative or episodic memory and habit memory, see Brenda Milner, Larry R. Squire, and Eric R. Kandel, "Cognitive Neuroscience and the Study of Memory," *Neuron* 20 (March 1998): 445–68. See also Daniel Schachter, *Searching for Memory: The Brain, the Mind and the Past* (New York: Basic Books, 1996), 134–60.

7. Yosef Hayyim Yerushalmi, *Zakhor: Jewish History, Jewish Memory* (New York: Schocken Books, 1989), 5.

8. William G. Little, "Surviving *Memento*," *Narrative* 13, no. 1 (January 2005), 67.

9. Deborah Knight and George McKnight, "Reconfiguring the Past: *Memento* and Neo-Noir," in *Memento: Philosophers on Film*, ed. Andrew Kania (New York: Routledge, 2009), 163.

10. Brenda Milner's famous studies of H.M., who suffered from anterograde amnesia, showed that despite his brain damage, H.M. was able to develop a new skill by practice and conditioning (drawing a star by looking into a mirror). This proves that amnesiacs have been able to retain and build on habit memory. See Milner et al., "Cognitive Neuroscience and the Study of Memory," 448 and 456.

11. According to Israeli neuropsychologist Daniel Levy, "a pure amnesiac would indeed not be able to remember a post-amnesia-onset incident at all, nor

assign it to a new context or frame. However, I have had contact with patients who had very bad but not total amnesia. Such a person might conceivably form a gist memory of a very salient, emotionally charged, event, and then associate it with preserved knowledge acquired pre-morbidly. So Leonard Shelby could have linked the very powerful impression of a woman dying of an insulin overdose administered by her husband with the case of Sammy Jankis, with which he was familiar from the period before the injury that caused his amnesia. That would not be a case of repression, but of confabulation, trying to make sense of a fragment of memory lacking a context by associating it with a preserved pre-morbid memory." E-mail correspondence, November 1, 2012.

12. See Hippolyte Bernheim, *Suggestive Therapeutics: A Treatise on the Nature and Uses of Hypnotism* (New York: G.P. Putnam's Sons, 1889). On the subject of police investigators or psychotherapists suggesting false memories into existence, see Elizabeth Loftus, "Our Changeable Memories: Legal and Practical Implications," *Nature Reviews* 4 (March 2003): 23–233. See also Schachter, "Reflections in a Curved Mirror," in *Searching for Memory*, 98–133.

13. Michael McKenna, "Moral Monster or Responsible Person? *Memento's* Leonard as a Case Study in Defective Agency," in *Memento*, ed. Andrew Kania (New York: Routledge, 2009), 25.

14. Yerushalmi, *Zakhor*, 5.

15. Jonathan Gottschalk, *The Storytelling Animal* (Boston: Houghton Mifflin Harcourt, 2012), 168.

16. David Ellenson, "History, Memory and Relationship," in *Memory and History in Christianity and Judaism* (Notre Dame: University of Notre Dame Press, 2001), 171–72.

17. Adriane Leveen, *Memory and Tradition in the Book of Numbers* (Cambridge: Cambridge University Press, 2008), 21.

18. Christopher Nolan, *Memento*, scene 44.

19. Yerushalmi, *Zakhor*, 94.

20. See Amos Funkenstein, "Collective Memory and Historical Consciousness," *History and Memory* 1 (Spring/Summer 1989): 5–26.

21. Yael Zerubavel, *Recovered Roots: Collective Memory and the Making of Israeli National Tradition* (Chicago: University of Chicago Press, 1995), 4–5. For responses to Yerushalmi's *Zakhor*, see "Forum: Recalling Zakhor: A Quarter-Century's Perspective," *JQR* 97, no. 4 (Fall 2007): 487–544. For more on the notion of history as construction or the transformation of chronicle into story, see Hayden White, *Metahistory: The Historical Imagination in Nineteenth-Century Europe* (Baltimore: Johns Hopkins University Press, 1973).

22. Eugene Borowitz, "God and Man in Judaism Today: A Reform Perspective," *Judaism* 23, no. 3 (Summer 1974): 303.

23. McKenna, "Moral Monster or Responsible Person?," 35.

24. On the subject of the pluralism of partial truths, see Irving Greenberg, "The Principles of Pluralism," *Sh'ma* (April 1999), 4.

25. Christopher Nolan, *Memento*, http://www.imsdb.com/scripts/Memento.html, scene 174.

26. Dan P. McAdams, *The Stories We Live By: Personal Myths and the Making of the Self* (New York: Guilford Press, 1993), 11. See also Michael White and David Epston, *Narrative Means to Therapeutic Ends* (New York, W. W. Norton & Company, 1990), 10, and Donnel Stern, *Partners in Thought* (New York: Routledge, 2010).

27. In using the adjective "commanding," I am referring to a distinction recently made by Yehuda Kurtzer between history and memory: "*Where history informs, memory commands.* History enables standing apart, outside, above the past . . . Memory, meanwhile, whether by design or accident, wields a commanding over those who remember." See Yehuda Kurtzer, *Shuva: The Future of the Jewish Past* (Waltham: Brandeis University Press, 2012), 26.

28. Christopher Nolan, *Memento*, scene 25.

29. Tony E. Jackson, "Graphism and Story-time in *Memento*," *Mosaic* 40, no. 3 (September 2007): 53, 54. The reference here to Plato is from *Phaedrus*, particularly in Socrates's speech at the end of the dialogue, http://classics.mit.edu/Plato/phaedrus.html.

30. Here Darnton is summarizing the theory of Rolf Engelsing. See Robert Darnton, "First Steps Toward a History of Reading," in *The Kiss of the Lamourette: Reflections in Cultural History* (New York: W.W. Norton & Co., 1990), 165.

31. Rosenzweig, "Upon the Opening of the Jüdisches Lehrhaus," 95–96.

32. Martin S. Jaffee, *Torah in the Mouth: Writing and Oral Tradition in Palestinian Judaism 200 BCE–400 CE* (New York: Oxford, 2001), 155.

33. Ibid., 147.

34. See the symposium on "The Jewish Literary Revival," *Tikkun* 12, no. 6 (November/December 1997).

35. Jonathan Safran Foer, *Everything is Illuminated* (New York: Perennial, 2003), 198.

36. Translation adapted from http://www.shechem.org/torah/avot.html#chap3.

37. Commentary on Pirkei Avot by Israel Lifschitz, German rabbi (1782–1860).

38. Cited in Pinkhas Kehati, *Mishnayot mevo'arot: Seder Nezikin 2*, commentary on Avot 3:8, "*Rak hishamer lekha*" (Jerusalem: Heikhal Shelomo, 1977), 352.

39. Angela Buchdahl, "Ordination Address," Temple Emanu-El, New York, 2012. Quoted with permission from the author. For a full copy of the address, see http://accantors.org/acc/system/files/Ordination+Address+Angela+Buchdahl+2012.pdf.

40. Rosenzweig, "Upon the Opening of the Jüdisches Lehrhaus," 98.

Chapter 5

1. Peter Steinfels, "Woody Allen Counts the Wages of Sin," *The New York Times* (October 15, 1989), http://www.nytimes.com/1989/10/15/movies/film-woody-allen-counts-the-wages-of-sin.html?src=pm&pagewanted=1.

2. Eugene Borowitz, "Heeding Ecclesiastes At Long Last," in Steinfels, "Woody Allen Counts the Wages of Sin."

3. See, for example, Sam Girgus, "The Eyes of God," in *The Films of Woody Allen* (Cambridge: Cambridge University Press, 1993), 129.

4. Pirkei Avot 4:2.

5. This challenge is made even more explicit in his later film *Match Point* (2005), which revisits the Judah Rosenthal plot without the comic elements of the Clifford plot line. In fact, Dr. Borowitz and I lectured on this later film on a number of occasions, including a CCAR convention. In this book, I have chosen in this chapter to focus on the earlier work, as I believe it offers a more textured and complex treatment of the issues of sin and the meaning of human action.

6. Danny Zemel, "Al Chet shechatanu: Collectively We Own Them All," in *We Have Sinned*, ed. Lawrence Hoffman (Woodstock, VT: Jewish Lights, 2012), 242.

7. *Love and Death* opens with the following comic monologue on the subject of human mortality and divine justice:

> To be executed for a crime I never committed. Of course, isn't all mankind in the same boat? Isn't all mankind ultimately executed for a crime it never committed? The difference is that all men go eventually; I'm supposed to go at 6 o'clock tomorrow morning. I was supposed to go at 5 o'clock but I've got a smart lawyer. Got leniency.

See *Love and Death*, Dir. Woody Allen. MGM, 1975. Film. For a discussion of Allen's God concerns as seen in his films, see Gary Commins, "Woody Allen's Theological Imagination," *Theology Today* 44, no. 2 (July 1987): 235–49.

8. R. A. Blake, "Looking for God: Profane and Sacred in the Films of Woody Allen," *Journal of Popular Film & Television* 19, no. 2 (Summer 1991). Accessed through the EBSCO articles database.

9. Greg Bachman, *Crimes and Misdemeanors:* Reflections on Reflexivity," in *A Companion to Woody Allen*, ed. Peter Bailey and Sam Girgus (Malden, MA: John Wiley, 2013), 179.

10. To be sure, Allen's real-life affair and subsequent marriage to Mia Farrow's daughter Soon-Yi (and the abuse charges leveled against him by Farrow) cast an eerie shadow on this and other on-screen relationships featuring Woody Allen and young girls. For more on this, see Crystal Downing, "Woody Allen's Blindness and Insight: The Palimpsests of *Crimes and Misdemeanors*," *Religion and the Arts* 1, no. 2 (Spring 1997): 73–92.

11. Mark W. Roche, "Justice and the Withdrawal of God in Woody Allen's *Crimes and Misdemeanors*," in *The Films of Woody Allen*, ed. Charles L. P. Silet (Lanham, MD: The Scarecrow Press, 2006), 271.

12. *Crimes and Misdemeanors*. Dir. Woody Allen. Orion Pictures, 1989. Film.

13. According to Gary Saul Morson,

> One of Raskolnikov's theories demands this murder on moral grounds. Kill her and give her money to the poor; "one death for hundreds of lives—it's simple arithmetic!" Another theory denies the existence of morality altogether. Good and evil are simply prejudices, "artificial terrors" inherited from religion, which means that, for the man who truly dares to transgress, "all is permitted." Indeed, Raskolnikov imagines that all the great men of history, from Solon to Napoleon, acted on precisely this principle, which justifies any crime if for no other reason than that there is no such thing as crime.

See Gary Saul Morson, "How to Read Crime and Punishment," *Commentary* (June 1992), https://www.commentarymagazine.com/article/how-to-read-crime-and-punishment/.

14. David Landry, "Faint Hope: A Theological Interpretation of Woody Allen's *Crimes and Misdemeanors*, *Journal of Religion and Popular Culture* 22, no. 1 (Spring 2010), para. 17.

15. Fyodor Dostoevsky, *Crime and Punishment*, part V, chap. 4, para. 129, http://www.bartleby.com/318/54.html.

16. *Crimes and Misdemeanors*, opening scene.

17. Sam Girgus, "The Eyes of God," in *The Films of Woody Allen*, 138.

18. Ibid., 135.

19. See Greg Bachman, "*Crimes and Misdemeanors*: Reflections on Reflexivity," in *A Companion to Woody Allen*, ed. Peter Bailey and Sam Girgus (Malden, MA: John Wiley, 2013), 170–87.

20. Landry, "Faint Hope," para. 19.

21. Meir Sternberg, "The Story of David and Bathsheba," in *The Poetics of Biblical Narrative* (Bloomington: Indiana University Press, 1987), 190.

22. David's use here of the term "*ben mavet*" is especially ironic, as this is the same term used by Saul to condemn David unfairly to death in 1 Samuel 30:31.

23. Translation adapted from http://www.mechon-mamre.org/p/pt/pt08b12.htm. The story of Jezebel's murder and dispossession of Navot in 1 Kings 21 serves as an interesting analogue to the David and Bathsheba story, as there too a prophet of God outs the sin, provoking a radical show of contrition. See 1 Kings 21: 17–29.

24. According to Mark Roche, "Judah's elliptical confession to Cliff suggests a need for intersubjectivity and absolution, even if it is not fully realized; the act

of confession suggests that Judah is in truth barely coping with his crime." See Roche, "Justice and the Withdrawal," 275. See also Landry, "Faint Hope," para. 32.

25. In response to a question posed by Sander Lee regarding the possibility that Judah might be still be guilt ridden at the end of the movie, Allen writes, "You are wrong about Judah; he feels no guilt and the rare time the events occur to him, his mild uneasiness (which sometimes doesn't come at all) is negligible." In general, Allen dismisses the conventional moral position as unrealistic or blind. See Sander Lee, *Woody Allen's Angst: Philosophical Commentaries on His Serious Films* (Jefferson, NC: McFarland & Company Inc., Publishers, 1997), 288. In another interview with Stij Björkman, Allen said, "Judah's never really in too much of a quandary. Any quandary he has, he's going to rationalize it away to do what he wants. And he does it and he gets away with it." See Bjorkman, *Woody Allen on Woody Allen* (New York: Grove Press, 1993), 226.

26. The only character in the present time of the film who upholds conventional morality is the rabbi. But, according to Allen, Ben doesn't really understand the reality of life: "One can argue that he understands it more deeply than the others. I don't think he does myself. I think he understands it less, and that's why I wanted to make him blind. I feel that his faith is blind. It will work, but it requires closing your eyes to reality." Quoted in Mark Conrad, "The Indifferent Universe: Woody Allen's *Crimes and Misdemeanors*, in *Movies and the Meaning of Life*, ed. Kimberly A Blessing and Paul J. Tudico (Chicago: Open Court, 2005), 117–18.

27. The notion that children suffer for the guilt of their parents, however disturbing, is not alien to the Bible. See Exodus 34:7.

28. Shmuel Herzefeld, "David and Batsheva: Echoes of Saul and the Gift of Forgiveness," in *The Book of Samuel*, ed. Nathaniel Helfgot (Teaneck, NJ: Ben Yehuda Press, 2006), 226. The idea that this episode is meant to be seen as a turning point seems evident already at the very beginning of 2 Samuel 11:1, with the opening verse: "*Vayehi litshuvat hashanah*" (and it came to pass at the turn of the year).

29. Amy Kalmanofksy, *Dangerous Sisters of the Hebrew Bible* (Minneapolis: Fortress Press, 2014), 101.

30. Robert Alter, *The David Story* (New York: W. W. Norton & Company, 1999), 249–50.

31. 2 Samuel 13:17.

32. For more on the metaphorical or symbolic language of sin, see Paul Ricoeur, *Symbolism of Evil* (Boston: Beacon Press, 1969). Gary Anderson builds on Ricoeur's exploration of the symbolic or metaphorical nature of evil and sin in his more recent *Sin: A History* (New Haven: Yale University Press, 2009), where he shows how Hebraic metaphorical conceptions of sin change greatly over time and in differing linguistic and historical circumstances, including later notions of debt and merit.

33. Marc Zvi Brettler, "Sin, Sanction, and Confession in the Bible," in Hoffman, *We Have Sinned*, 32.

34. Anderson, *Sin: A History*, 16.

35. Ibid., 6.

36. Ibid., 23, 24.

37. Brettler, 36.

38. Adapted from http://www.mechon-mamre.org/e/et/et2651.htm.

39. For a discussion of this verse in terms of theories of original sin, human frailty, and sexuality, as well as the collective sinfulness of Israel, see J. K. Zink, "Uncleanness and Sin: A Study of Job XIV 4 and Psalm LI 7, *Vetus Testamentum* 17, no. 3 (July 1967): 354–61.

40. A similar idea arises in Lady Macbeth's "Out, damned spot!" speech in Shakespeare's *Macbeth*, act 5, scene 1. Allen may very well have had this in mind, as he has Judah's father, Sol, refer in the Seder scene to how "murder will always out, whether in the Bible or in Shakespeare."

41. Edward R. Dalglish, *Psalm Fifty-One in Light of Ancient Near Eastern Patternism* (Leiden: E.J. Brill, 1962), 155.

42. Ibid., 202. See Benjamin J. Segal, "Psalm 51," in *A New Psalm: Psalms as Literature* (Jerusalem: Gefen, 2013), 232–37. Segal's commentary includes mention of the importance of verse 7 in the development of the Pauline doctrine of original sin (235). In terms of Jewish liturgy, Segal also notes that verse 17 serves as the opening of the silent Amidah, while verse 20 figures in the ceremony of taking the Torah out of the ark at the beginning of the Torah service (237).

43. James Kugel, *The Great Poems of the Bible: A Reader's Companion with New Translations* (New York: Free Press, 2008), 153.

44. Amos Hakham, *Sefer tehilim* (Israel: Mossad Harav Kook, 1990), שׁו.

45. Adapted from *The Soncino Talmud, Tractate Shabbath*, trans. H. Freedman, http://www.come-and-hear.com/shabbath/shabbath_56.html.

46. Thanks go out to my husband, Daniel Feit, for pointing out the context of this passage and offering this reading.

47. See BT Rosh Hashanah 25a.

48. Lyden, "The Definition of Religion," in *Film as Religion*, 44.

49. Ibid., 48.

50. Commins, "Woody Allen's Theological Imagination," 249.

51. According to Mary P. Nichols, "Only rabbi Ben plays parts in both plot and subplot—for he is Judah's confidant and foil and also Lester's brother—and it is at his daughter's wedding that Judah and Cliff meet. Ben connects the serious drama with the comedy, but he does not know that he is doing so." Mary P. Nichols, *Deconstructing Woody* (Lanham, MD: Rowman & Littlefield, 1998), 161–62. One might argue, however, given the rabbi's enduring faith and optimism, that this allows his "viewpoint," however blind, to exert a considerable influence over one's interpretation of the film. As Nichols herself notes at

the end of her chapter on *Crimes*, "Just as the rabbi's literal blindness does not imply an inability to see the truth, the blindness of God in the simple sense is required by his goodness" (164).

52. *Crimes and Misdemeanors*, closing scene.

53. According to Crystal Downing, Woody Allen read and admired the work of Primo Levi. She also notes that in 1988, a translation of Levi's *The Drowned and the Saved* was published by Raymond Rosenthal, a clue perhaps to Allen's choice to name his protagonist Judah Rosenthal. See Downing, "Blindness and Insight," 76.

Chapter 6

1. *Forrest Gump*. Dir. Robert Zemeckis. Paramount, 1994. Film

2. Winston Groom, *Forrest Gump* (New York: Pocket Books, 1986), 1; Isaac Bashevis Singer, "Gimpel the Fool," in *Collected Stories* (New York: Farrar Strauss and Giroux, 1982), 1.

3. See Enid Welsford, *The Fool: His Social and Literary History* (Gloucester, MA: Peter Smith 1966), and Sandra Billington, *A Social History of the Fool* (New York: St. Martin's Press 1984), 16.

4. All this can be contrasted with professional buffoons, clowns, court jesters, or court fools, such as those featured in the plays of Shakespeare. According to Siegel, "[t]he court jester was either a feeble-minded person who evoked amusement by his inaneness or his antics. He might also be someone who pretended to be a fool and used his assumed folly as a license for his wit." See Paul Siegel, "Gimpel and the Archetype of the Wise Fool," in *The Achievement of Isaac Bashevis Singer*, ed. Marcia Allentuck (Carbondale: Southern Illinois University Press, 1969), 159.

5. Dave Kehr, "Who Framed Forrest?," *Film Comment* 31, no. 2 (March–April 1995): 50–51.

6. Thomas B. Beyers, "History Re-Membered: *Forrest Gump*, Postfeminist Masculinity, and the Burial of the Counterculture," *Modern Fiction Studies* 42, no. 2 (1996): 419–44.

7. Steven D. Scott, 'Like a Box of Chocolates': Forrest Gump and Postmodernism, *Literature/Film Quarterly* 29, no. 1 (2001), 25.

8. Ibid., 27.

9. Steven Cohan and Ina Rae Hark, introduction to *The Road Movie Book* (New York: Routledge 1997), 1.

10. For more on the road in American culture, see *Hit the Road, Jack: Essays on the Culture of the American Road*, ed. Gordon E. Slethaug and Stacilee Ford (Montreal: McGill-Queen's University Press, 2012).

11. See Jerzy Kosinzky, *Being There* (1970; repr., New York: Grove Press, 1999).

12. Billington, *A Social History of the* Fool, 16.

13. Sanford Pinsker, *The Schlemiel as Metaphor: Studies in Yiddish and American Jewish Fiction* (Carbondale: Southern Illinois University Press 1991), 19.

14. Ruth Wisse, *The Schlemiel as Modern Hero* (Chicago: University of Chicago Press, 1971), 21.

15. Quoted in Arthur Green, *Tormented Master* (Tuscaloosa: University of Alabama Press, 1979), 51.

16. Martin Buber, *The Tales of Rabbi Nachman* (Atlantic Highlands, NJ: Humanities Press International, 1988), 94.

17. Wisse, *Schlemiel as Modern Hero*, 21.

18. Adapted from Isaac Bashevis Singer, "Gimpel the Fool," trans. Saul Bellow, in *Collected Stories* (New York: Farrar, Strauss and Giroux 1982), 3.

19. In the Yiddish original, the words used here for fool are *shoyteh* (idiot) and *nar* (fool), respectively. See "Gimpl Tam," in *Der Shpigl un andere dertsyalungen* (Jerusalem: Tcherikover Publishers/Hebrew University, 1975), 34.

20. Singer, "Gimpel the Fool," 4.

21. Ibid., 13. In Bellow's translation, Elka scolds him for being a fool, but this is not accurate. In the original Yiddish, Elka says to Gimpel, "*Du tam, un az Elka is falsh iz shoyn alts lign?*" This can be translated either as "You simpleton," "You [are] *tam*," that is, you are by nature whole and blameless and you should continue in this way. See "*Gimpl tam*," 45.

22. Ibid., 14

23. Paul Kresh, *Isaac Bashevis Singer: The Magician of 86th Street* (New York: Dial Press, 1979), 41.

24. Ibid., 203.

25. For an application of the notion of second naïveté to the Jewish theological issue of divine revelation and authority, see Neil Gillman, *Sacred Fragments: Recovering Theology for the Modern Jew* (Philadelphia: JPS, 1990), 39–61.

26. Ricoeur, *The Symbolism of Evil*, 352.

Chapter 7

1. For a discussion of the relationship between animal speech and stuttering, see Marc Shell, "Animals That Talk," *Stutter*, 76–101.

2. *The King's Speech*. Dir. Tom Hooper. Weinstein Company, 2011. Film. The wife of Lionel Logue plays a similar role in the film, urging Lionel, who mentions an argument he had with an unnamed patient (Bertie), to apologize, saying it will be good for them both.

3. Lionel Logue kept a diary, but it did not include records of his meetings with the duke/king. Academy Award–winning screenwriter David Seidler, who was born in England and moved to Long Island in his later childhood, stuttered

himself as a child. His parents would frequently point to George VI as an inspirational example of someone who overcame his speech impediment and learned to give eloquent speeches. While writing the screenplay, Seidler discovered that his uncle David, who also stuttered as a child, was treated by Lionel Logue, which gave Seidler further insight into Logue's techniques. For more on the writing of the original screenplay for *The King's Speech*, see Derek Sante's interview with Seidler, https://www.youtube.com/watch?v=4Q6t_5sKTUk.

4. According to Lisa Schwarzman, each of these musical selections is meaningful and contributes to one's understanding of the scenes. The selection of the overture from *The Marriage of Figaro* for the first therapy session signifies that the "opera" plot concerning Bertie's speech therapy has begun. The subsequent choice of the Concerto for Clarinet in A Major suggests that, like the clarinet and the other instruments in the concerto, Lionel and Bertie are now working together. The choice of Beethoven's Seventh Symphony in A Major for Bertie's first wartime speech is especially significant. Here is "[m]ajestic music composed by a musical titan who was losing his hearing, chosen to intensify the effect of words spoken by a monarch just coming into his voice." See Lisa Schwarzman, "The Director of the 'King's Speech' Owes His DGA Award to Two Other Guys," *Entertainment Weekly*, February 1, 2011, http://www.ew.com/article/2011/02/01/kings-speech-tom-hooper-dga-award.

5. The various Freudian aspects of Logue's treatment strategy that attribute stuttering to psychological trauma have been discredited by some more recent studies that emphasize genetic and mechanical factors. For more on this, see Jonah Lehrer, "What *The King's Speech* Gets Wrong About Stuttering," *The Wall Street Journal*, January 24, 2011, http://blogs.wsj.com/ideas-market/2011/01/24/re-thinking-stutterers/.

6. In David Shields' novel *Dead Languages*, the stuttering adolescent protagonist makes a similar observation: "I came to think that all fluent speech was 'fascistic' (a word I had learned form Mother); was an assertion of authority in the one enterprise in which any authority struck me as ludicrous." See David Shields, *Dead Languages* (Saint Paul, MN: Graywolf Press, 1989), 36.

7. Exodus 4:10. My translation.

8. Ella Shohat, "Sacred Word, Profane Image: Theologies of Adaptation," in *A Companion to Literature and Film*, ed. Robert Stam and Alessandra Raengo (Oxford: Blackwell, 2004), 25.

9. Rashbam on Exodus 4:11, *Torat ḥayyim* (Jerusalem: Mossad HaRav Kook, 1993), 44. Ibn Ezra (1089–1164) seems to straddle the interpretive camps, suggesting that Moses's professed slowness "of mouth" refers to a hereditary impediment, while "slowness of tongue," refers to his rusty Egyptian, given that he had not spoken it in years. See Ibn Ezra on Exodus 4:10, *Torat Ḥayyim*, 44.

10. For a study of Moses's heaviness of mouth and tongue against the backdrop of ancient Near Eastern sources that supports the argument that Moses

did indeed have a speech impediment, see Jeffrey Tigay, "'Heavy of Mouth' and 'Heavy of Tongue' on Moses' Speech Difficulty," *BASOR* 231 (1978): 57–67.

11. Exodus Rabbah 1:26, *The Midrash Rabbah: Exodus, Leviticus*, trans. H. Freedman and Maurice Simon (London: Soncino, 1977), 33–34. Philo offers an even more extensive description of Moses's precociousness and beauty, offering descriptions of Moses's exceptional intellect and capacity to accumulate wisdom, such that in "a short time he surpassed all their [his teachers'] knowledge, anticipating all their lessons by the excellent natural endowments of his own genius." See Philo, *On the Life of Moses* 6, no. 25, http://www.earlyjewishwritings.com/text/philo/book24.html.

12. This midrash brings to mind Isaiah 6:17, where coal is seen as purifying an unclean prophetic tongue. Toddler Moses's placing of the coal in his mouth both purifies and encumbers his tongue, suggesting that "heaviness" is somehow linked to a readiness to speak God's word.

13. An explicit connection between barrenness/pregnancy and Moses's heaviness of mouth is drawn in a midrash from Tanhuma. According to this midrash, when Moses rejects God's call to him on the grounds that he is a "*kevad peh*," God declares that he will transform Moses into a new "*beriyah*" [creature] "like a woman who becomes pregnant and gives birth [*harah veyoledet*]." The midrash draws this connection between Moses's speech and barrenness/pregnancy by playing on the similarity between the words "*harah*" (pregnant) and "*lehorot*" (to teach) based on Exodus 4:12, where God promises to teach Moses what to say ("*vehoreitikha asher tedabber*"). Tanhuma Shemot 18. Accessed through the Bar Ilan Responsa Project, version 14.

14. Rashi on Exodus 4:11, *Torat Hayyim*, 44.

15. My translation.

16. *Otsar Midrashim*, Eisenstein, 357. My translation.

17. Brian Britt, *Rewriting Moses: The Narrative Eclipse of the Text* (London: T & T Clark International, 2004), 123.

18. For more on Martin's Buber's understanding of *leitwörter*, see Michael Fishbane, "Martin Buber's Moses," in *The Garments of Torah* (Bloomington: Indiana University Press, 1989), 94.

19. Martin Buber, *Moses: The Revelation and the Covenant* (New York: Harper Torchbooks, 1946), 50.

20. Ibid., 59.

21. Shell, *Stutter*, 106. Shell also detects stuttering in certain symbolic words and practices, such as the placing of *tzstzit* (ritual fringes) on a four-cornered garment. See 132.

22. Daniel Boyarin, *Intertextuality and the Reading of Midrash* (Bloomington: Indiana University Press, 1990), 39. See also Gerald Bruns, *Hermeneutics Ancient and Modern* (New Haven: Yale University Press, 1992), 110.

23. Joseph Heinemann, "The Nature of Aggadah" (1974, repr. in *Midrash and Literature*, ed. Geoffrey H. Hartman and Sanford Budick [New Haven: Yale University Press, 1986]), 42. Again, this is not to say that earlier, pre-exilic readers of the Hebrew Bible did not also demonstrate a need to reread the Bible in light of their own concerns and times. As Michael Fishbane has shown, the enterprise of rereading the Hebrew Bible actually begins within the Hebrew Bible itself. See Michael Fishbane, *Biblical Interpretation in Ancient Israel* (Oxford: Clarendon Press, 1985). And, as Gary Porton further explains,

> Just as we should not view the rabbinic interpretations of the Bible as a process begun only after the Bible had been canonized, so also we should not conclude that the small group of Jews we have described as "rabbis" were the only Jews of the postbiblical period to exegete the Hebrew Bible. That those Jews and non-Jews who eventually became Christians elucidated the Hebrew Bible is a well-known fact. In addition, the small community of Jews who lived on the bluff overlooking the north end of the Dead Sea at Qumran also explained the Bible, and some of their interpretations, known as *pesharim* after the word *pesher* ("interpretation") with which many of the relevant passages open, have come down to us.

See Gary G. Porton, *Understanding Rabbinic Midrash* (Hoboken: K'tav, 1985), 5. See also note 31 to the introduction of this volume.

24. The one exception to this erasure are the names of the midwives, Shifrah and Puah, who help maintain Israelite life. Names endure in the text, only on a subsistence level.

25. Sholem Asch, *Moses*, trans. Maurice Samuel (New York: G.P. Putnam's Sons, 1951), 42.

26. Ibid., 29.

27. See Fishbane, 97.

28. Phil Schneider, *Transcending Stuttering*, http://vimeo.com/16695172.

29. Cushing Stahlberg, *Sustaining Fictions*, 216.

Chapter 8

1. "Reclusive Deity Hasn't Written A New Book In 2,000 Years," *The Onion* 50, no. 37 (September 16, 2014), http://www.theonion.com/article/reclusive-deity-hasnt-written-a-new-book-in-2000-y-36936.

2. Abraham Joshua Heschel, *God in Search of Man* (New York: Farrar Strauss & Giroux, 1955), 179.

3. Moses Maimonides, *Mishneh Torah*, in "Hilkhot yesodei hatorah 1, no. 9" (Jerusalem: Pardes, 1959), 2–3.

4. Sally McFague, *Models of God: Theology for an Ecological, Nuclear Age* (Philadelphia: Fortress Press, 1987), xii.

5. Mark Twain, *Following the Equator* (1897), chap. 15, http://www.gutenberg.org/files/2895/2895-h/2895-h.htm.

6. *Stranger than Fiction*. Dir. Marc Forester. Columbia Pictures, 2006. Film. Quote taken from Zach Helm, screenplay for *Stranger than Fiction*, 26–27, http://www.dailyscript.com/scripts/Stranger-Than-Fiction.pdf.

7. Eliezer Berkovitz, *God, Man and History* (Jerusalem: Shalem Press, 2004), 22–23.

8. Gene C. Fant Jr., *God as Author: A Biblical Approach to Narrative* (Nashville, TN: B & H Academic, 2010), 45.

9. Helm, screenplay for *Stranger than Fiction*, 37–38.

10. Ibid., 39.

11. For a biblical source for this notion of the divine Book, see Exodus 32:33–34, where in the aftermath of the sin of the Golden Calf, Moses implores God that if he cannot forgive the people, to wipe him out of his book, whereupon God retorts, "Only one who has sinned against me will I erase from my record."

12. This exchange in these words appears in the actual film rather than the script. *Stranger than Fiction*, 36:35–37:00.

13. McFague, *Models of God*, 111.

14. My translation.

15. Helm, screenplay for *Stranger than Fiction*, 119.

16. Jeffrey Rubinstein, *Rabbinic Stories* (Mahwah, NJ: Paulist Press, 2002), 216.

17. Helm, *Stranger than Fiction*, 1.

18. Italo Calvino, *If on a Winter's Night a Traveler*, trans. William Weaver (San Diego: Harcourt Inc., 1981), 259.

19. Elizabeth Bernstein, "Researchers Study Awe and Find It Is Good for Relationships," *The Wall Street Journal*, February 23, 2015, http://www.wsj.com/articles/researchers-study-awe-and-find-it-is-good-for-relationships-1424717882.

20. Heschel, *God in Search of Man*, 131.

21. *Midrash Rabbah: Exodus*, trans. S. M. Lehrman (London: Soncino Press, 1977), 171.

22. Heschel, *God in Search of Man*, 136.

23. Anne Lamott, *Bird by Bird* (New York: Anchor Books, 1994), 99–100.

Chapter 9

1. *A Serious Man*. Dir. Ethan and Joel Coen. Focus Features, 2009. Film.

2. Many Jews in Minneapolis have taken issue with this portrayal, arguing that their rabbis and Hebrew school were not at all like those portrayed in the film. The Coen brothers' own mother came from a family of Hebrew educators and was herself a teacher in the synagogue Hebrew school. For more on this, see Riv Ellen Prell, "*A Serious Man* in Situ: Fear and Loathing in St. Louis Park," *AJS Review* 35, no. 2 (November 2011): 365–76.

3. The parable genre also plays a significant role in the New Testament and in Christian theology, though scholars acknowledge its Hebrew biblical and rabbinic literary origins. For more on this, see David Flusser, *Jewish Sources in Early Christianity*, trans. John Glucker (Tel Aviv: MOD Books, 1989), 61–66; and Brad H. Young, *The Parables: Jewish Tradition and Christian Interpretation* (Grand Rapids, MI: Baker Academic, 1998).

4. Shai Ginsburg, "The Physics of Being Jewish, or On Cats and Jews," *AJS Review* 35, no. 2 (November 2011): 358.

5. Ethan Coen, as interviewed by Andrew O'Hehir, "Goys, God, Dentistry, and 'A Serious Man,'" http://www.salon.com/2009/10/01/coens/.

6. Stern, *Parables in Midrash*, 4.

7. Ibid., 18.

8. Translation from Raymond P. Scheindlin, *The Book of Job* (New York: W. W. Norton & Company, 1998), 56.

9. See, for example, Frank Lidz, "Biblical Adversity in a '60s Suburb," *New York Times*, September 23, 2009, http://www.nytimes.com/2009/09/27/movies/27lidz.html?pagewanted=all&_r=0; David Tollerton, "Job of Suburbia: *A Serious Man* and Viewer Perceptions of the Biblical," *Film and Religion* 15, no. 2 (October 2011), http://www.unomaha.edu/jrf/Vol15no2/JobSeriousMan.html.

10. BT Bava Batra 15a. For discussion of other instances where the rabbis view a biblical story as a mashal, see Eugene Borowitz, *The Talmud's Theological Language-Game* (Albany: State University of New York Press, 2006), 88–89.

11. Scheindlin, *The Book of Job*, 149.

12. Ibid., 26.

13. See, for example, Abraham Joshua Heschel, *God in Search of Man* (New York: Farrar, Strauss and Giroux, 1955), 45–48.

14. See Martin Buber, *I and Thou*, trans. Walter Kaufmann (New York: Charles Scribner, 1970).

15. Joel and Ethan Coen, script of *A Serious Man*, http://www.imsdb.com/scripts/A-Serious-Man.html, scene 81.

16. Ibid., scene 87.

17. Ibid.

18. Ibid.

19. John H. Lienhard, no. 347: SCHRÖDINGER'S CAT," *Engines of Our Ingenuity*, http://www.uh.edu/engines/epi347.htm.

20. See http://www.imsdb.com/scripts/A-Serious-Man.html, 19.

21. Because of the success and popularity of the film and its use of this song, one can find the lyrics to this song on several sites on the Internet. For a transliteration of the Yiddish and another translation, see http://www.richard silverstein.com/2003/09/12/dem-milners-tre/.

22. Song of Songs Rabbah 1:1, 8–9. Accessed from the Bar Ilan Responsa Project, version 14. My translation.

23. Stern, *Parables in Midrash*, 67.

24. See http://www.imdb.com/title/tt1019452/trivia.

25. Joseph Telushkin, "The Rebbe's Big Idea," *JTA*, June 26, 2014, http://www.jta.org/2014/06/16/news-opinion/opinion/op-ed-the-rebbes-big-idea-2.

26. Dermot Cox, *The Triumph of Impotence* (Rome: Universita Gregoriana, 1978), 160.

27. Sallie McFague, *Speaking in Parables: A Study in Metaphor and Theology* (Philadelphia: Fortress Press, 1975), http://www.religion-online.org/showchapter.asp?title=452&C=362.

Chapter 10

1. In Genesis 22, as we will see later in this chapter, God tests Abraham by asking him to sacrifice Isaac. Elsewhere in the Penateuch, the people are enjoined not to heed the message of a prophet who urges them to worship other gods, but rather to view this as a test from God meant to show their devotion (Deut. 13:2–4). When chosen by an angel of God to wage war against the Midianites, Gideon subjects God to two tests involving wool and dew to ascertain that God is with him (Judges 6:36–40). In his bid to slay Goliath, the young shepherd David, untried in the ways of war, refuses to wear Saul's armor because he is inexperienced in wearing this kind of garb, trusting instead in God, who has previously enabled him to vanquish a lion and a bear. Not wearing the armor effectively amounts to David testing God (see I Samuel 17:37–39).

2. *Exam*. Dir. Stuart Hazeldine. Hazeldine Films, 2009. Film. Quotation from Stuart Hazeldine, *Exam*, shooting script, http://www.chrisjonesblog.com/images/2012/05/EXAM-SHOOTING-SCRIPT1.pdf, 7–8. Quotation modified to take into account differences between script and what is actually said in the film.

3. Ibid., 9.

4. "The days of our lives are seventy years, and if virile, eighty years" (Psalms 90:10).

5. Hazeldine himself involves *Lord of the Flies* in a web interview, referring to it as an influence in the making of the film, insofar as the novel and the film both ask whether we, as human beings, "can retain our humanity under intense pressure or do we revert to an animalistic state." See http://www.dreadcentral.com/news/18658/exclusive-stuart-hazeldine-talks-exam-paradise-lost-and-tripods/

(July 29, 2010). See also William Golding, *Lord of the Flies* (New York: Riverhead Books, 1954).

6. Pierre Teilhard de Chardin, *The Divine Milieu* (New York: Harper & Row, 1960), 54. Writer-director Stuart Hazeldine echoes the same idea in a published interview:

> To me life itself is a blank page. It's a mystery and we have a limited amount of time. We don't know how much. We have a limited amount of time to figure out what it means if we should so desire, if not . . . we can just eat, drink, and sleep until we drop. But we have the option to figure out whether there is a purpose to be in this world and what that purpose might be, whether it's political, or religious or familial or whatever it may be.

See http://www.dreadcentral.com/news/18658/exclusive-stuart-hazeldine-talks-exam-paradise-lost-and-tripods/.

7. Hazeldine, *Exam*, shooting script, 32.

8. Pierre Teilhard de Chardin, *The Phenomenon of Man* (New York: Harper & Row, 1959), 31.

9. Hazeldine, *Exam*, shooting script, 92.

10. Lawrence Kohlberg, *The Philosophy of Moral Development*, vol. I (New York; Harper & Row, 1981), 27.

11. Ibid., 12–13.

12. Ibid., 17.

13. Carol Gilligan, *In a Different Voice: Psychological Theory and Women's Development* (Cambridge, MA: Harvard University Press, 1982), 18. Gilligan's theories have provoked serious critique, including among feminists who are concerned about a retrograde reinscribing of gender roles. As Zella Luria writes, "What do we want today as women and feminists? Do we truly gain by returning to a modern cult of true womanhood?" See Zella Luria, "A Methodological Critique," *Signs* 11, no. 2 (Winter 1986): 320; as well as the other articles in this issue dedicated to Gilligan's book. See also Dennis H. Senchik, *Listening to a Different Voice: A Feminist Critique of Gilligan*," *Studies in Philosophy and Education* 10 (1999): 233–49.

14. Gilligan, *In a Different Voice*, 18, 19. As noted above, Gilligan's theory is not without its detractors, most vitriolic among them Christina Hoff Sommers, *The War Against Boys: How Misguided Feminism Is Harming Our Young Men* (New York: Simon & Schuster, 2001). See also the Interdisciplinary Forum on Gilligan's *In a Different Voice* in *Signs* 11, no. 2 (Winter 1986), 304–33.

15. Laura Mulvey, "Visual Pleasure and Narrative Cinema," in *Film Theory and Criticism*, ed. Gerald Mast and Marshall Cohen (New York: Oxford University Press, 1985), 811.

16. Thanks to Linda Daitz for the Kim Novak reference.

17. Translation adapted from *The Midrash Rabbah: Genesis*, ed. H. Friedman and M. Simons (London: Soncino Press, 1977), 250.

18. Nahmanides, commentary on Genesis 22:1, *Torat hayyim*, vol. 1 (Jerusalem: Mossad HaRav Kook, 1986), 252. My translation. Similar observations are made by Sforno (22:1, 252), who speaks of the test enabling the one tested to convert potential into action, and Ibn Ezra (Gen. 22:1), who views the test as an opportunity for the one tested to reap a reward, 253.

19. Classical Jewish sources enumerate these trials in different ways. See, for example, Avot deRabbi Natan 1:23.

20. See Simeon ben Zemah Duran (Rashbatz), *Magen Avot* commentary on Mishnah Avot 5:3. Accessed through the Bar Ilan Responsa Project, version 14.

21. For more on this, see Shalom Spiegel, *The Last Trial: On the Legends and Lore of the Command to Abraham to Offer Isaac as a Sacrifice: The Akedah*, trans. Judah Goldin (New York: Pantheon Books, 1967).

22. See also Genesis 21, where an angel of God calls out to Hagar to arise and take hold of her son. Immediately thereafter, however, in Genesis 21:19, God (not an angel of God) opens Hagar's eyes such that she sees the lifesaving well. By contrast, it is an angel of God, rather than God directly, who speaks to Abraham, and Abraham on his own espies the ram.

23. Scholar Omri Boehm uses source criticism to argue that the original story comprised Genesis 1–10 and then 13–14 and that the angel sections were part of a later tradition. According to Boehm, Abraham himself looked up, saw the ram, and made the decision to disobey God and substitute the ram for Isaac. Boehm's reading elevates disobedience rather than obedience in this context. See Omri Boehm, *The Binding of Isaac: A Religious Model of Disobedience* (London: Bloomsbury T & T Clark, 2007). For a broad consideration of Jewish, Muslim, and Christian sources on the Akedah, see James Goodman, *But Where Is the Lamb?* (New York: Schocken, 2013).

24. Translation adapted from *The Torah: A Woman's Commentary*, 1123.

25. For an earlier version of this feminist reading of Genesis 22, see Wendy Zierler, "In Search of a Feminist Reading of the Akedah," *Nashim* (June 2005): 10–26.

26. Nancy Chodorow, *The Reproduction of Mothering* (Berkeley: University of California Press, 1978), 167. For the story of the mother who relinquishes truth to save her child, see I Kings 3:16–28.

27. Gilligan, *In a Different Voice*, 35.

28. Ibid., 104.

29. Nel Noddings, *Caring: A Feminine Approach to Ethics and Morality* (Berkeley: University of California Press, 1984), 44.

30. Phyllis Trible, "Genesis 22: The Sacrifice of Sarah," in *Women in the Hebrew Bible*, ed. Alice Bach (New York: Routledge, 1999), 285.

31. Pierre Teilhard de Chardin, *The Phenomenon of Man*, 31. Quoted in Lawrence Kohlberg with Clark Power, "Moral Development, Religious Thinking,

and the Question of a Seventh Stage," in *The Philosophy of Moral Development: Moral Stages and Idea of Justice* (New York: Harper & Row, 1981), 365.

Chapter 11

1. Plate, *Religion and Film: Cinema and The Re-Creation of the World*, 2.

2. Jeffery Weiss, "The Hunger Games Snubs Religion," *Star Tribune* (March 26, 2012), quoted in Ruth Schuster, "Finding Jesus in *The Hunger Games*," *Ha'aretz* (November 28, 2013), http://www.haaretz.com/israel-news/culture/leisure/1.560731.

3. The one exception in the first *Hunger Games* film to this absence of references to the divine figures in the soundtrack, which includes a song by Arcade called "Abraham's Daughter," explicitly linking the whole system of tributes to the narrative of the Binding of Isaac from Genesis 22. Implied in the song is the idea that Katniss, in provoking resistance to the Capitol, plays the role of a kind of Abraham's daughter who opposes the sacrifice of Isaac.

4. Abraham Joshua Heschel, *The Sabbath* (New York: Farrar Strauss and Giroux, 1951), 18.

5. Though many of the names in the trilogy derive from ancient Rome, the name Everdeen comes from Bathsheva Everdeen, the feisty female protagonist of Thomas Hardy's *Far From the Madding Crowd*. See Tina Jordan, "Suzanne Collins Comments on the Books She Loves," *Entertainment Weekly*, August 12, 2010, http://www.ew.com/article/2010/08/12/suzanne-collins-on-the-books-she-loves.

6. Suzanne Collins, *The Hunger Games* (New York: Scholastic, 2008), 52. All further citations from this book are noted in parenthesis within the body of the chapter.

7. *The Hunger Games*. Dir. Gary Ross. Lionsgate, 2012. Film.

8. Mishnah Avot 2:5.

9. In the novel, no such film is screened at the Reaping. Instead, the mayor of District 12 reads a script of the history of Panem, "the country that rose out of the ashes of a place that was once called North America." Katniss notes that it's "the same story every year," implying that the government has turned the recitation of this version of history into a ritual of commemoration and collective punishment. See Collins, *The Hunger Games*, 18.

10. According to Tammy Gant, music serves the function of religion or spirituality for Katniss. For more on this, see "Hungering for Righteousness: Music, Spirituality and Katniss Everdeen," in *Of Bread, Blood and* The Hunger Games, ed. Mary F. Pharar and Leisa A. Clark (Jefferson, NC: McFarland & Company, 2008), 89–97.

11. William James, *The Varieties of Religious Experience* (New York: Barnes and Noble Classics, 2004), 240–42.

12. Viktor Frankl refers to love in these terms, as he discusses his own experiences in a Nazi concentration camp:

> A thought transfixed me: for the first time in my life I saw the truth as it is set into song by so many poets, proclaimed as the final wisdom by so many thinkers. The truth—that love is the ultimate and highest goal to which man can aspire. Then I grasped the meaning of the greatest secret that human poetry and human thought and belief have to impart: *The salvation of man is through love and in love.* I understood how a man who has nothing left in this world still may know bliss, be it only for brief moment, in the contemplation of his beloved. . . . For this first time in my life, I was able to understand the meaning of the words, "The angels are lost in perpetual contemplation of infinite glory."

See Viktor Frankl, *Man's Search For Meaning* (Boston: Beacon Press, 1992), 48–49.

13. Ibid., 60.

14. Ibid., 135.

15. Diana Butler Bass, "*The Hunger Games*: Spiritual, but Not Religious," *On Faith*, March 22, 2012, http://www.faithstreet.com/onfaith/2012/03/22/the-hunger-games-spiritual-but-not-religious/15570.

16. Laura Snider, "The Theology of the Hunger Games," *Christianity Today*, November 13, 2013, http://www.christianitytoday.com/women/2013/october/theology-of-hunger-games.html.

17. Jamey Heit, *The Politics of* The Hunger Games (Jefferson, NC: McFarland & Co., 2015), 1. The Christian-centeredness of this book is noteworthy given its ostensible secular political subject and its subtle anti-Semitism. Heit begins his book with this New Testament reference to Herod and then quotes historian Heinrich Graetz's damning description of the Jewish Herod as "the evil genius of the Judean nation," referring to Graetz (1812–1891) simply as a nineteenth-century German historian, an odd designation given that Graetz was first and foremost a Jewish historian, one with strong ties to the Jewish community. Heit goes on repeatedly thereafter to refer to Christian scripture and Christian theologians in reference to the trilogy. He also quotes Holocaust survivor Victor Frankl's famous book *Man's Search for Meaning* without mentioning the Holocaust context of Frankl's book (see Heit, 75–77).

18. See Matthew 2:12–18.

19. Plutarch Heavensbee, former head gamemaker-turned-rebel, explains the origin of the name Panem in *Mockingjay*, the third book of the trilogy: "It's a saying from thousands of years ago, written in a language called Latin about a place called Rome. *Panem et circuses* translates into 'Bread and Circuses.' The writer [Juvenal] was saying that in return for full bellies and entertainment, his people had given up their political responsibilities and therefore their power." See Suzanne Collins, *Mockingjay* (New York: Scholastic, 2010), 223. All further citations from this novel are noted within the body of the chapter in parentheses.

20. http://christiananswers.net/spotlight/movies/2012/hungergames2012.

html. For more Christian readings, see *The Hunger Games and the Gospel* (Englewood, CO: Patheos, 2012); and Selena Sarns, *Finding God in the Hunger Games* (TheBiblePeople.com, 2013).

21. Heit, *The Politics of* The Hunger Games, 73. This image, while present in the film, is conspicuously absent in the original novel, *Catching Fire*. It is also worth noting that Katniss's pose might also be construed as mimicking the form and outstretched wings of the Mockingjay, a rare breed of bird that the Capitol never expected to survive and thrive, which Katniss comes to symbolize for the cause of rebellion. See Suzanne Collins, *Catching Fire* (New York: Scholastic, 2009).

22. The one possible exception to this is the last name of the second Head Gamemaker, Plutarch Heavensbee, which refers to heaven, generally understood to be the province of God. Insofar as Heavensbee turns out to be a rebel leader, he is shown to be on the side of good versus evil, though even the rebel faction proves to have its moral blind spots.

23. Robert Bellah, Richard Madsen, William M. Sullivan, Ann Swidler, and Steven M. Tipton, preface to the 1996 edition, *Habits of the Heart* (Berkeley: University of California Press, 2008), xv.

24. For an extensive treatment of Holocaust references in *The Hunger Games* or for a reading of the trilogy as "an analogy to the Holocaust," see Alice Chudnovsky's website, "Hunger Games vs. the Holocaust," http://hungergamesvsholocaust.weebly.com/.

25. According to Adam Levin, the electrified, barbed-wired fence imagery throughout the trilogy also serves as an allusion to the Holocaust, while the first-person, present-tense narration of the novels provokes parallels with *Anne Frank: Diary of a Young Girl*. See Adam Levin, "Recreating the Holocaust: YA Dystopia and the Young Jewish Reader," in *Space and Place in the Hunger Games* (Jefferson, NC: McFarland & Company, 2014), 124–43.

26. Irving Greenberg, "Cloud of Smoke, Pillar of Fire," in *Auschwitz, The Beginning of a New Era: Reflections on the Holocaust*, ed. Eva Fleischner (Jersey City: Ktav, 1977), 320.

27. See Harvey Cox, "The Secular City 25 Year Later," http://www.religion-online.org/showarticle.asp?title=206. Originally published in *The Christian Century* (November 7, 1990): 1025–29.

28. Harvey Cox, *The Secular City*, 19–20.

29. Greenberg, 333.

30. Ibid., 331.

31. James Orr, *God's Image in Man and Its Defacement in the Light of Modern Denials* (Grand Rapids, MI: William B. Eerdmans Publishing Company, 1948), 36. Quoted in Mark J. Mangano, *The Image of God* (Lanham, MD: University Press of America, 2008), xvii.

32. For an in-depth study of the concept of *tzelem Elohim* in rabbinic literature, including rabbinic homilies that offer commentary on the biblical story of human creation, see Yair Lorberbaum, *In God's Image: Myth, Theology and*

Law in Classical Judaism (New York: Cambridge University Press, 2015). For a comparison of Jewish and Christian understandings of this concept, including medieval Jewish sources, see Alexander Altmann, *Homo Imago Dei* in Jewish and Christian Theology," *Journal of Religion* 48, no. 3 (July 1968): 235–59.

33. Nehama Leibowitz, *Studies in the Book of Genesis* (Jerusalem: World Zionist Organization, 1972), 1. Harold S. Kushner explains this preamble as indicating man's similarity both to the animals and to God. Having created the animals and the beasts, God says to them, "Let us arrange for a new kind of creature to emerge, a human being, in *our* image, yours and Mine. Let us fashion a creature who will be like you, an animal, in some ways—needing to eat, sleep, to mate—and will be like Me in other ways, rising above the animal level." See Harold S. Kushner, *When Bad Things Happen to Good People* (New York: Avon Books, 1981), 73.

34. According to Hebrew University historian Yuval Noah Harari, what allowed *Homo sapiens* to triumph over the physically superior Neanderthals was precisely this faculty of the imagination: "The ability to create an imagined reality out of words enabled large numbers of strangers to co-operate effectively . . . *Homo sapiens* soon far outstripped and animal species in its ability to co-operate." See Yuval Noah Hararai, *Sapiens* (London: Vintage Books, 2011), 36.

35. Joseph B. Soloveitchik, *The Lonely Man of Faith* (New York: Doubleday, 2006), 12.

36. W. Randall Garr, *In His Own Image and Likeness: Humanity, Divinity, and Monotheism* (Leiden: Brill, 2003), 132.

37. Ibid., 157–58.

38. *The Midrash Rabbah: Genesis* (London: Soncino Press, 1977), 196.

39. Nachum M. Sarna, *Understanding Genesis* (New York: Schocken Books, 1966), 15–16.

40. Ibid.

41. Abraham Joshua Heschel, *Man's Quest for God* (New York: Charles Scribner's Sons, 1954), 120–21, 124.

42. Lorberbaum, *In God's Image*, 2. See, for example, *Mekhilta de-Rabbi Yishmael*, ba-Hodesh 8 and Tosefta Yevamot 8:7.

43. Ibid., 7.

44. Tosefta Yevamot 8:7. Translation from Lorberbaum, *In God's Image*, 165. See also Genesis Rabbah 34:14, in *The Midrash Rabbah: Genesis*, vol. 1 (London: Soncino Press, 1977), 280.

45. Mishnah Makkot 1:10, in *Mishnayot: Seder Nezikin*, trans. Shalom Shraga Blackman (Gateshead: Judaica Press, 1963), 310. This is not to suggest, of course, that Jewish tradition prohibits capital punishment, murder in self-defense, or in the context of war. For more on that, see Mangano, *The Image of God*, 98–99.

46. Jack Miles, *God: A Biography* (New York: Alfred A. Knopf, 1995), 44.

47. See Dan Pagis, "'Edut,'" in *Points of Departure*, trans. Stephen Mitchell

(Philadelphia; JPS, 1981), 24–25. For this and other Pagis poems related to the Holocaust, see http://www.yadvashem.org/yv/en/education/lesson_plans/dan_pagis.asp.

48. Collins, *Catching Fire*, 38.

49. Katniss also harbors a reluctance to get caught up in romantic entanglements, an attitude clearly reminiscent of her literary namesake, Thomas Hardy's protofeminist heroine Bathsheba Everdene from *Far From The Madding Crowd*, who takes particular pride that "her waist had never been encircled in a lover's arm." See Thomas Hardy, *Far From the Madding Crowd* (London: Pan Books, 1967), 273.

50. *Catching Fire* actually includes a reference to a rainbow. While speaking with the dying morphling during the Quarter Quell, Peeta laments that "I haven't figured out a rainbow yet. They come so quickly and leave so soon. Just a little bit of blue here or purple there. And they fade away again, back into the air." Peeta's inability at this point in the trilogy to figure out the rainbow fits with the fact that he and Katniss are still in the sealed ark/arena of the Hunger Games, looking for a way out and a new beginning. See Collins, *Catching Fire*, 313.

51. Lorberbaum, *In God's Image*, 2.

52. Leviticus Rabbah XXXIV, 3, in *The Midrash Rabbah: Exodus Leviticus*, trans. H. Freedman and Maurice Simon (London: The Soncino Press, 1977), 428.

53. Mishnah, Sanhedrin 4:5. Translation adapted from *Mishnayot: Seder Nezikin*, trans. Shalom Shraga Blackman (Gateshead: Judaica Press, 1963), 254; and *The Soncino Babylonian Talmud*, trans. Jacob Shachter (London: Soncino Press, 1969), 37a, http://www.come-and-hear.com/sanhedrin/sanhedrin_37.html.

54. Irving Greenberg and Shalom Freedman, *Living in the Image of God: Conversations with Rabbi Irving Greenberg* (Lanham, MD: Jason Aronson, 1998), 67–69.

55. Collins's reference to this idyllic place as "the Meadow" is interesting in light of Viktor Frankl's description of the difficulties experienced by former concentration camp prisoners in restoring their sense of humanity: "We came to a meadow full of flowers. We saw and realized that we were there, but we had no feelings about them . . . We had literally lost the ability to feel pleased and had to relearn it slowly." See Frankl, *Man's Search For Meaning*, 95.

56. Frankl, *Man's Search For Meaning*, 115.

57. See Mangano, *The Image of God*, 23–40.

Conclusion

1. *Moonrise Kingdom*. Dir. Wes Anderson. Indian Paintbrush, 2012. Film.

2. For an excellent overview of the distinctive features of Wes Anderson's style in relation to classic Japanese director Yoshiro Ozu, see Anna Catley, "Wes Anderson and Yoshiro Ozu: A Visual Essay," https://www.youtube.com/watch?v=rbXRpiVO1po.

Bibliography

Adorno, Theodor. *The Culture Industry: Selected Essays on Mass Culture*. London: Routledge, 1991.
Allentuck, Marcia, ed. *The Achievement of Isaac Bashevis Singer*. Carbondale: Southern Illinois University Press, 1969.
Alter, Robert. *The David Story*. New York: W.W. Norton & Company, 1999.
Anderson, Gary. *Sin: A History*. New Haven: Yale University Press, 2009.
Anderson, Paul Thomas. *Magnolia: The Shooting Draft*, http://www.dailyscript.com/scripts/magnolia.html.
Anker, Roy M. *Catching Light: Looking for God in the Movies*. Grand Rapids, MI: William B. Eerdmans Publishing Company, 2004.
Asch, Sholem. *Moses*. Translated by Maurice Samuel. New York: G.P. Putnam's Sons, 1951.
Bach, Alice. *Women in the Hebrew Bible*. New York: Routledge, 1999.
Bailey, Peter, and Sam Girgus, eds. *A Companion to Woody Allen*. Malden, MA: John Wiley, 2013.
Bakhos, Carol, ed. *Current Trends in the Study of Midrash*. Leiden: Brill, 2006.
Bass, Diana Butler. "*The Hunger Games*: Spiritual, but Not Religious." *On Faith*, March 22, 2012.
Batnitzky, Leora. *Idolatry and Representation: The Philosophy of Franz Rosenzweig*. Princeton: Princeton University Press, 2000.
Beaudoin, Tom. *Virtual Faith: The Irreverent Spiritual Quest of Generation X*. San Francisco: Jossey Bass Publishers, 1998.
Bellah, Robert N., Richard Madsen, William M. Sullivan, Ann Swidler, and Steven M. Tipton. *Habits of the Heart*. Berkeley: University of California Press, 2008.
Berkovitz, Eliezer. *God, Man and History*. Jerusalem: Shalem Press, 2004.
Bernstein, Elizabeth. "Researchers Study Awe and Find It Is Good for Relationships." *The Wall Street Journal*, February 23, 2015.
Beyers, Thomas B. "History Re-Membered: *Forrest Gump*, Postfeminist Masculinity, and the Burial of the Counterculture." *Modern Fiction Studies* 42, no. 2 (1996): 419–44.
Billington, Sandra. *A Social History of the Fool*. New York: St. Martin's Press, 1984.

Bird, Michael, and John May, eds. *Religion and Film*. Knoxville: University of Tennessee Press, 1982.

Blake, R. A. "Looking for God: Profane and Sacred in the Films of Woody Allen." *Journal of Popular Film & Television* 19, no. 2 (Summer 1991): 58–67.

Blessing, Kimberly A., and Paul J. Tudico, eds. *Movies and the Meaning of Life: Philosophers Take on Hollywood*. Chicago: Open Court, 2005.

Blizek, William L., ed. *The Continuum Companion to Religion and Film*. London: Continuum, 2009.

Bjorkman, Stij. *Woody Allen on Woody Allen*. New York: Grove Press, 1993.

Boehm, Omri. *The Binding of Isaac: A Religious Model of Disobedience*. London: Bloomsbury T & T Clark, 2007.

The Book of Job. Translated by Raymond P. Scheindlin. New York: W. W. Norton & Company, 1998.

Bordwell, David. *Film Art: An Introduction*. New York: McGraw Hill Education, 2012.

Borowitz, Eugene. "God and Man in Judaism Today: A Reform Perspective." *Judaism* 23, no. 3 (Summer 1974): 298–308.

———. *The Mask Jews Wear*. 2nd ed. New York: Sh'ma, 1980.

———. *Renewing the Covenant*. Philadelphia: JPS, 1991.

———. *The Talmud's Theological Language-Game*. Albany: State University of New York Press, 2006.

Boyarin, Daniel. *Intertextuality and the Reading of Midrash*. Bloomington: Indiana University Press, 1990.

Boyd, Malcolm. "Theology and the Movies." *Theology Today* 14, no. 3 (1957): 359–75.

Brant, Jonathan. *Paul Tillich and the Possibility of Revelation Through Film*. Oxford: Oxford University Press, 2012.

Britt, Brian. *Rewriting Moses: The Narrative Eclipse of the Text*. London: T & T Clark International, 2004.

Brooklyn College Film Department, "Film Glossary." http://userhome.brooklyn.cuny.edu/anthro/jbeatty/COURSES/glossary.htm.

Bruns, Gerald. *Hermeneutics Ancient and Modern*. New Haven: Yale University Press, 1992.

Buber, Martin. *Moses: The Revelation and the Covenant*. New York: Harper Torchbooks, 1946.

———. *I and Thou*. Translated by Walter Kaufmann. New York: Charles Scribner, 1970.

———. *The Tales of Rabbi Nachman*. Atlantic Highlands, NJ: Humanities Press International, 1988.

Calvino, Italo. *If on a Winter's Night a Traveler*. Translated by William Weaver. San Diego: Harcourt Inc., 1981.

Chodorow, Nancy. *The Reproduction of Mothering.* Berkeley: University of California Press, 1978.
Clarke, Anthony J., and Paul Fiddes. *Flickering Images: Theology and Film in Dialogue.* Oxford: Regent's Park College Oxford, 2005.
Coen, Joel, and Ethan. Script of *A Serious Man.* http://www.imsdb.com/scripts/A-Serious-Man.html.
Cohan, Steven, and Ina Rae Hark. *The Road Movie Book.* New York: Routledge 1997.
Cohen, Arthur A., and Paul Mendes Flohr, eds. *Contemporary Jewish Religious Thought.* New York: Free Press, 1987.
Collins, Suzanne. *The Hunger Games.* New York: Scholastic, 2008.
———. *Catching Fire.* New York: Scholastic, 2009.
———. *Mockingjay.* New York: Scholastic, 2010.
Commins, Gary. "Woody Allen's Theological Imagination." *Theology Today* 44, no. 2 (July 1987): 235–49.
Cooper, John C., and Carl Skrade, eds. *Celluloid and Symbols.* Philadelphia: Fortress Press, 1970.
Cox, Dermot. *The Triumph of Impotence.* Rome: Universita Gregoriana, 1978.
Cox, Harvey G. "Theological Reflections on Cinema." *Andover Newton Quarterly* 3, no. 2 (1962): 28–40.
———. *The Secular City.* New York: Macmillan, 1965.
———. "The Secular City 25 Year Later." *The Christian Century*, November 7, 1990.
Christianson, Eric S., Peter Francis, and William Telford, eds. *Cinéma Divinité.* London: SCM Press, 2005.
Crimes and Misdemeanors. Directed by Woody Allen. Orion Pictures, 1989. Film.
Dalglish, Edward R. *Psalm Fifty-One in Light of Ancient Near Eastern Patternism.* Leiden: E.J. Brill, 1962.
Dark, David. *Everyday Apocalypse: The Sacred Revealed in Radiohead, The Simpsons, and Other Pop Culture Icons.* Grand Rapids, MI: Brazos Press, 2002.
Darnton, Robert. *The Kiss of the Lamourette: Reflections in Cultural History.* New York: W.W. Norton & Co., 1990.
Deacy, Christopher. *Faith and Film: Religious Themes in Contemporary Cinema.* Burlington, VT: Ashgate, 2005.
———, and Gaye Williams Ortiz, eds. *Theology and Film: Challenging the Sacred/Secular Divide.* Malden, MA: Wiley Blackwell, 2008.
The Descendants. Directed by Alexander Payne. Fox Searchlight, 2011. Film.
DeGiglio-Bellemare, Mario. "Magnolia and the Signs of the Times: A Theological Reflection." *Film and Religion* 4, no. 2 (October 2000). http://www.unomaha.edu/jrf/magnolia.htm.
Detweiler, Craig, and Barry Taylor. *A Matrix of Meanings: Finding God in Popular Culture.* Grand Rapids, MI: Baker Academic, 2003.
Dorsky, Nathaniel. *Devotional Cinema.* Berkeley, CA: Tuumba Press, 2003.
Dostoevsky, Fyodor. *Crime and Punishment.* http://www.bartleby.com/318/54.html.

Downing, Crystal. "Woody Allen's Blindness and Insight: The Palimpsests of *Crimes and Misdemeanors*. *Religion and the Arts* 1 (1997): 73–92.
Edges, Chris. *Empire of Illusion: The End of Literacy and the Triumph of Spectacle*. New York: Nation Books, 2009.
Eisenstein, J. D. "Midrash Yonah." In *Otzar hamidrashim*. New York: J. D. Eisenstein, 1915.
Ellenson, David. "History, Memory and Relationship." In *Memory and History in Christianity and Judaism*. Notre Dame: University of Notre Dame Press, 2001.
Ellis, John. *Visible Fictions*. New York: Routledge, 2002.
Eskenazi, Tamara, and Andrea Weiss, eds. *The Torah: A Woman's Commentary*. New York: Women of Reform Judaism, 2008.
Exam. Directed by Stuart Hazeldine. Hazeldine Films, 2009. Film.
Fant, Gene C., Jr. *God as Author: A Biblical Approach to Narrative*. Nashville: B & H Academic, 2010.
Fishbane, Michael. *Biblical Interpretation in Ancient Israel*. Oxford: Clarendon Press, 1985.
———. *The Exegetical Imagination*. Cambridge, MA: Harvard University Press, 1998.
———. *The Garments of Torah*. Bloomington: Indiana University Press, 1989.
Flusser, David. *Jewish Sources in Early Christianity*. Translated by John Glucker. Tel Aviv: MOD Books, 1989.
Foer, Jonathan Safran. *Everything Is Illuminated*. New York: Perennial, 2003.
Forrest Gump. Directed by Robert Zemeckis. Paramount, 1994. Film.
Frankl, Viktor. *Man's Search for Meaning*. Boston: Beacon Press, 1992.
Freud, Sigmund. *Jokes and Their Relation to the Unconscious*. New York: W.W. Norton & Company, 1960.
Funkenstein, Amos. "Collective Memory and Historical Consciousness." *History and Memory* 1 (Spring/Summer 1989): 5–26.
Galpaz-Feller, Penina. *Yonah: masa el haḥofesh*. Jerusalem: Carmel, 2009.
Garr, W. Randall. *In His Own Image and Likeness: Humanity, Divinity, and Monotheism*. Leiden: Brill, 2003.
Garriott, Deidre Anne Evans, Whitney Elaine Jones, and Julie Elizabeth Tyler. *Space and Place in the Hunger Games*. Jefferson, NC: McFarland & Company, 2014.
Genesis Rabbah. Edited by Theodor Albeck. Bar Ilan Responsa Project, version 14.
Giannetti, Louis. *Understanding Movies*. 13th ed. New York: Pearson, 2013.
Gilligan, Carol. *In a Different Voice: Psychological Theory and Women's Development*. Cambridge, MA: Harvard University Press, 1982.
Gillman, Neil. *Sacred Fragments: Recovering Theology for the Modern Jew*. Philadelphia: JPS, 1990.
Ginsburg, Shai. "The Physics of Being Jewish, or On Cats and Jews." *AJS Review* 35, no. 2 (November 2011): 357–64.

Girgus, Sam. *The Films of Woody Allen*. Cambridge: Cambridge University Press, 1993.
Golding, William. *Lord of the Flies*. New York: Riverhead Books, 1954.
Goodman, James. *But Where Is the Lamb?* New York: Schocken, 2013.
Gottschalk, Jonathan. *The Storytelling Animal*. Boston: Houghton Mifflin Harcourt, 2012.
Green, Arthur. *Tormented Master*. Tuscaloosa: University of Alabama Press, 1979.
Greenberg, Irving. "Cloud of Smoke, Pillar of Fire." In *Auschwitz, the Beginning of a New Era: Reflections on the Holocaust*, edited by Eva Fleischner. Jersey City: Ktav, 1977.
———. *The Jewish Way*. New York: Touchstone, 1993.
———, and Shalom Freedman. *Living in the Image of God: Conversations with Rabbi Irving Greenberg*. Lanham, MD: Jason Aronson, 1998.
Groom, Winston. *Forrest Gump*. New York: Pocket Books, 1986.
Halbertal, Moshe, and Avishai Margalit. *Idolatry*. Cambridge: Harvard University Press, 1992.
Hakham, Amos. *Sefer tehilim*. Israel: Mossad Harav Kook, 1990.
Harari, Yuval Noah. *Sapiens*. London: Vintage Books, 2011.
Hazeldine, Stuart. *Exam* shooting script, http://www.chrisjonesblog.com/images/2012/05/EXAM-SHOOTING-SCRIPT1.pdf.
Heinemann, Joseph. "The Nature of Aggadah." 1974. Reprinted in *Midrash and Literature*. Edited by Geoffrey H. Hartman and Sanford Budick. New Haven: Yale University Press, 1986.
Heit, Jamey. *The Politics of* The Hunger Games. Jefferson, NC: McFarland & Co., 2015.
Helfgot, Nathaniel, ed. *The Book of Samuel*. Teaneck: Ben Yehuda Press, 2006.
Helm, Zach. Screenplay for *Stranger than Fiction*, http://www.dailyscript.com/scripts/Stranger-Than-Fiction.pdf.
Hemmings, Kaui Hart. *The Descendants*. New York: Random House, 2008.
Heschel, Abraham Joshua. *The Sabbath*. New York: Farrar Strauss and Giroux, 1951.
———. *Man's Quest for God*. New York: Charles Scribner's Sons, 1954.
———. *God in Search of Man*. New York: Farrar Strauss & Giroux, 1955.
Higgins, Gareth. *How Movies Helped Save My Soul: Finding Spiritual Fingerprints in Culturally Significant Films*. Lake Marie, FL: Relevant Books, 2003.
Hoffman, Lawrence, ed. *We Have Sinned: Sin and Confession in Judaism*. Woodstock, VT: Jewish Lights, 2012.
The Hunger Games. Directed by Gary Ross. Color Force Productions, 2012. Film.
Hurley, Neil. *Theology Through Film*. New York: Harper & Row, 1970.
———. *The Reel Revolution*. Maryknoll, NY: Orbis Books, 1978.
Jackson, Tony E. "Graphism and Story-time in *Memento*." *Mosaic* 40, no. 3 (September 2007): 51–66.

Jacobs, Louis. *The Jewish Religion: A Companion*. Oxford: Oxford University Press, 1995.
Jaffee, Martin S. *Torah in the Mouth: Writing and Oral Tradition in Palestinian Judaism 200 BCE–400 CE*. New York: Oxford, 2001.
James, William. *The Varieties of Religious Experience*. New York: Barnes and Noble Classics, 2004.
Jerusalem Talmud. Tractate Avodah Zarah. Bar Ilan Responsa Project, version 14.
Jewett, Robert. *Saint Paul at the Movies*. Louisville, KY: Westminster/John Knox Press, 1993.
———. *Saint Paul Returns to the Movies: Triumph Over Shame*. Grand Rapids, MI: William. B. Eerdmans Publishing Co., 1998.
Johnston, Robert K. *Reel Spirituality*. Grand Rapids, MI: Baker Academic, 2000.
———. *Useless Beauty: Ecclesiastes Through the Lens of Contemporary Film*. Grand Rapids, MI: Baker Academic, 2004.
———. *Reframing Theology and Film: New Focus for an Emerging Discipline*. Grand Rapids, MI: Baker Academic, 2007.
———, and Catherine Barsotti. *Finding God in the Movies*. Grand Rapids, MI: Baker Academic, 2004.
Jordan, Tina. "Suzanne Collins Comments on the Books She Loves." *Entertainment Weekly*, August 12, 2010.
Jump, Herbert A. "The Religious Possibilities of the Motion Picture (1910). *Film History* 14, no. 2 (2002): 216–28.
Kalmanofksy, Amy. *Dangerous Sisters of the Hebrew Bible*. Minneapolis: Fortress Press, 2014.
Kania, Andrew, ed. *Memento: Philosophers on Film*. New York: Routledge, 2009.
Kates, Judith, and Gail Reimer Twersky, eds. *Beginning Anew: A Woman's Companion to the High Holidays*. New York: Simon & Schuster, 1997.
Kaunfer, Elie. "Limmud on One Leg." http://limmud.org/publications/limmudononeleg/5771/vayeshev/.
Kehati, Pinkhas. *Mishnayot mevo'arot: Seder Nezikin*. Jerusalem: Heikhal Shelomo, 1977.
Kehr, Dave. "Who Framed Forrest?" *Film Comment* 31, no. 2 (March–April 1995): 50–51.
Kepnes, Steven, ed. *Interpreting Judaism in a Postmodern Age*. New York: New York University Press, 1996.
The King's Speech. Directed by Tom Hooper. Weinstein Company, 2011. Film.
Klein, A. M. *The Collected Poems of A.M. Klein*. McGraw Hill, 1974.
Kohlberg, Lawrence. *The Philosophy of Moral Development: Moral Stages and the Idea of Justice*. New York: Harper & Row, 1981.
Kolodny, Annette. *The Lay of the Land: Metaphor as Experience and History in American Life and Letters*. Chapel Hill: University of North Carolina Press, 1975.

Kresh, Paul. *Isaac Bashevis Singer: The Magician of 86th Street.* New York: Dial Press, 1979.
Kugel, James L. *The Great Poems of the Bible: A Reader's Companion with New Translations.* New York: Free Press, 2008.
———. *In Potiphar's House: The Interpretive Life of Biblical Texts.* New York: HarperSanFrancisco, 1990.
Kurtzer, Yehuda. *Shuva: The Future of the Jewish Past.* Waltham: Brandeis University Press, 2012.
Kushner, Harold S. *When Bad Things Happen to Good People.* New York: Avon Books, 1981.
Landry, David. "Faint Hope: A Theological Interpretation of Woody Allen's *Crimes and Misdemeanors*. *Journal of Religion and Popular Culture* 22, no. 1 (Spring 2010): 1–19.
Lamott, Anne. *Bird by Bird.* New York: Anchor Books, 1994.
Lee, Sander. *Woody Allen's Angst: Philosophical Commentaries on His Serious Films.* Jefferson, NC: McFarland & Company Inc., Publishers, 1997.
Lehrer, Jonah. "What *The King's Speech* Gets Wrong About Stuttering." *The Wall Street Journal*, January 24, 2011.
Leibowitz, Nehama. *Studies in the Book of Genesis.* Jerusalem: World Zionist Organization, 1972.
Leonard, Richard, SJ. *Movies That Matter.* Chicago: Loyola Press, 2006.
Leveen, Adriane. *Memory and Tradition in the Book of Numbers.* Cambridge: Cambridge University Press, 2008.
Levinas, Emmanuel. *In the Time of the Nations.* Translated by Michael B. Smith. Bloomington: Indiana University Press, 1994.
Lidz, Frank. "Biblical Adversity in a '60s Suburb." *New York Times*, September 23, 2009.
Lindvall, Terry. "Religion and Film: Part 1: History and Criticism." *Communication Research Trends* 23, no. 4 (2004).
Little, William G. "Surviving *Memento.*" *Narrative* 13, no. 1 (January 2005): 67–83.
Lorberbaum, Yair. *In God's Image: Myth, Theology and Law in Classical Judaism.* New York: Cambridge University Press, 2015.
Love and Death. Directed by Woody Allen. MGM, 1975. Film.
Lyden, John C. *Film as Religion: Myth, Morals and Rituals.* New York: New York University Press, 2003.
———, ed. *The Routledge Companion to Religion and Film.* New York: Routledge, 2009.
Lynch, Gordon. *Understanding Theology and Popular Culture.* Malden, MA: Blackwell, 2005.
Lynch, William F., S.J. *The Image Industries.* New York: Sheed and Ward, 1959.
Magnolia. Directed by Paul Thomas Anderson. New Line Productions, 1999. Film.

Maimonides. "Hilkhot teshuvah." *Mishneh Torah*. Bar Ilan Responsa Project, version 14.
Mangano, Mark J. *The Image of God*. Lanham, MD: University Press of America, 2008.
Mann, Vivian B. *Jewish Texts on the Visual Arts*. Cambridge: Cambridge University Press, 2000.
Marsh, Clive, and Gaye Ortiz, eds. *Explorations in Theology and Film*. Malden, MA: Blackwell, 1997.
Martin, J. W., and Conrad Oswalt. *Screening the Sacred*. Boulder: Westview, 1995.
Mast, Gerald, and Marshall Cohen, eds. *Film Theory and Criticism*. New York: Oxford University Press, 1985.
May, John R., ed. *New Image of Religious Film*. Kansas City: Sheed & Ward, 1997.
Mazur, Eric. *The Encyclopedia of Religion and Film*. Santa Barbara, CA: ABC-CLIO, 2011.
McAdams, Dan P. *The Stories We Live By: Personal Myths and the Making of the Self*. New York: Guilford Press, 1993.
McFague, Sally. *Models of God: Theology for an Ecological, Nuclear Age*. Philadelphia: Fortress Press, 1987.
———. *Speaking in Parables: A Study in Metaphor and Theology*. Philadelphia: Fortress Press, 1975.
Mechon-mamre.org. *Hebrew-English Bible According to the JPS 1917 Translation*. http://www.mechon-mamre.org/p/pt/pt0.htm.
Memento. Directed by Christopher Nolan. Newmarket, 2001. Film.
Mercadante, Linda A. "The God Behind the Screen: *Pleasantville* & *The Truman Show*." *Journal of Religion and Film* 5, no. 2 (October 2001). http://www.unomaha.edu/jrf/truman.htm.
The Midrash Rabbah. Translated by H. Freedman and Maurice Simon. London: Soncino, 1977.
Midrash Tanhuma. Bar Ilan Responsa Project, version 14.
Miles, Jack. *God: A Biography*. New York: Alfred A. Knopf, 1995.
Milner, Brenda, Larry R. Squire, and Eric R. Kandel. "Cognitive Neuroscience and the Study of Memory." *Neuron* 20 (March 1998): 445–68.
Mishnayot: Seder Nezikin. Translated by Shalom Shraga Blackman. London: Judaica Press, 1963.
Mitchell, Jolyon, and S. Brent Plate, eds. *The Religion and Film Reader*. New York: Routledge, 2007.
———, and Sophia Marriage, eds. *Mediating Religion: Conversations in Media, Religion and Culture*. London: T & T Clark, 2003.
Monaco, James. *How to Read a Film*. New York: Oxford University Press, 2000.
Moonrise Kingdom. Directed by Wes Anderson. Indian Paintbrush, 2012. Film.
Morreall, John. *Comedy, Tragedy and Religion*. Albany: State University of New York Press, 1999.

Morson, Gary Saul. "How to Read Crime and Punishment." *Commentary*, June 1992, https://www.commentarymagazine.com/article/how-to-read-crime-and-punishment/.

Nichols, Mary P. *Deconstructing Woody*. Lanham, MD: Rowman & Littlefield, 1998.

Noddings, Nel. *Caring: A Feminine Approach to Ethics and Morality*. Berkeley: University of California Press, 1984.

Nolan, Christopher. *Memento*, shooting script, http://www.imsdb.com/scripts/Memento.html.

Norich, Anita, and Yaron Z. Eliav, eds. *Jewish Literatures and Cultures: Context and Intertext*. Providence, RI: Brown Judaic Studies, 2008.

Ochs, Peter, and Nancy Leveen, eds. *Textual Reasonings: Jewish Philosophy and Text Study at the End of the Twentieth Century*. Grand Rapids, MI: William B. Eerdmans Publishing Company, 2002.

O'Hehir, Andrew. "Goys, God, Dentistry, and 'A Serious Man,'" http://www.salon.com/2009/10/01/coens/.

Orr, James. *God's Image in Man and Its Defacement in the Light of Modern Denials*. Grand Rapids, MI: William B. Eerdmans Publishing Company, 1948.

Owen, Stephen. *Remembrances*. Cambridge, MA: Harvard University Press, 1986.

Pagis, Dan. *Points of Departure*. Translated by Stephen Mitchell. Philadelphia: JPS, 1981.

Payne, Alexander, Nat Faxon, and Jim Rash. *The Descendants*, shooting script, http://www.imsdb.com/scripts/Descendants,-The.html.

Pesikta deRav Kahanah. Bar Ilan Responsa Project, version 14.

Pharar, Mary F., and Leisa A. Clark, eds. *Of Bread, Blood and* The Hunger Games. Jefferson, NC: McFarland & Company, 2008.

Philips, William H. *Film: An Introduction*. 4th ed. New York: Bedford/St. Martin's, 2009.

Pinsker, Sanford. *The Schlemiel as Metaphor: Studies in Yiddish and American Jewish Fiction*. Carbondale: Southern Illinois University Press, 1991.

Plate, S. Brent. "Religion/Literature/Film: Toward a Religious Visuality of Film." *Literature and Theology* 12, no. 1 (1998): 16–38.

———. *Religion and Film: Cinema and the Re-Creation of the World*. London: Wallflower, 2009.

Porton, Gary G. *Understanding Rabbinic Midrash*. Hoboken: K'tav, 1985.

Prell, Riv Ellen. "*A Serious Man* in Situ: 'Fear and Loathing in St. Louis Park.'" *AJS Review* 35, no. 2 (November 2011): 365–76.

Reinhartz, Adele. *Scripture on the Silver Screen*. Louisville, KY: Westminster Press, 2003.

Ricoeur, Paul. *Symbolism of Evil*. Boston: Beacon Press, 1969.

Romanowski, William D. *Eyes Wide Open: Looking for God in Popular Culture*. Grand Rapids, MI: Brazos Press, 2007.

Rosenzweig, Franz. *On Jewish Learning*. Edited by N. N. Glatzer. New York: Schocken Books, 1955.
Rubinstein, Jeffrey. *Rabbinic Stories*. Mahwah, NJ: Paulist Press, 2002.
Sarna, Nachum M. *Understanding Genesis*. New York: Schocken Books, 1966.
Schachter, Daniel. *Searching for Memory: The Brain, the Mind and the Past*. New York: Basic Books, 1996.
Schneider, Phil. *Transcending Stuttering*. http://vimeo.com/16695172.
Schrader, Paul. *Transcendental Style in Film: Ozu, Bresson, Dreyer*. New York: Da Capo, 1988.
Schwarzman, Lisa. "The Director of the 'King's Speech' Owes His DGA Award to Two Other Guys." *Entertainment Weekly*, February 1, 2011.
Scott, Steven D. 'Like a Box of Chocolates': *Forrest Gump* and Postmodernism. *Literature/Film Quarterly* 29, no. 1 (2001): 23–31.
Segal, Benjamin J. *A New Psalm: Psalms as Literature*. Jerusalem: Gefen, 2013.
A Serious Man. Directed by Ethan and Joel Coen. Focus Features, 2009. Film.
Shalev, Meir. *Reishit*. Tel Aviv: Am Oved, 2008.
Shell, Marc. *Stutter*. Cambridge, MA: Harvard University Press, 2006.
Sherwood, Yvonne. *A Biblical Text and Its Afterlives: The Survival of Jonah in Western Culture*. Cambridge: Cambridge University Press, 2000.
Shields, David. *Dead Languages*. St. Paul, MN: Graywolf Press, 1989.
Silet, Charles L. P., ed. *The Films of Woody Allen*. Lanham, MD: The Scarecrow Press, 2006.
Simon, Uriel. *JPS Bible Commentary: Yonah*. Philadelphia: JPS, 1999.
Singer, Isaac Bashevis. *Collected Stories*. New York: Farrar Strauss and Giroux, 1982.
———. "Gimpl tam." In *Der Shpigl un andere dertsyalungen*. Jerusalem: Tcherikover Publishers/Hebrew University, 1975.
Snider, Laura. "The Theology of the Hunger Games." *Christianity Today*, November 13, 2013.
Sollors, Werner. *Beyond Ethnicity: Consent and Descent in American Culture*. New York: Oxford University Press, 1986.
Soloveitchik, Joseph B. *The Lonely Man of Faith*. New York: Doubleday, 2006.
The Soncino Babylonian Talmud. Edited by I. Epstein. London: Soncino Press, 1969, 1973, 1977,
Stahlberg, Lesleigh Cushing. *Sustaining Fictions: Intertextuality, Midrash, Translation, and the Literary Afterlife of the Bible*. New York: T & T Clark, 2008.
Stam, Robert, and Alessandra Raengo, eds. *A Companion to Literature and Film*. Oxford: Blackwell, 2004.
Steinfels, Peter. "Woody Allen Counts the Wages of Sin." *New York Times*, October 15, 1989, http://www.nytimes.com/1989/10/15/movies/film-woody-allen-counts-the-wages-of-sin.html?src=pm&pagewanted=1.
Stern, David. *Parables in Midrash: Narrative and Exegesis in Rabbinic Literature*. Cambridge, MA: Harvard University Press, 1991.

Sternberg, Meir. *The Poetics of Biblical Narrative*. Bloomington: Indiana University Press, 1985.
Stone, Bryan. *Faith and Film: Theological Themes at the Cinema*. Saint Louis: Chalice Press, 2000.
Stranger than Fiction. Directed by Marc Forester. Columbia Pictures, 2006. Film.
Teilhard de Chardin, Pierre. *The Phenomenon of Man*. New York: Harper & Row, 1959.
———. *The Divine Milieu*. New York: Harper & Row, 1960.
Tigay, Jeffrey. "'Heavy of Mouth' and 'Heavy of Tongue' on Moses' Speech Difficulty." *BASOR* 231 (1978): 57–67.
Tillich, Paul. *Theology of Culture*. New York: Oxford University Press, 1959.
Tollerton, David. "Job of Suburbia: *A Serious Man* and Viewer Perceptions of the Biblical." *Film and Religion* 15, no. 2 (October 2011). http://www.unomaha.edu/jrf/Vol15no2/JobSeriousMan.html.
Torat ḥayyim. Jerusalem: Mossad HaRav Kook, 1986.
Travers, Peter. Review of *Magnolia*. *Rolling Stone*, February 27, 2001, http://www.rollingstone.com/movies/reviews/magnolia-20010227.
The Truman Show. Directed by Peter Weir. Paramount, 1998. Film.
Vaux, Sara Anson. *Finding Meaning at the Movies*. Nashville, TN: Abingdon Press, 1999.
Vawter, Bruce. *Job & Jonah: Questioning the Hidden God*. Ramsey, NJ: Paulist Press, 1983.
Ventura, Elbert. "Palm Tree of Life: The Sneaky Profundity of The Descendants." *Slate*, February 23, 2012, http://www.slate.com/articles/arts/culturebox/2012/02/the_descendants_alexander_payne_s_movie_is_as_profound_as_terrence_malick_s_tree_of_life_.html.
Vermes, Geza. *Scripture and Tradition in Judaism*. Leiden: Brill, 1961.
Wall, James M. *Church and Cinema*. Grand Rapids, MI: William B. Eerdmans Publishing Company, 1971.
Watkins, Gregory, ed. *Teaching Religion and Film*. New York: Oxford University Press, 2008.
Weiss, Jeffery. "The Hunger Games Snubs Religion." *Star Tribune*, March 26, 2012.
Welsford, Enid. *The Fool: His Social and Literary History*. Gloucester, MA: Peter Smith, 1966.
Wiesel, Elie. *Five Biblical Portraits*. Notre Dame: University of Notre Dame Press, 1981.
Wisse, Ruth. *The Schlemiel as Modern Hero*. Chicago: University of Chicago Press, 1971.
Wright, Melanie J. *Religion and Film: An Introduction*. London: I.B. Tauris, 2007.
Yerushalmi, Yosef Hayyim. *Zakhor: Jewish History and Jewish Memory*. New York: Schocken, 1989.
Yosef, Ovadiah. *Shut yehaveh da'at*. Bar Ilan Responsa Project, version 14.

Young, Brad H. *The Parables: Jewish Tradition and Christian Interpretation*. Grand Rapids, MI: Baker Academic, 1998.

Zerubavel, Yael. *Recovered Roots: Collective Memory and the Making of Israeli National Tradition*. Chicago: University of Chicago Press, 1995.

Zierler, Wendy. "Fools on the American Road: 'Gimpel the Fool,' *The Frisco Kid*, and *Forrest Gump*." In *Hit the Road Jack: Essays on the Culture of the American Road*, edited by Gordon Slethaug and Stacilee Ford, 214–33. Montreal: McGill-Queen's University Press, 2012.

———. "In Search of a Feminist Reading of the Akedah." *Nashim* (June 2005): 10–26.

Zink, J. K. "Uncleanness and Sin: A Study of Job XIV 4 and Psalm LI 7." *Vetus Testamentum* 17, no. 3 (July 1967): 354–61.

Zsengeller, Jozsef, ed. *Rewritten Bible After Fifty Years*. Leiden: Brill, 2014.

Index

Abel and Cain, 53, 223, 226, 229
Abraham, 202, 203
Adam and Eve, 53, 125, 155, 223, 230–31. *See also* Garden of Eden
Adler, Rachel, 38–39
aggadah, xii, 147
Akedah. *See* Binding of Isaac
Akiva, Rabbi, 159, 160, 225, 228
Allen, Woody, 245, 265n10. *See also Crimes and Misdemeanors* on Judah Rosenthal, 267n25
altruism, 75, 211, 212, 214
American Beauty (film), xii, 243
American Pastoral (Roth), 4, 243, 247
amnesia, 262n11. *See also Memento*
Anderson, Gary, 107, 267n32
Anderson, Paul Thomas, 41, 258n3, 259n13. *See also Magnolia*
Anderson, Wes, 233. *See also Moonrise Kingdom*
anger, 138–39
Anker, Roy, 258n7
Asch, Sholem, 148
atonement, 114, 229. *See also* forgiveness; repentance; Yom Kippur
attachment, feminist theory of, 205–8
autonomy vs. determinism, 156
Avodah Zarah, 21–22

Avot, 91–92, 202–3

Babylonian Talmud, 21, 22, 111–13, 127, 159, 160, 174. *See also* Avodah Zarah
Bachman, Greg, 97, 102
Bass, Diana Butler, 217
Bathsheba and David, 102–6
Beaudoin, Tom, 9
Bellah, Robert N., 219
Ben Bag Bag, 180
Berkovitz, Eliezer, 154
betzelem Elohim. *See* created in the image of God
Beyers, Thomas B., 119–20
Billington, Sandra, 126
Binding of Isaac (Akedah), 56, 202–7, 276n1, 278n23, 279n3
birthright (*bekhorah*)
  betrayal of, 62
  concept and meaning of, 70, 71, 73
  in *The Descendants*, 60, 62, 64–66, 68, 69, 72–74
  embracing vs. renouncing, 64, 68–75
  vs. individual achievement, 59
  Jacob, Esau, and, 69–75
  notion of enduring, 60
  reclaiming, 66

Black (character in *Exam*), 190, 192, 196–98
black and white vs. color, 79–80
blacks, 122, 190–91
blank sheet, life as a, 194–95
blindness, real and metaphorical, 100, 101, 114, 115, 267n26, 268n51
Blonde (character in *Exam*), 190, 192–93, 195, 196, 198–200
Boehm, Omri, 278n23
Borowitz, Eugene "Gene" B., 12
   American Beauty and, 243
   on creative alienation, 20
   Crimes and Misdemeanors and, 95, 97
   The Descendants and, 68–69
   emails from Zierler to, 240–42
   emails to Zierler, 237–40
   Hebrew Union College–Jewish Institute of Religion and, 1–3
   on inverted midrash, 14
   on *Memento*, 86–87
   on midrash, 239, 242
   My Big Fat Greek Wedding and, 245, 253n30
   overview, xi
   philosophical beliefs, 86
   on power of the forbidden, 246
   Reel Theology and, 2, 3, 86–87, 246
   Tuesdays with Morrie and, 246
   writings
     The Mask Jews Wear, 12, 20
     Renewing the Covenant: A Theology for the Postmodern Jew, xi, 241, 245, 253n30
   Zierler's early encounters with, 1–3
Boyarin, Daniel, 147
Brant, Jonathan, 9–10
Brettler, Marc, 107, 108
Buber, Martin, 146, 148, 176
Buchdahl, Angela, 92
burning bush, 146

Cain and Abel, 53, 223, 226, 229
Calvino, Italo, 163
capital punishment, 229
care, ethics of, 211
Catching Fire (Collins), 216, 227, 228, 281n21, 283n50
Catching Fire (film), 216, 218
Chodorow, Nancy, 205
Christian precedents of Jewish "Reel Theology," 6–12
Christian religious right, 261n15
Christian vs. Jewish confession, 259n12
Christianity, 155, 252n23. *See also under* Jewish "Reel Theology"; New Testament
   faith and theology as synonymous with, 11
   and film, books on, 241
   Hunger Games trilogy and, 217–18
   wise/holy fool in, 118
Christmas, 137, 245–46
Christology, 11. *See also* Jesus; "Son of man"
circumcision (*milah*), 141
"Clever Man and the Simple Man, The" (R. Nachman), 241
cleverness, 117, 118, 121, 182–83
Coen, Joel and Ethan, 169–72, 275n2. *See also Serious Man*
Collins, Suzanne. *See Hunger Games* trilogy
color, 190. *See also Exam*
   vs. black and white, 79–80
comedy, 38
   compared with religion, 39
   tragedy and, 98–99
Commins, Gary, 114
confession (*vidui*), 54, 57. *See also* repentance; *vidui*
   of Daniel, 55

of David, 104–6, 109, 112
deathbed, 49, 259n10
etymology of the term, 57
first biblical, 53
of Jonah, 37
Judah and, 52–54
of Judah Rosenthal in *Crimes and Misdemeanors*, 99, 104, 105, 108–9, 266n24
in Leviticus, 54
in *Magnolia*, 42, 44, 48–52, 241, 259n12
overview and nature of, 57
to a third party, 259n12
connection, testing for, 205–8
conservatism
Christian religious right, 261n15
Forrest Gump and, 119–20
Cox, Dermot, 187
Cox, Harvey G., 7, 12, 220–21
created in the image of God (*betzelem Elohim/tzelem Elohim*), 23, 29, 35, 221–31, 281n32
creation narrative, Genesis, 19, 23, 28, 29, 221–22. *See also* Adam and Eve; Garden of Eden
"let there be light," 26
creative alienation, 20. *See also* re-creative alienation
Crime and Punishment (Dostoyevsky), 99, 100
Crimes and Misdemeanors (film), 95, 205n10
category confusion in, 97–100
David and Bathsheba and, 102–6
Jewish worldview vs. the worldview of, 108–9
Judah Rosenthal (character), 95–102, 104–5, 108–9, 115, 265n5, 266–67nn24–25, 268n51
many metaphors of sin in, 106–11

(not) seeing and (not) being seen in, 100–102
Rabbi Ben, 100, 101, 114, 267n26, 268n51
real and imagined worlds in, 114–15
and the wages of sin, 95–97
Cushing, Lesleigh. *See* Stahlberg, Lesleigh Cushing.

Dalglish, Edward, 111
Daniel, book of, 55
Darnton, Robert, 90
David, King
Bathsheba and, 102–6
confession (vidui), 104–6, 109, 112
sin and, 106–14
Deaf (character in *Exam*), 190, 192–96, 199
Descendants, The (film), 60–68
birthright (*bekhorah*), 60, 62, 64–66, 68, 69, 72–74
descent/consent, Jacob/Esau, and, 68–75
plot, 69–67
and re-embracing the motherland, 74–75
descent relations, 59
Destroyer, God as, 226
destruction, 4, 229–30
determinism vs. autonomy, 156
dilemma(s). *See also* moral dilemma(s)
Heinz, 197
Dostoyevsky, Fyodor, 99, 100
Doubt (film), 243–44
doubt and faith, 130, 244
dove (*yonah*), 31

Eden, 61, 62, 64, 230–31, 233. *See also* Garden of Eden

Egypt. *See* Pharaoh; Plagues of Egypt
Eliav, Yaron Z., 21, 22
Elijah, 56, 260n24
Ellis, John, 41
emet, 35, 36, 75
empiricism, 85, 86, 127
Esau and Jacob, 56, 69–75
ethical dilemmas. *See* moral dilemma(s)
ethics of altruism and care, 211. *See also* altruism
ethnicity, 189–90. See also *Exam*
Eve. *See* Adam and Eve
evil, 112. *See also* sin
Exam (film)
  characters, 190
  interpersonal dilemmas in, 197
  and life as a blank sheet, 194–95
  plot and overview, 189–93
  testing for the elect, 189–93
Exodus, 50–51. *See also* Moses; *Shemot*
  films about, 145
Ezekiel, book of, 155

faith, 127–29, 170, 203, 206. *See also* trials (of faith)
  biblical, 7, 16
    paradox of, 166
  blind, 267n26
  Christianity and, 11, 252n23
  and doubt, 130, 244
  in God, 114
  in the modern age, 130
  and obedience (vs. disobedience), 203
  reason and, 86, 127, 128
Faith and Film (Deacy), 11
Faith and Film (Stone), 8, 241
faithfulness, law of, 235
Fant, Gene C., 155

father, God as, 56, 57
father-son relationships in Bible, 55–57
fear, test of, 204. *See also* Binding of Isaac
Feit, Daniel, 2–6, 258n27, 268n46
female psychological development, 205
feminism, 10, 12, 120, 157
  Judaism and, 92, 206, 247
  Orthodox Judaism and, 1, 13
feminist messages and themes in films, 74, 242, 247. See also *Descendants, The*
feminist perspectives, 15, 198–200. *See also* gender
  on attachment, detachment, and female development, 199, 205–7. *See also* moral development
  on Bible, 157, 206
  on Kohlberg and moral development, 198–200, 205–7
  patriarchy and, 247
feminist theological writings, 152, 247
feminists, 157, 206, 207, 277n13
film. *See also specific topics*
  writings on Jewish faith and, 6, 20
Film as Religion: Myth, Morals and Rituals (Lyden), 9
Flood, 227, 235. See also Noah's Ark
  after the, 31, 224, 227, 228, 231
Foer, Jonathan Safran, 91
fool(s), 269n4
  holy, 117–26
  in Jewish tradition, 126–31
  synonyms and related terms, 126
forgetting, 75, 84, 88, 91–92, 241. *See also* forgiveness; *Memento*
forgiveness, 39–40, 48, 66, 108. *See also* forgetting
  from God, 34, 37, 39–40, 107, 110, 111, 274n11
  in Psalm 51, 110, 111

Forrest Gump (film), 241
  conservative/right-wing messages in, 119–20
  and the fool in Jewish tradition, 126–31
  holy fools and, 117–26
  plot, 122–26
  precedents of Forrest's character type in Western literature, 118
Frankl, Viktor Emil, 217, 279n12
free will, 31, 36
Freud, Sigmund, 38
Frisco Kid, The (film), 241
frog rain, 50–52, 57

Gamliel, Rabban, 22
Garden of Eden, 53, 55, 62, 125, 162, 223, 230–31, 256n3. *See also* Adam and Eve; Eden
Garr, W. Randall, 222–23, 228
gender, 62, 277n13. *See also* feminism; feminist perspectives; masculinity; patriarchy
  God and, 157–58, 166, 230
gender roles and stereotypes, 200
Genesis, 28, 226–27, 278n23. *See also specific topics*
  "be fruitful and multiply," 222–24, 228
George V. See *King's Speech, The*
Germany, 220. *See also* Nazi Germany
Gilligan, Carol, 198–99, 205, 207, 277n13
gimgum, 143–44
"Gimpel the Fool" (Singer), 117, 128–30, 241
Girgus, Sam, 102
goat
  in Joseph/Judah cycle, 53, 54
  vidui (confession) and, 54. *See also* scapegoat
God, 17, 231. *See also Stranger than Fiction*; *specific topics*
  as artist vs. parent, 158
  in the book of Jonah, 28, 32–40
  gender and, 157–58, 166, 230
  Golden Calf and, 35, 274n11
  humans as created in the image of, 23, 29, 35, 221–31
  images and characterizations of, 57, 166, 221, 225, 226
  Moses and, 15, 29, 35, 140, 141, 143–46, 149, 157, 159, 160, 272nn12–13, 274n11, 281
  nature of, 17, 28, 56, 57, 148, 158, 202, 226
  rhetorical question at end of the book of Jonah, 36
  as stuttering, 146
  terminology for, 226
God-as-writer metaphor, 157
goodness, 216
  acts of, 231
  experiencing and witnessing, 231
Gottschalk, Jonathan, 84
Graetz, Heinrich, 280n17
gratitude. See goodness
Greenberg, Irving, 220, 259n10
guilt, admission of, 52–54. *See also* confession; repentance

Hagar, 278n22
Halbertal, Moshe, 86
Harari, Yuval Noah, 282n34
Harry Potter and the Sorcerer's Stone (Rowling), 244
Hassidism, 127
Hawaii, 60–66
Hazeldine, Stuart, 276–77nn5–6. *See also Exam*

heaven, 281n22
heavy of mouth and tongue, 141, 145, 148. See also *kevad peh*; Moses: speech impediment
Hebrew Union College-Jewish Institute of Religion (HUC-JIR), 1-3, 92
Heinemann, Joseph, 147
Heinz dilemma, 197
Heisenberg's uncertainty principle, 179-80
Heit, Jeremy, 217-18, 280n17
Helm, Zach. See *Stranger than Fiction*
Hemmings, Hart, 260n5
Heschel, Abraham Joshua, 151, 164, 166, 176, 210, 225, 244
ḥesed shel emet, 75
Hitler, Adolf, 139, 148
Holocaust (Shoah), 129, 217, 219-21, 226, 281nn24-25
Hours, The (film), 242, 244-45
human creation in the divine image, 23, 29, 35, 221-31
humor. See comedy
Hunger Games, The (film), 209, 279n3, 281n21
  and duty and dignity in the absence of religion, 209-17
Hunger Games trilogy (novels), 209, 279n9, 280n17, 280n19
  Panem and the Flood generation, 227-31
  toward a theological reading of, 217-21
Hurley, Neil P., 23-24, 254n41

I and Thou (Buber), 178
idolatry
  film and, 20-23, 209, 254n41
  images, interpretive imagination, re-creative alienation, and, 20-24, 209
  prohibition against, 12, 20-23

images. See also under idolatry
  Jewish stance toward, 21
individualism, 218-19
innocence, 126, 130-31, 235
  children and, 42, 43, 105, 118. See also Binding of Isaac
  Forrest Gump and, 117, 118, 125
  of Job, 174
  King David and, 105
  of Moses, 142
  sin and, 42-43, 126
  state of, 63
  of Adam and Eve and the Garden of Eden, 62, 125, 233
  resurrection of the lost, 62, 130
  transfer of, 105
intellectualism, 120, 127, 129
  vs. anti-intellectualism, 119, 120. See also *Forrest Gump*
inverted midrash, 14-19, 169, 243
Isaac, 204, 206-8. See also Binding of Isaac
  Jacob and, 53, 56

Jackson, Tony, 89-90
Jacob, 36, 71, 72, 74-75, 128, 147, 241
  characterizations of, 36, 128, 241
  Esau and, 56, 69-75
  Isaac and, 53, 56
  Joseph and, 52, 56
  Judah and, 52
Jacobs, Louis, 259n12
Jaffee, Martin, 90-91
James, William, 216
Jesus, 178. See also Christology; "Son of man"
  death, 217, 218
Jethro, 142
Jewish, meaning/essence of being, 52
Jewish position in contemporary culture, 20
Jewish "Reel Theology," 20
  Christian precedents, 6-12

defined, 6
toward a, 12–14
Job, book of, 174, 186, 189
Johnston, Robert K., 258n5
Jonah, 32, 38
  confession, 37
  death wish, 31, 33, 35, 36, 257n14
  God and, 32–40
  journey, 31–34
  meanings of his name, 30–31
  personality, 33–34, 38, 39
  in whale's belly, 32–35, 38
Jonah, book of, 52
  central teachings, 34
  as comedy, 37–40
  ending, 36
  forgiveness in, 34, 37, 39–40
  God in, 28, 32–40
  interpretations of, 256n9, 257n14, 257n16
  Nineveh in, 31, 32, 34, 36–38
  repentance in, 34–38
  Truman Show and, 28, 30–40
Joseph, 253n31
Judah (son of Jacob), 54
  confession (*vidui*) and, 52–54
  contrasted with Woody Allen's Judah Rosenthal (character), 104
  Joseph and, 52–54, 56
  overview and life history, 52–53
  Tamar and, 52–54
Judah, tribe of, 54, 102
Judah Rosenthal (character in *Crimes and Misdemeanors*), 95–102, 104–5, 108–9, 115, 265n5, 266–67nn24–25, 268n51
Judah the Prince, 112–15
"Judah-ism," 52–54
Judaism. *See also specific topics*
  as confession, 52–55

Kafka, Franz, 28
Kaunfer, Elie, 52

Kehr, David, 119, 120
kevad peh (heavy of mouth), 141, 143, 272n13. *See also* heavy of mouth and tongue
King's Speech, The (film), 133, 138–40
  Moses's speech and, 140–49
  plot, 133–38
Klein, A. M., 33
Kohlberg, Lawrence, 196–99, 201, 203, 205, 207
Kresh, Paul, 130
Kugel, James, 111, 253n31
Kushner, Harold S., 282n33
kvd, 145, 146, 148

Lamott, Anne, 166–67
Landry, David, 99, 102–3
Lange, Dorothea, 203
language, 47
learning in reverse order, 14. *See also* inverted midrash
  modern Jewish, 77–78
Lee, Sander, 267n25
Leonard, Richard, 30
"let there be light," 26
Levy, Daniel, 262n11
Levy, Louis, 114–15
Liberal Judaism, 12–13. *See also* Reform Judaism
Lienhard, John H., 179
literal-mindedness, 151–52
Lorberbaum, Yair, 225
Lord of the Flies (Golding), 195, 276n5
love, 158
  salvation through, 280n12
  superseding law, 235
  test of, 204. *See also* Binding of Isaac
  Viktor Frankl on, 279n12
Love and Death (film), 265n7
Lyden, John, 23, 114
Lynch, S. J. William F., 254n41

Madsen, Richard, 219
Magnolia (film), 41–48, 241
  characters, 42, 44–47
  confession and repentance in, 42, 44, 48–52, 241, 259n12
  reconciliation between fathers and sons in, 56
  redemption of fathers in, 55–57
Maimonides, 152
Makkot, 225
Malachi, book of, 56, 260n24
Mann, Aimee, 44, 49–50, 52
Mann, Vivian B., 21
March of the Penguins (film), 67, 261n15
Marty, James, 255n53
masculinity, 74, 200, 230. *See also* feminist perspectives; patriarchy
  God and, 157, 166
mashal, 17–18, 54, 152, 165, 178, 182–84
mashal (meshalim). See also *Serious Man, A*
  book of Job as a, 174
  rabbinic, 127
  A Serious Man prologue as a, 172–73
mashal lemah hadavar domeh, 14, 170, 242
Mask Jews Wear, The (Borowitz), 12, 20
Match Point (film), 265n5
McAdams, Dan P., 88
McFague, Sally, 152, 158, 187
McKenna, Michael, 83, 87
meaning, quest for, 217, 220
Meir, Rabbi, 22, 91
Meir, Samuel ben (Rashbam), 73, 141
Memento (film)
  history, memory, and, 241
  (post)modern Jewish memory and, 83–89

  plot, 79–82
  reading, 78–83
memory. *See also* remembering
  and concept of self, 214
  ethics and, 214
  imagination and, 89–93
  Jews and, 91
  remaking. See *Memento*
Menahot 29b, 159, 160
messiah, 113, 155
messianic redemption, 155–56
Micah, book of, 36
Midnight in Paris (film), 245
midrash, 16–17, 147, 173, 182, 239, 242. *See also specific topics*
  analogy between movies and, 17
Midrash Yonah, 37
milah, 141
Miles, Jack, 226
"Miller's Tears, The" (Mark Warshawsky), 181–82
Milner, Brenda, 262n10
miracles, 202–3
  trials and, 201–2
Mishnah Avot, 91–92, 202–3
Mishnah in Sanhedrin, 229, 230. *See also* Sanhedrin
Mishnah in Tractate Avodah Zarah, 21–22
Mishnah Makkot, 225
Moonrise Kingdom (film), 233–36
moral development, Kohlberg's stages of, 198–99, 205
moral dilemma(s)
  biblical, 205–6
  as test, Kohlberg/Gilligan/Noddings and, 195–201
Morreall, John, 39
Morson, Gary Saul, 206n13
Moses, 92, 142–45
  childhood, 141–43
  in film, 145

God and, 15, 29, 35, 140, 141, 143–46, 149, 157, 159, 160, 272nn12–13, 274n11, 281
Harry Potter and, 244
leadership, 140, 144–45
overview and characterizations of, 140, 141, 144, 145, 148, 272n11
Pharaoh and, 140–46, 160
Philo on, 272n11
Rabbi Akiva and, 159, 160
sin, forgiveness, and, 274n11
"Song of the Sea," 148
speech impediment, 140–49, 160, 271–72nn9–13
speeches, 92, 160
Talmudic story about, 159
Ten Commandments, Mount Sinai, and, 29, 35, 92, 157, 159, 254n41, 281
Torah and, 29, 159, 160
Moses (Asch), 146
Mulvey, Laura, 200
My Big Fat Greek Wedding (film), 245

Nachman of Bratzlav, 127–28
Nahmani, Samuel bar, 112–13, 182
naïveté, second, 130, 170
Nathan, 104–6, 109
Nazi Germany, 139, 148, 226. See also Holocaust
New Testament, 126, 176, 235, 241, 280n17
Nichols, Mary P., 268n51
nihilism, 86, 112, 175
9/11 terrorist attacks, 1–3
Nineveh, 31, 32, 34, 36–38
Noah, 228, 230
after the Flood, 224, 228, 231. See also Flood: after the
characterizations of, 126, 128, 224
generation of, 128, 224, 227

Noah's Ark, story of, 228, 230. See also Flood
book of Jonah and, 31
dove in, 31
God in, 226, 228
Noddings, Nel., 206, 207
Nolan, Christopher. See *Memento*

obedience vs. disobedience, 203
Ochs, Peter, 13, 35
Orr, James, 221

Pagis, Dan, 226, 246
parables, 5, 14, 152, 182, 234, 275n3
 God revealed through, 17
 merits of, 183
 a theology informed by, 187
 in Torah, 18–19, 182–83
partial truths, the meaningfulness of, 83–89
Pascal, Blaise, 154–55
patriarchy, 74, 247. See also *Descendants, The*; feminist perspectives
penance, 259n12. See also penitence; repentance
penitence, 109. See also penance
 paradigm of sin and, 111–14
perpetuities, rule against, 60
Pharaoh, 51, 56, 140–46
 Moses and, 140–46, 160
Philo, 272n11
physics. See also under *Serious Man, A*
 quantum, 179–80
Pinsker, Sanford, 126
Pirkei Avot. See Avot
Plagues of Egypt, 50–51, 145, 202, 203. See also frog rain
Plate, Brent, 19, 209
Porton, Gary G., 273n23
postmodern condition, 78, 83
postmodernism, 1, 13, 86, 122, 237, 241. See also under *Memento*

Potiphar, 160, 253n31
Proclos, 21–22
profanity, 47
projection, 255n53
psychoanalytic perspectives on female psychological development, 205
psychological development. *See* female psychological development; moral development

quantum theory, 179–80

rabbis. *See Crimes and Misdemeanors*: Rabbi Ben
race, 189–90. *See also Exam*
racial reconciliation, 119
Ramses, 145
randomness/change, idea of, 44
Rashbam (Samuel ben Meir), 73, 141
Rashbatz (Simeon ben Zemah Duran), 202
re-creative alienation
  images, idols, and interpretive imagination, 20–24
  stance of, 20, 209
reality TV, 25, 30, 42
reason and faith, 86, 127, 128
Rebecca, 69, 71, 72, 207–8
recreation, nature of, 19
recreational nature of film, 19
redemption, 141, 163, 165, 166
  confession and, 52, 55
  of fathers in *Magnolia*, 55–57
  hoped-for ideal of future, 114
  King David and, 113, 114
"Reel Theology." *See also* Jewish "Reel Theology"
  design of, 237–42
  Eugene Borowitz, z"l, and the beginnings of, 1–6
Reel Theology course, 2, 5, 12, 246
  books, movies, and TV shows studied/covered in, xii, 2, 4, 237, 239–44, 246, 247, 253n30
  conceptual framework for and purposes and design of, xiii, 3, 5, 237–42
  inverted midrash and, 14
  midrash and, 242
  Rabbi Borowitz and, 2, 3, 253n30
  Rabbi Borowitz on, xi–xiii, 237–40
  Rabbi Borowitz's correspondence with Zierler regarding, 237–42
  reasons for teaching, xiii
  students' experience of, xiii, 237–38
  syllabus, 5
  themes covered in, 4–5, 239–40, 253n30
Reform Judaism, xii–xiii, 12, 92, 243. *See also* Liberal Judaism
religion. *See also specific topics*
  compared with comedy, 39
  duty and dignity in the absence of, 209–17
  ways of writing about, 239
religious right, Christian, 261n15
remembering, 91–92. *See also* forgetting; *Memento*
  inner, 77–78, 90, 93
Renewing the Covenant: A Theology for the Postmodern Jew (Borowitz), xi, 241, 245, 253n30
repentance (*teshuvah*), 50, 53, 55–57, 109, 241, 259n12. *See also* atonement; confession; *Magnolia*: confession and repentance in; Yom Kippur
  in book of Daniel, 55
  in book of Jonah, 34–38
  of King David, 104, 105, 113
  messianic and utopian aspects, 55–56
  as a return of fathers to sons and sons to fathers, 55–57

responsibility, accepting/taking, 52–54. *See also* confession; repentance
Reuben, 113
revenge, 80, 81, 87, 247. *See also Memento*
Ricoeur, Paul, 130
Roche, Mark, 266n24
Rosenzweig, Frank, 14, 77, 78, 90, 92–93
Rotenstreich, Nathan, 73
Roth, Philip, xi, 3, 4, 243
Rubinstein, Jeffrey, 160

Sabbath, 83
sacrifice. *See* Binding of Isaac
saintliness and the saintly character, 216
salvation, 38, 39, 144, 178, 211, 280n12. *See also tikkun olam*
   through love, 280n12
Samuel bar Nahmani, 112–13, 182
Sanhedrin (tractate), 112, 225, 229, 230, 246
Sarah, 206, 207
Sarna, Nachum, 224
Satan in the book of Job, 174, 189
scapegoat, Yom Kippur ritual of the, 54, 107–8
Scheindlin, Raymond P., 175
schlemiel, 38, 126–27. *See also* fool(s); Jonah; simpleton
   defined, 126
Schneerson, Menachem Mendel, 185
Schneider, Phil, 148–49
Schrödinger's cat, 179, 180
Schwarzman, Lisa, 271n4
Scott, Steven D., 121
second naïveté, 130, 170
secular, the, 220
   God and, 220–21
   and the religious, 7
   and the sacred, 8, 12, 239
secular city, 220, 221

Secular City, The (Cox), 7, 220–21
secular cultural movement, 221
secular humanistic culture, 220
secular individualism, 218–19
secular learning, 77
secularization, 7, 12, 221
   moral limits of, 221
seeing, 195, 208. *See also* vision motifs
Segal, Benjamin J., 268n42
Seidler, David, 136, 270n3. *See also King's Speech*
September 11 attacks, 1–3
Serious Man, A (film), 169–70
   comedy in, 175–76
   epigraph, 170–71
   parables and, 175–80, 182–84, 186–87
   prologue, 171–73, 180
   where physics and theology meet, 179–87
Seth, 223
sexual violation, 105–6
sexuality, 60, 63–64, 105–6
Shalev, Meir, 39
Shemot, 147, 149. *See also* Exodus
Sherwood, Yvonne, 34
Shields, David, 271n6
Shir Hashirim Rabbah. *See* Song of Songs Rabbah
Shoah. *See* Holocaust
Shohat, Ella, 141
shtetl, 91, 127, 171, 173
shtetl Jews, 126
Simeon ben Zemah Duran (Rashbatz), 202
simpleton, 117, 127, 128, 130, 131, 270n21. *See also Forrest Gump*
   Jewish, 127. *See also* schlemiel
simplicity, 117, 126. *See also Forrest Gump*
   vs. cleverness, 117, 127–28, 241

simplicity *(continued)*
   receiving everything that happens to you with, 170–71, 174
sin, 95. *See also* confession; *Crimes and Misdemeanors*; redemption; repentance
   admitting, 52–54
   innocence and, 42–43, 126
   King David and, 106–14
   metaphorical or symbolic language of, 267n32
   metaphors of, 106–11
   and penitence, paradigm of, 111–14
   synonyms and related terms, 96, 106–7, 126
   use of the word, 96, 106, 107
   wages of, 95–97
Singer, Isaac Bashevis, ix, 117, 128–30
Skrade, Carle, 7–8
Smoke (film), 242, 245–46
smoke, image and motif on, 242
Snider, Laura, 217
Soleveitchik, Joseph, 222
Sollors, Werner, 59
Son of Man, The (Magritte), 155
"Son of man," 155
Song of Songs, 234
Song of Songs Rabbah, 182
Stahlberg, Lesleigh Cushing., 16
Stern, David, 17–18, 173, 184
Sternberg, Meir, 103
Stone, Bryan, 8
Stranger than Fiction (film), 152–61
   man in search of God the author/God the author in search of man, 161–64
   moments of awe and how a wristwatch saved Harold Crick, 164–67
   plot, 152–53
stuttering, 146. *See also* Moses: speech impediment

Sullivan, William M., 219
Swidler, Ann, 219

"Tale about a Clever Man and a Tam, A" (R. Nachman), 127
Talmud. *See* Babylonian Talmud
tam, 126–29, 174, 241
   connotations of the word, 126
Tamar, 53, 104
technology, use of, 121–22
Teilhard de Chardin, Pierre, 194, 195, 208
Telford, William, 11
ten biblical plagues, 50–51, 145, 202, 203
Ten Commandments, 29, 35, 83, 92, 157, 203, 254n41. *See also under* Moses
"tens," 202–3
teshuvah. *See* repentance
testing. *See also* Binding of Isaac; Job; trials
   for connection, 205–8
   for the elect, 189–93
   of the elect, Jewish, 200–5
theology, definitions of, 11
Thomas, Hardy, 283n49
tikkun ha-adam (the repair of Adam), 230
tikkun olam (repairing and salvation of the world), 230, 240
Tillich, Paul, 7
Tipton, Steven M., 219
Torah, 239. *See also Torah she-bikhtav*
   Moses and the, 29, 159, 160
   parables in the, 18–19, 182–83
Torah she-be'al peh (Oral Torah), 89–91
Torah she-bikhtav (written Torah), 90. *See also* Torah
Torah study, 24
Traffic (film), 246

tragedy and comedy, 98–99
trials (of faith), 189, 191, 201, 202.
    See also Binding of Isaac; Job;
    testing
  miracles and, 201–2
Trible, Phyllis, 206
Truman Show, The (film), 25, 37–41,
    256nn2–3
  book of Jonah and, 28, 30–40
  Christof compared with God,
    27–29
  Magnolia and, 41–42
  plot, 25–29
  Stranger than Fiction and, 152
  truth, God, humankind, and, 30–37
truth. See also partial truths; Truman
    Show, The
  humor and. See Jonah, book of: as
    comedy
  revealing hidden, 39
Tuesdays with Morrie (Albom), 2, 246
Tuesdays with Morrie (film), 2, 246
tzelem Elohim. See created in the
    image of God

uncertainty principle, 179–80
Unforgiven (film), 247

vidui (confession), 48–50, 52–55,
    259n10. See also confession
violence, 105–6. See also specific topics
  cultures of, 227, 229–30
  in Genesis, 226–27, 229–30

Virtual Faith: The Irreverent
    Spiritual Quest of Generation X
    (Beaudoin), 8–9
virtue, 216. See also goodness
vision motifs, 100–2, 190, 194–95.
    See also Moonrise Kingdom;
    seeing

Warshawsky, Mark, 181
weather, 50–51. See also frog rain
Whalerider (film), 242, 247
White (character in Exam), 190, 192,
    193, 195–200
Wiesel, Elie, 33–34
will to meaning (Frankl), 217, 220
wisdom, 118. See also Forrest Gump
"wising up," 49–50
Wisse, Ruth, 128
writing
  oral tradition and, 90–91
  practice of, 166–67

Yerushalmi, Yosef Hayim, 82, 83,
    85–86
Yezierska, Anzia, 245
Yom Kippur, 36, 39, 48, 259n10
Yom Kippur ritual of the scapegoat,
    54, 107–8
"Yonah," 30–31, 256n9. See also
    Jonah

Zemel, Danny, 96
Zornberg, Aviva, 31

www.ingramcontent.com/pod-product-compliance
Ingram Content Group UK Ltd.
Pitfield, Milton Keynes, MK11 3LW, UK
UKHW041923140426
5217IPUK00014B/293